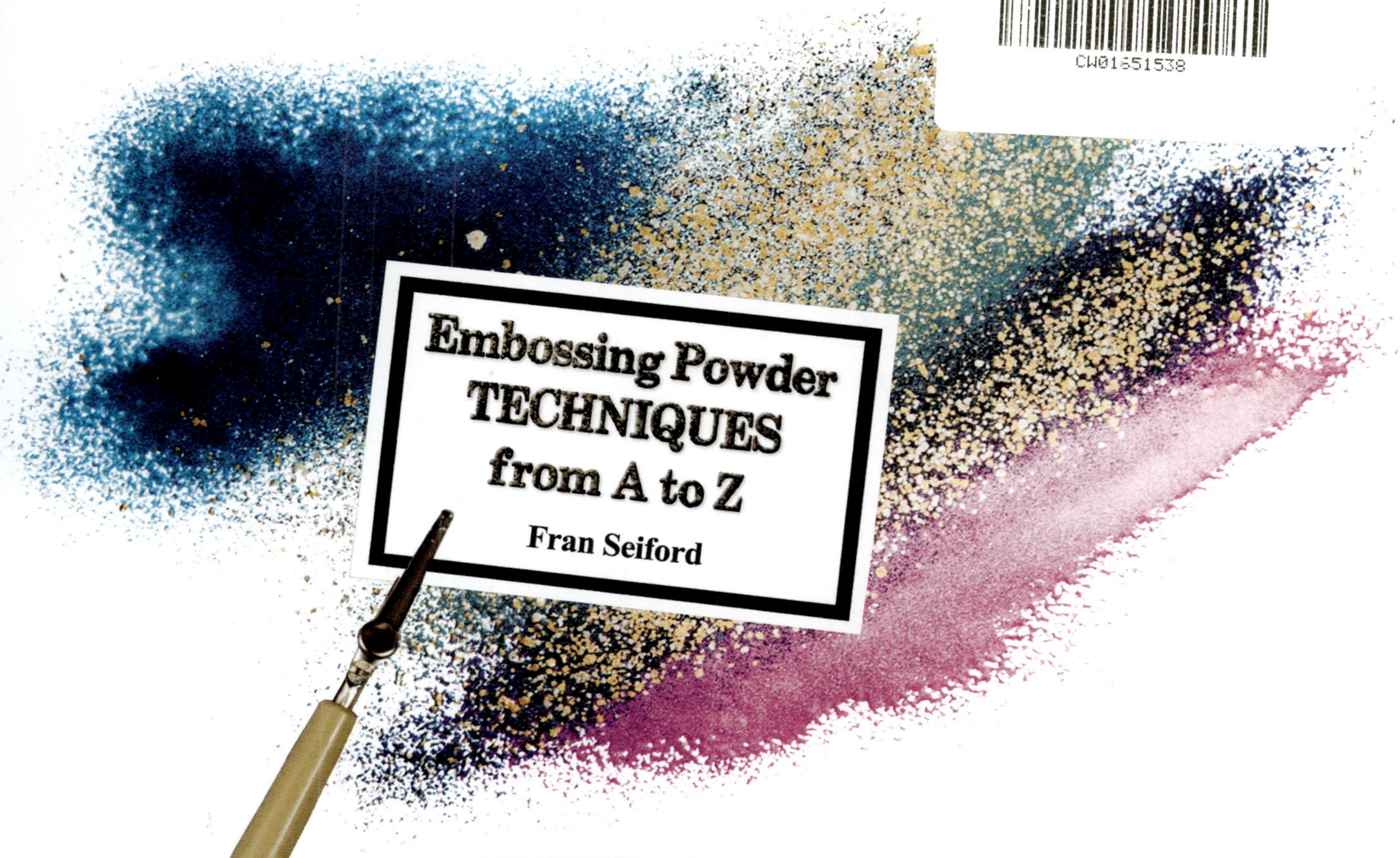

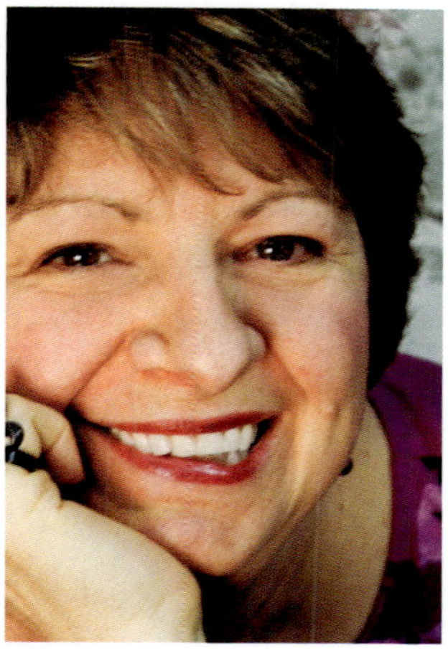

This book has a focus of Embossing Techniques. I've exclusively used my Stampendous stamps and Embossing Powders, because that is what I know best, and we offer an incredibly wide variety. We'll cover techniques from A to Z, from simple to most complex. Basics are at the beginning and it builds from there. There are charts and reference materials that will save you lots of trial and error. It is not my expectation that you will repeat these projects so much as use them to learn a technique. I hope you will try your hand at these techniques and discover your own unique style. These techniques will work with any stamps and embossing powders.

Fran

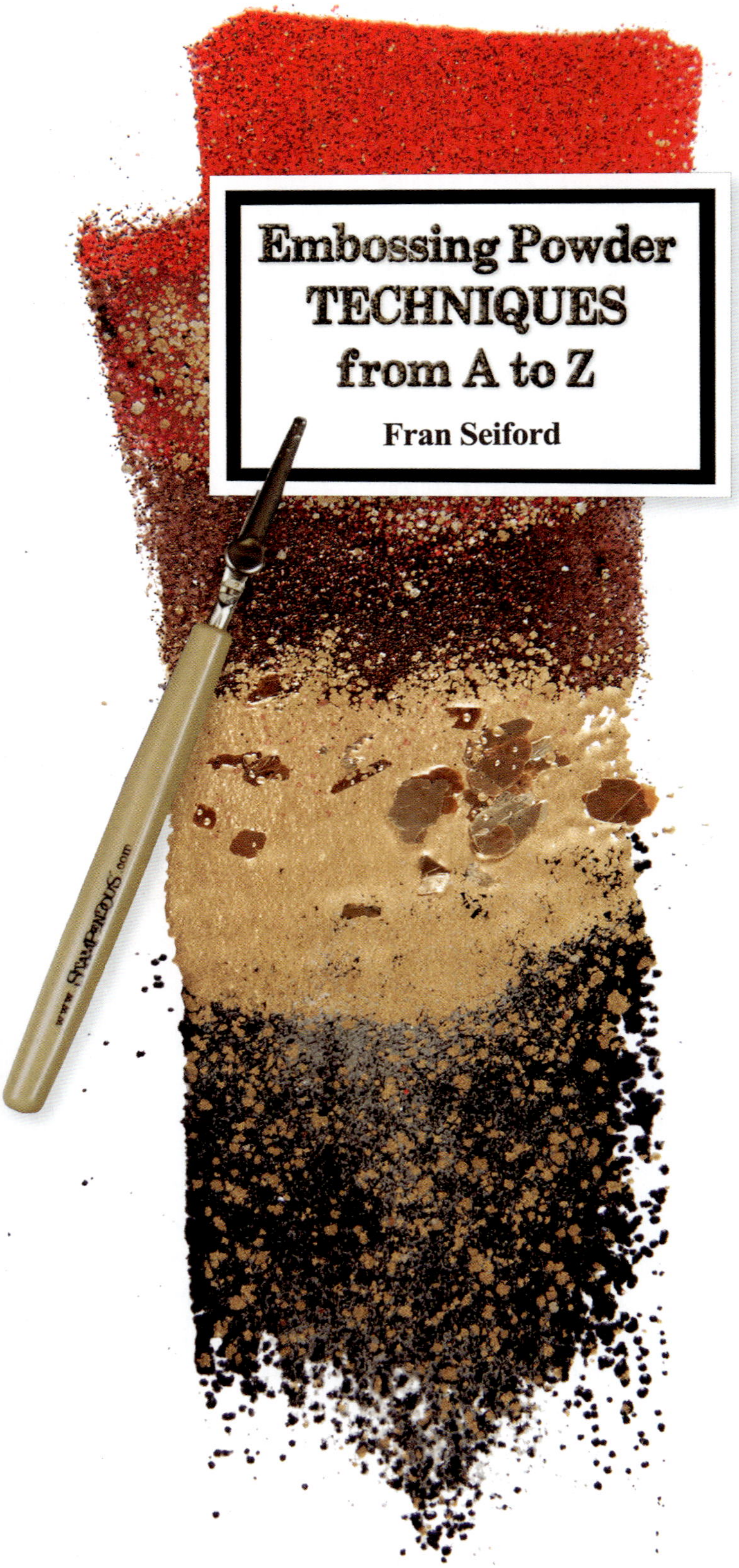

Table of Contents

BASIC SUPPLIES FOR HEAT EMBOSSING

In the crafting world and beyond, the word "embossing" can mean many different things. This book is about ***Heat Embossing*** with melted powders to create shiny raised impressions. It can be done in minutes by hand with Embossing Powders, rubber stamps, and a heat source.

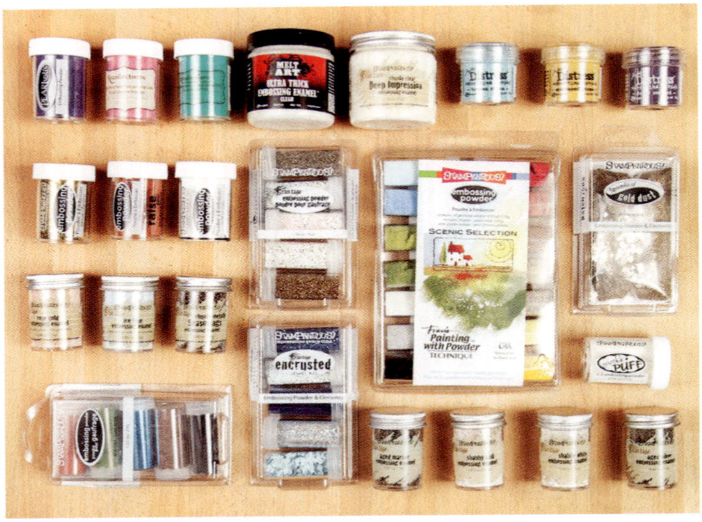

EMBOSSING POWDERS or Thermography Powders are finely ground plastic particles which come in a wide variety of types, granulations and colors. They melt at relatively low temperatures and cool for a shiny, raised, durable finish. Powders can be applied in many ways to many surfaces for fabulous results.

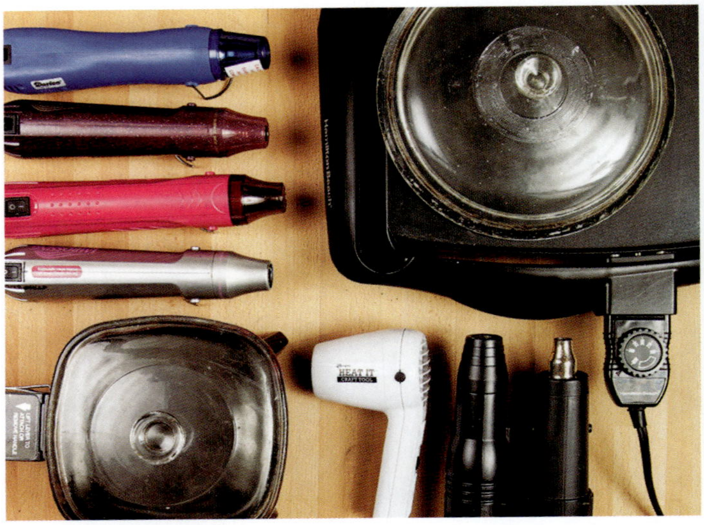

HEAT TOOLS are used to melt Embossing Powders. Regardless of brand, style, color or shape of the tool, it generates heat to melt powders without just blowing it all around as a hair dryer would do. Heat tools range in color, style, wattage and pricing. Electric skillets, pancake griddles, toaster ovens, and melting pots can be used as well. Unplug when not in use.

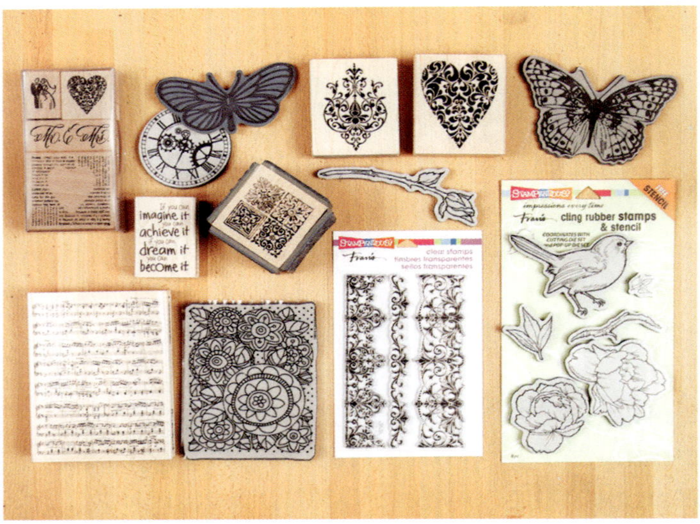

RUBBER STAMPS that are wood mounted or cling or even clear polymer are all ideal for providing imagery to heat emboss. They allow you to work quickly and do a wide variety of techniques, colors and styles. Stamps with very fine lines, bold silhouettes, or in between can all be embossed for beautiful classic results.

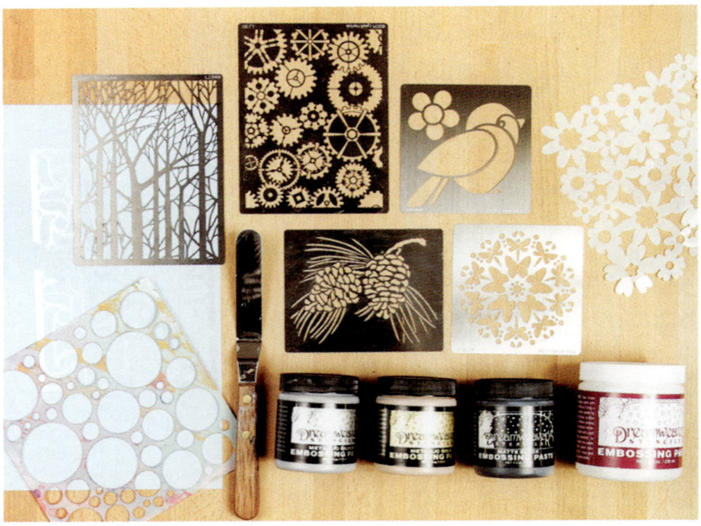

STENCILS of metal or plastic can be used to apply wet ink patterns that can then be heat embossed. Apply wet ink directly or indirectly on daubers through stencil pattern. Powders dusted over ink will find the wet pattern and the excess will fall away. Keep your stencils away from heat: metal will get very hot; plastic ones will melt and be ruined.

What is Thermographic Printing? Traditionally, wedding invitations or business cards have shiny raised lettering you can feel if you run your fingers over the surface. Printers call this process "Thermography". "Thermo" implies heat. The process involves a printing press, coating wet ink with powder, vacuuming away excess and running it through a heat tunnel to melt the fine letters. Crafters can do this same process by hand with rubber stamps.

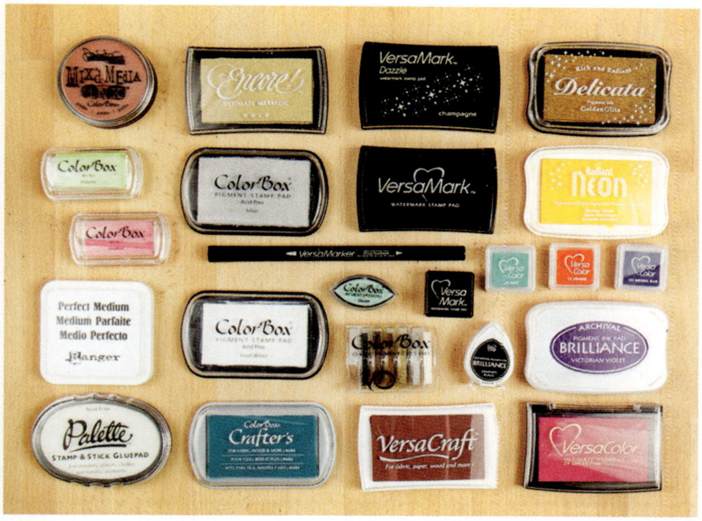

INKS need to stay wet long enough to be dusted with embossing powder. Some slow-drying inks are tinted or clear like VersaMark™ or Perfect Medium. Look for pads, cubes, pens, or bottles with dauber top. Pigment inks of any color work well. Most dye inks dry too quickly. Chalk and permanent inks dry too quickly to work for embossing.

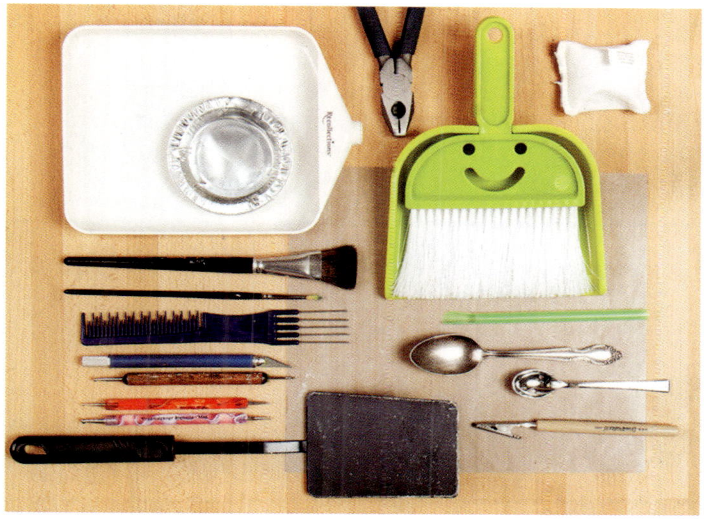

EMBOSSING AIDS include: alligator clip tool or a wooden clothespin to hold paper away from heat, trays designed for catching and funneling powders back into jars, containers with lids, spoons or small scoops, brushes, stencil tools and craft knife for touch-ups. Reduce static as needed with anti-static pouch, talcum powder or dryer sheets.

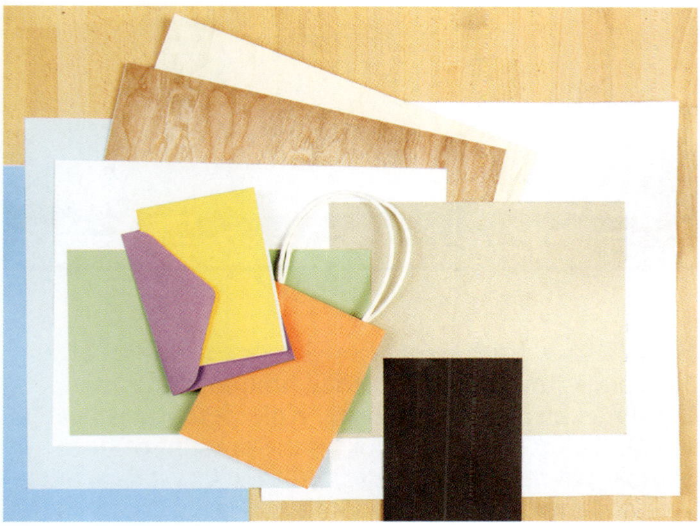

PAPERS best suited to heat embossing have a somewhat porous finish. Select postcard weight or heavier to sustain Embossing Powders. Select smooth papers for fine detail stamps. Embossing Powders may chip off slick or pearlized papers. Very porous papers absorb inks quickly. Try textured watercolor paper. Test small scrap pieces for best results.

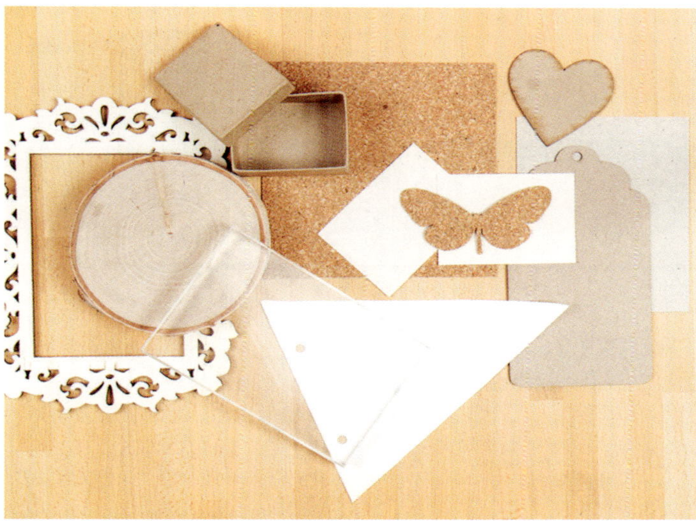

OTHER SURFACES that are porous can easily be embossed such as wood, paper mache, chipboard, slate, etc. Work carefully with metal to not burn fingers. Non-porous surfaces such as glass, ceramic or glazed tiles may emboss okay, but chip off easily. Avoid surfaces that will melt like plastics or thin glass that may shatter with heat. See more on page 52.

TYPES OF EMBOSSING POWDER

Whatever the names given by different suppliers, there are certain categories or "families" of Embossing Powders that have unique characteristics. Understanding these types will help you determine what you select for different techniques and looks. Samples have been embossed over a black swatch so you can see how opaque or translucent a powder is when melted.

METALLIC Embossing Powders are classic, shiny, and come in a wide range of variations from detail to chunky. They heat the quickest and remain the shiniest even if overheated. Sample colors shown left to right are: Pirate Gold, Sterling Silver, and Copper.

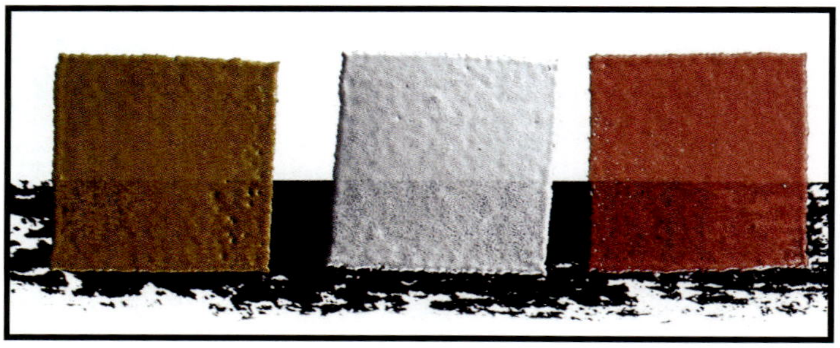

PEARL Embossing Powders are similar to Metallic but more colorful and shimmery. Some colors are more translucent than others. They heat quickly and remain shiny even if overheated. Interference tints look white until heated over dark papers. Samples: PEARLustre™ Carnelian, Jade, and Sapphire.

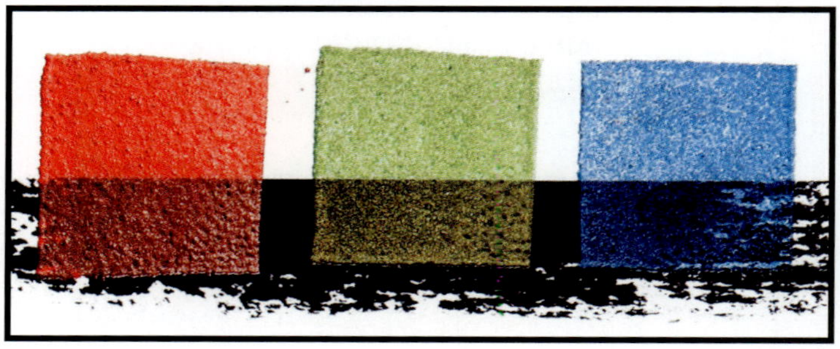

CLEAR COLOR Embossing Powders are shiny and translucent until you get into the darkest colors like black. Clear is a favorite in detail, regular or chunky size granulations. The smaller the granules, the quicker they heat. Sample colors shown left to right are Clear, Clear Lemon, and Clear Bark.

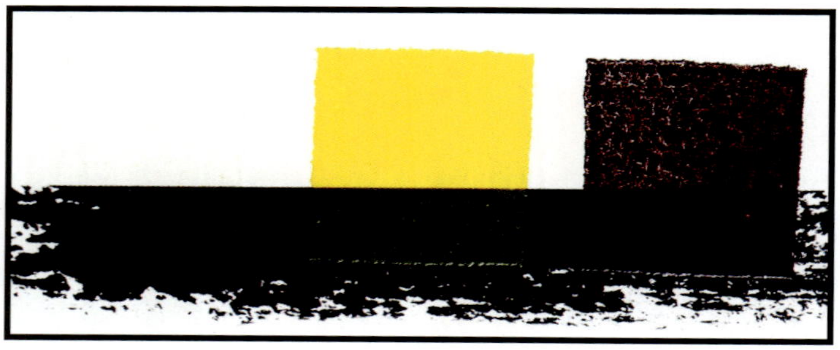

OPAQUE Embossing Powders are shiny and will cover whatever ink or paper is underneath. They have a white base or core and when overheated may look more white. They take a bit more time to heat than clear base powders. Neon colors fit this category. Samples shown are Aqua, Lettuce, and Olive.

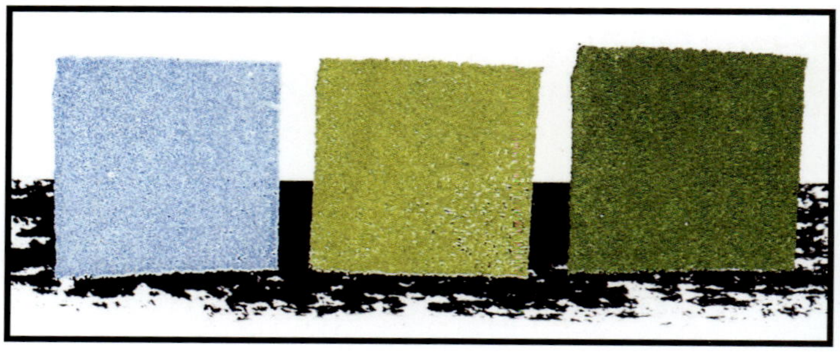

TINSEL Embossing Powders are sparkly with lots of Glitter added to any other type of Embossing Powder base. Glitters vary in granulation, color and sparkle. They are the most sensitive to overheating and may go dull. Sample colors shown left to right are Blue Tinsel, Red Tinsel, and Vintage Lilac.

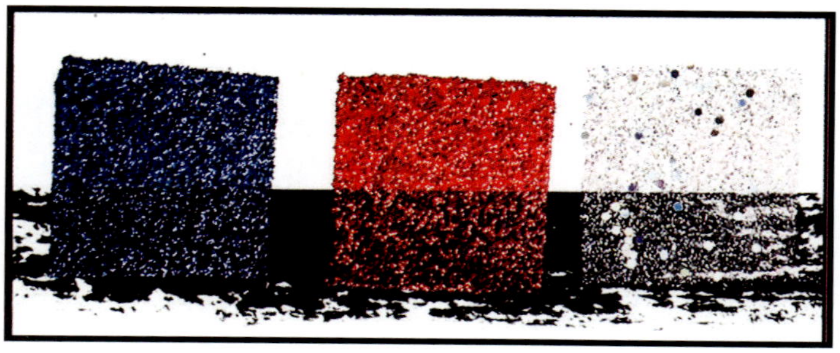

SPARKLY Embossing Powders are mixes of clear or opaque powders with varied amounts of glitter. Crystal is an all-time favorite. Kaleidescope is heat sensitive and changes color by the amount of heat. Sample colors shown left to right are Crystal, Winter Wonderland, and Jeweled Gold.

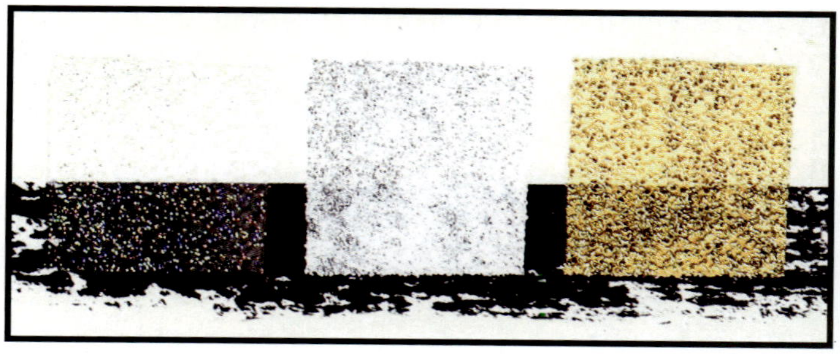

GRANULATION Embossing Powders can be ground to varied size particles. If not labeled otherwise, most powders will be considered "regular" granulation. Finely ground Detail or large Chunky granulations will be labeled accordingly with a variety of names. Powder types could potentially be available in any granulation. Different granulations serve different purposes. See Granulation Comparison on page 20.

DETAILED Embossing Powders are finely ground powders. They may also be called ultra fine. Available in metallic, clear, and some colors. Detailed powders are best for fine line stamps. Static may be more pronounced. Impressions will not be as raised. Samples: Detailed Black, White, and Silver.

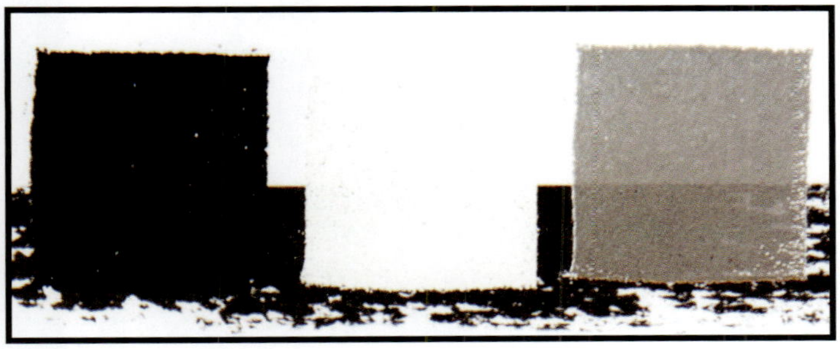

CHUNKY or Ultra-Thick Embossing Enamels are usually available in Metallic or Clear and some colors. They create a thicker, more dimpled shiny surface which can be stamped into for a Deep Impression. Samples: Gold, Aged Silver, and Black.

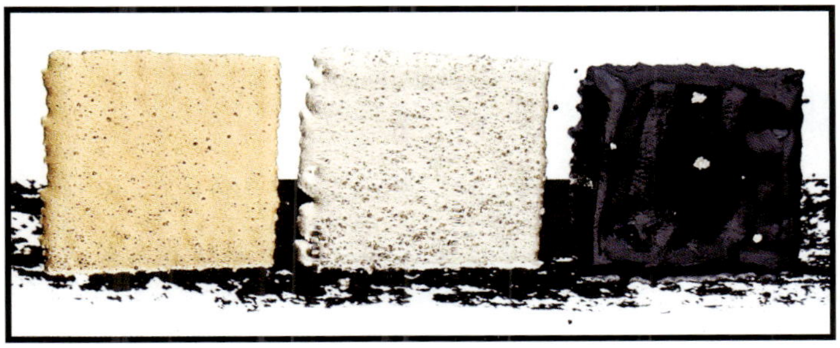

FRANTAGE Embossing Enamels are Fran Seiford's specialty mixes. They offer a unique, irregular, vintage look. Most include some chunky powders and are often heated from underneath. Some are available as Spoonful Mixes. Samples shown are Shabby Pink, Aged Silver, and Aged Marine.

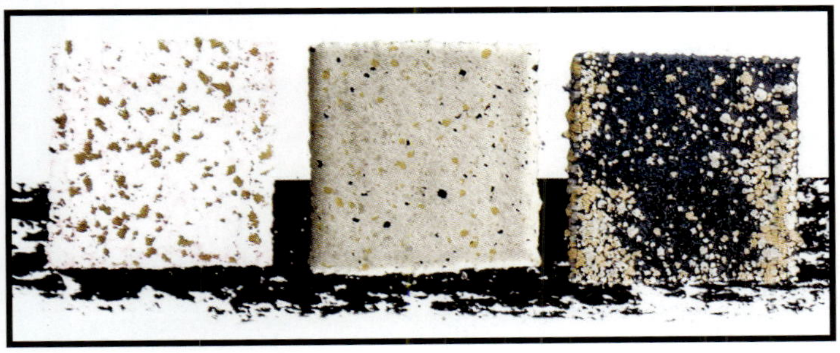

COLOR MIX Embossing Powders could be a mix of anything you like. Opaque colors are often combined to achieve a dappled color. They show best when melted in a large area to see the beautiful colors of varied values from light to dark. Sample colors shown are Golden Sand, Verdigris, and Twilight.

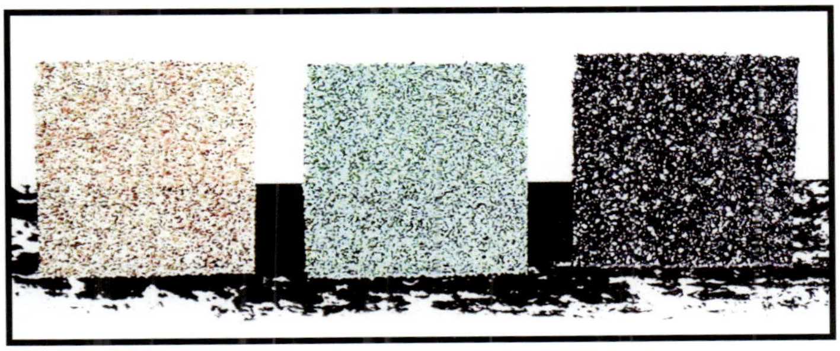

DISTRESS Embossing Powders are a specialty powder developed by Tim Holtz® for Ranger®. They are opaque colors with a matte or sandy "grit" to give an instantly aged or distressed look and texture. Sample colors left to right are Broken China, Scattered Straw, and Weathered Wood.

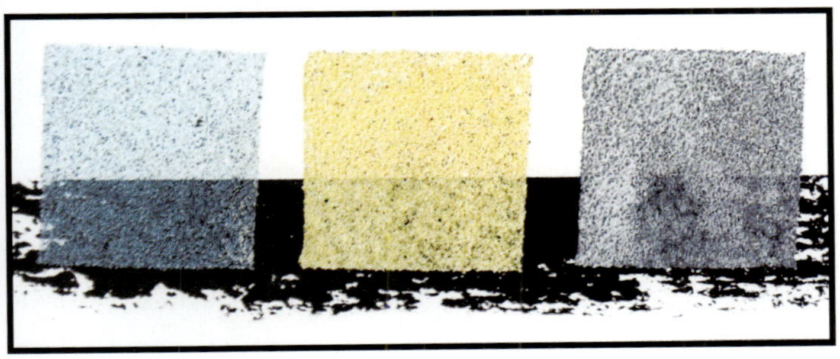

PUFF Embossing Powders are a specialty item which is very raised but not shiny--rather almost rubbery. Available in white or colors and different granulations. Sparkle Puff has crystal glitter in the mix and is ideal for snow. Samples shown left to right are Chunky White, Puff, and Sparkle Puff.

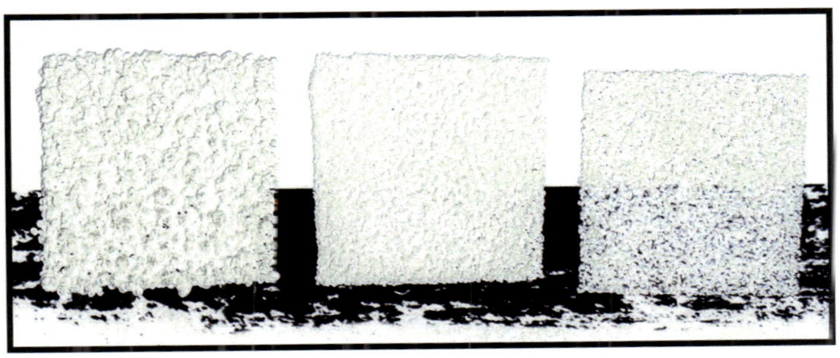

BASIC
EMBOSSING POWDER TECHNIQUE

A

The most basic steps to the embossing process are shown here in detail. Refer to these expanded steps as we build and add other variations from simplest to more complex techniques. VersaMark™ Watermark Ink is clear and the most versatile embossing ink. However, a color pigment ink will be helpful when making multiple impressions which can be dusted and heated all at once.

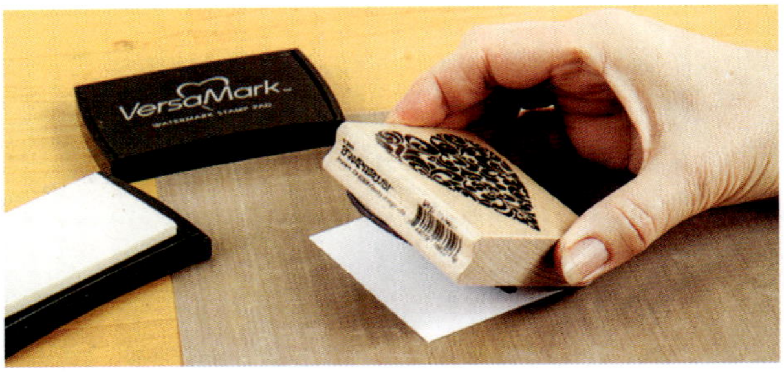

1. Stamp: Stamp image in a slow drying ink like clear VersaMark™ or any pigment ink color. You do not need a matching ink since most inks will be covered by the color of the Embossing Powder.

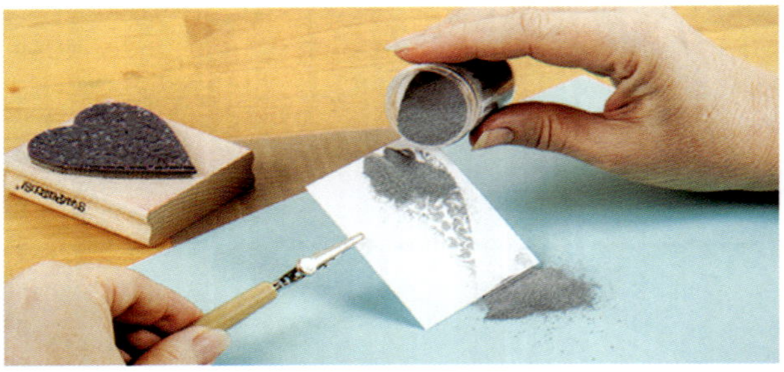

2. Dust: Place folded scrap paper under work area. Sprinkle Embossing Powder over still wet ink impression. Shake off excess or tap lightly on the back of paper. Use a small dry brush to remove unwanted powder BEFORE you begin to heat.

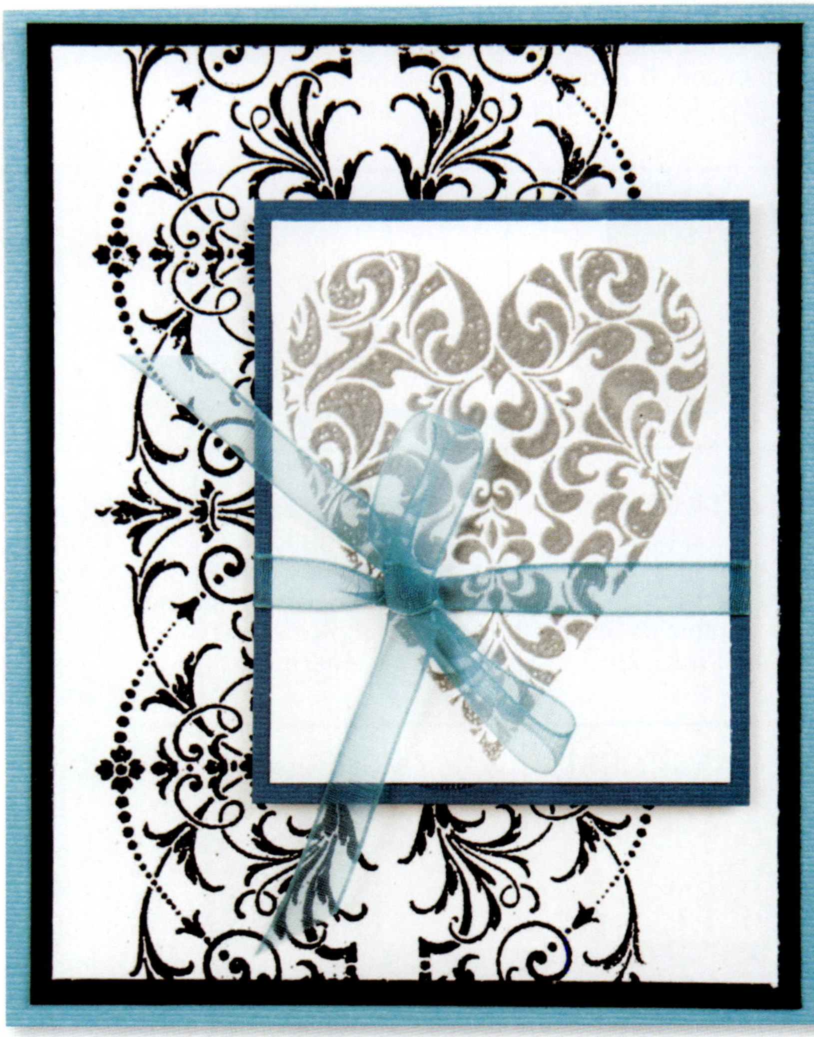

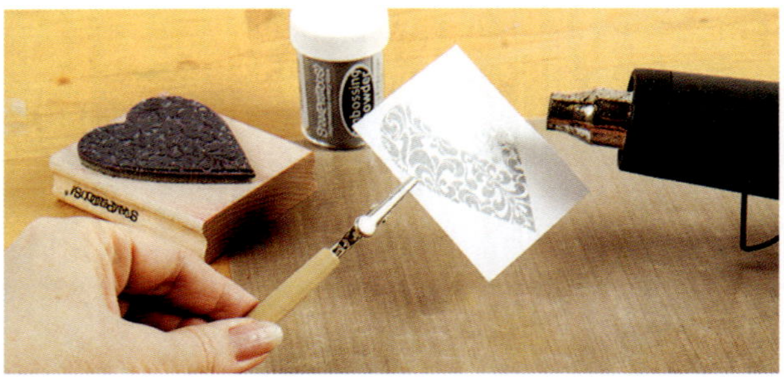

3. Heat: Hold small papers with a clip tool to keep from burning fingers. Apply heat tool starting in one corner to concentrate heat until powder changes color and gets shiny, then proceed to evenly heat entire panel. Overheating in one place may scorch paper.

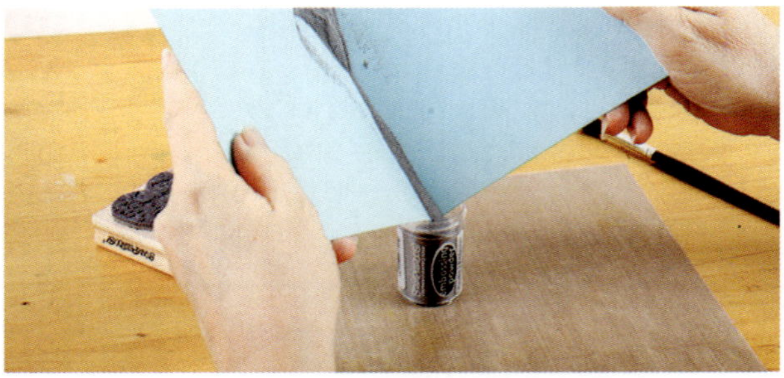

4. Collect excess: Funnel the Embossing Powder in the fold of scrap paper back into jar.

STAMPED LAYERS
EMBOSSING POWDER TECHNIQUE

B

Try stamping and embossing layer upon layer for wonderful results. In this approach you will want to heat each layer. Vary the colors and types of powder and the paper colors. Clear Embossing Powders over clear ink will give you a tone-on-tone darker shade. Smooth or textured paper will vary the look as well.

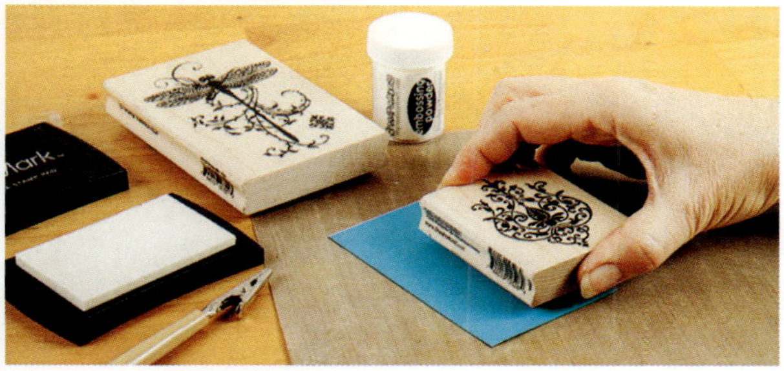

1. Stamp and emboss first layer: Stamp image in clear VersaMark™ ink. Hold with clip tool and apply heat to melt powder.

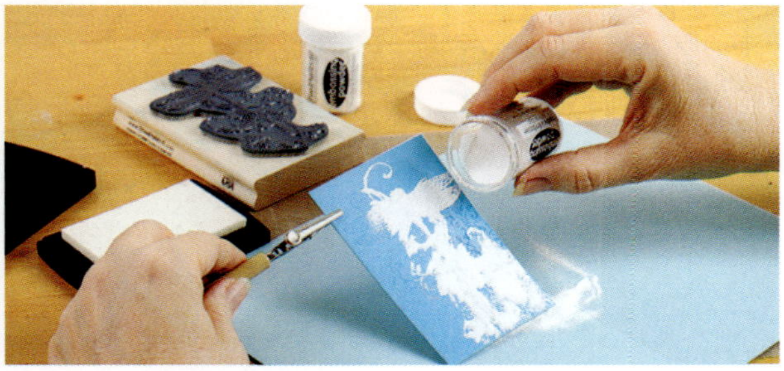

2. Stamp and emboss second layer: Repeat process with another stamp and use another color of Embossing Powder. Heat set.

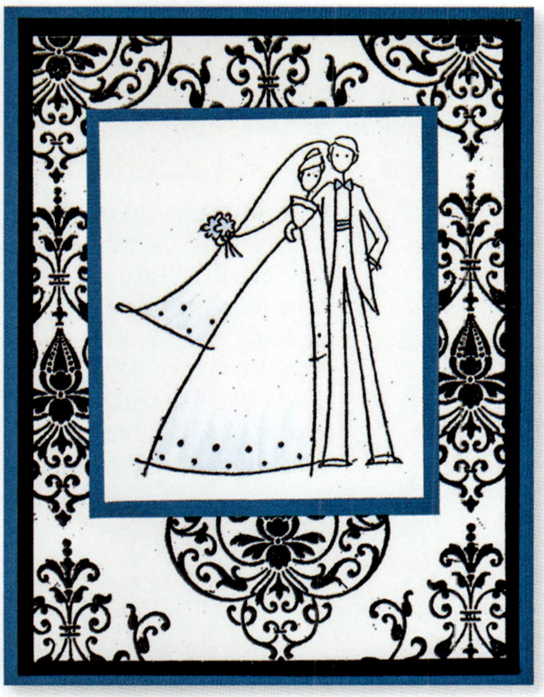

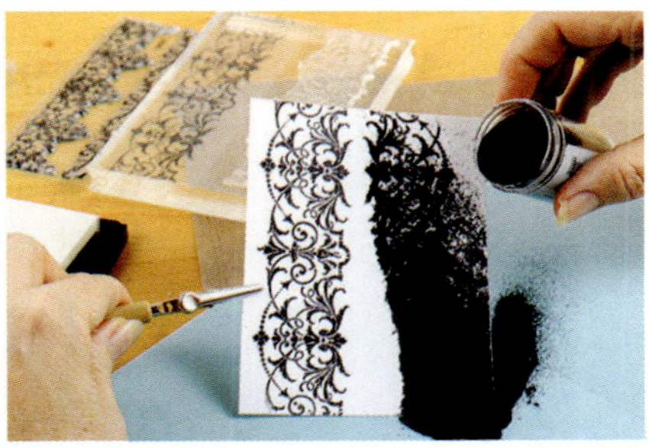

Multiple Stamping Tip: Stamp and dust first impression. Once powder is in place it can wait to be heated. Stamp and dust second impression. Now heat both impressions at once.

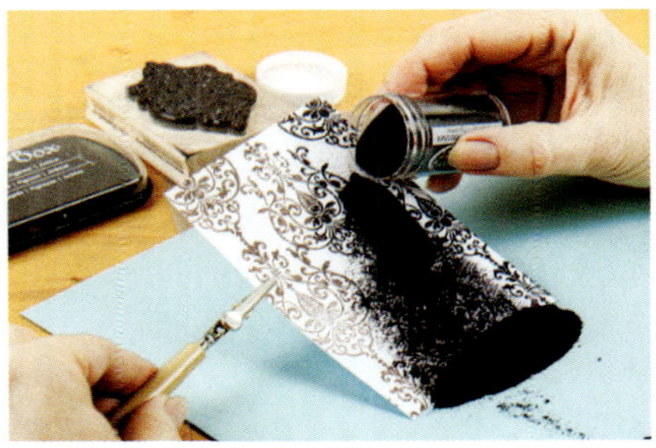

Background Pattern Tip: Stamp in a slow-drying color ink for close placement of images all across panel. Then dust and heat all at once.

BASIC STAMPING TIPS
FOR HEAT EMBOSSING

Stamping is the basis of embossing and the one builds on the other. So if you are struggling, these basic tips may help you discover the problem. If your stamped impression is not right, fix it before going forward with Embossing Powder or heating.

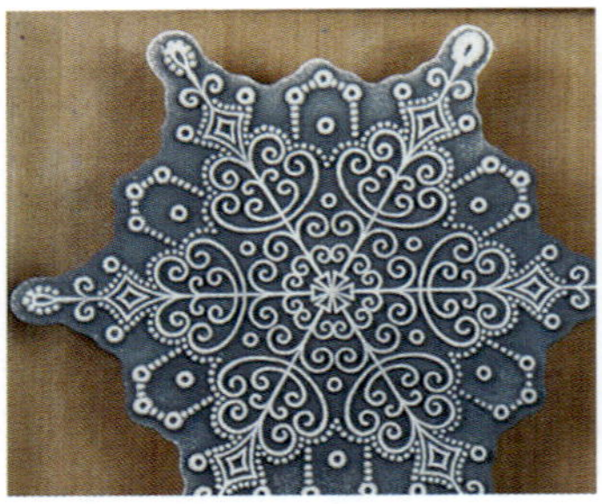

Ideal inking is evenly and entirely covered on the surface design area without excess ink in the recessed areas.

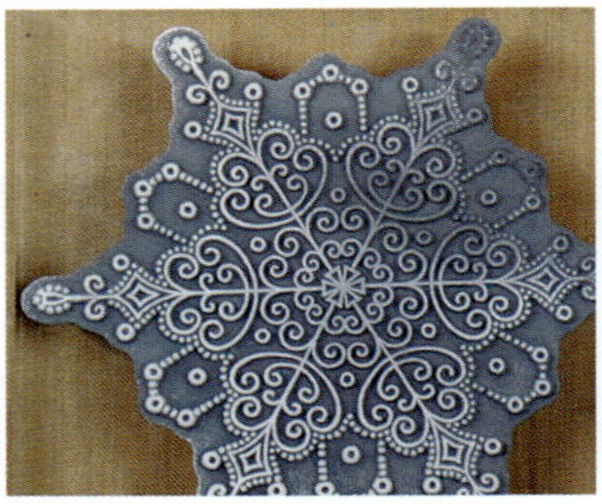

Missed ink areas happen most often in the center of a large stamp that could use a bit more finger pressure to ensure a complete covering of ink. With clear ink, check for shiny or dull areas.

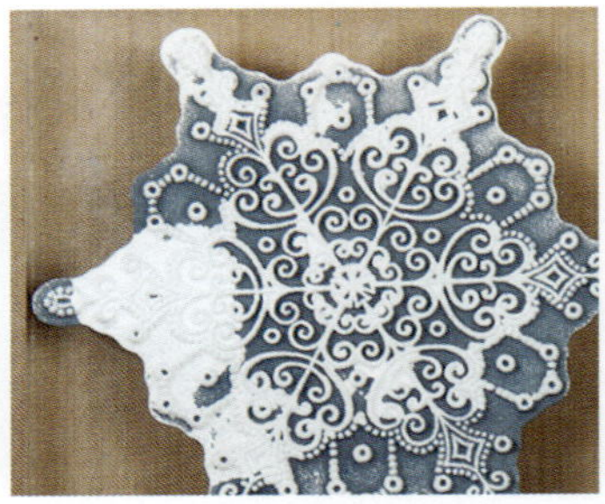

Over-inking with a very wet, new or gooshy pigment in a foam ink pad will cause a fine line impression to increase in size. Press lightly or clean stamp and try again. Good impressions are the right combination of ink and pressure. Each stamp may have a different feel.

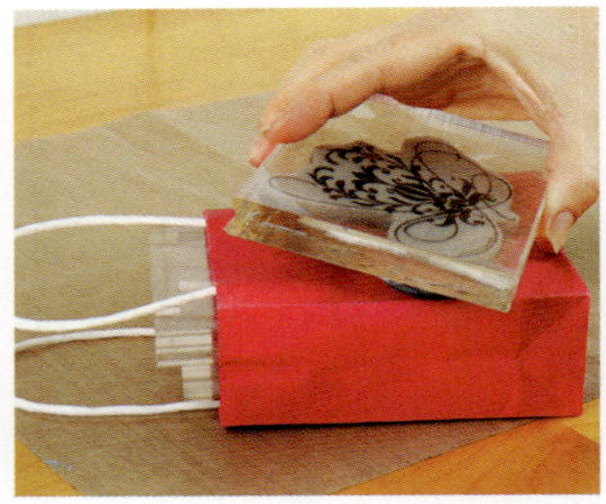

What is underneath should be smooth. Put block handles inside gift bag for a level even surface. Some like a cushioned surface. Most rubber stamps have a cushion. Stamps on handles usually give the best impressions. Large stamps will need more finger pressure in the middle of the stamp.

Clean-Up

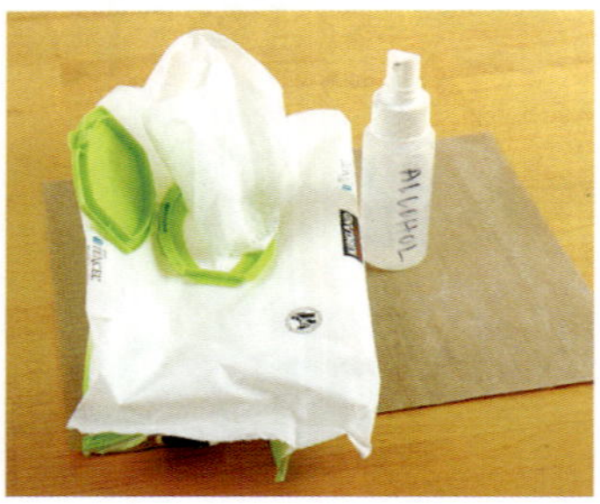

Clean hands to start with will minimize oily or wet smudges on paper. Sometimes ink on your hands will get on your papers. Use wet wipes, rubber stamp cleaners, water or rubbing alcohol in spray bottles. When you dust with Embossing Powders, sticky smudges will capture powder.

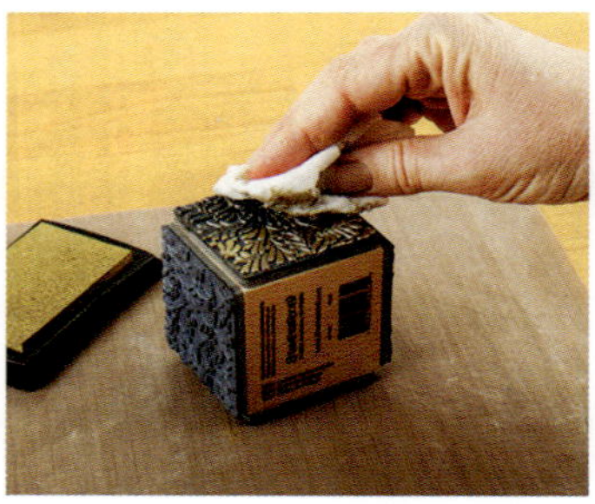

Wet wipes are fine with most inks. VersaMark™ ink is clear, but remains sticky so it helps to clean stamps before storing.

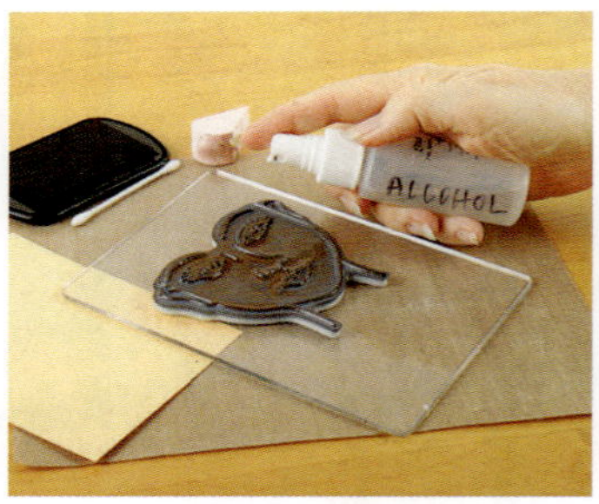

Stamp cleaners or alcohol in a spray bottle can be used on stamps if you need a stronger or wetter option in the studio than going to the sink.

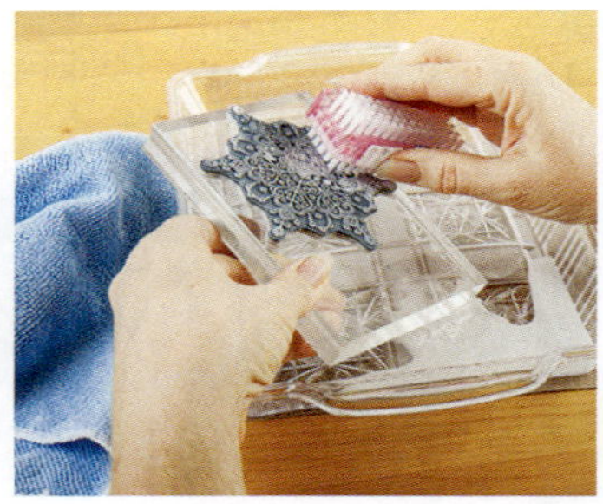

Wet scrub is quick in a tray or sink. Scrub with soft brush. Cling rubber stamps with imprinted indexes can be soaked in a shallow tray of scalding hot water or spritzed with alcohol to remove even dried-on acrylic paints.

WORKING & STORAGE TIPS
FOR HEAT EMBOSSING

The more colors of powders you use in your project, the more it will help to consider these storage and work options. Some more complicated techniques require quick access to multiple powders. It is helpful to have many powders in easy reach and put them all away at the end.

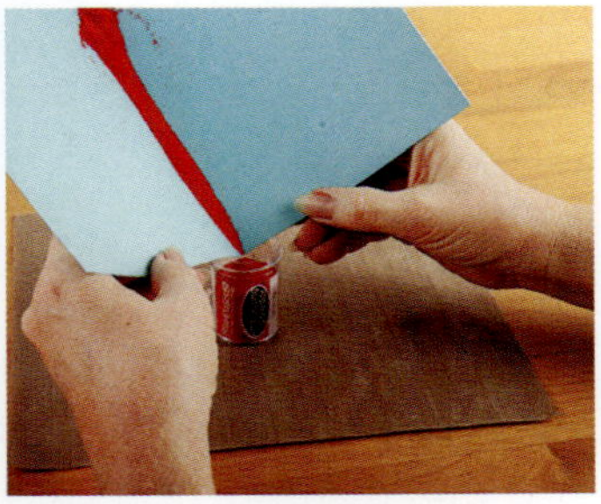

Folded paper underneath will catch the excess powder and make it easy to funnel it back into jar. If you need to work quickly with multiple colors, papers require lots of space to spread them out.

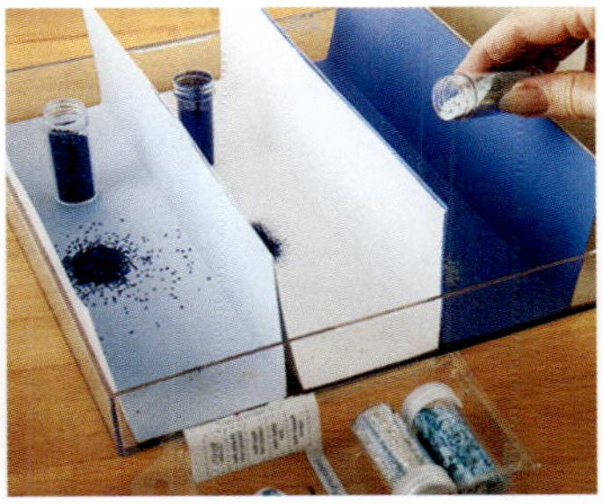

Double-fold papers will stand up and take up less space for multiple colors. If you stand them up in a tray, you can access each color more easily with less risk of spilling over.

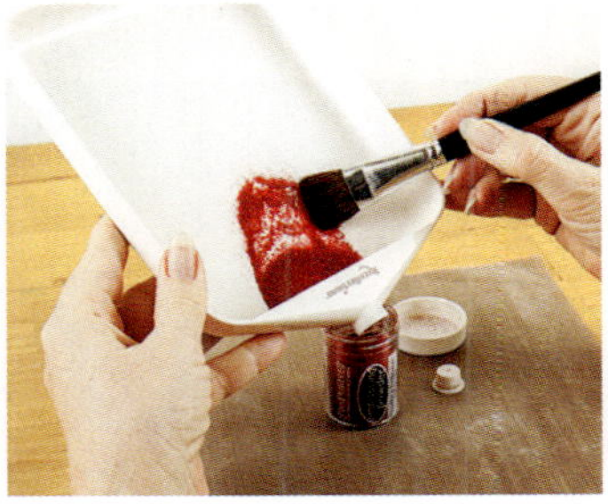

Glitter trays have a spout with a stopper to hold and then funnel powders back into jar. Again you can only work with one color at a time. Tray must be cleaned before next color.

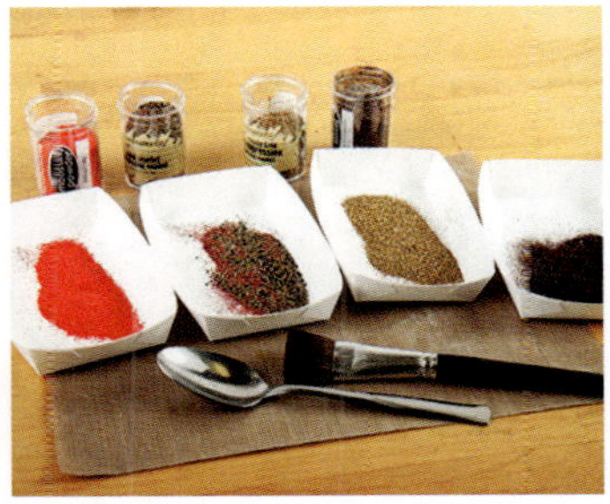

Paper food trays are inexpensive and great for temporary use. These trays are a great option for workshops.

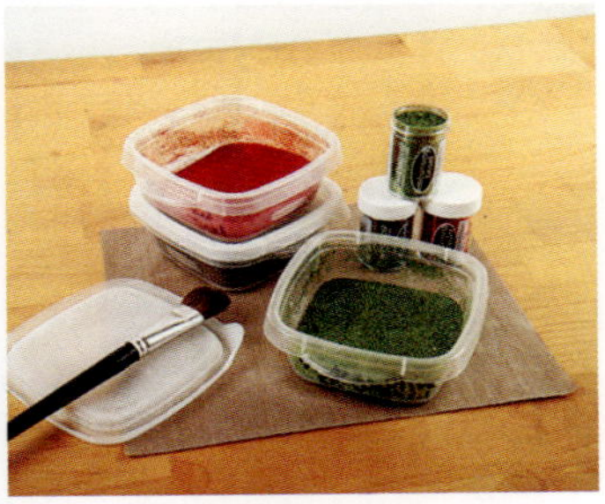

Plastic containers with lids will work well for temporary or permanent storage. Select shallow, wide sizes big enough to catch powders under your card or project.

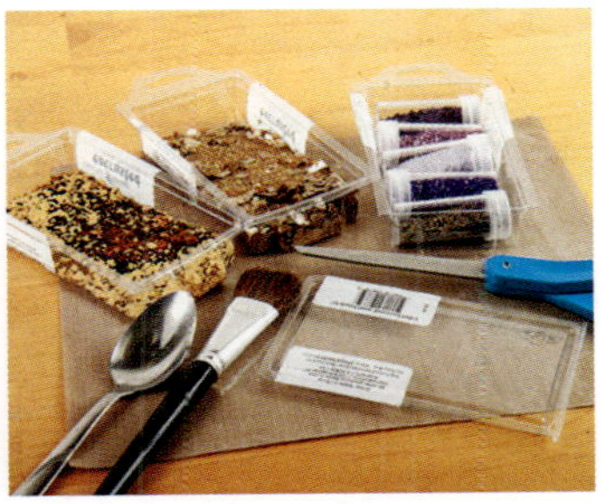

Clam shell packaging of 5 jar or Spoonful Kit is just big enough for an A2 sized card. Use scissors to cut lid off at the hinge. Lid will snap back on but not be air tight so it is okay for studio when it is stored level. This is not safely portable.

Tip: A soft, dry brush will work to gather powders out of any of these containers to return them to jar.

Powder Mix-Ups

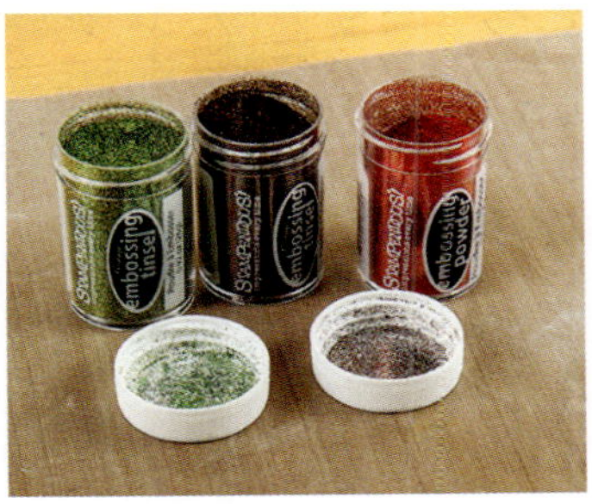

Contaminated powders might simply be thrown away OR, if you want to keep them, but not mix them back in, find another bottle or container to keep the mix. Avoid switching lids. Frantage™ mixes started with an accident that became a happy surprise. You can have an "end of the road" mix that is ever-changing.

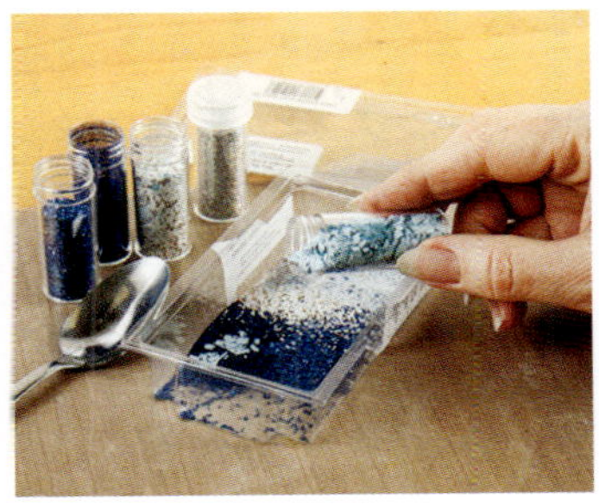

Custom mixes are lots of fun. Intentionally pre-mix powders for splashes of color for Encrusted Jewel Technique. See page 42. Mix different types of powders for special effects. Mix small quantity of powder first and test. Add other elements such as glitter, crushed glass glitter, color fragments, mica fragments or Shaved Ice.

Protection

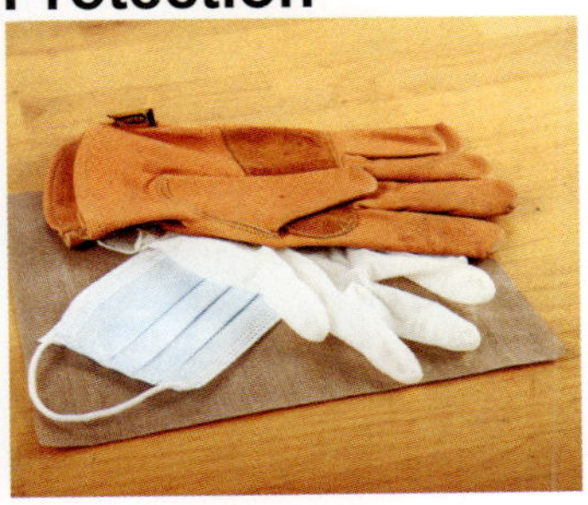

Crafters with sensitive skin may want to wear gloves. A mask and good ventilation are advised when melting powders on griddle. Some folks are especially sensitive to fumes. Do not cook with items used for crafting.

PROBLEM SOLVING TIPS
AND FAQs FOR HEAT EMBOSSING

If you are not having any problems, skip these pages. Come back if you run into difficulties and can not figure out what is going wrong. Damp, cold, or humidity may affect results.

Powder DOESN'T stick where it should, what am I missing?

Here are some things to check to have more consistent results every time.

Wrong ink type such as quick drying chalk, dye or permanent ink could be your problem. Fast drying inks will not stay wet long enough to capture powders evenly. Inks will dry out more quickly in hot, arid conditions. Even a ceiling fan can dry ink too quickly.

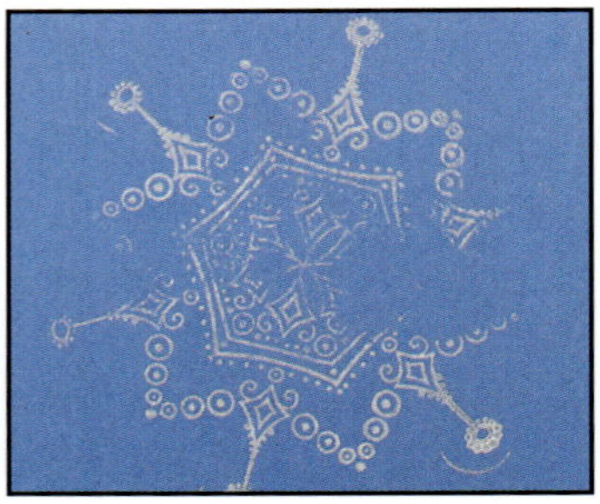

Missed ink may occur in areas that simply did not connect with the ink pad or, when pressed unevenly, missed a spot. Clear inks may be difficult to see. Look for shiny or dull areas. Unmounted stamps are more difficult to press completely and evenly.

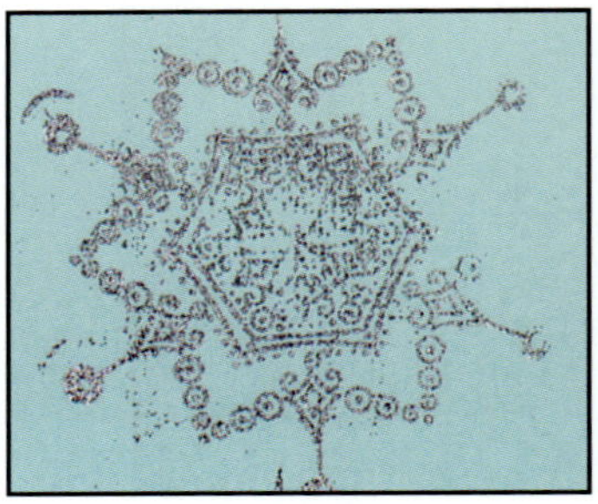

Messy, careless stamping will be magnified when you dust with Embossing Powder. Be sure to touch up BEFORE heating.

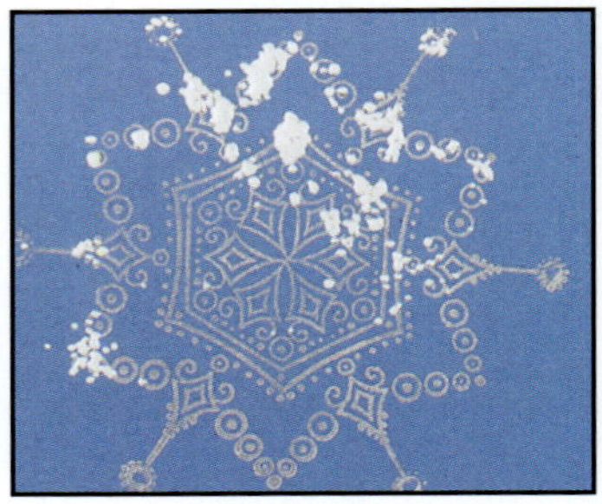

Wrong combinations of chunky powders on fine line stamp impressions will be uneven at best. For best results: dust quickly, tap minimally, and heat from underneath. Chunky granules will get larger when melted.

Powder sticks where I DON'T want it, what can I do to clean it up?

Here are some options that can be done BEFORE heating.

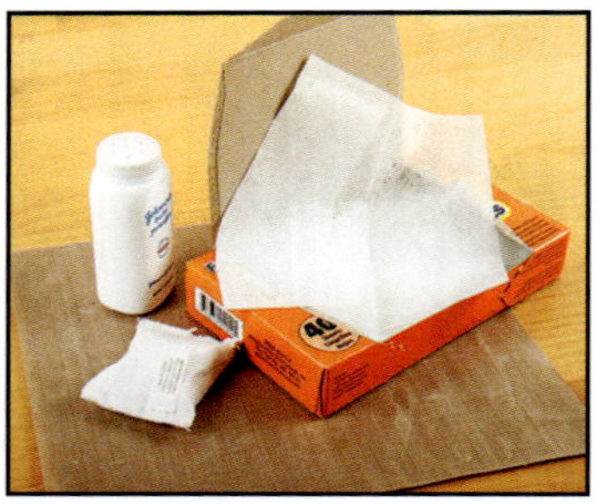

Anti-static pouch or talcum powder or a quick brush of a dryer sheet across the paper may be needed BEFORE you begin in order to reduce static. This is especially true with detail powders.

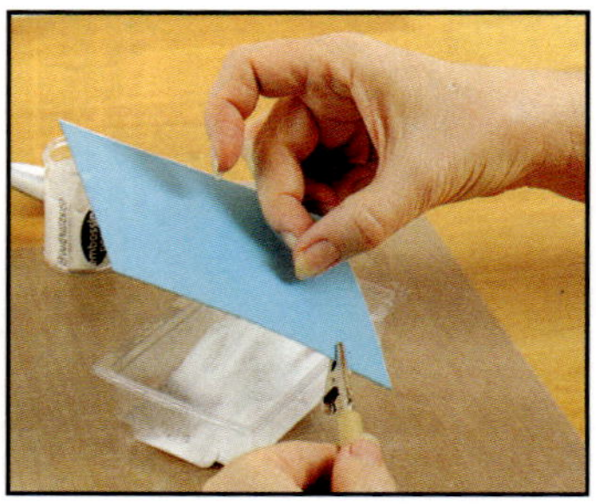

Tapping on the back of the paper releases most of the unwanted powders. Blow away small bits. If needed, try a firmer snap or flick from the back. If it removes too much, dust again with powder. Heat when you are satisfied.

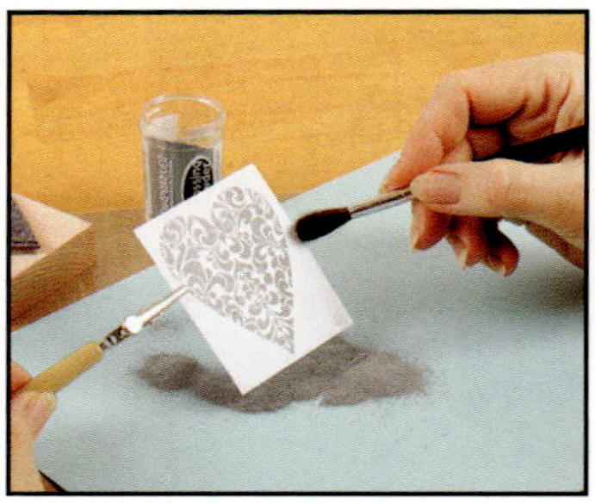

Small brushes, stencil tool, or tip of craft knife will allow you to remove particles in small places. If you disturb areas you want you can dust again, but then you may have to clean again, too.

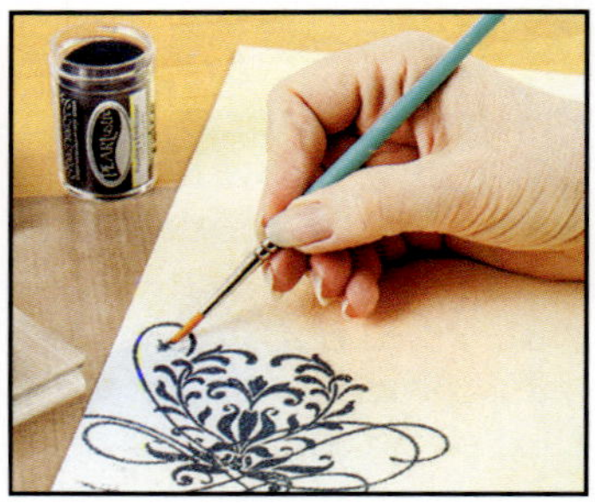

Open areas on some designs will imprint ink and catch powder. Use a small dry brush to remove any unwanted powder BEFORE heating.

Can I OVERHEAT Embossing Powder?

Yes,but here are some suggestions to avoid burning.

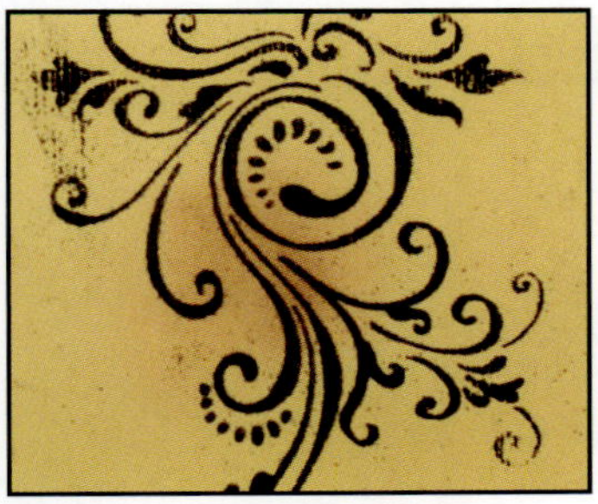

Scorching paper may occur if you hold the heat in any one place too long. For best results, heat in one area until you see a change, then move heat slowly and consistently on to the next area.

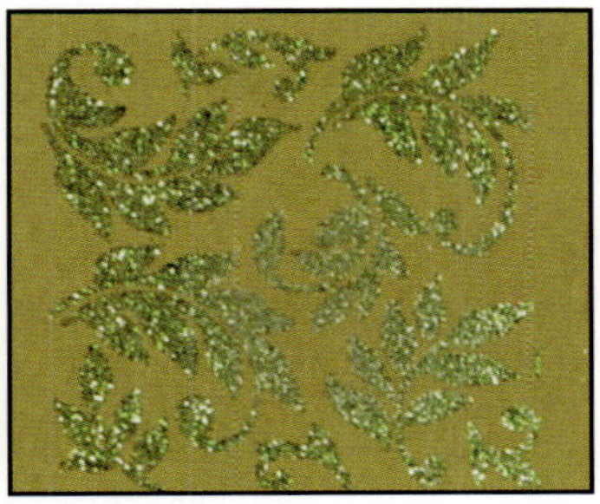

Burning powder may occur if you hold the heat in any one place too long. When Metallics, and especially Tinsel or glittery powders, are overheated they burn out and become dull and flat.

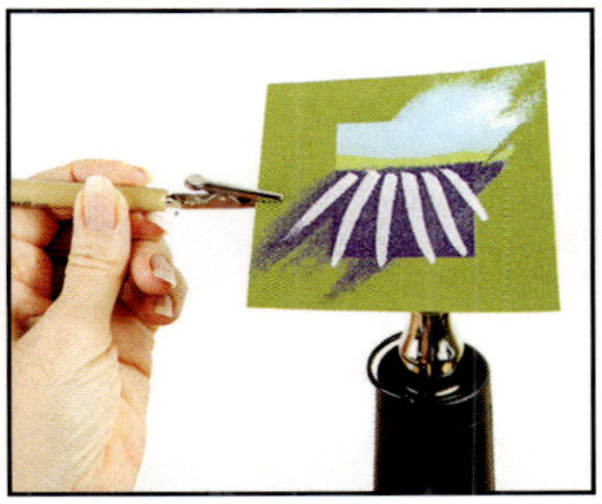

Don't burn fingers and instead use clip tools to hold away from heat tool. Do not ever touch molten Embossing Powder; it burns your fingers and disturbs the impression. Instead, wait several seconds to be sure it is cool. Test carefully. **Heat tools should only be used by an adult.**

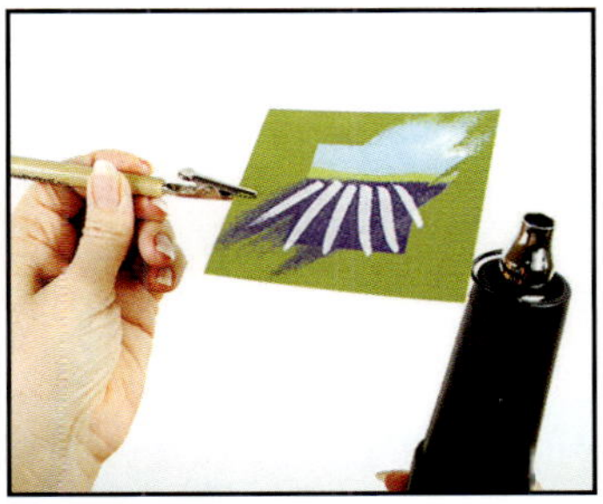

Heat tool smoking may occur for a few minutes with a new heat tool. Otherwise, a very hot tool held too closely under the paper may be trapping air. Simply move heat tool to the side to get more air and move back in to continue heating. An old heat tool may smoke or rattle when it is almost burned out.

REPAIRING TIPS FOR HEAT EMBOSSING

Can I REPAIR an imperfect impression?

Try these options that can still be done AFTER heating.

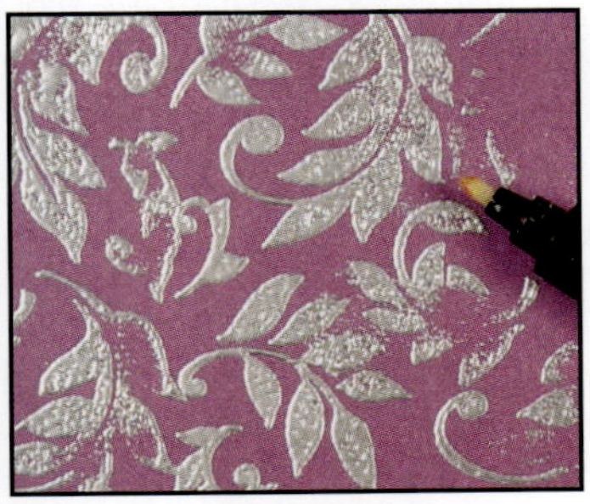

Touch up small areas with little lines or dots using a ballpoint pen or VersaMarker™. Dust and heat again.

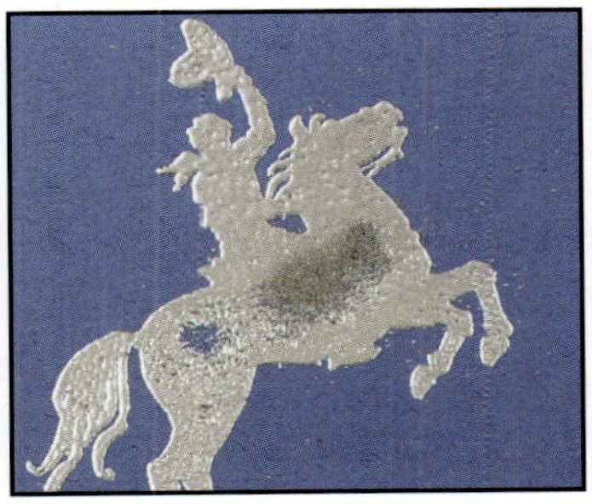

Fill in larger background areas without adding ink. Simply sprinkle powder lightly, hold level with clip tool, and heat from underneath to melt it in without looking lumpy.

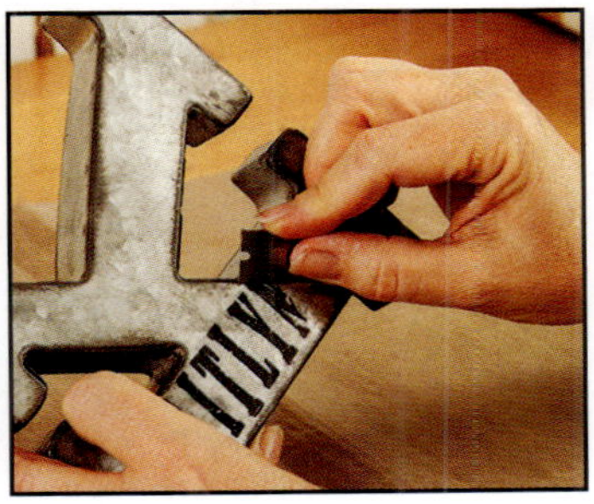

Replace it: In some cases, such as non-porous surfaces, you can use a razor blade to remove melted powder. See page 60 for repair tips on metal surfaces.

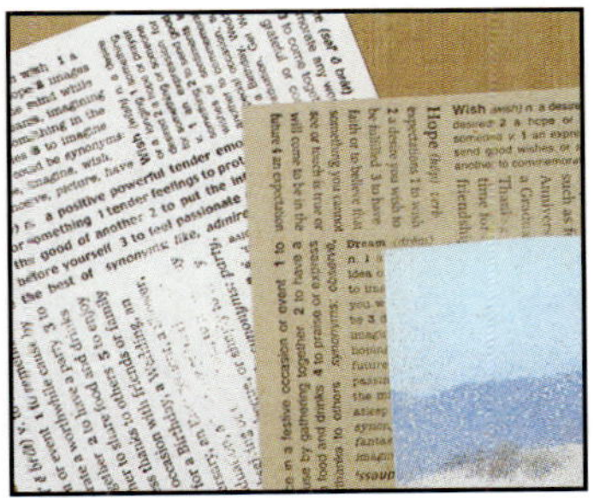

Cover it when all else fails by stamping or embossing another image over it. Tear it, add another layer, a cut out or a 3D embellishment. Use it for a collage in a mixed media journal. You may have created a one-of-a-kind masterpiece.

MULTIPLE COLOR & CONTINUOUS PATTERN
EMBOSSING POWDER TECHNIQUES

C

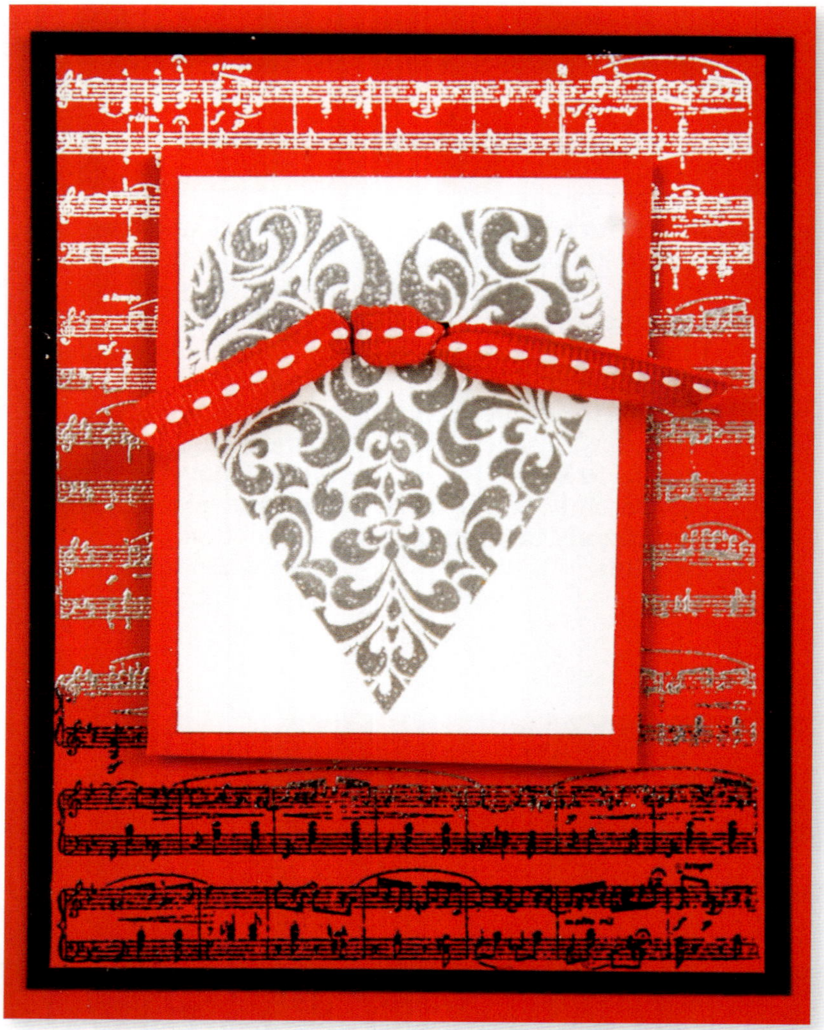

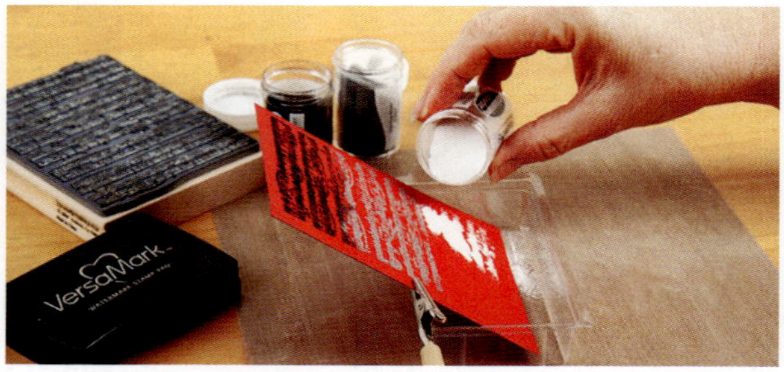

Multiple color powders: Stamp large image in wet ink and dust with one or MORE colors. Use an open container or separate folded scrap paper for each color if you don't want to mix your Embossing Powders. Heat all at once.

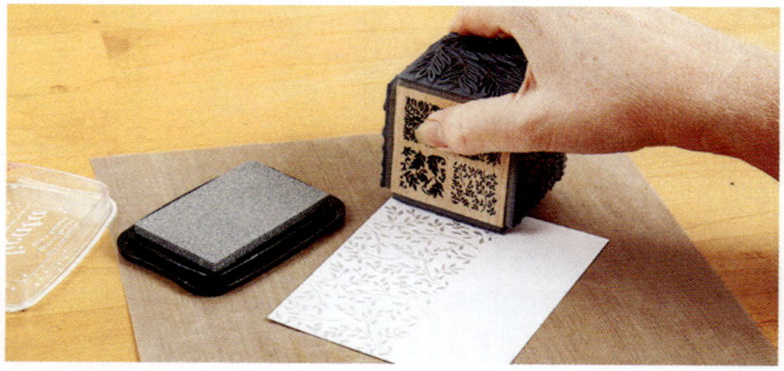

Continuous patterns can be stamped and embossed most easily with a pigment ink pad so you can see to line up the pattern and have time to cover entire panel. Start in one corner and continue in rows. It is better to overlap patterns than to leave gaps. Texture Cubes are designed for easy registration. Dust entire card with one or more powders and heat.

Timing Tip: Dust powder over wet ink as soon as possible, but then as long as you don't disturb it, you do not have to hurry to heat it. Dust a batch and heat all at once.

Touch-Up Tip: If you miss a spot, dust it again. If you get powder where it shouldn't be, tap gently on the back of the paper or use a small dry brush to remove it BEFORE heating. Many imperfections can be fixed. Fill in small spots with a ballpoint pen or VersaMarker™.

Remember, a handstamped card is special because you made it, not because it looks as perfect as if a machine printed it.

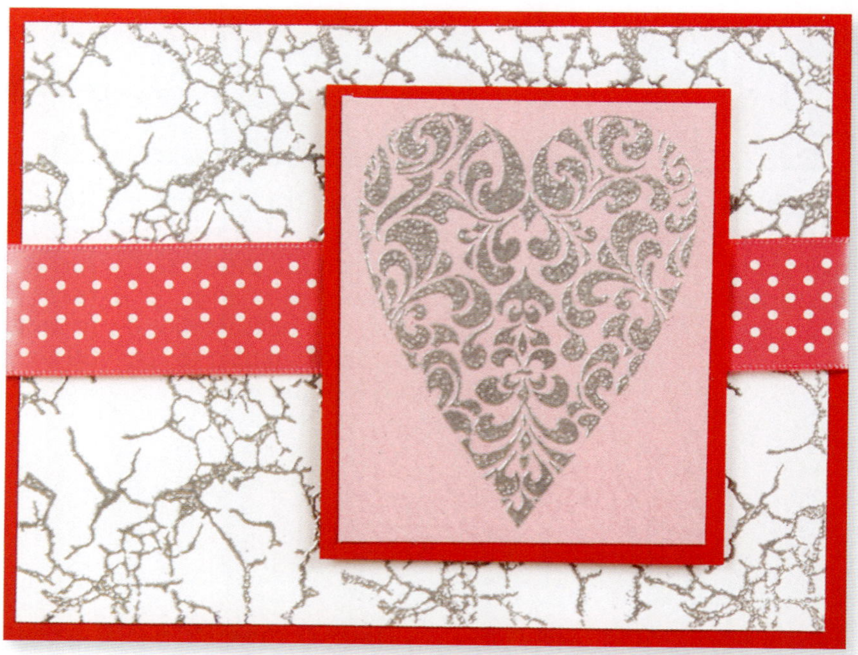

D

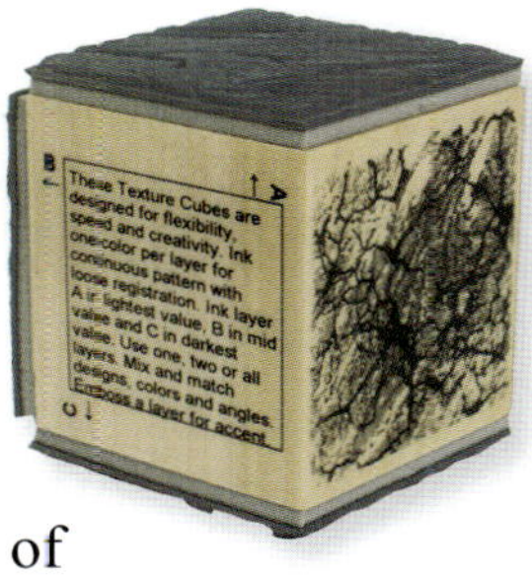

Texture Cubes have 3 or 4 stamp designs. Some are designed to work in layers one on top of another such as the Marble Texture Cube. For best alignment of patterns, keep the same grip and switch from one design to the next with a spin of the block. Test your colors.

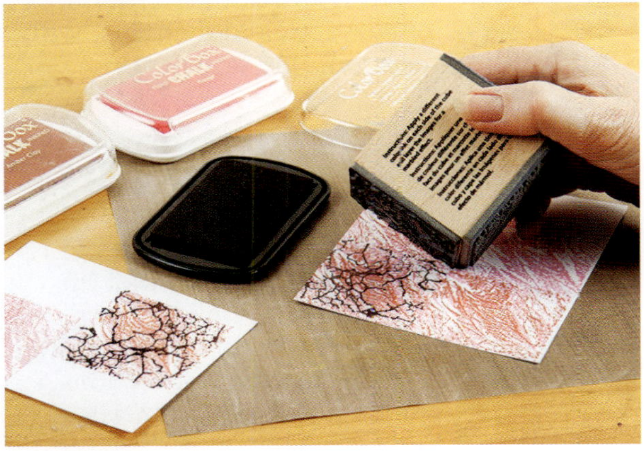

Texture Cube Layers: Stamp one pattern all across the card. Each ink layer will need to be COMPLETELY dry before you can dust and emboss a layer. Repeat process with a different color ink or Embossing Powder.

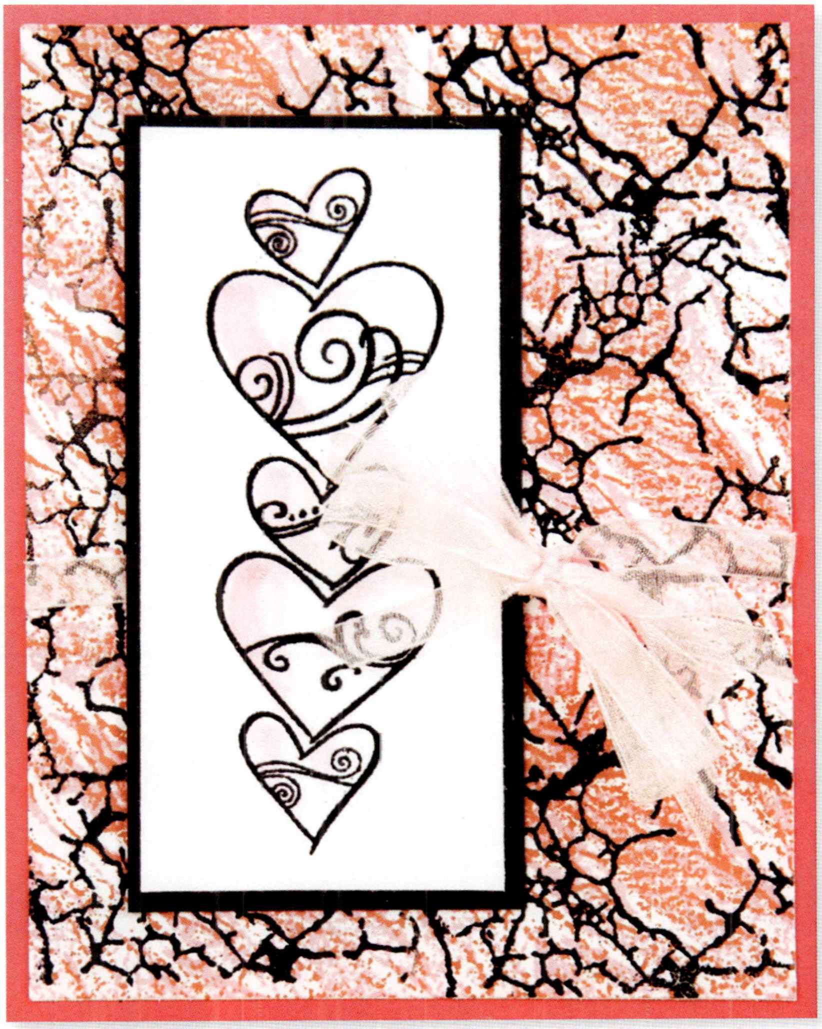

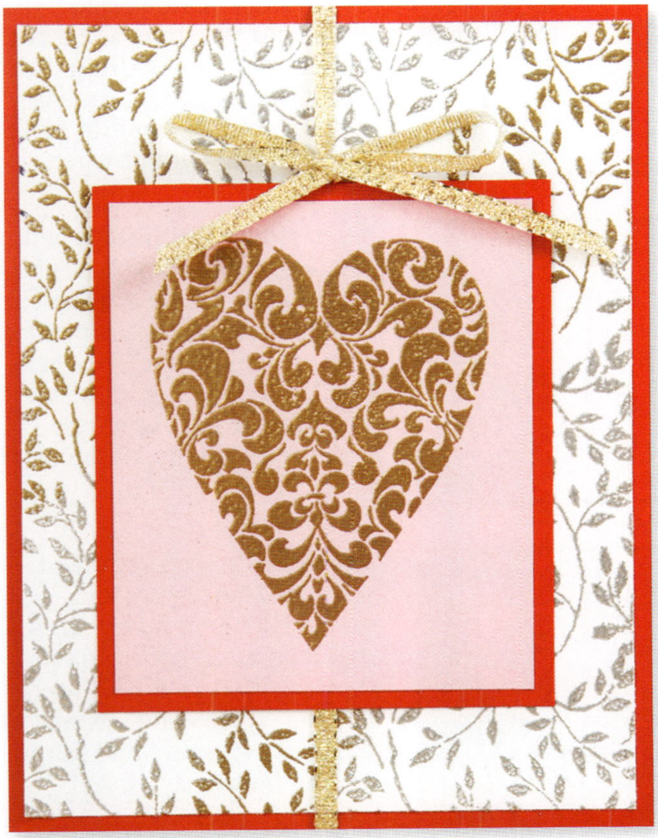

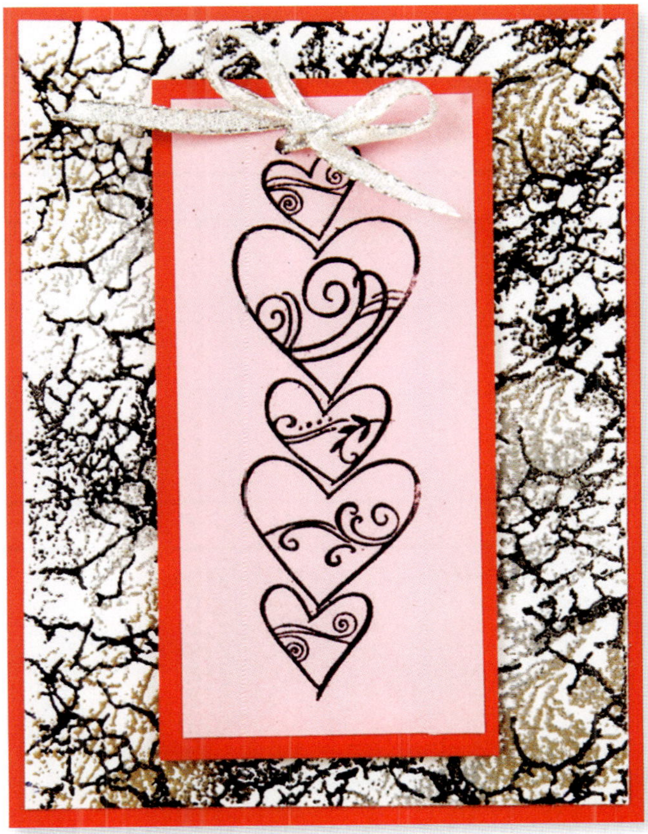

APPLICATOR OPTIONS FOR EMBOSSING POWDERS

E

While ink on a stamp is the most common way to emboss, here are more options for the doodler or mixed media artist who wants to personalize cards or journals, add a border, or touch up an incomplete impression. Test markers and pens in your stash to see how many will stay wet long enough to work well for embossing. Work in small sections if needed.

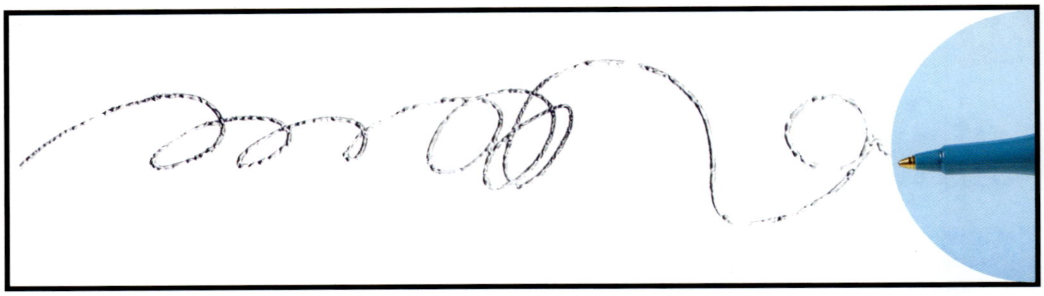

Ballpoint pens with varied widths or colors will generally remain wet long enough to doodle or write messages and then dust with Embossing Powders.

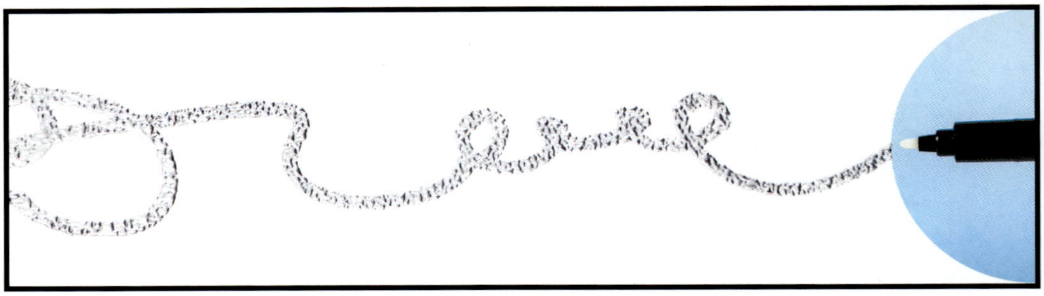

Clear embossing pens or VersaMarker™'s bullet tip give medium width lines, ideal for writing or doodling. Write and dust in sections, then heat all at once. Clear markings may be difficult to see as you go. Ink dries quicker on matte paper.

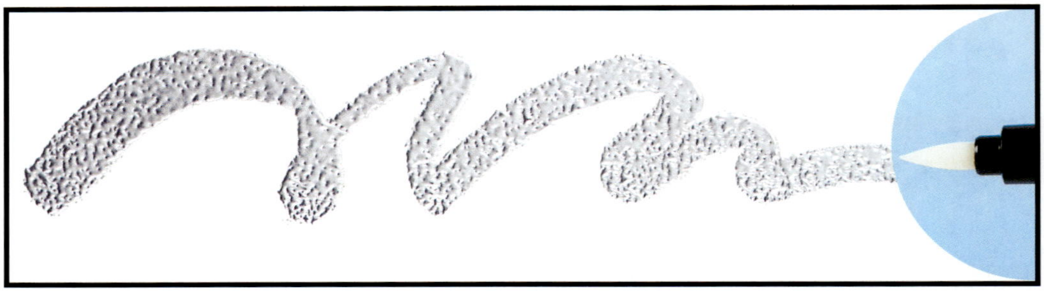

VersaMarker™ with clear watermark ink is double ended and has a flexible brush tip. Create varied thick and thin lines ideal for calligraphy or doodling. Ink dries slowly giving time to work, but is difficult to see until dusted with powder.

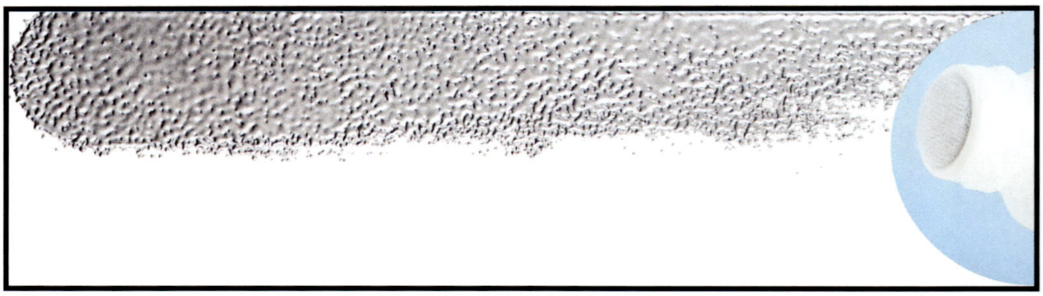

Embossing ink bottles with dauber top allow you to make polka dots, create wonderful brush strokes or ink a portion of a stamp design. Try spray bottles with water, glazes, or glue like Goosebumps Texture Spray by Tsukineko®.

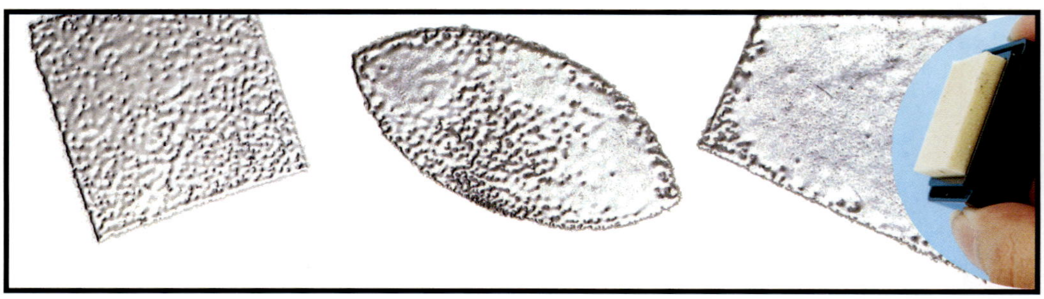

Ink pads that are pigment will be slow drying and are available in many sizes and shapes. Clear or tinted embossing inks are slow-drying. VersaMark™ is one of the most versatile and long-lasting watermark inks.

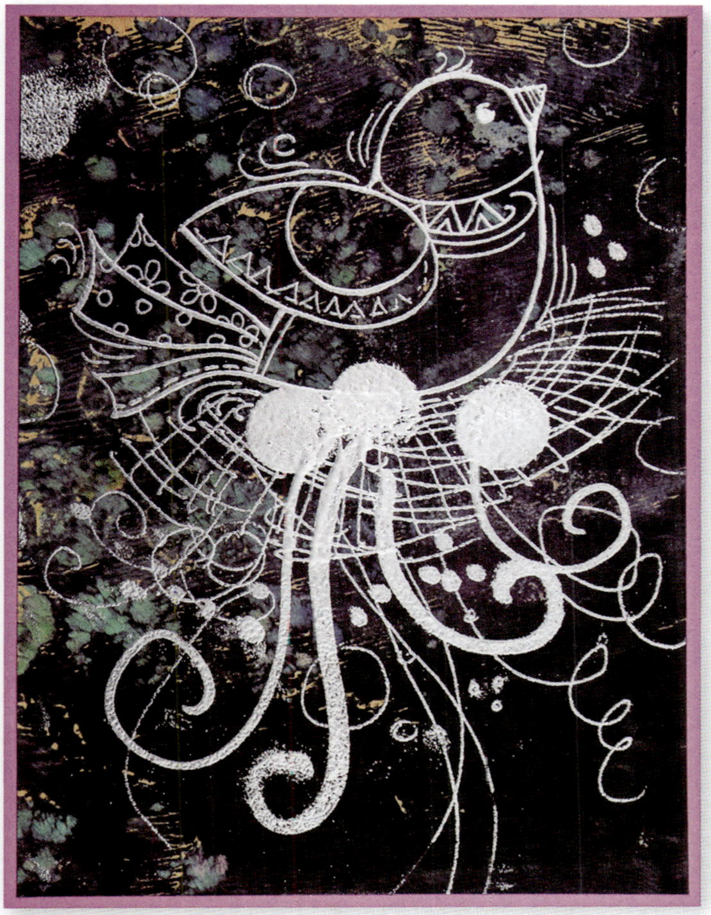

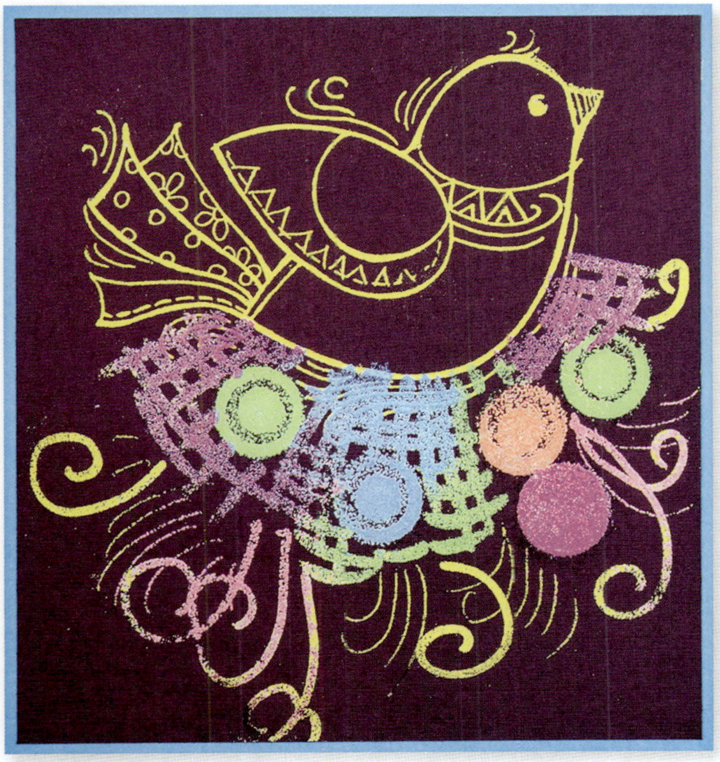

Colorful Tips: Silver and Neon Embossing Powders were used on these cards.

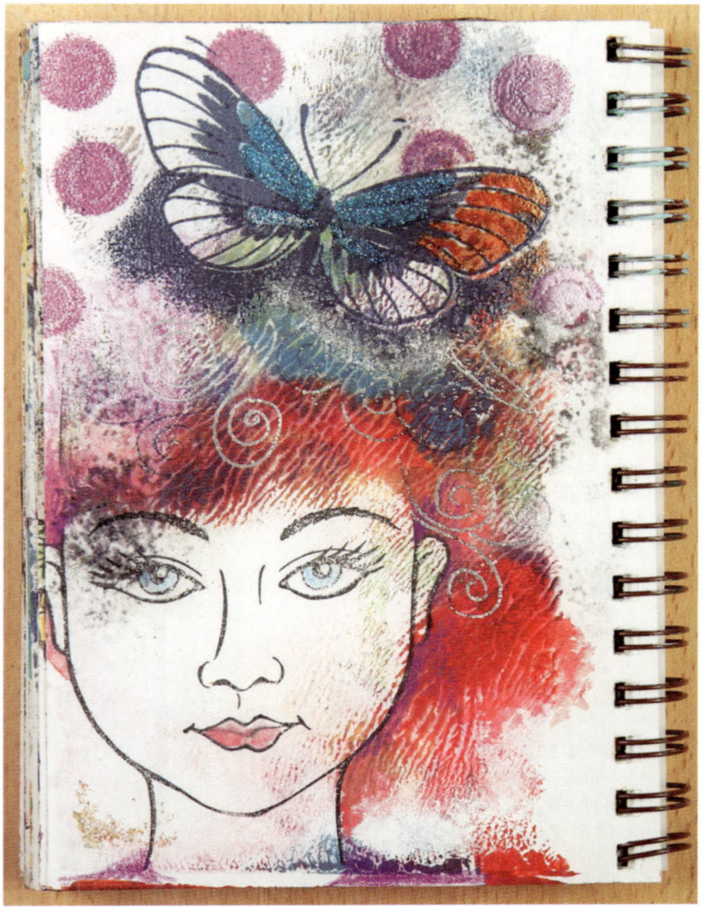

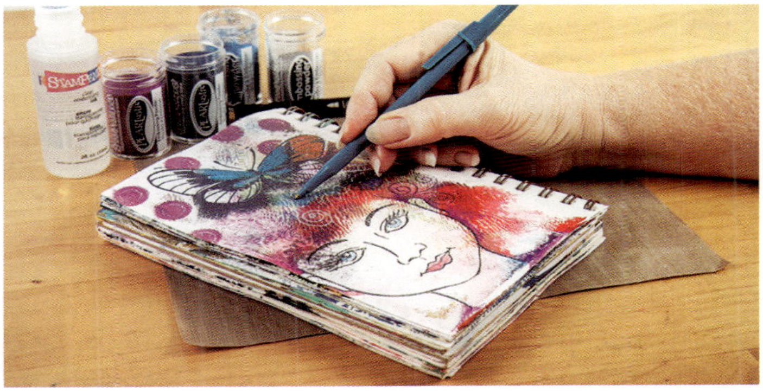

Doodling can be done with any combination of applicators. Stamped images are quick to emboss. Mixed media journals give endless opportunities for embellishing with drawn or handwritten messages.

GRANULATION: DETAIL TO CHUNKY
EMBOSSING POWDERS

Embossing Powders are available in very fine "detailed", "regular", or "chunky" particles. They may be labeled with a variety of names. The same design is shown here in three different granulations so you can see the results and select according to the stamp design you wish to emboss.

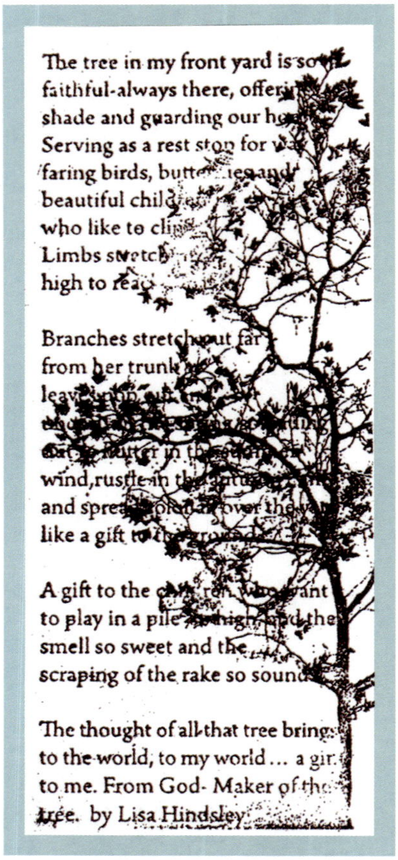

Detail: For best results select a fine stamp and make a light impression with VersaMark™ ink and not a pigment ink with a squishy foam pad.

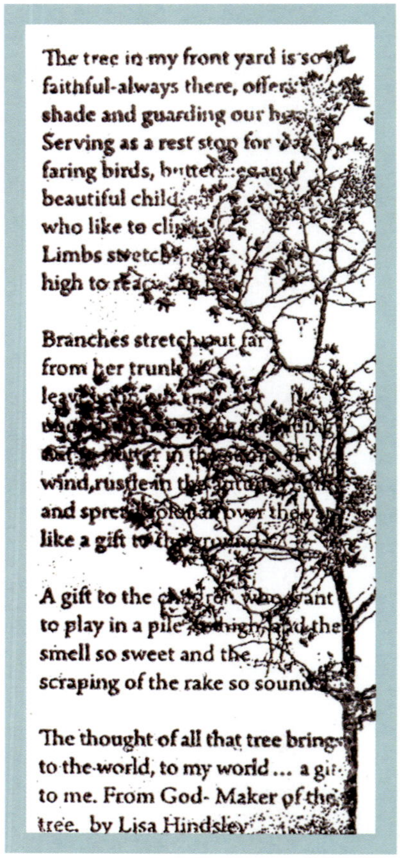

Regular: Gives good results with fine, varied, or bold stamps. Regular is your best all-around option and available in widest range.

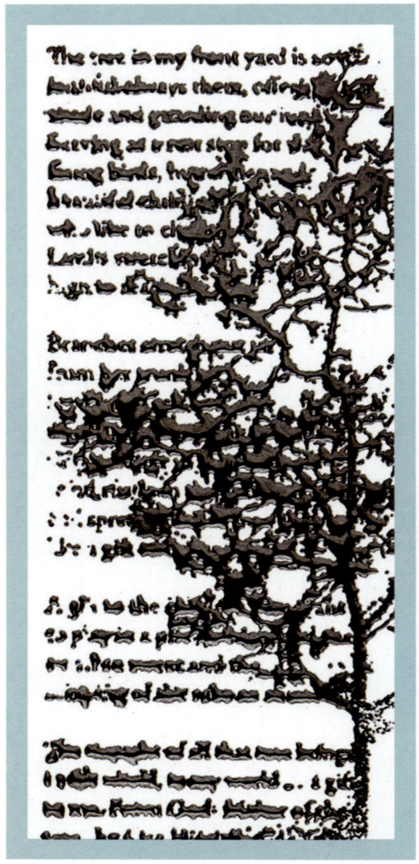

Chunky: May not attach to fine details unless heated from beneath. Best for bold images, sprinkling and more advanced "Deep Impression Techniques".

These samples show coverage over VersaMark™ Ink Cube and are sprinkled to show granulation differences.

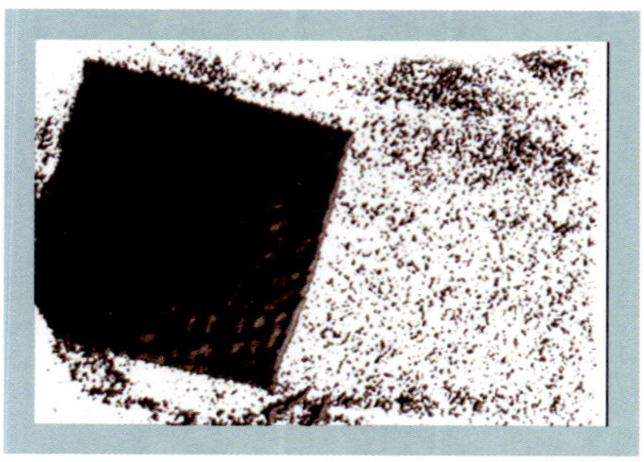

Detail Powders may seem very fly-away. Static makes returning powder to the jar a challenge. Use anti-static pouch, talcum powder, or dryer sheet on paper.

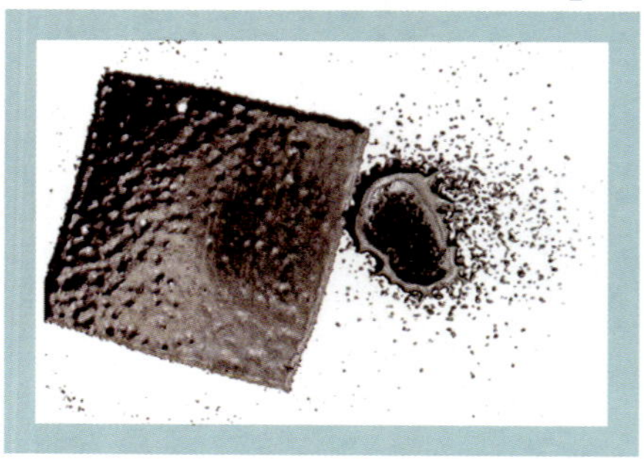

Regular is easy to work with in most any application. Sprinkling doesn't look nearly as interesting as Chunky granules.

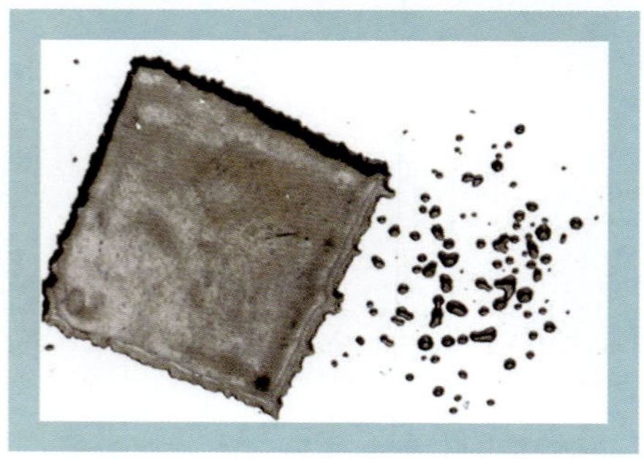

Chunky is the quickest way to get a thick layer. Sprinkled particles get larger when melted and are ideal for Encrusted Jewel Techniques on page 42-47.

TIPS FOR WORKING WITH DETAIL
EMBOSSING POWDERS

Detail Embossing Powders are ideal for capturing the finest details of a stamp. Because they are so fine, they seem very fly-away, and it may take a bit of practice to achieve the perfect impression. Static is also an issue, and an anti-static pouch or a dusting of talcum powder before stamping is recommended. For the perfectionist, detail may be the granulation of choice.

Tip: When stamping a very fine stamp, you may find that a firmer stamping surface and a lighter touch will give you the finest impression. Avoid excessively wet pigment inks with squishy foam pads and cushioned stamping surfaces. These may cause the impression to increase in size and fill in the fine details even with detail powder. Test the amount of pressure best for each type of stamp.

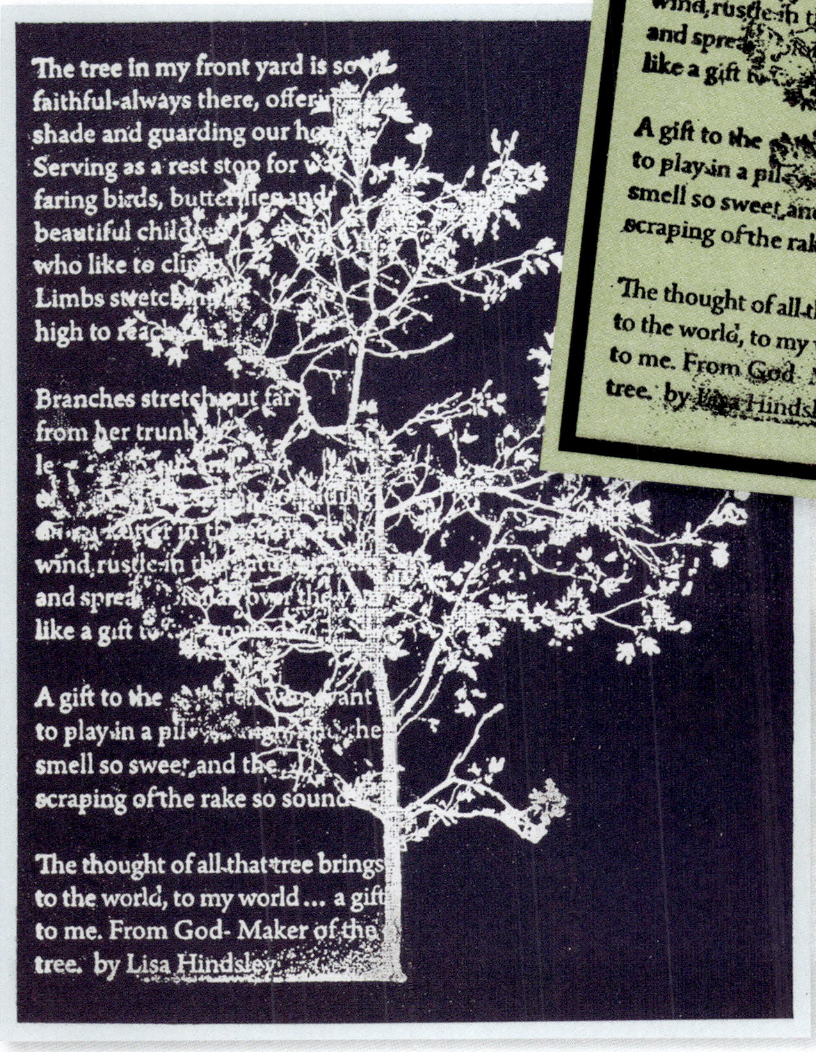

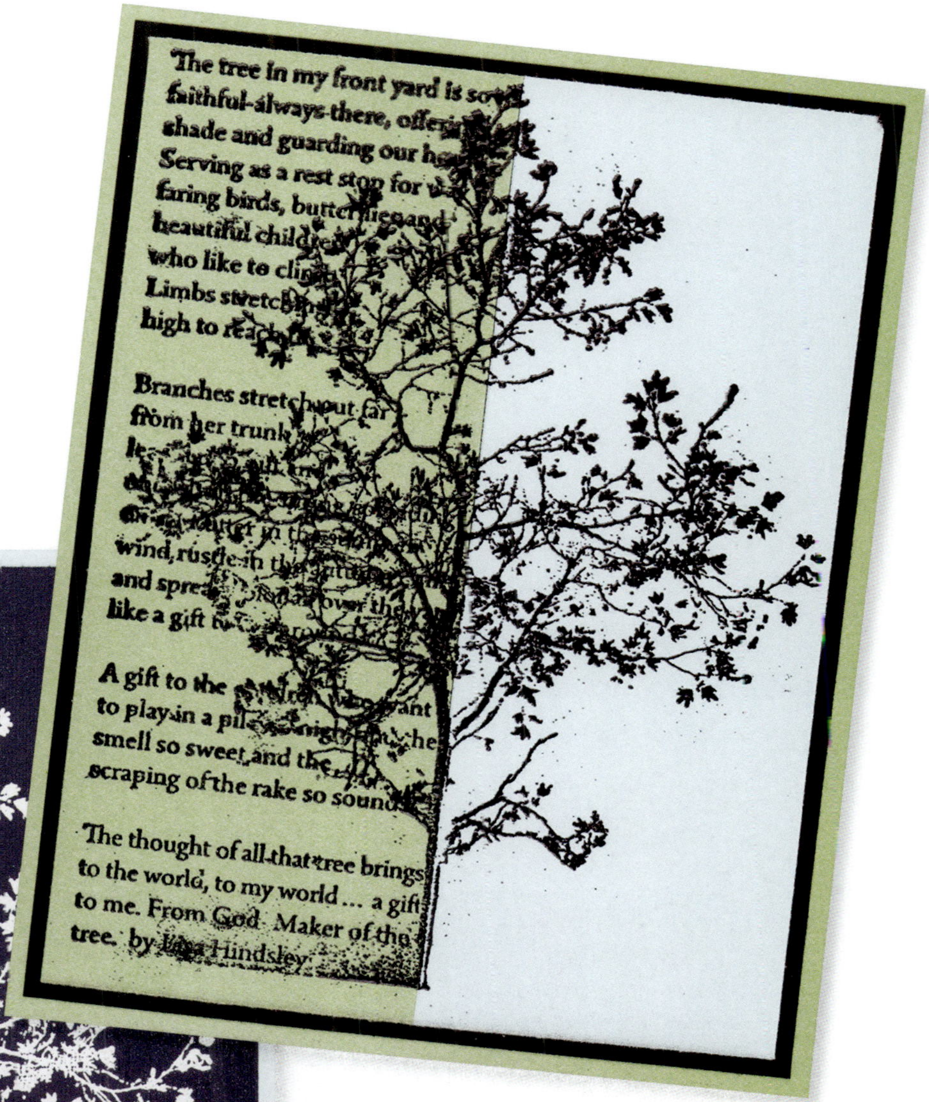

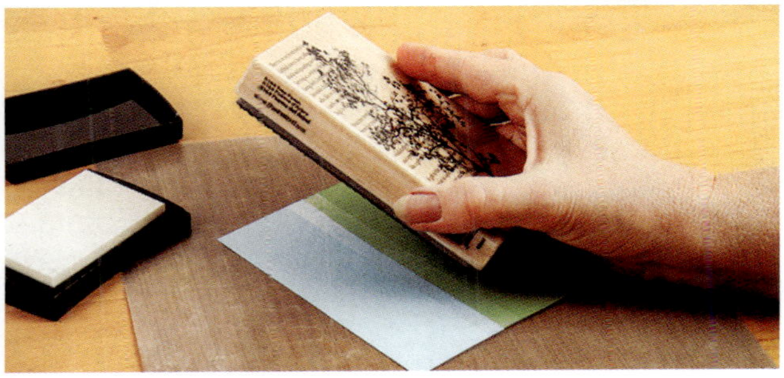

Two-Tone Tip: Trim and tape papers together on the back before stamping and embossing. Otherwise two impressions may be difficult to align and trim.

CLEAR: SHEEN & SHINE
EMBOSSING POWDERS

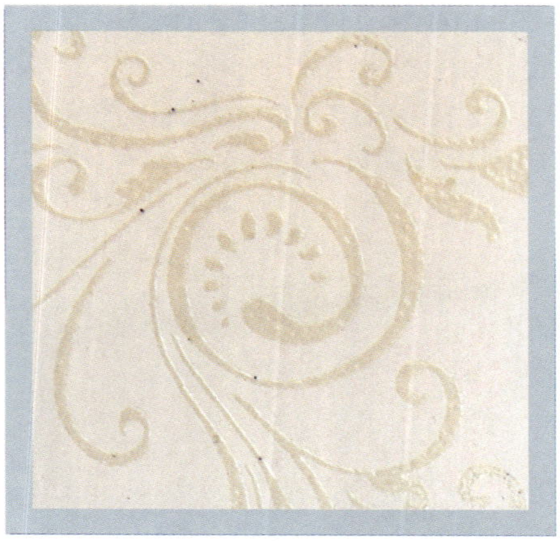

Clear and translucent Embossing Powders offer subtle, elegant impressions often used for wedding invitations.

CLEAR Embossing Powder over clear VersaMark™ ink on matte white paper.

CLEAR Embossing Powder over clear VersaMark™ ink on matte black paper.

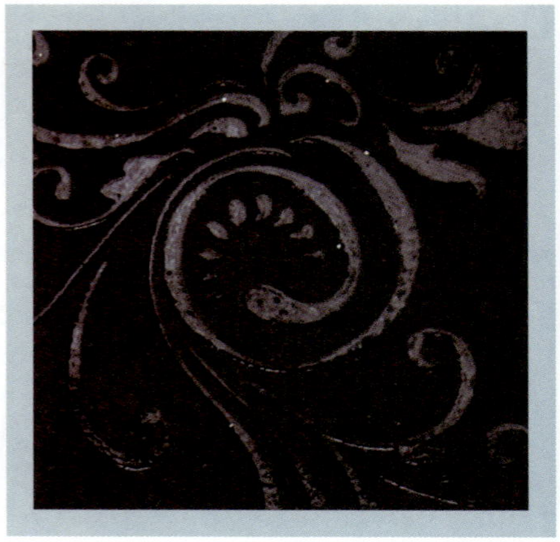

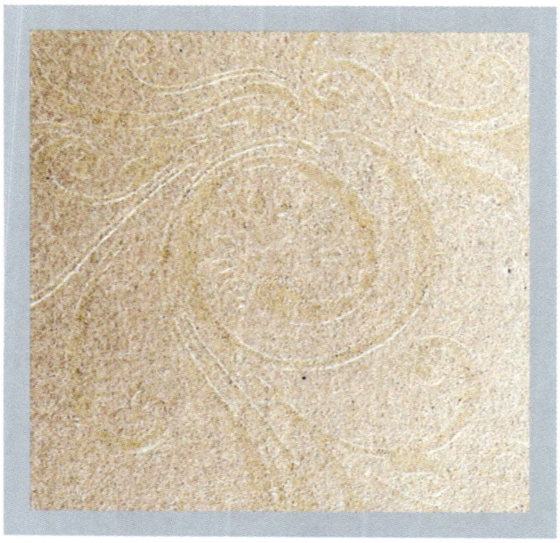

PEARL Embossing Powder over clear VersaMark™ ink on pearlescent ivory paper.

PEARL Embossing Powder over clear VersaMark™ ink on matte black paper.

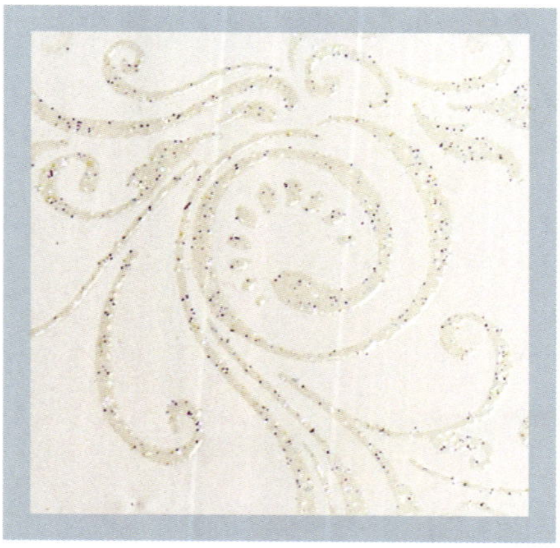

CRYSTAL Embossing Powder over clear VersaMark™ ink on matte white paper.

CRYSTAL Embossing Powder over clear VersaMark™ ink on matte black paper.

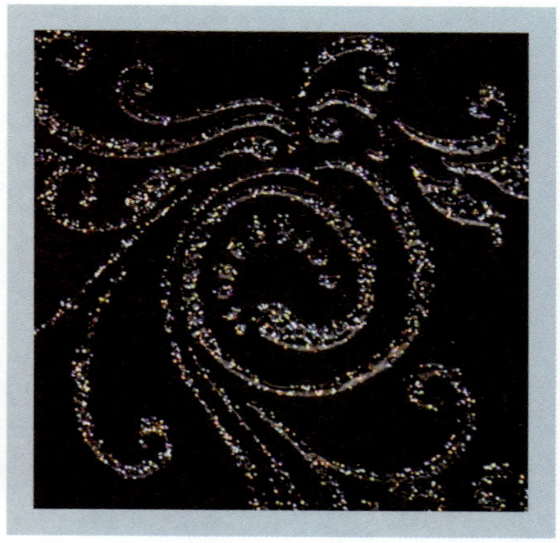

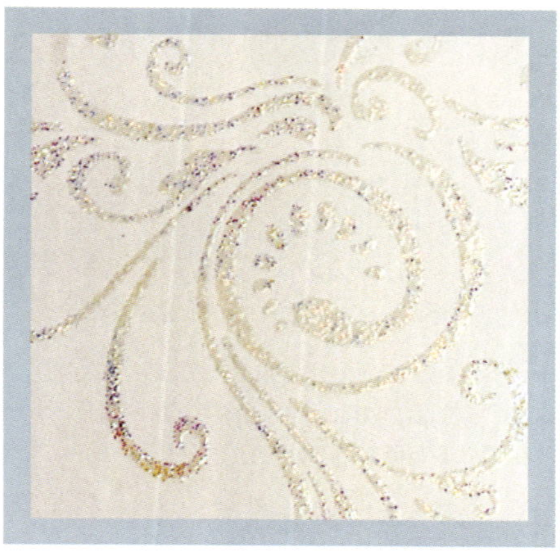

KALEIDOSCOPE Embossing Powder over clear VersaMark™ ink on matte white paper.

KALEIDOSCOPE Embossing Powder over clear VersaMark™ ink is heat sensitive and shows best on black paper. Heating longer takes the look from blue greens to orange yellows.

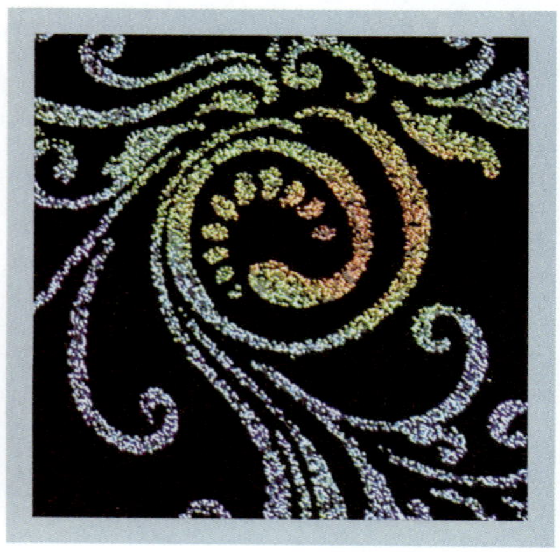

CLEAR & TRANSLUCENT
EMBOSSING POWDERS

Clear and translucent embossing powders offer Glossy "varnish" accents. It is difficult to photograph the sheen on a handmade sample. Use a CLEAN VersaMark™ ink pad and apply directly over stamped art or apply indirectly with a dauber through stencils of any kind.

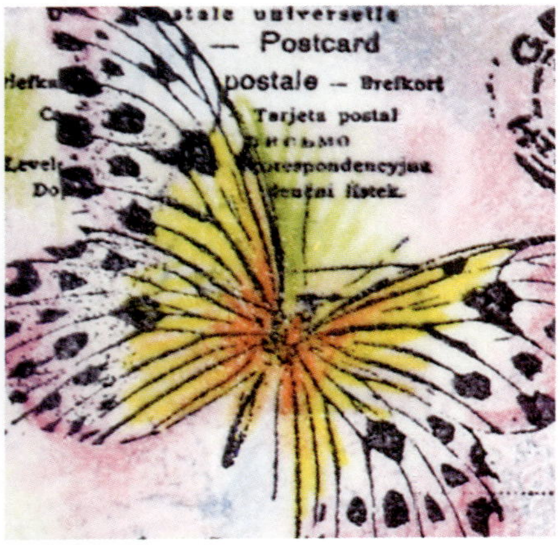

CLEAR Embossing Powder over clear VersaMark™ ink on stamped paper. Try Chunky Clear for an even thicker layer.

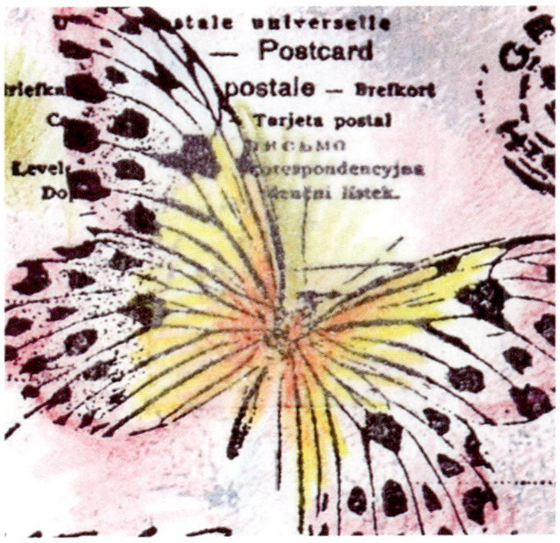

PEARLustre™ WHITE Embossing Powder over clear VersaMark™ ink on stamped paper.

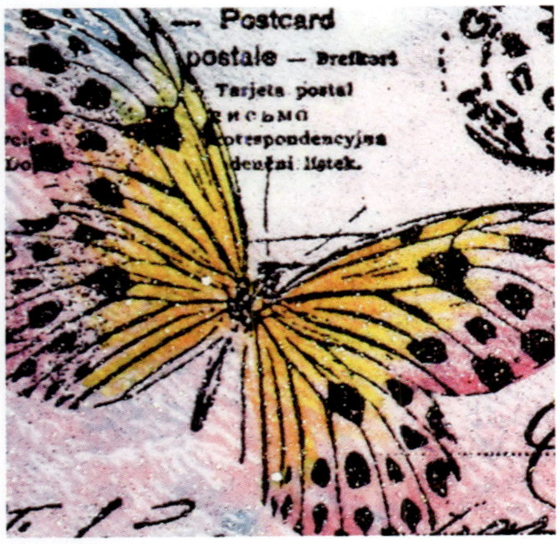

CRYSTAL Embossing Powder over clear VersaMark™ ink on stamped paper.

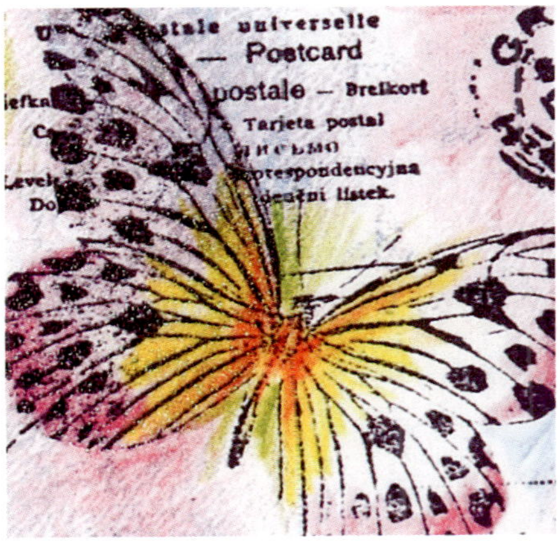

CRYSTAL Embossing Powder over clear VersaMark™ ink applied to only one wing on stamped paper.

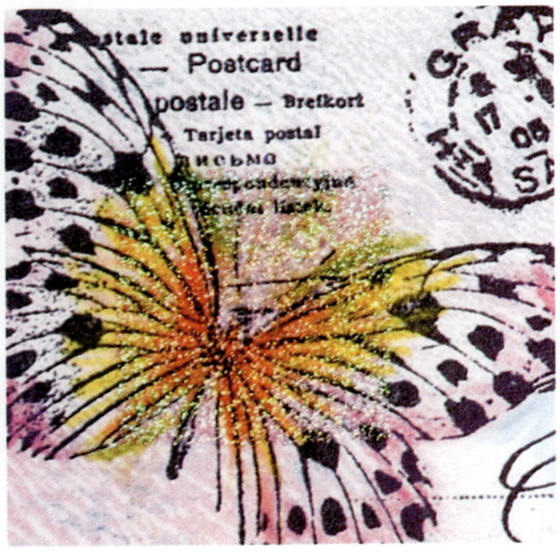

KALEIDOSCOPE Embossing Powder over clear VersaMark™ ink cube on stamped paper.

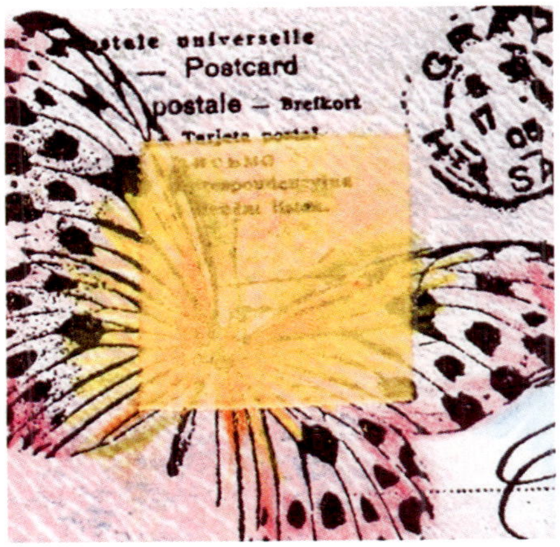

PEARLustre™ TOPAZ Embossing Powder over clear VersaMark™ ink cube on stamped paper.

Tip: Test clear ink over a scrap of stamped art to ensure that colors will not bleed when moisture is applied. For example: aquarelle colored pencil may brighten or may run. Try over printed paper patterns. Be sure to get complete and even coverage where you want it, because patching a second layer will show overlap.

SPOT GLOSS & CLEAR SEAL
EMBOSSING POWDER TECHNIQUE

F

Clear or Crystal Embossing Powders can be used to coat and give shine to a surface to look like glass for a vase, water, or a wet puddle. A coating of clear will add durability and protect the colors sealed in below. Test sample to be sure you don't have colors or inks that will run when the moisture of the ink pad or marker is applied.

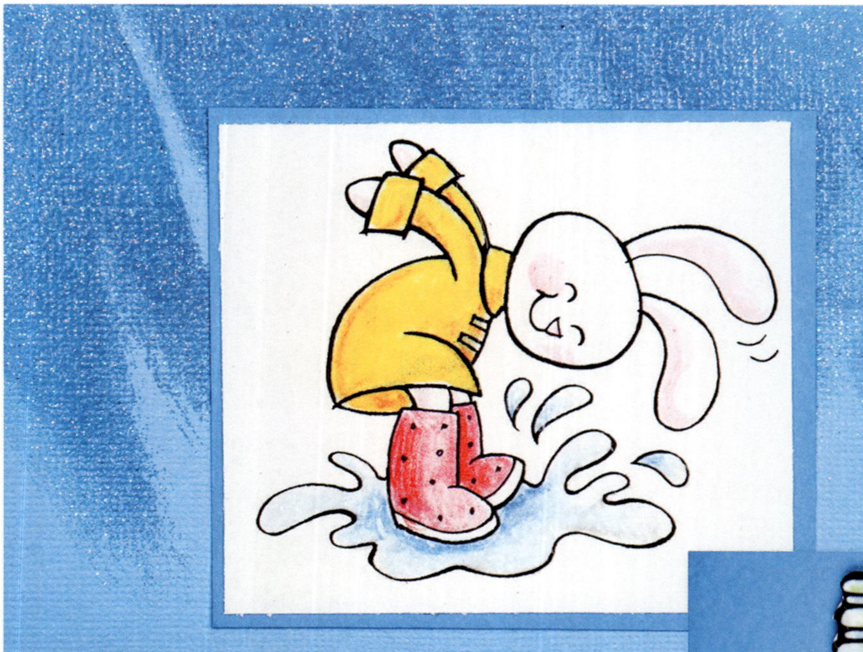

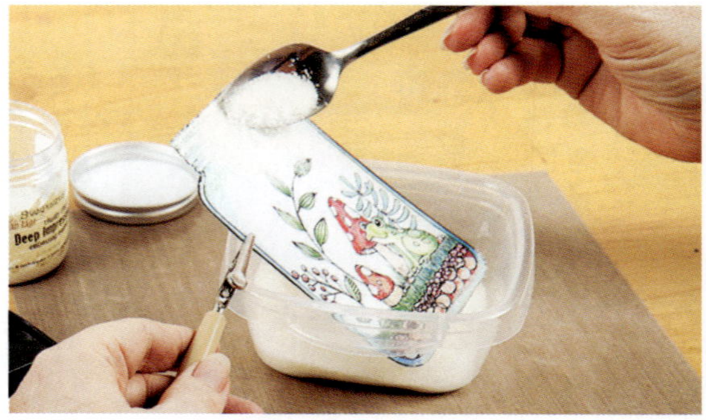

Clear seal: Quickly coat the entire surface with clear VersaMark™ ink pad. Dust with clear powder while still wet. Chunky Clear will be more raised and dimpled than finer clear powders, but a second coat will be smooth as glass.

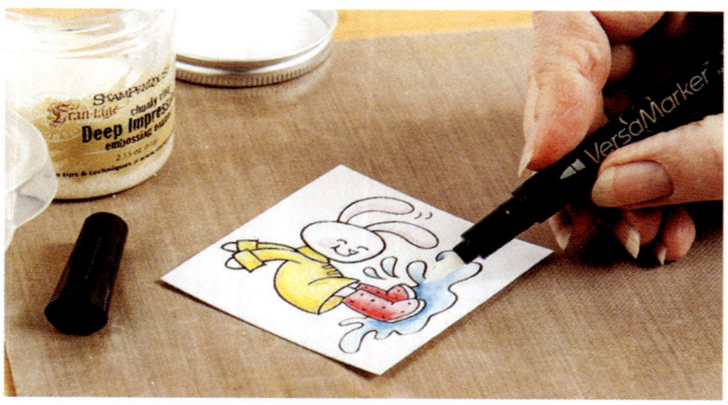

Add spot colors: Stamp and color in image. Test and work carefully with any water based colors so as not to smear them when adding the VersaMarker™ over the top. Apply brush tip to color in one area at a time. Use bullet tip for small details. Clean tips if needed between colors. Dust with Clear or Crystal Embossing Powders while marker areas are still wet.

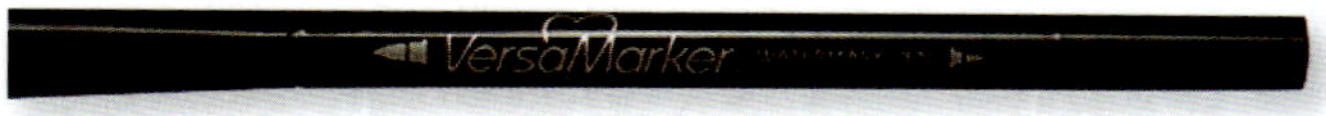

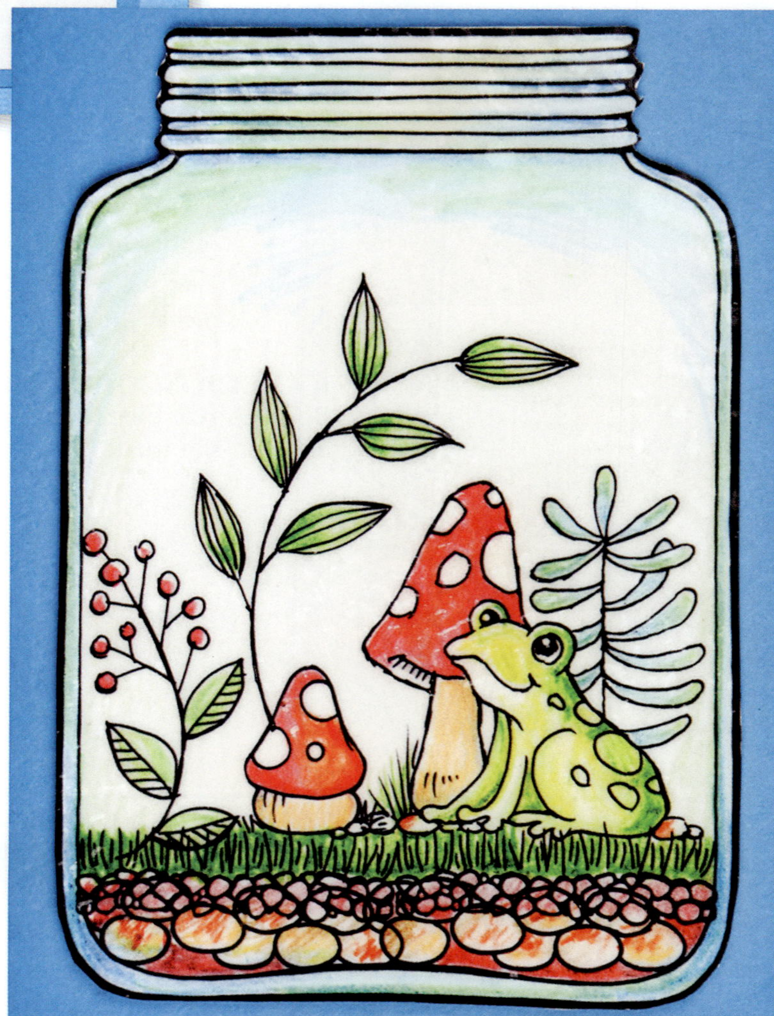

SPOT COLOR
EMBOSSING POWDER TECHNIQUE

Embossing Powders in different colors can be used to "paint" in embossed compartments for colorful results. This cloisonné approach is actually very easy to do and gives entirely different results based on choice of stamp design and embossing powder selection.

Add Spot Colors: Stamp and emboss image to be colored in. Use VersaMarker™ brush tip to color in one color at a time. Dust with powder. Repeat many more colored compartments and heat all at once.

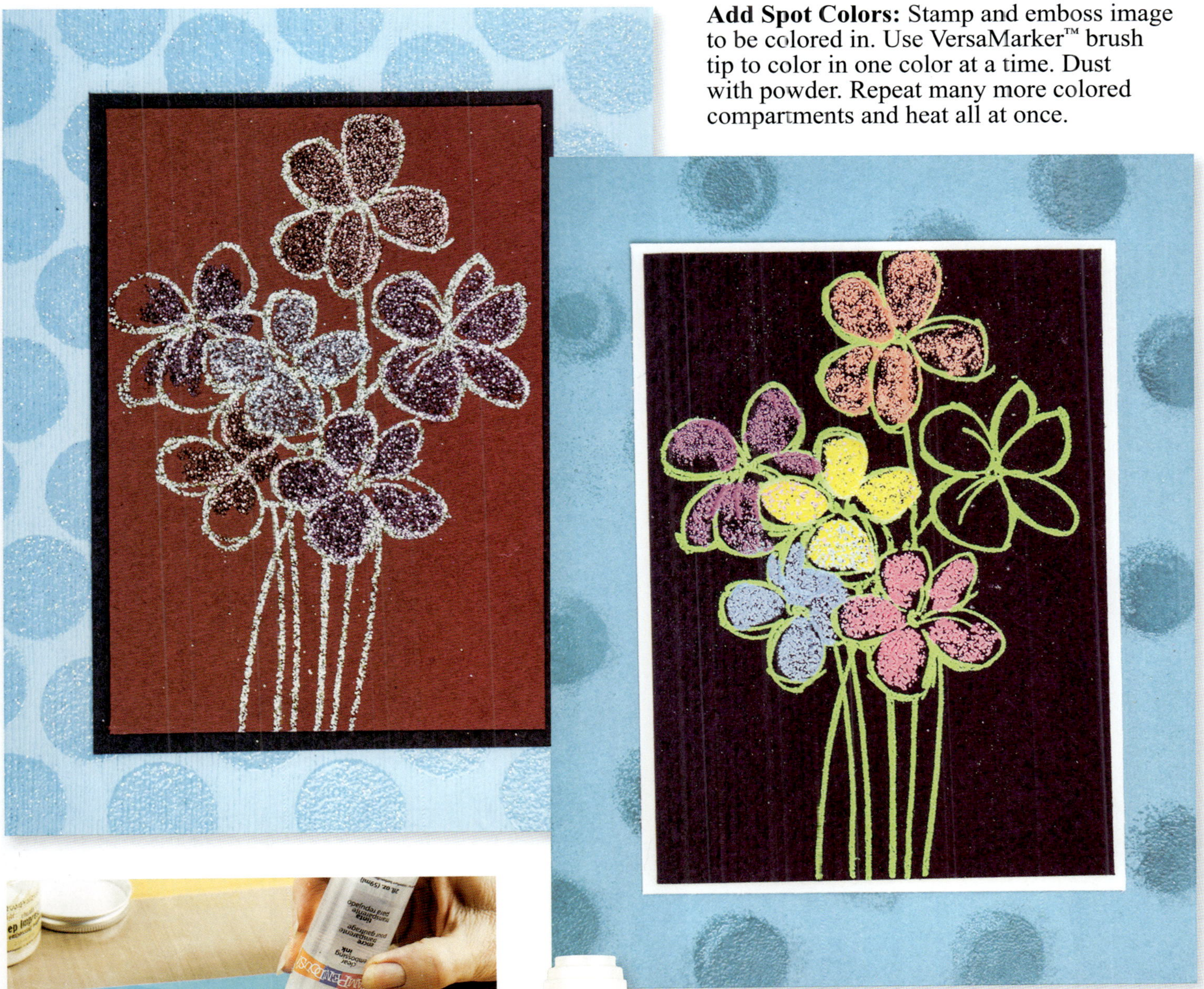

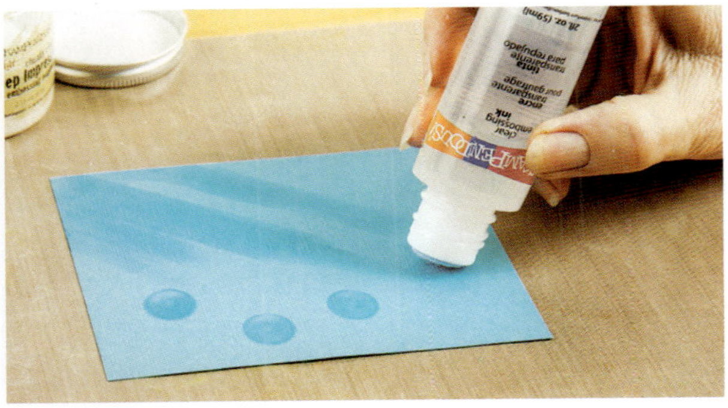

Dauber top will make interesting brush strokes or polka dots. Dust with Clear, Crystal, or any color Embossing Powder.

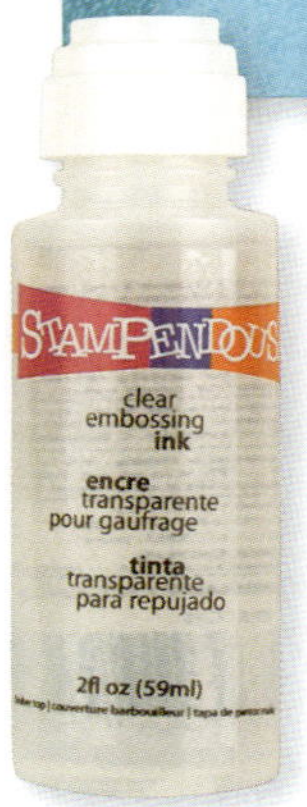

Embossing Ink Tip: Remove dauber top if you want to use clear embossing ink with a brush or other applicators.

SCORCHING & DECKLED EDGE
EMBOSSING POWDER TECHNIQUE

Creating rough, aged, or vintage looking papers is quick, easy, and less expensive than buying old, ephemera papers. If you want a rough look, scrunch up the edges and tear it in spots. Cardmakers often worry about overheating and scorching light color paper. With this look you can use it to your advantage. A faux deckled edge is easy with a quick swipe of ink around the edges.

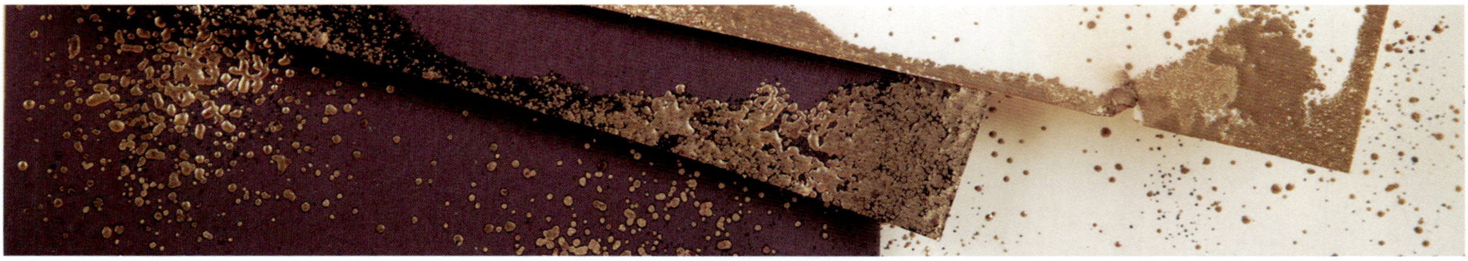

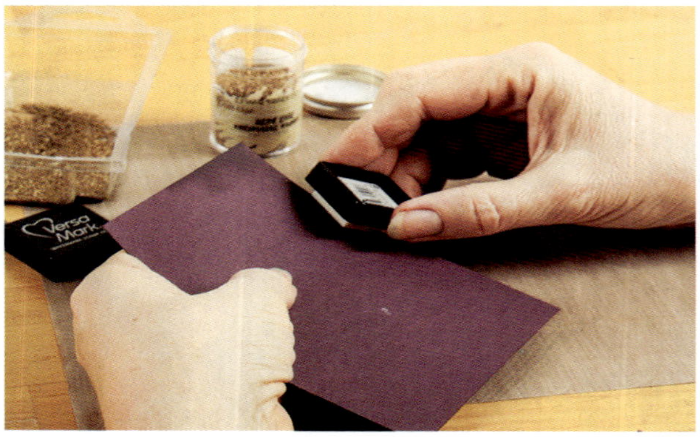

Ink the edges: Rough up, or even tear it in places, before or after you brush VersaMark™ ink at an angle along the edges. Use a dry brush to remove unwanted powder.

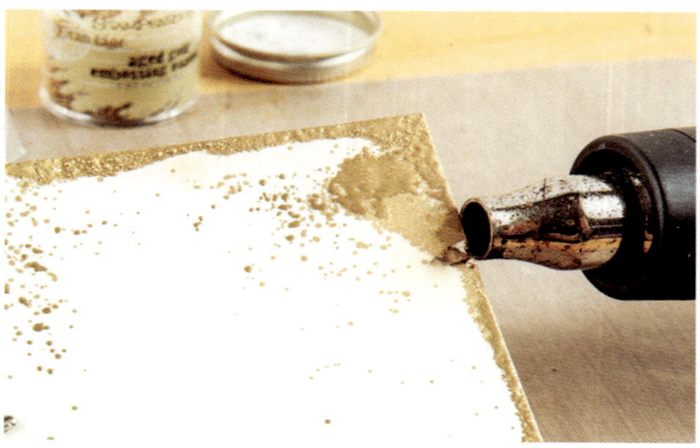

Dust and overheat: Dust with one or more metallic or Frantage™ Aged Embossing Powders. Heat from top or bottom and intentionally hold heat tool in one place long enough to scorch the paper for aging. Hold the heat tool to the side of a tear and watch the scorching travel in from that point.

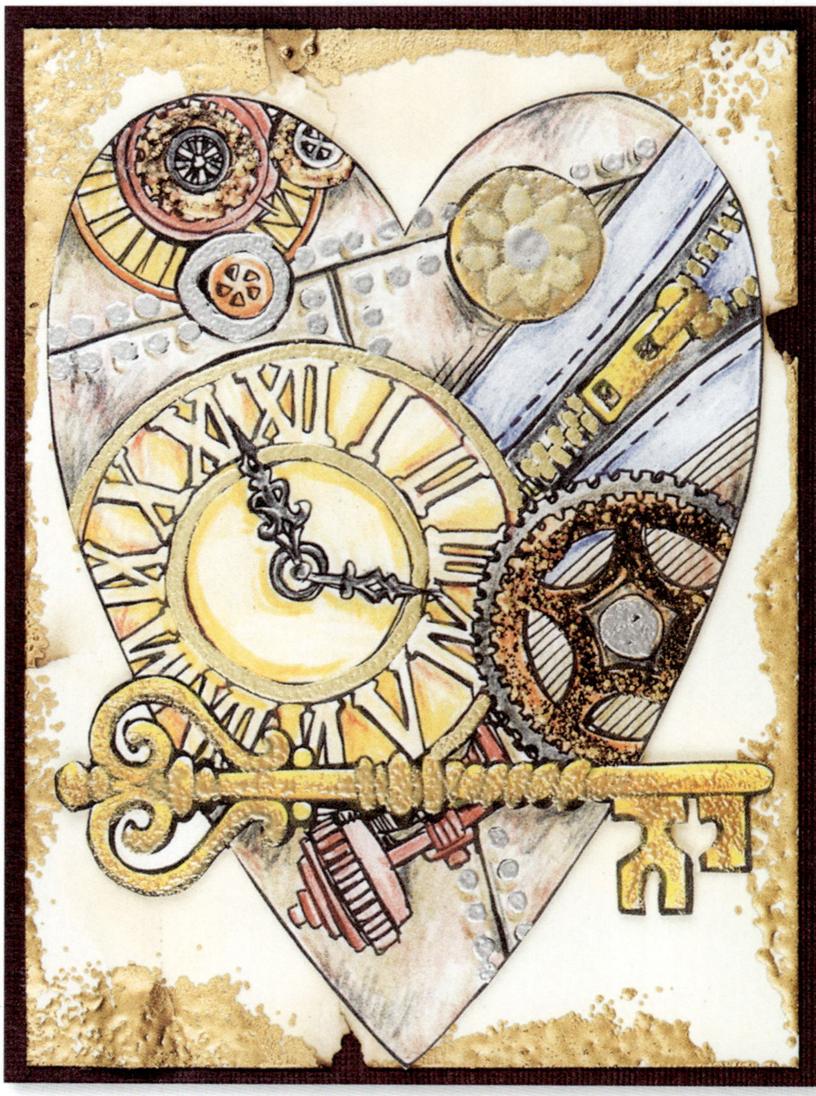

Add spot metallic accents: Apply VersaMarker™ brush or bullet tip to color in one area at a time. Dust with any number of Metallic Embossing Powders and heat.

VINTAGE CRACKED GLASS
EMBOSSING POWDER TECHNIQUE

H

This technique takes advantage of the fact that Embossing Powder, after it cools, will be brittle if you can bend the paper surface underneath. It is a very fun technique for “instant aging” when you want a vintage or mixed media look.

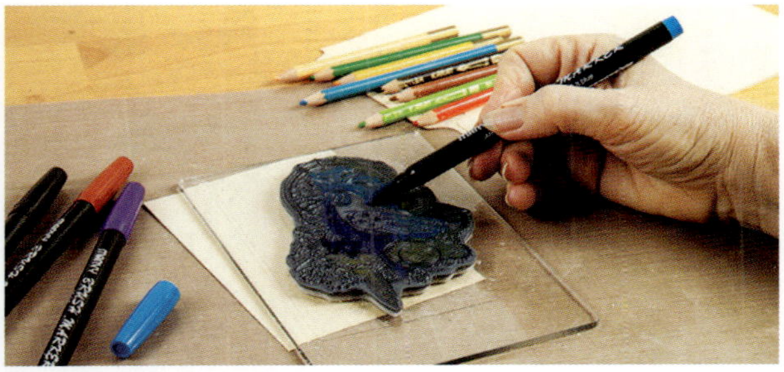

Color it: Apply water-based markers to rubber stamp for multiple color impression. Color in with colored pencils.

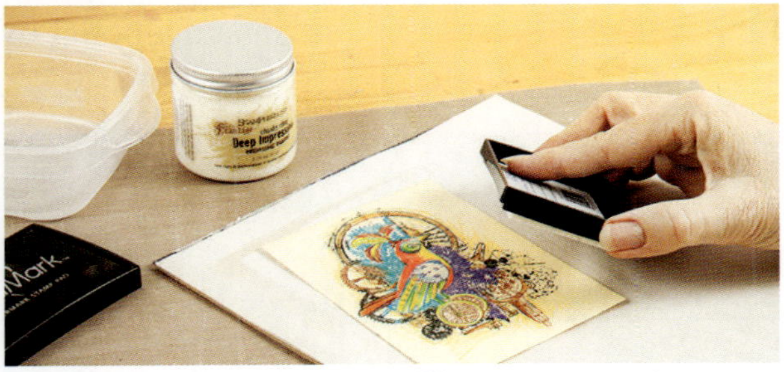

Ink it: Apply VersaMark™ ink over entire surface. Dust with Chunky Clear Embossing Powder for first thick layer.

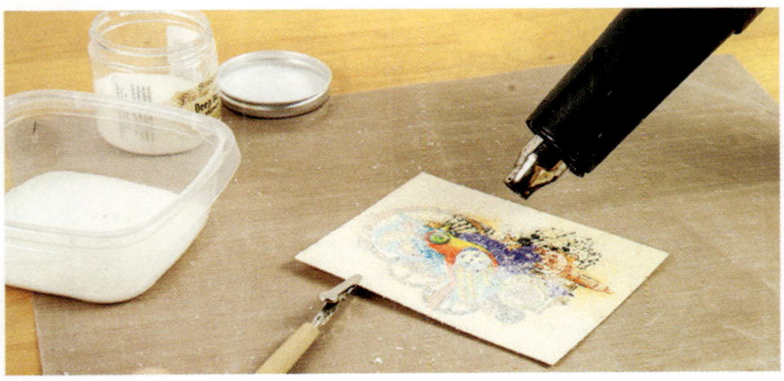

Emboss it: Heat emboss first layer. Let cool. Repeat ink, powder and heat for second thick layer for best crackle results.

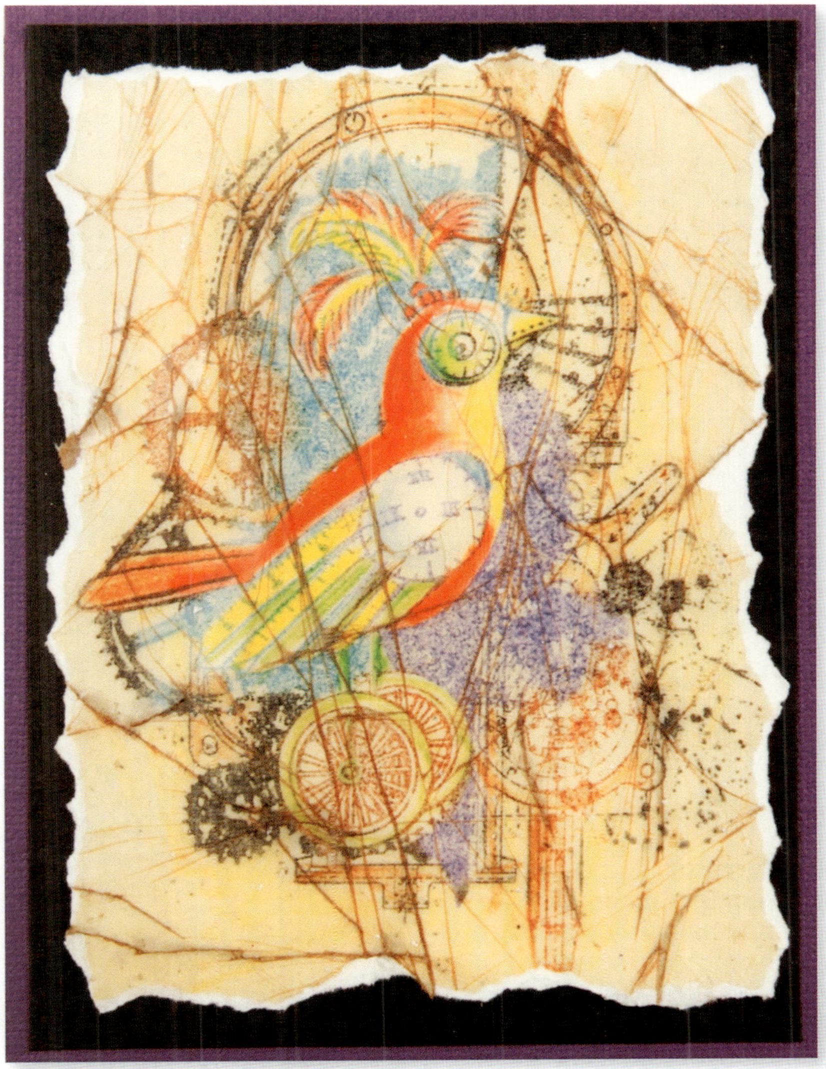

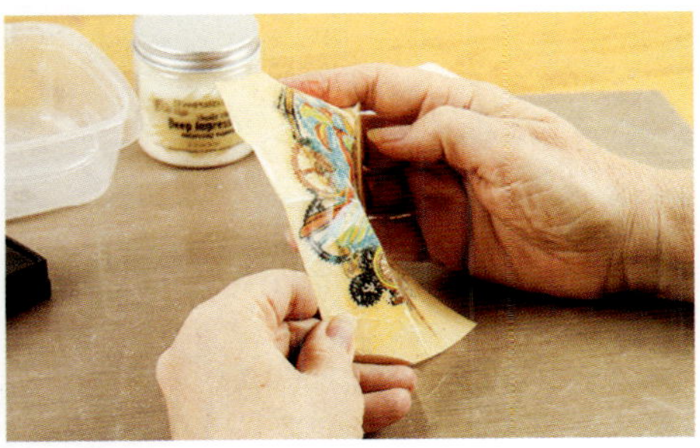

Crack it: Put it in the freezer to harden. Crumple and crack the clear embossed surface.

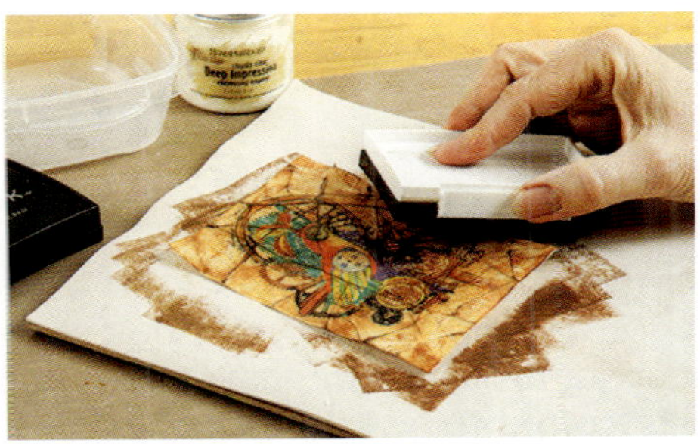

Ink it: To make the cracks even more pronounced, rub a water-based dye ink across the surface.

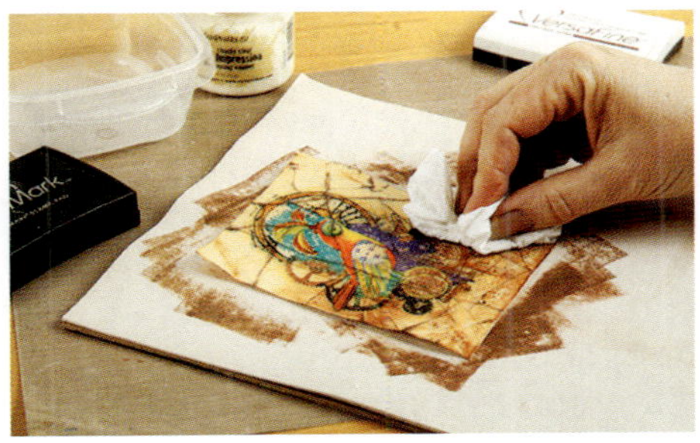

Wipe it: Excess will wipe off embossed areas leaving color in the cracked recesses. Tear edges.

WATERCOLOR RESIST WITH BLACK EMBOSSING POWDER

I

Stamped images embossed in black are easy to watercolor with any number of water-based colors, paints, pigments, or markers. The raised lines create compartments that are easy to fill with separate colors. An acrylic block or plastic lid will work as a mixing palette. Use small brushes or water brushes. A jar of water to clean colors and paper towels to blot will be helpful.

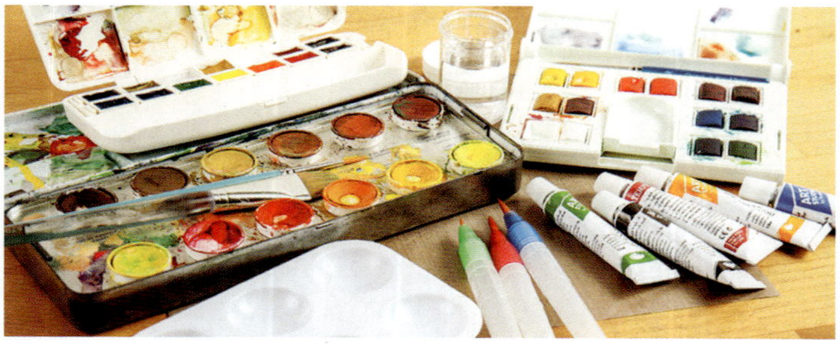

Watercolor sets: Try any water-based colors in a paint set or in tubes. Experiment with color range and try mixing colors on brush or palette.

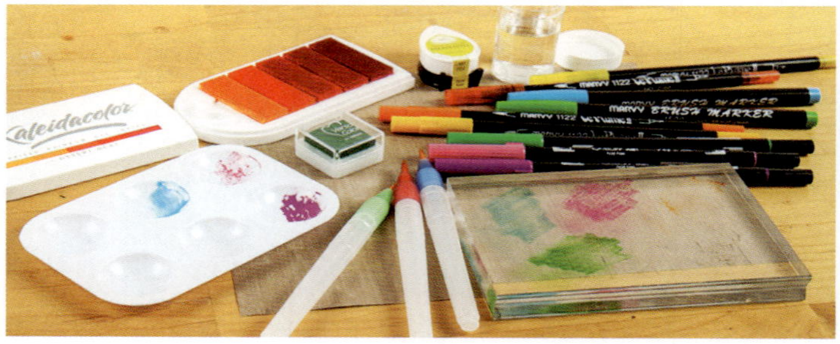

Water-based inks and markers: Coloring with markers directly on paper will give bold colors. Indirect application of color with brush and amount of water used will allow you to create soft colors.

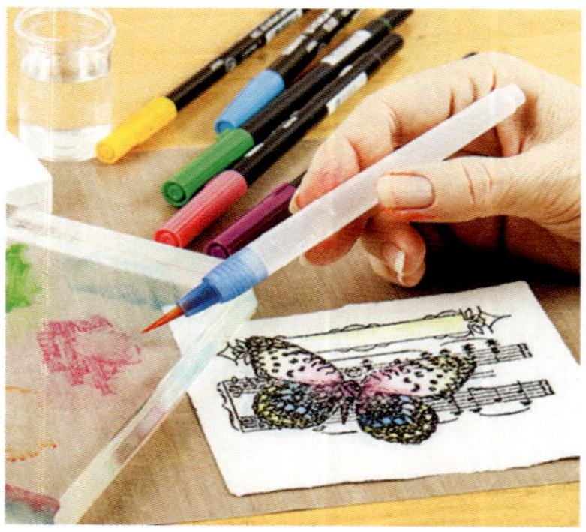

Watercolor: Apply water to a compartment you wish to paint, then add a little color and see how it dries. Blot while wet if you want to remove color. Remember, the more water, the more colors will travel and blend. Colors may dry lighter than applied.

Paper Tip: The better the quality of watercolor paper you select, the more water it will absorb without warping. Smooth or textured surfaces add to the delight of a miniature watercolor painting.

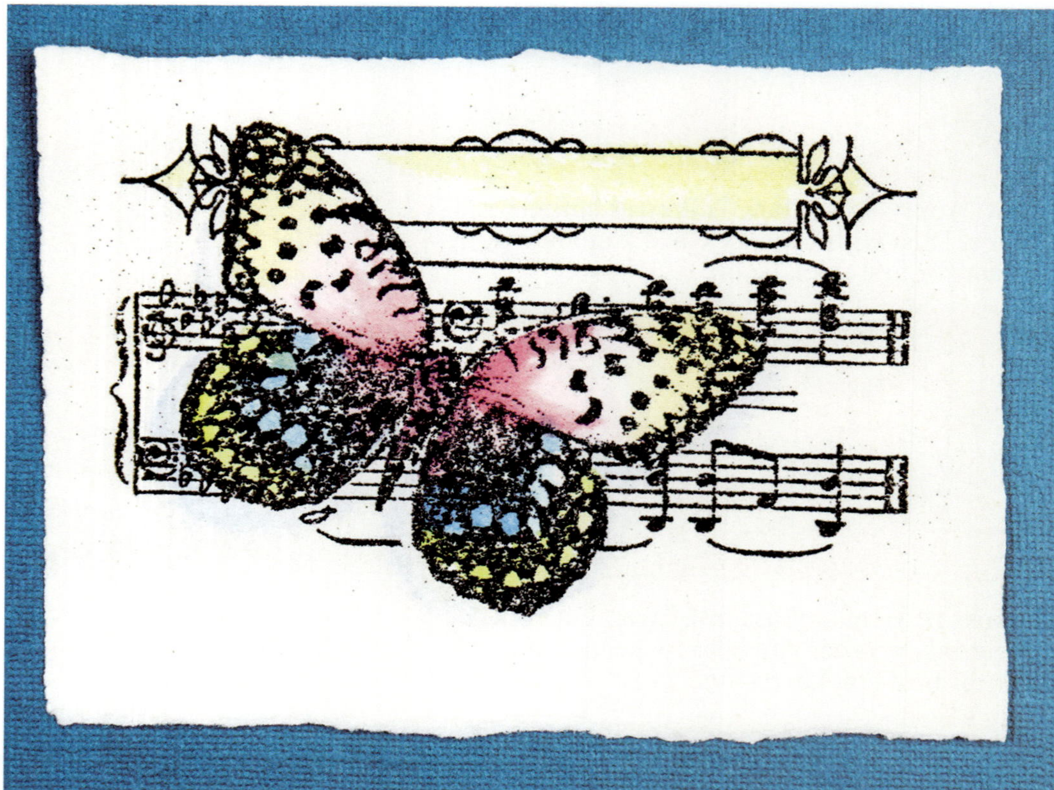

Embossing Tip: Test papers and water-based colorants to check results before starting a large project. Look at embossed impression carefully at different angles to ensure that heat has not missed any spots before you begin the watercolor process. Large papers should be taped on the edges to take lots of water without warping.

WATERCOLOR RESIST WITH WHITE EMBOSSING POWDER

J

Stamped images embossed in white offer an easy way to add watercolor washes to paint the negative space with any number of water-based colors, paints, or pigments. The raised lines will resist watercolor pigments. Clear Embossing Powder may be used on white paper as well.

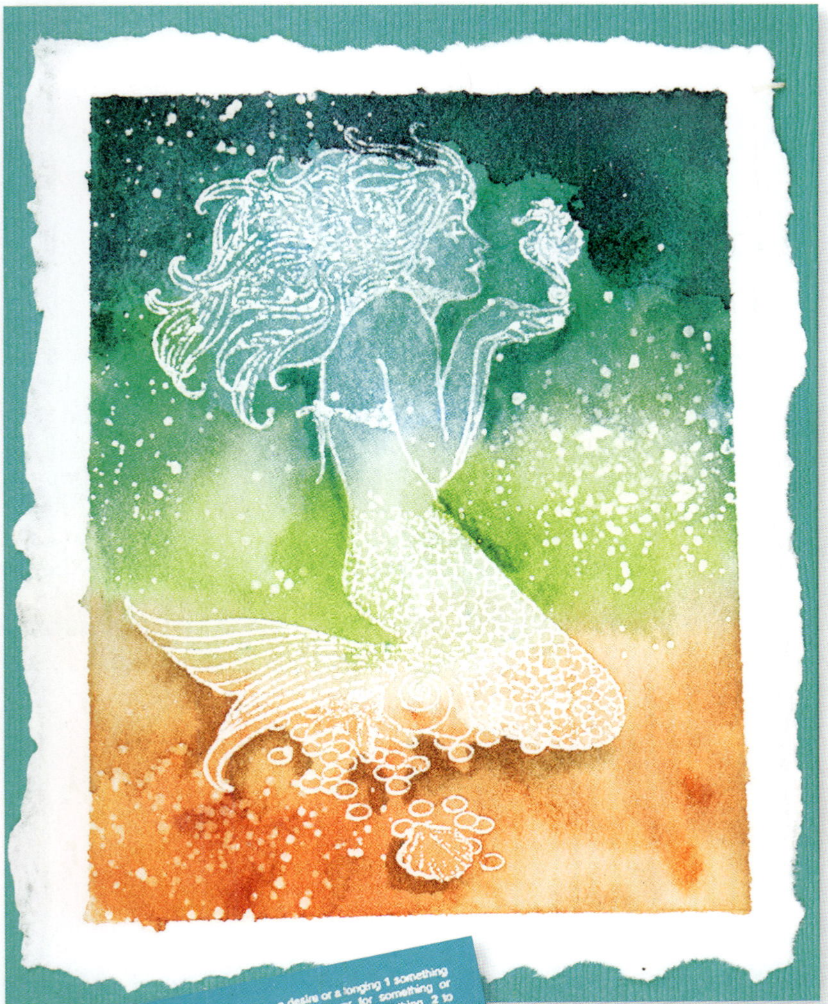

1. Deckled edges: Create classic watercolor paper edges by hand for an irregular border or a more uniform deckled edge by pulling 1/4" or so of edge against a straight edge ruler.

2.Tape edges: Create a classic watercolor white "frame" by taping deckled edge panel to a firm, non-absorbent surface such as a clipboard or jumbo acrylic handle. Use a masking tape that can be removed without tearing after paper has dried. Hand press tape along edges to seal.

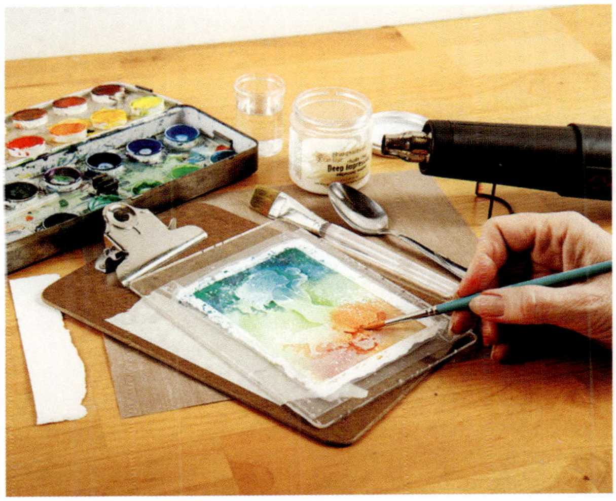

3. Wet brush: Use a large brush to wet the background. Add pigment on brush and allow watermarks to develop. Remember colors will travel wherever the water allows.

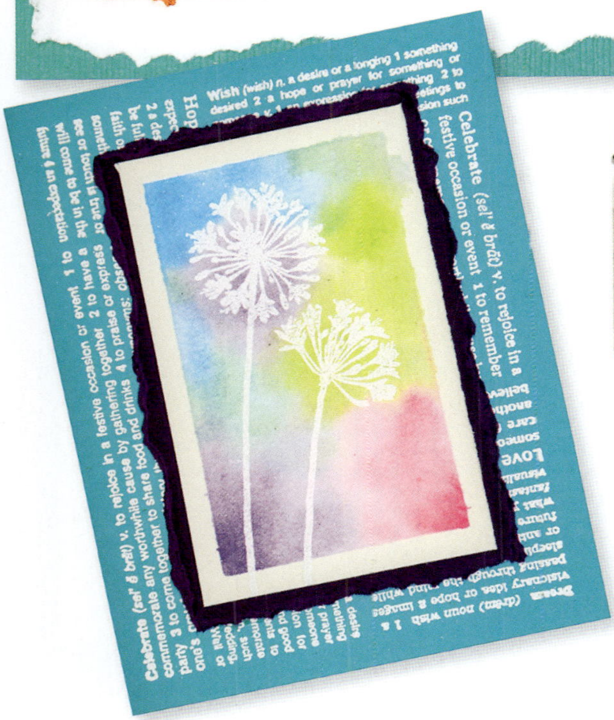

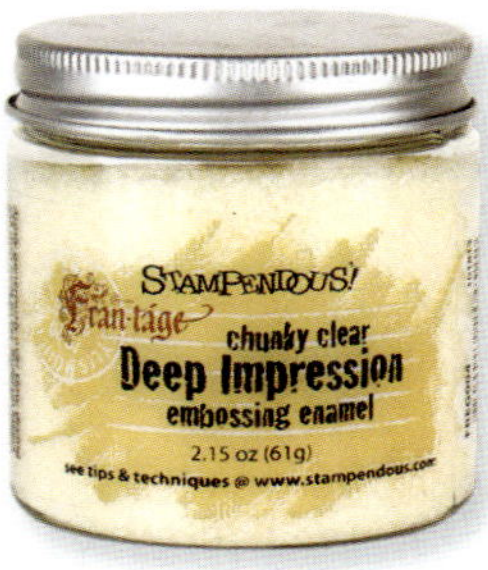

4. "Salt" resist: Before painting, Chunky Clear or Chunky White Embossing Powder will give the look of salt resist. Since heat will not come through clipboard, lift paper with tape and sprinkle Embossing Powder. Hold level and heat from underneath.

5. Remove tape only after paper is dry to reveal classic watercolor edge.

Framing Tip: For watercolor of any size you wish to have framed with matboard, instead of a deckle edge, allow an inch or so perimeter.

INK PAD "BATIK" RESIST
WITH WHITE EMBOSSING POWDER

K

Stamped images embossed in white will give you the look of batik when you overstamp with water-based ink pads. The raised impression will resist water-based pigments and can simply be wiped clean of any ink coverage. Bold line stamp designs give most dramatic results.

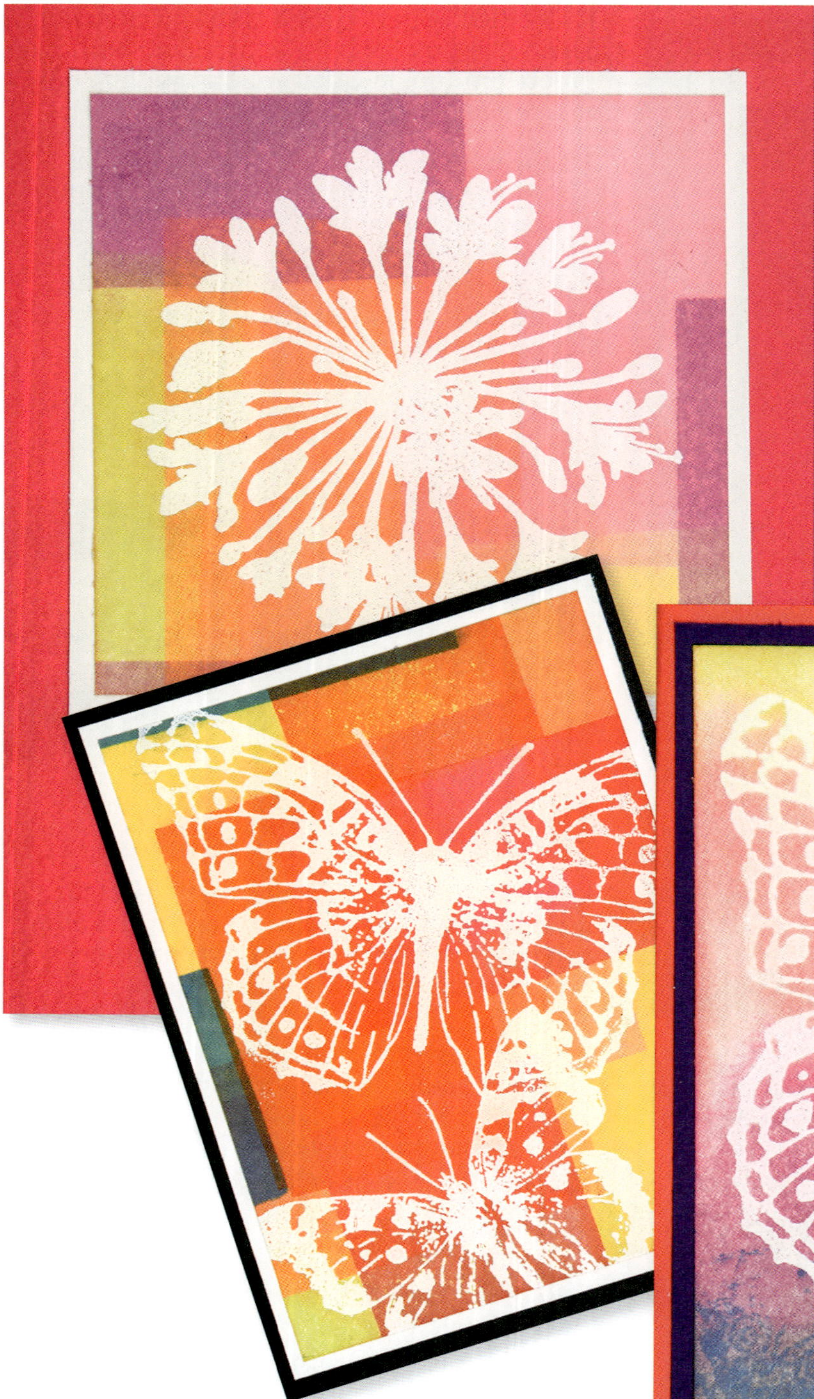

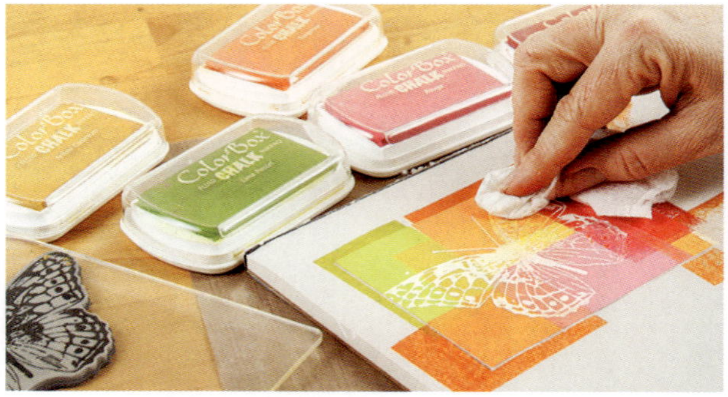

Direct to paper: Stamp in wet ink, emboss with white and heat set. Select ink pad colors and apply directly to paper over embossed image. Overlapping impressions of ink pad creates interesting designs. Use a dry paper towel to burnish and remove ink from white impression. Some inks may tint the white Embossing Powder.

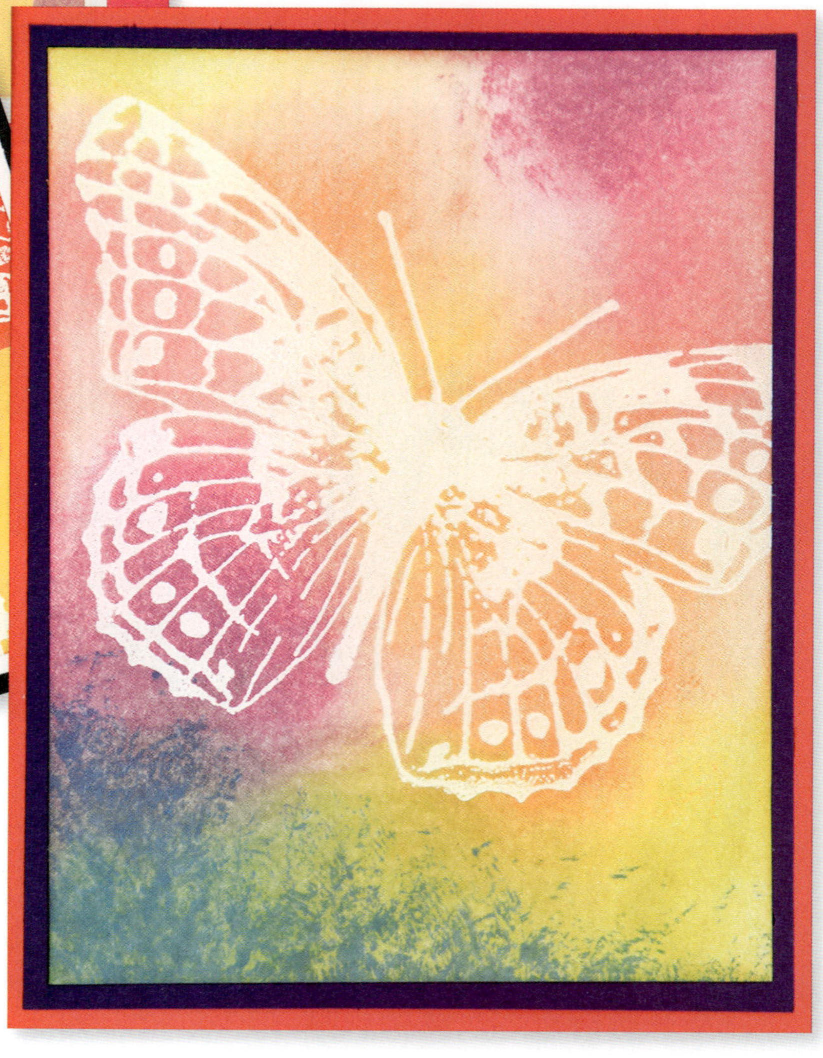

Color Transfer: For a more dappled look, apply ink to daubers or paper toweling and dab across embossed impression. Burnish away excess ink at the end.

BATIK RESIST INK CHART
FOR EMBOSSING POWDERS

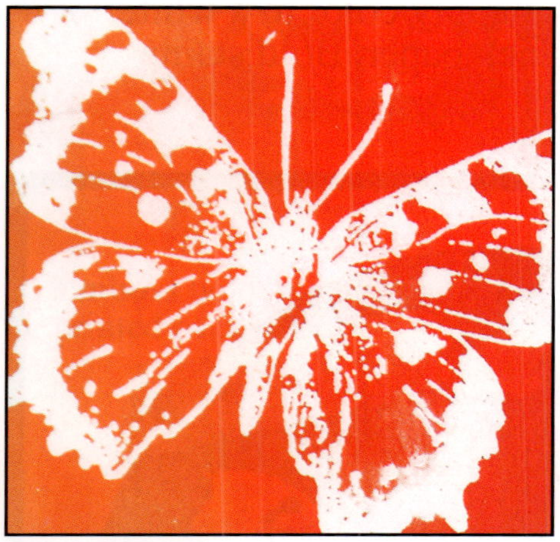

Dye ink over white Embossing Powder looks about the same as over Clear Embossing Powder.

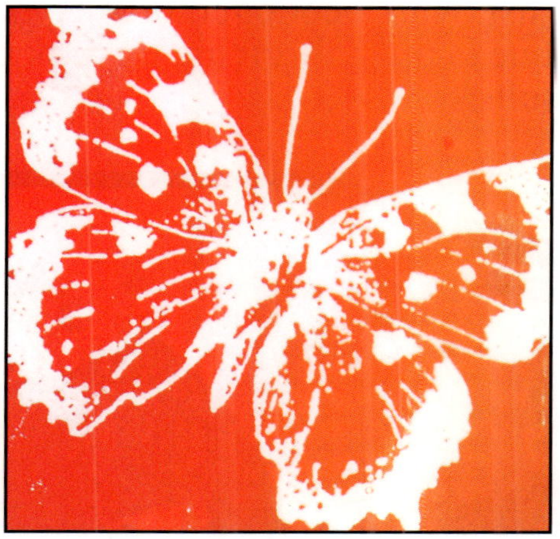

Dye ink over clear Embossing Powder instead of White. Kaleidocolor blend dye ink pad.

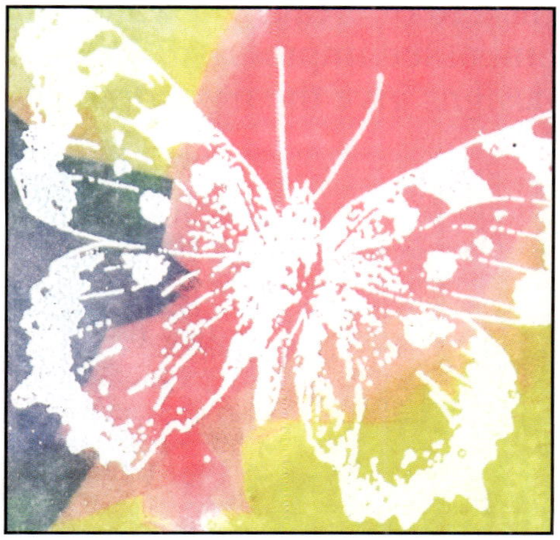

Chalk ink pads offer a wide range of colors and wipe away nicely. Darker colors may leave a tint.

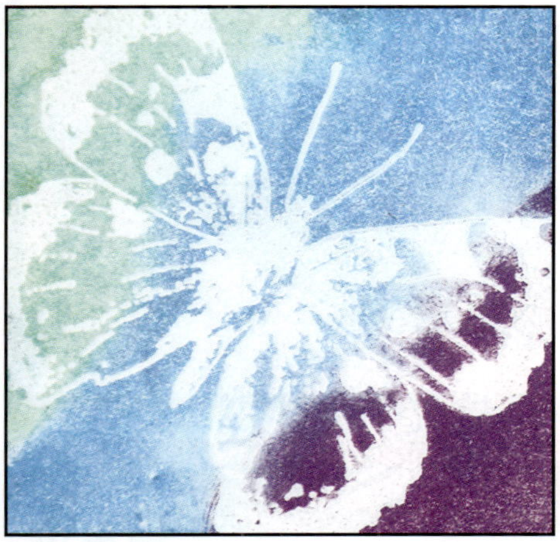

Dye ink pads offer a wide range of colors and wipe away nicely. Darker colors may leave a tint.

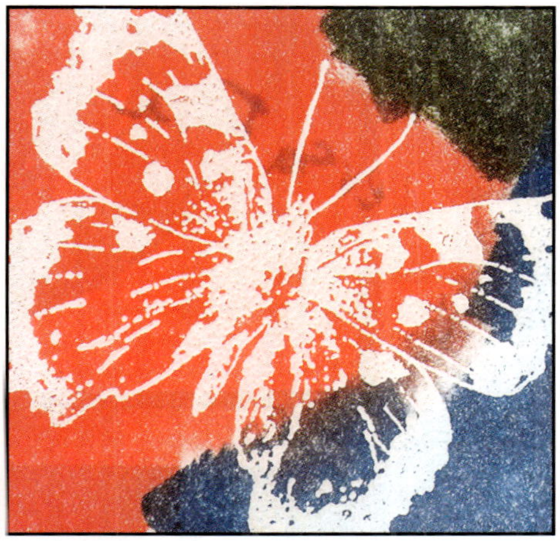

VersaFine™ instant dry pigment inks offer a wide range of colors. Darker colors will leave a tint.

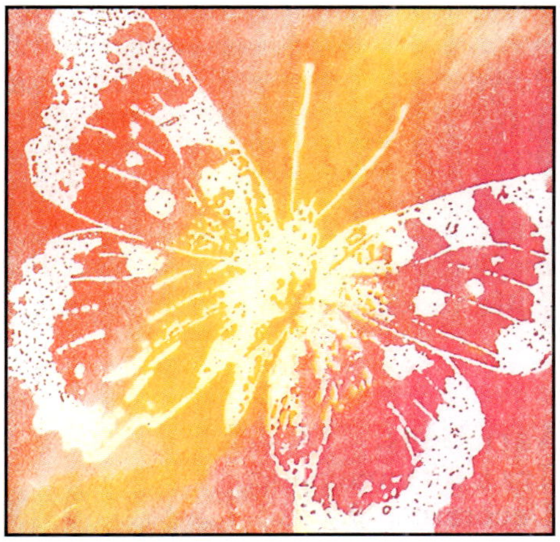

Pigment ink pads offer a wide range of colors and wipe away the easiest leaving little to no tint.

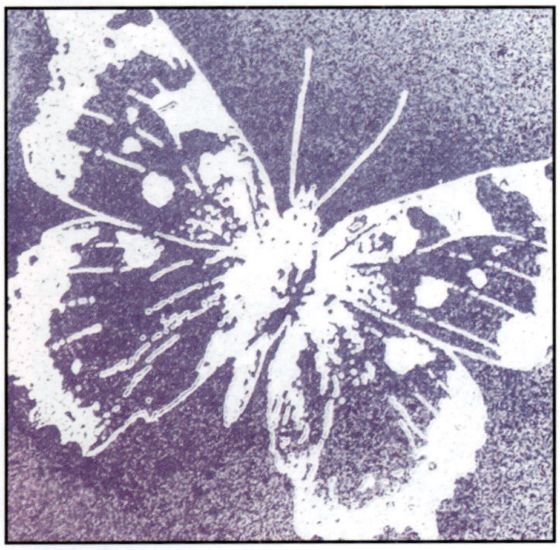

Dye ink sprayed on makes interesting patterns. Wipe off carefully to not disturb spots.

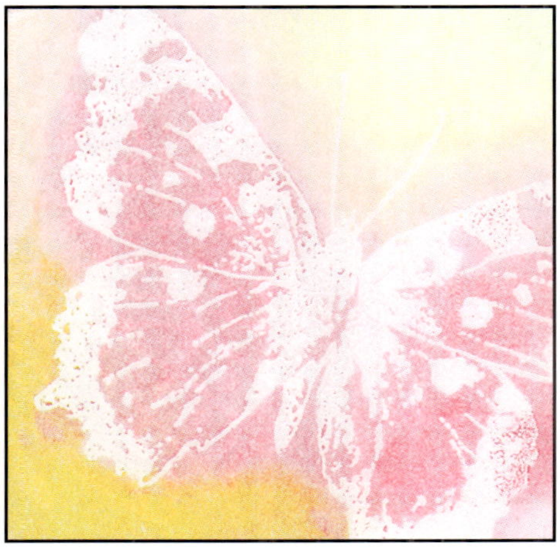

Gelatos can be rubbed on and burnished away. Burnishing lightens the colors quite a bit.

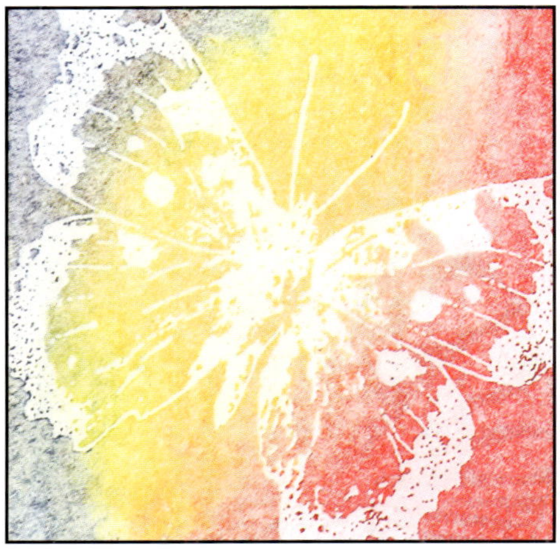

Oil pastel sticks can be rubbed on and burnished away. Burnishing removes most of the dark values.

IRON-OFF RESIST
EMBOSSING POWDER TECHNIQUE

M

This Embossing Powder technique is a twist on any of the resist techniques. After embossing and applying your colors over the top, there is another step which can be done with an iron to completely remove the Embossing Powder leaving a flat but perfectly reversed out image. This process is similar to what is done in batik. Place your embossed work between several layers of newsprint and craft sheet to protect the surface of the iron. Remove sticky blotters and iron further as needed.

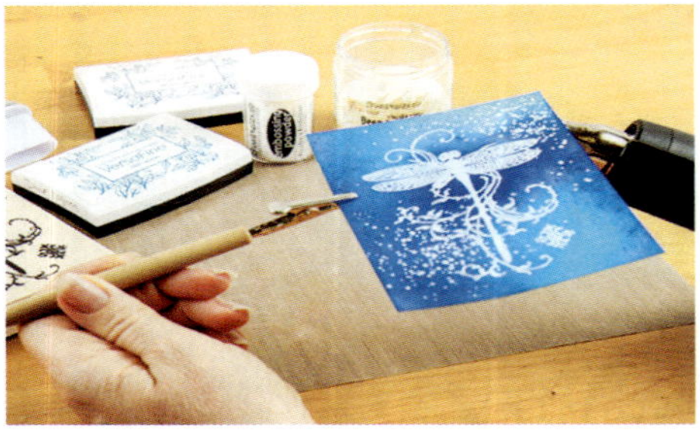

1. Stamp, emboss, and ink it: Add Chunky Clear or Chunky White sprinkles at the end and heat from underneath.

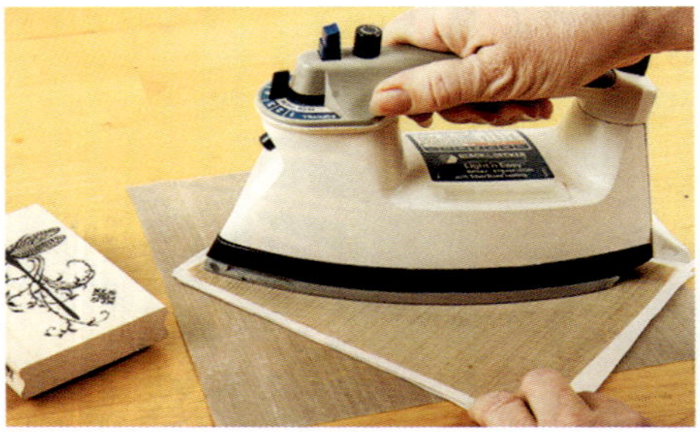

2. Iron it: Use iron on medium heat setting. Layer newsprint between craft sheets. Press firmly without shifting the blotters.

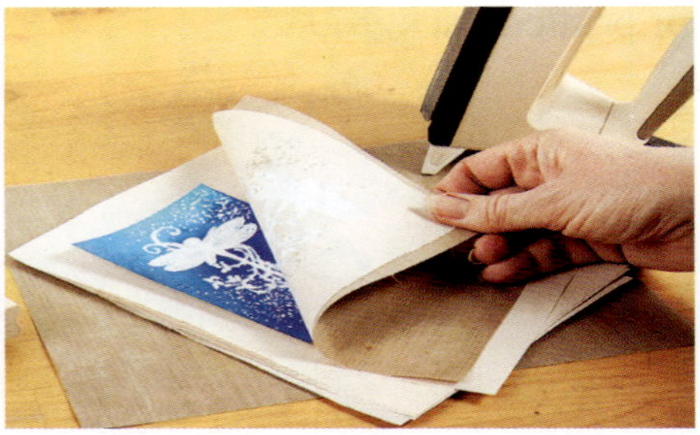

3. Blot it: Carefully remove each blotter and repeat as needed until all Embossing Powder is gone leaving only the resist impression.

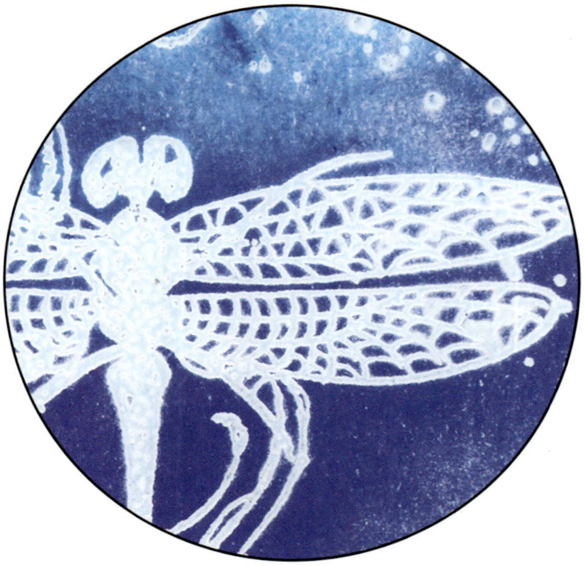

BEFORE ironing there is some tint of the inks.

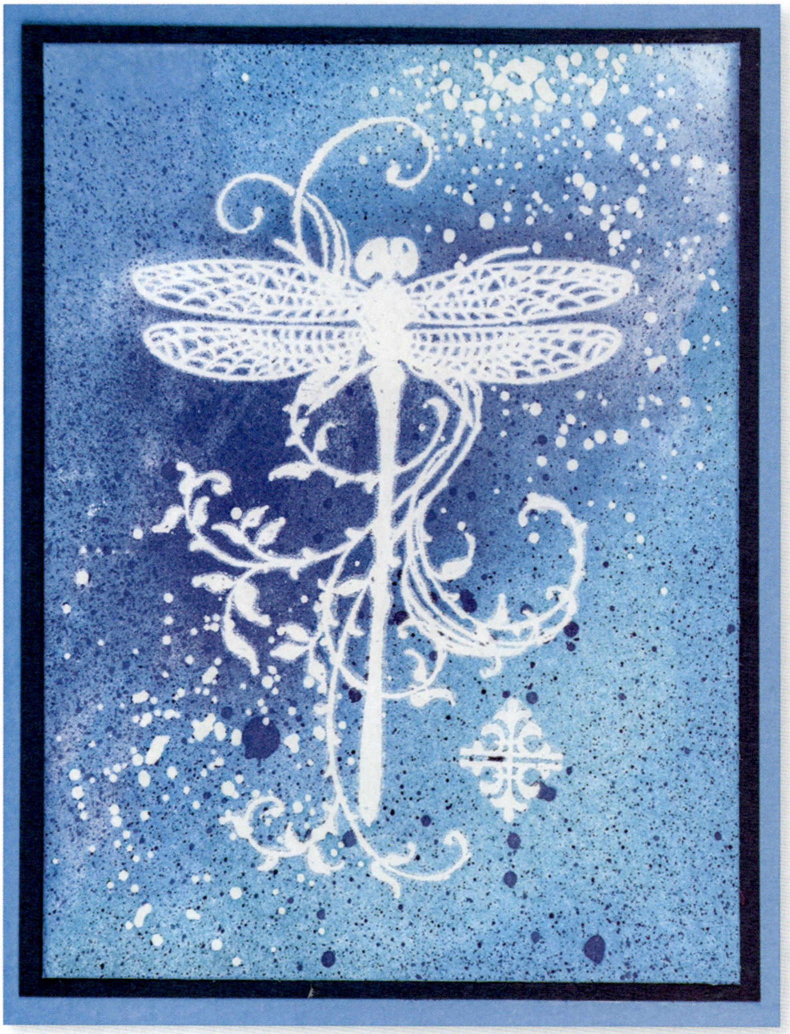

AFTER ironing there is a sharp contrast of paper color coming through.

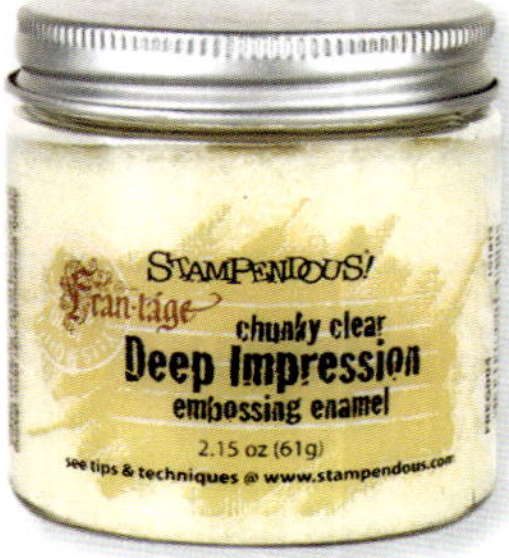

"Salt" Tip: Sprinkle Chunky Embossing Powder and heat from UNDERNEATH before inking. Then ink and iron as instructed.

IRON-ON FOIL
EMBOSSING POWDER TECHNIQUE

Many Embossing Powders will work as "glue" when molten to attach foil sheets to paper or other surfaces. Stamp N' Bond or other embossing powders with similar names, bonding powder, even White and Clear Embossing Powders will all work for this technique. While some use laminating machines or dry-mount presses, an iron will work as well. This process will work with foil on a release carrier sheet, but not foil leafing flakes or foil sheets with backing materials. Experiment with leftover "reverse" foil pieces too.

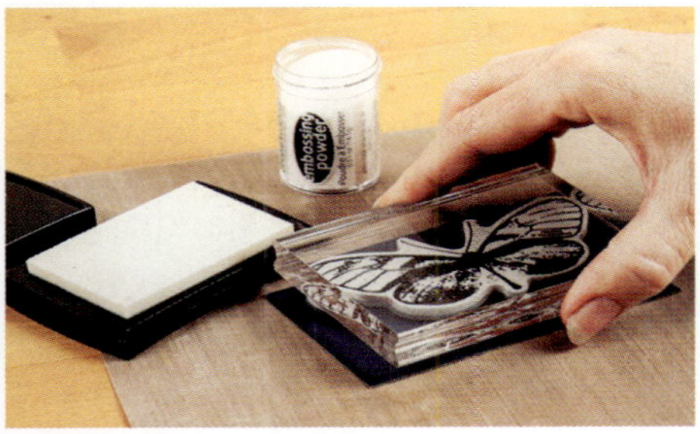

1. Stamp with VersaMark™ ink.

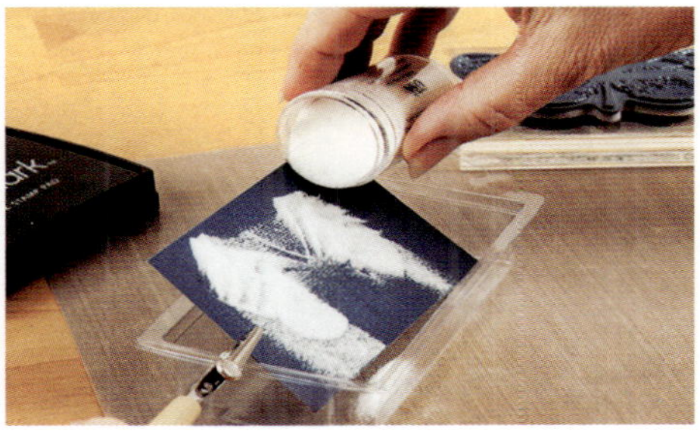

2. Dust with Clear Embossing Powder. No need to use heat tool.

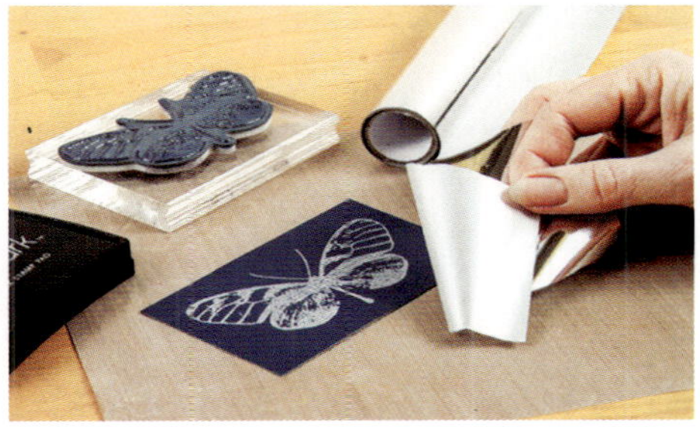

3. Layer with a trimmed piece of foil, dull side down, shiny side up.

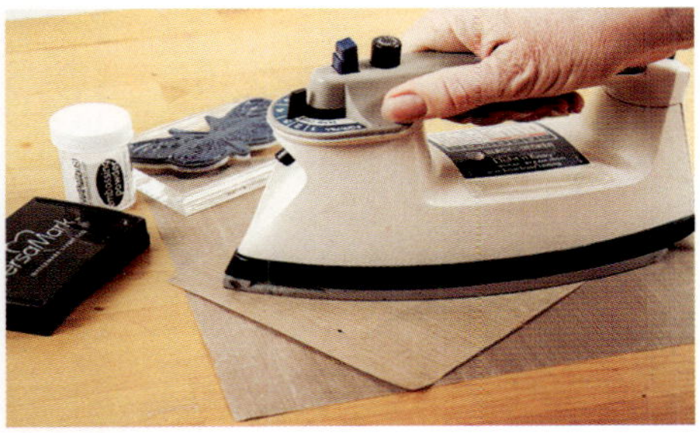

4. Iron on a medium heat setting for a few seconds, moving the iron firmly but not shifting the layers.

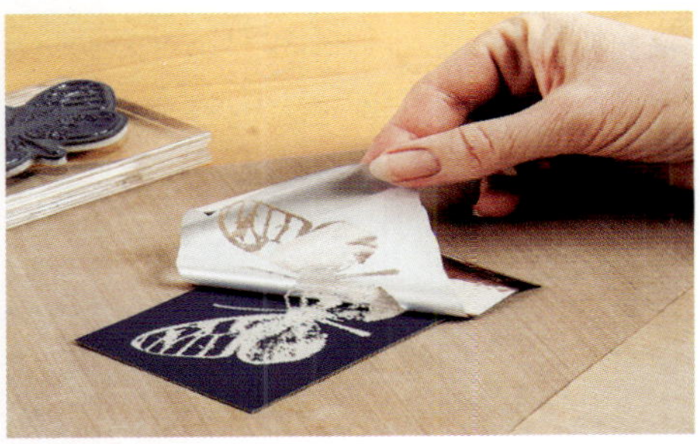

5. Burnish and let it cool. You will see where it has bonded through the foil. Remove foil very carefully.

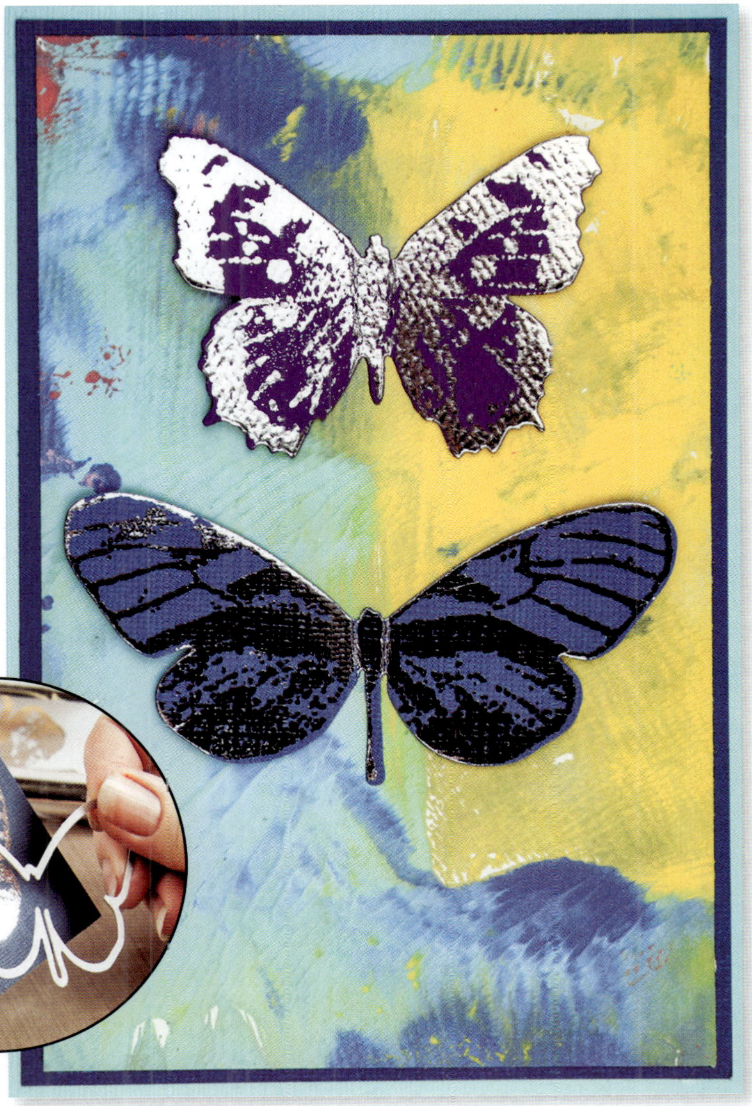

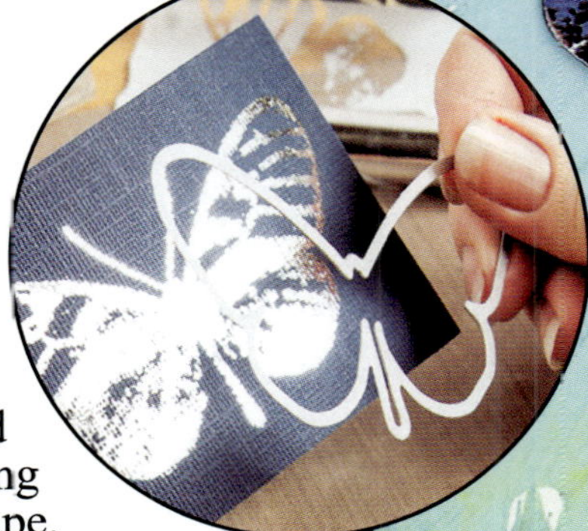

Tip: Butterfly stamp can be hand trimmed or used with matching wafer die shape.

SAND PAINTING
WITH STENCILS & EMBOSSING POWDERS

O

Sand Painting is a good description for this Dreamweaver® Stencils variation of the Double Glitter Technique. Here we use Embossing Powders instead. A variety of opaque colors allows you to create some beautiful scenic shading. It does not have to be perfect to have a lovely, quaint look.

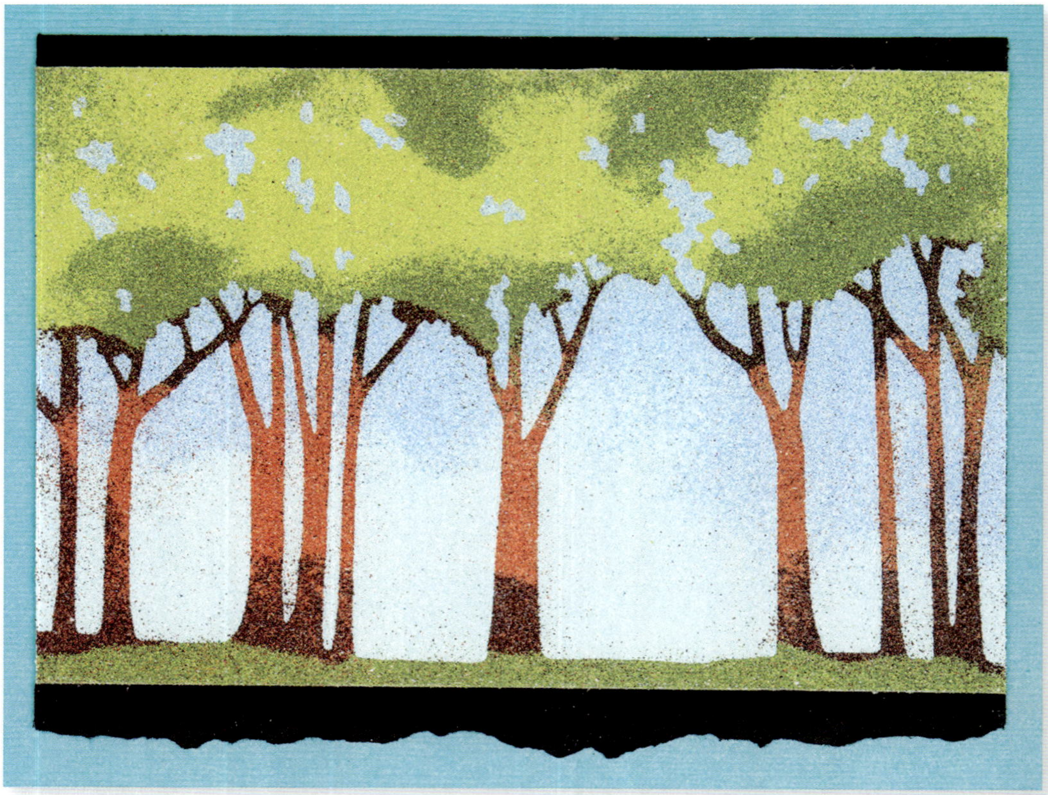

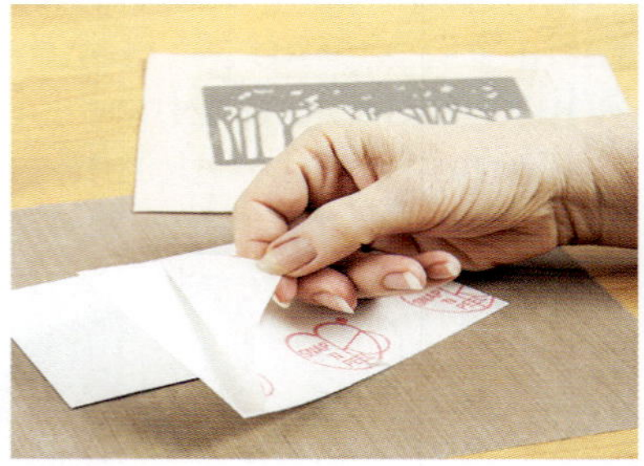

1. Double-sided adhesive panel is trimmed and adhered to card stock for stability.

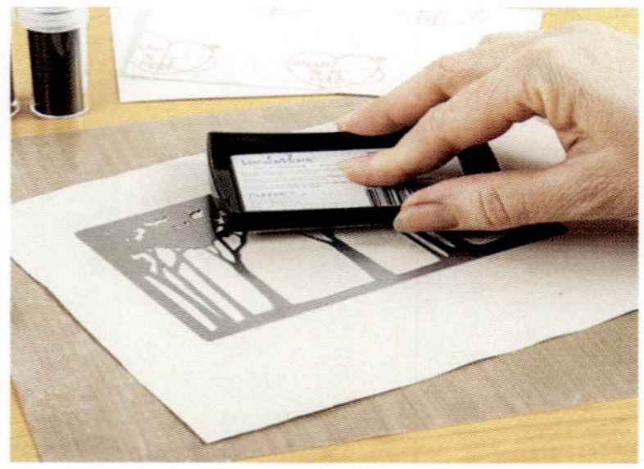

2. Protect stencil by creating a "resist" on the back with a complete, even coating of VersaMark™ ink.

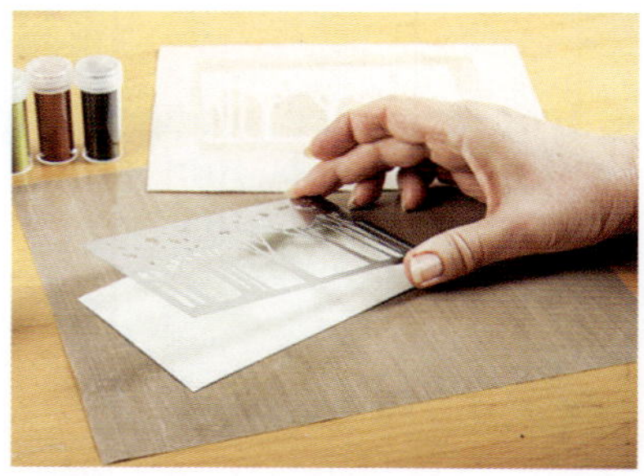

3. Position stencil on sticky side of adhesive panel.

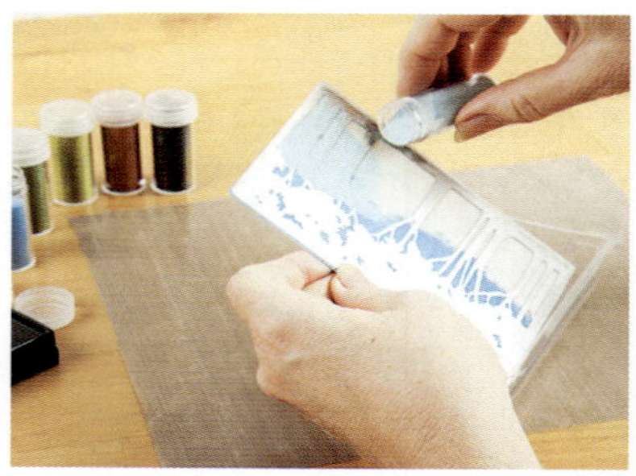

4. Apply background color powders one by one until all the open sticky areas are filled. Let color fall away.

Note: VersaMark™ ink is a simple alternative to Dreamweaver®'s recommended use of protecting the back of the stencil with soap. A bar of canning wax also works. With soap or wax it is important to then remove excess crumbs out of the stencil compartments before positioning stencil on adhesive.

Tip: 14 Jar Embossing Powder Kit was developed for the Painting with Powder Technique. It offers a great value with its variety of opaque colors as well as a few special mixes and clear color or two. A little jar goes a long way for making a wide variety of scenic projects.

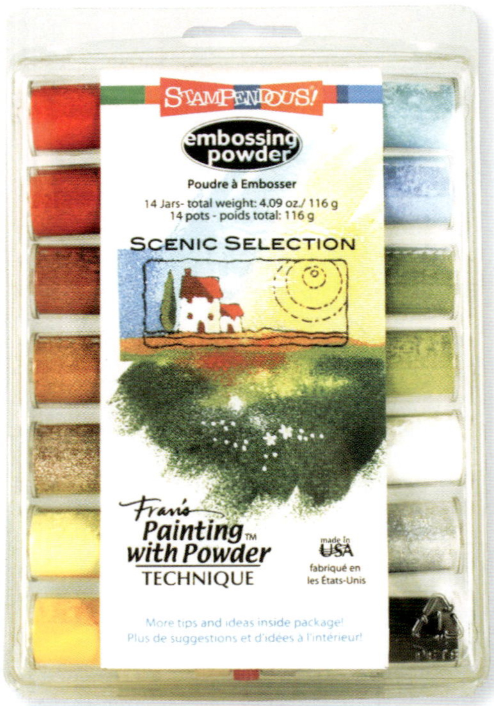

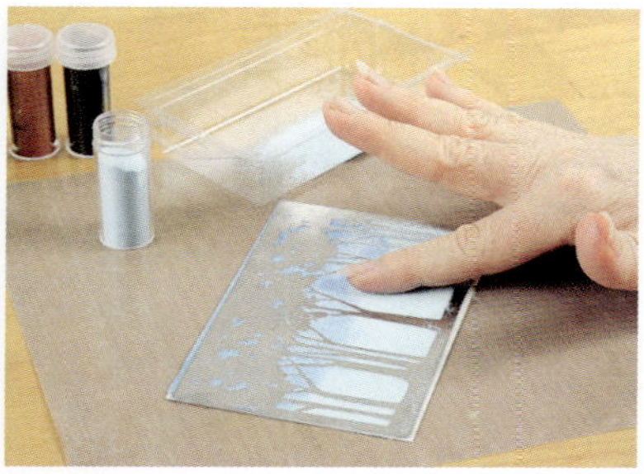

5. Press powder into adhesive for best coverage. Keep fingers off adhesive until powder is covering an area. Add one color at a time letting it fall away to the edge each time as needed.

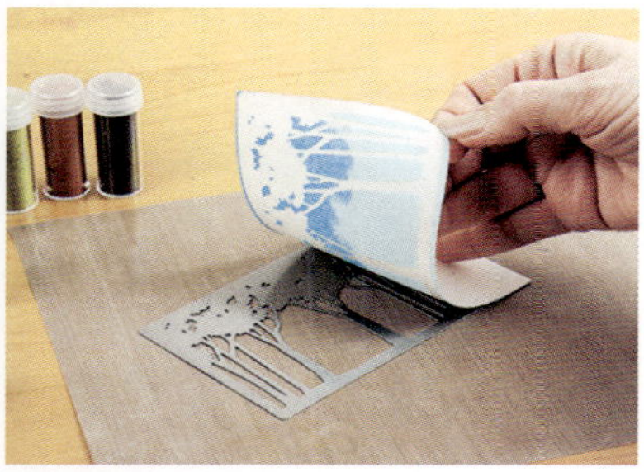

6. Remove stencil carefully by turning over flat on table and bending paper away.

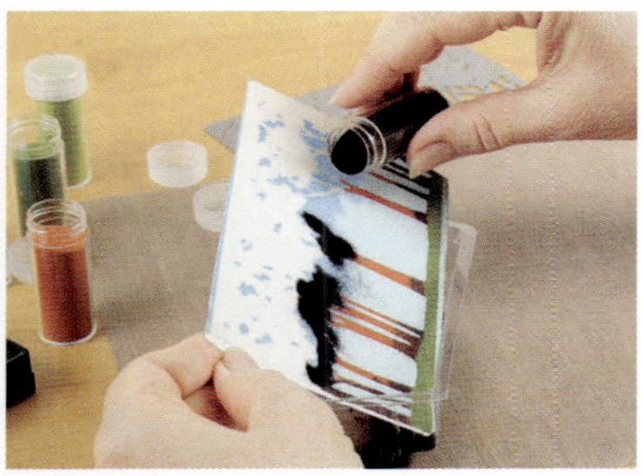

7. Add foreground color powders to the remaining sticky areas now uncovered.

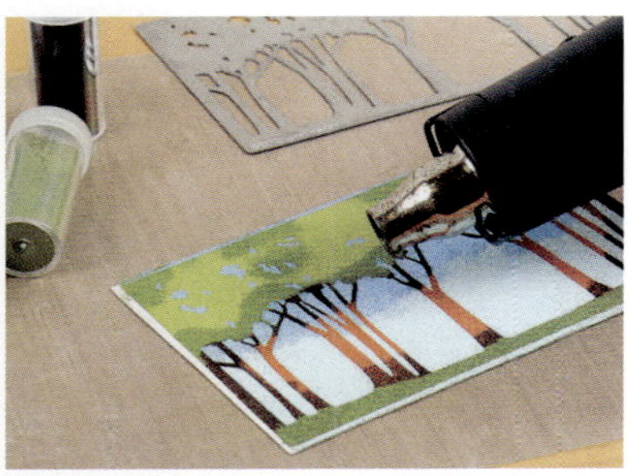

8. Optional quick heat set will secure Embossing Powders without so much heat that it gets shiny.

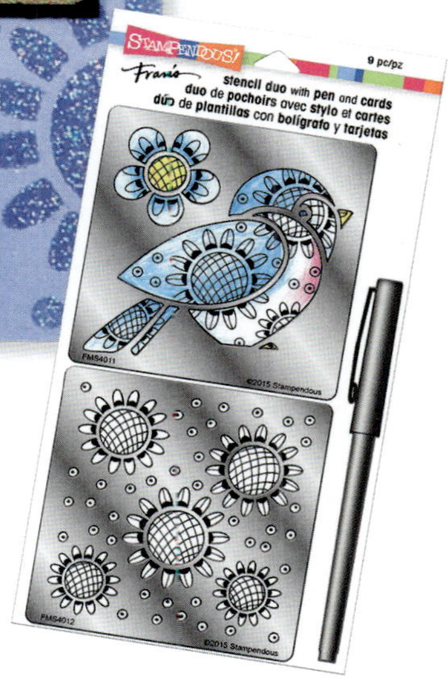

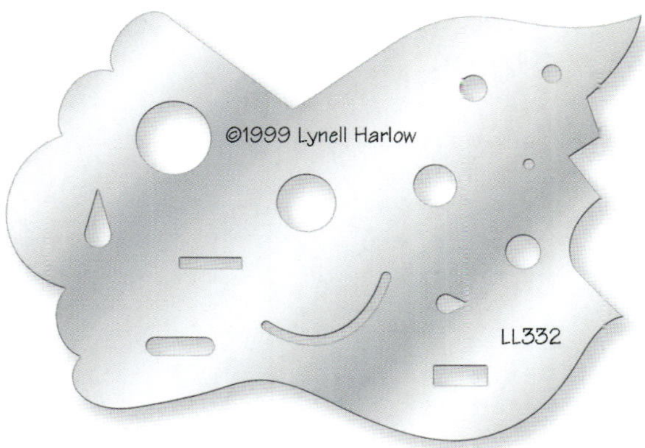

Tip: Stencil Duos with Pen are ideal for doodling as well as many other techniques.

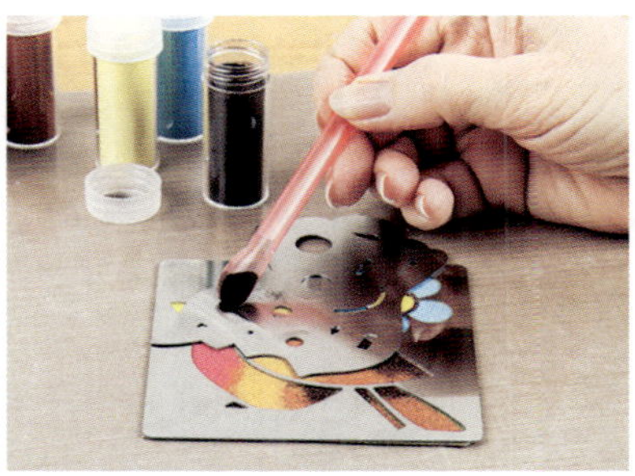

Picasso Stencil Tip: This unusually shaped stencil can mask and reveal small areas for powder, glitter, or color application.

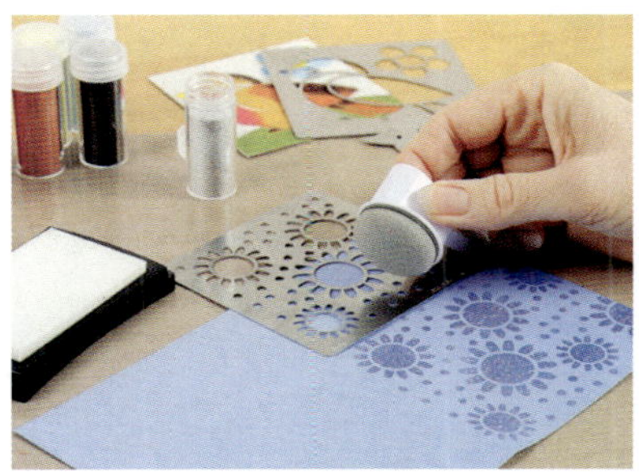

Background Tip: Use a dauber to apply VersaMark™ Ink through stencil. Dust and emboss with Stardust for a coordinated background.

MOLTEN MAGIC
EMBOSSING POWDER TECHNIQUE

P

Molten Magic is a Dreamweaver® Stencils technique that works best with Metallic or Glossy Dreamweaver® Pastes and Metallic Embossing Powders. Heating cures the paste and powders all at once for an amazing raised, textured finish.

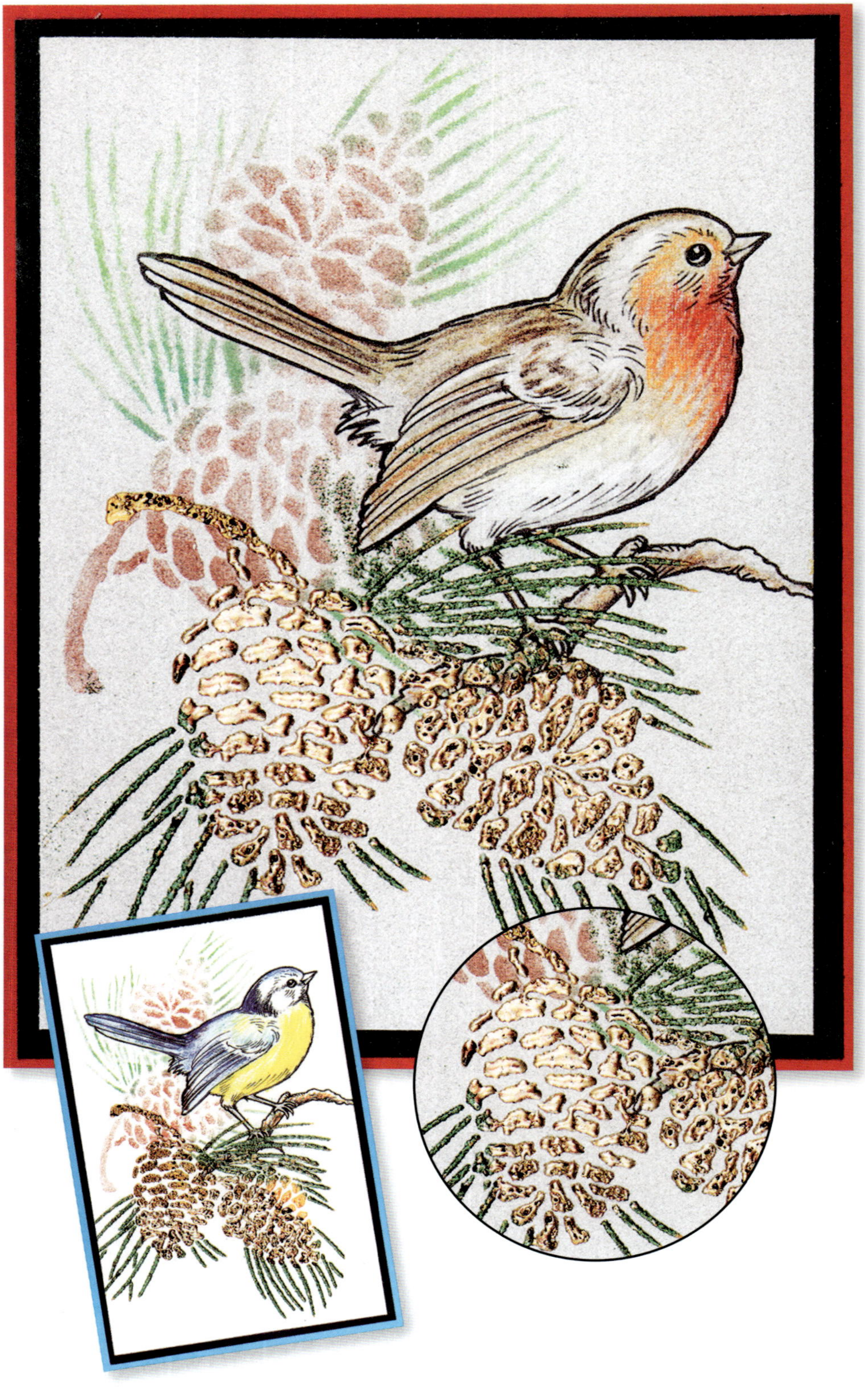

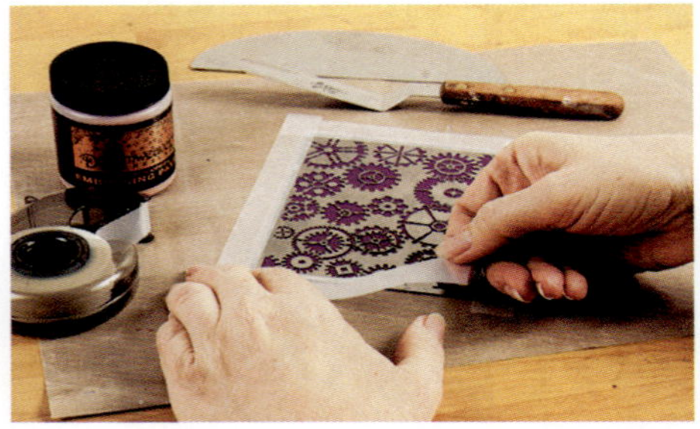

1. Tape it: Use a removable tape to seal all four sides to hold the stencil to paper and keep paste off the edge of the paper.

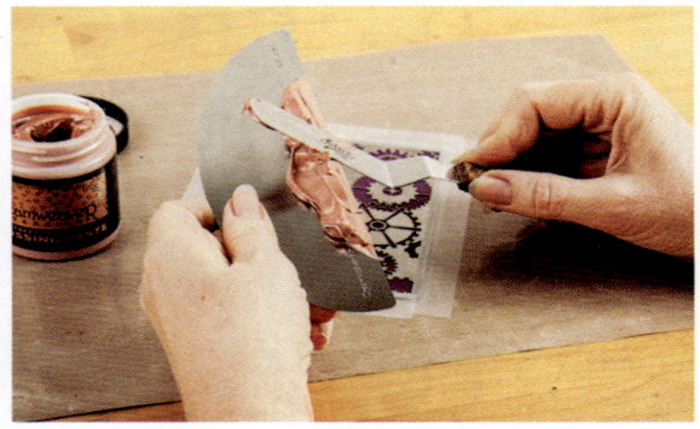

2. Load spreader with paste using palette knife, particularly for large stencils.

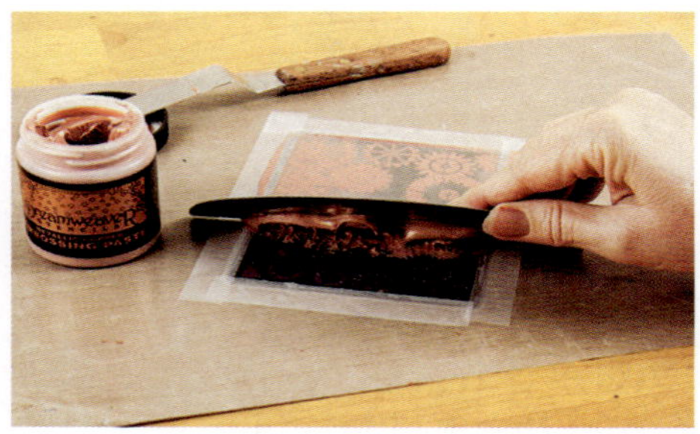

3. Apply paste as evenly and completely as possible. The more passes you make, the more the paper will warp with the moisture.

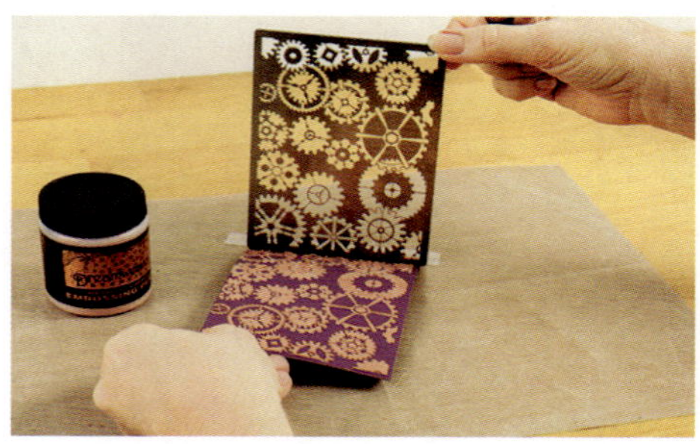

4. Remove tape and stencil by lifting stencil carefully on hinge side of tape.

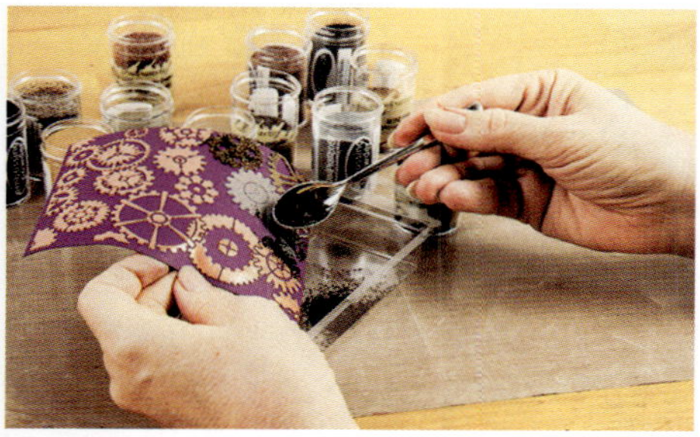

5. Dust it with a variety of metallic powders. Start on an edge and let powders fall away one by one.

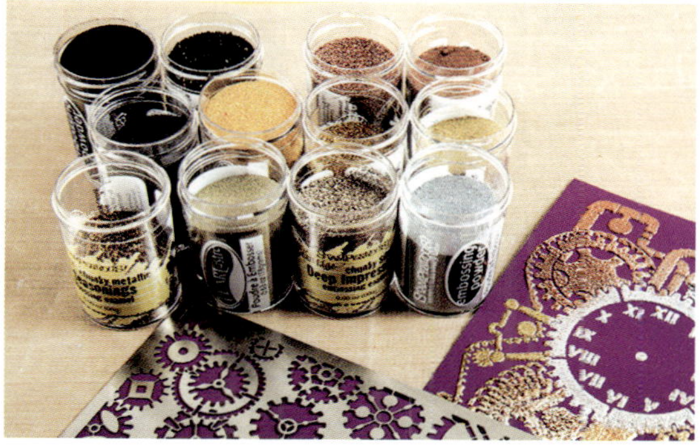

Metallic Embossing Powders are available in a variety of granulations, colors, and mixes such as the Frantage™ series. PEARLustres™ will also work for this technique. White based powders will take longer to fully heat and are less predictable.

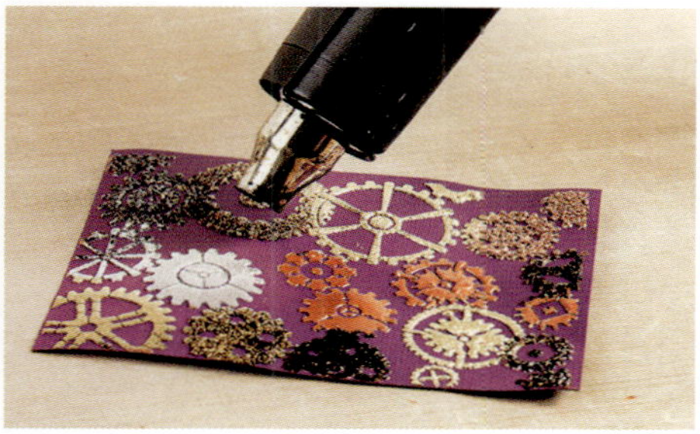

6. Heat it: Apply heat tool and watch paste raise, bubble, and then cure from crusty to a molten three dimensional texture.

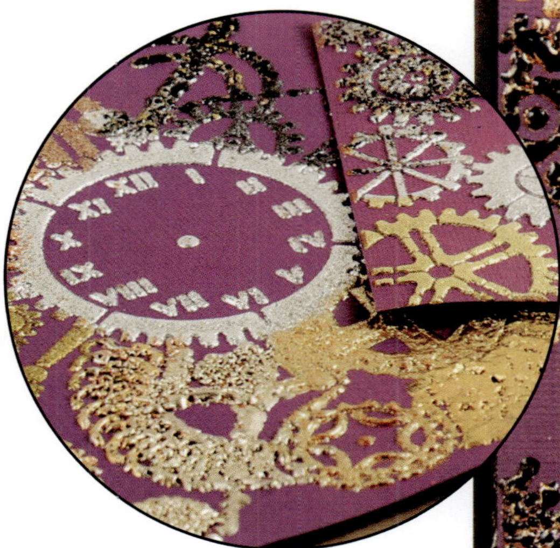

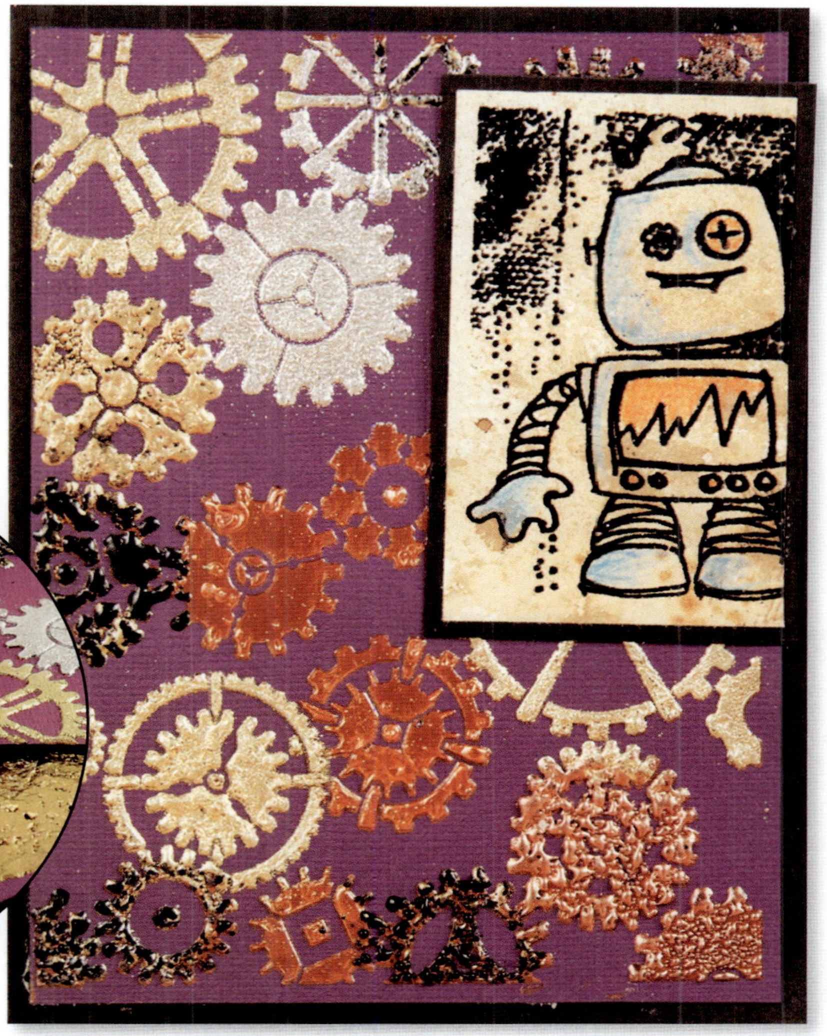

Basic Pasting Tips:

Metal Stencils should always be kept perfectly flat and clean.

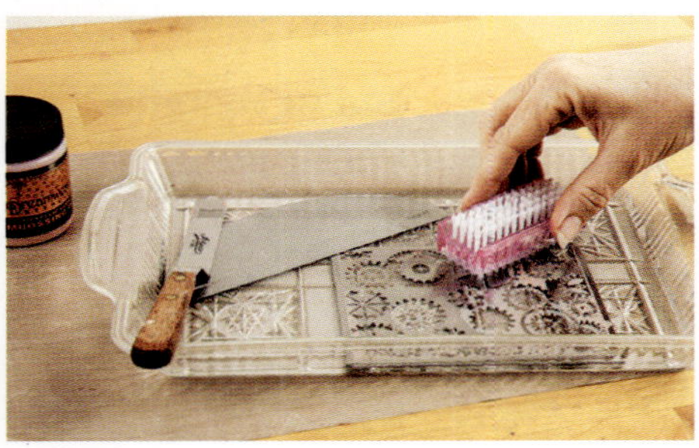

A. Soak stencil in flat bottom tray with water as soon as you remove tape. Scrub later with soft brush and pat dry with soft cloth.

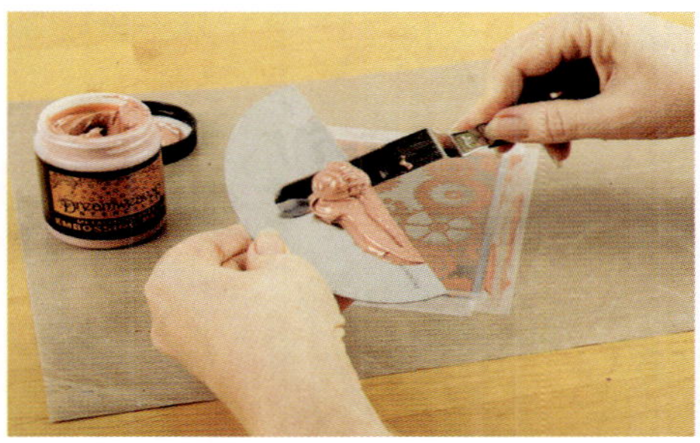

B. Recover excess paste: Apply paste generously for ease of application. Most returns to jar and will last for many applications.

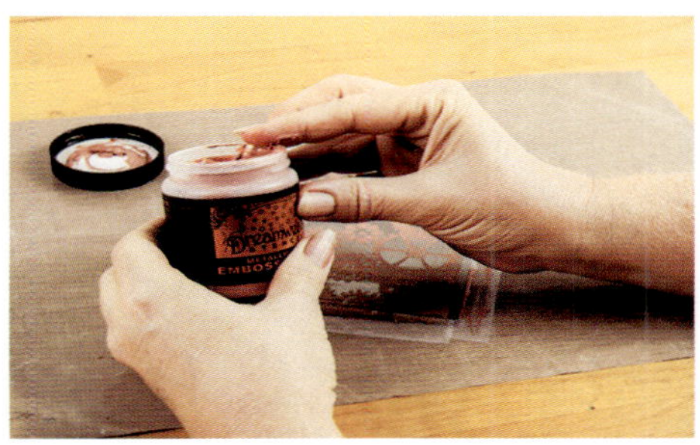

C. Clean rim and seal paste: Tap remaining paste down in jar and clean the rim of paste before securing lid on air tight jar.

TIPS FOR NON-POROUS SURFACES
TO BE EMBOSSED

Embossing on acetate, pearlized papers, vellum, or metallic foil can be tricky, but worth the unique results. Test materials such as acetate to be sure they can take heat with minimum warping. Work carefully to keep surface clean, dry and static free. See "Glass" on page 63.

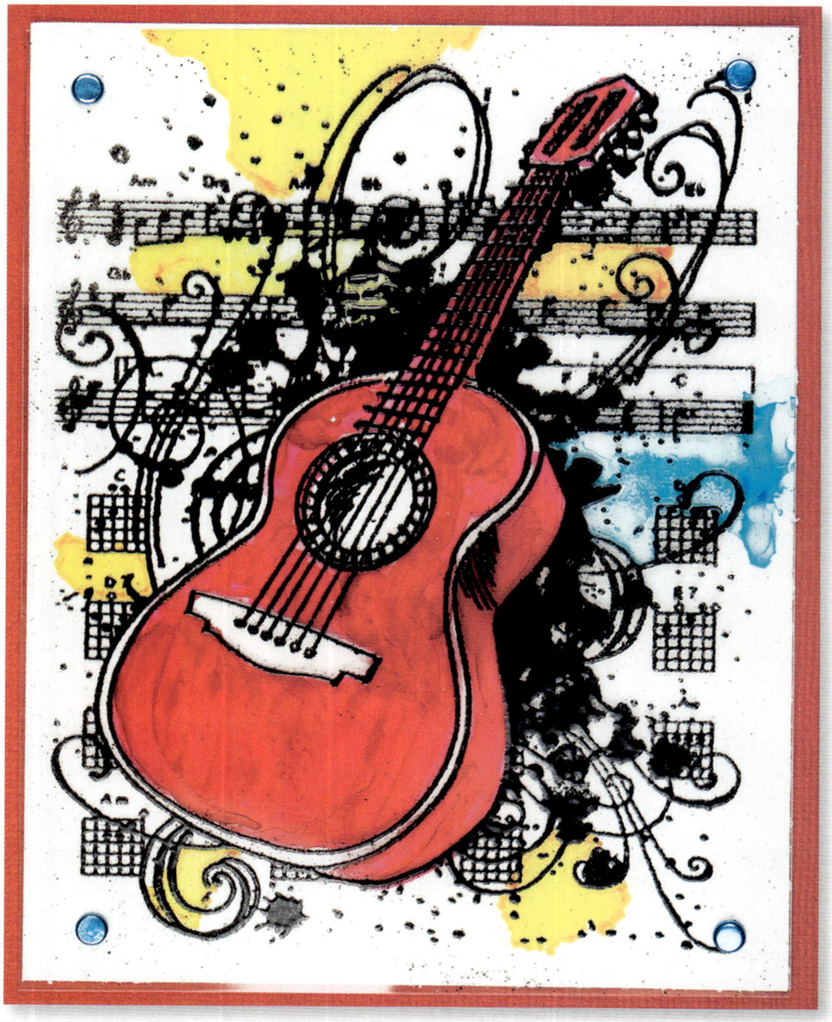

Layers Tip: Securing translucent layers is best done with hole punching to attach with brads or ribbon ties.

Specialty papers with embossed images are very elegant and often used for wedding invitations.

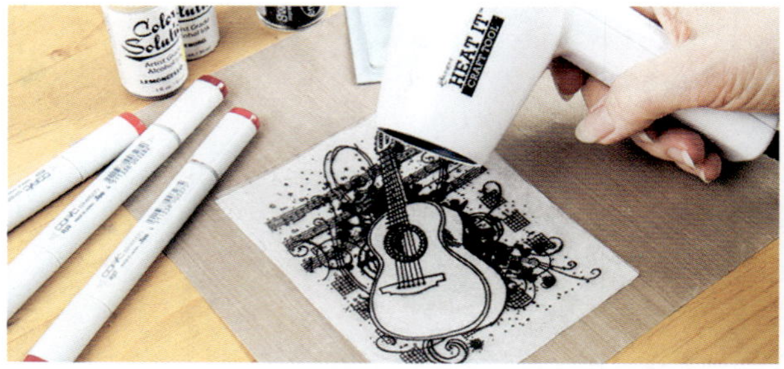

1. Stamp and emboss acetate: Use anti-static pouch. Brush away unwanted particles. Use low wattage heat tool and move evenly to minimize warping.

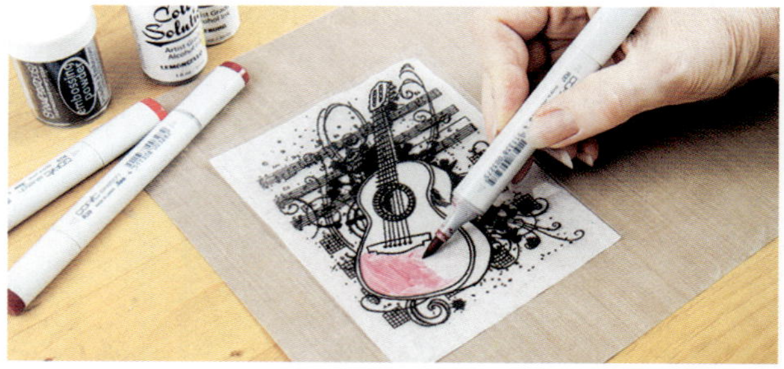

2. Alcohol markers can be used to color from front and back. Avoid letting marker tip contact embossed area.

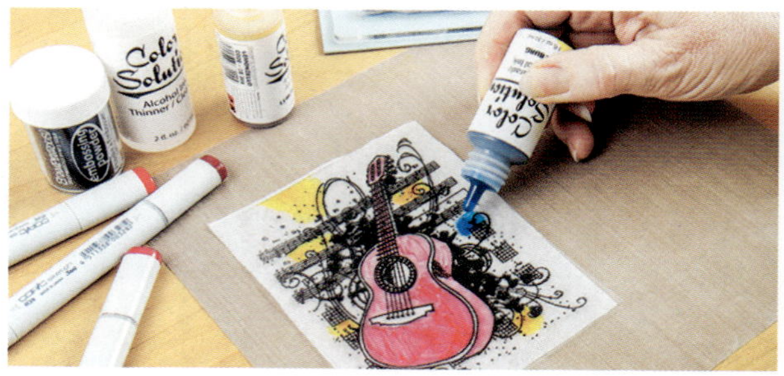

3. Alcohol inks can also be applied front or back. Squirt, spray or dab colors on.

Try **pearlized** papers with PEARLustre™ powders.

Use **vellum** sheets for translucent overlays.

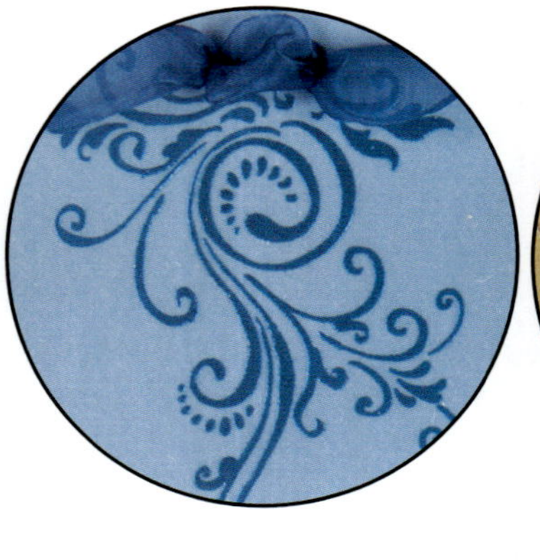

Use **foil or metallic** papers with metallic or PEARLustre™ Embossing Powders.

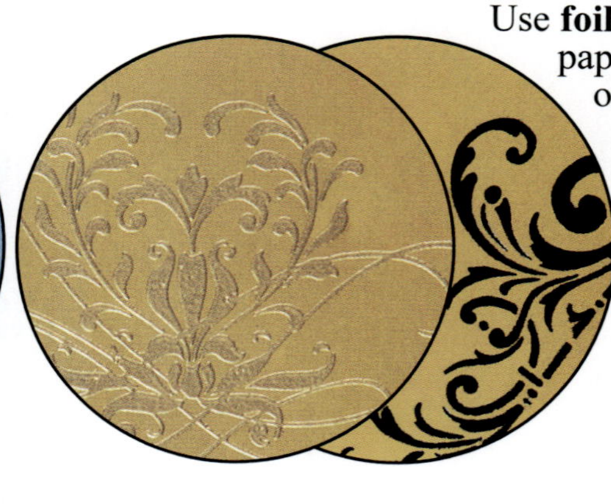

TIPS FOR POROUS SURFACES
TO BE EMBOSSED

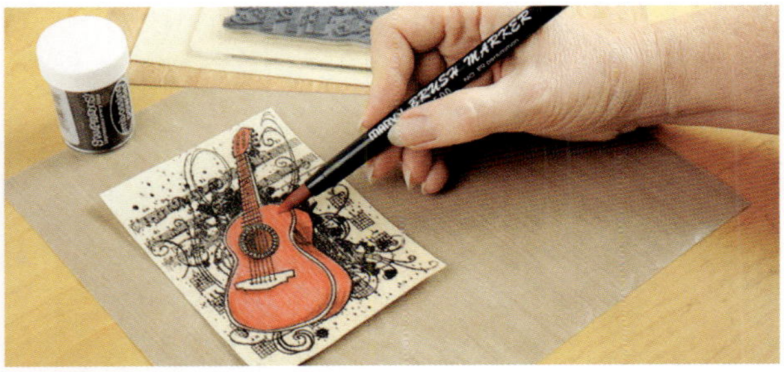

1. Wood veneer comes in many types and colors. If it has a sticky back adhesive, it may be best to adhere it to a sturdy paper panel before you stamp and emboss to minimize warping. Regular powders work best, detail powders seep into the grain.

2. Brush away any unwanted particles BEFORE heating.

3. Color in with water-based markers or paints, etc.

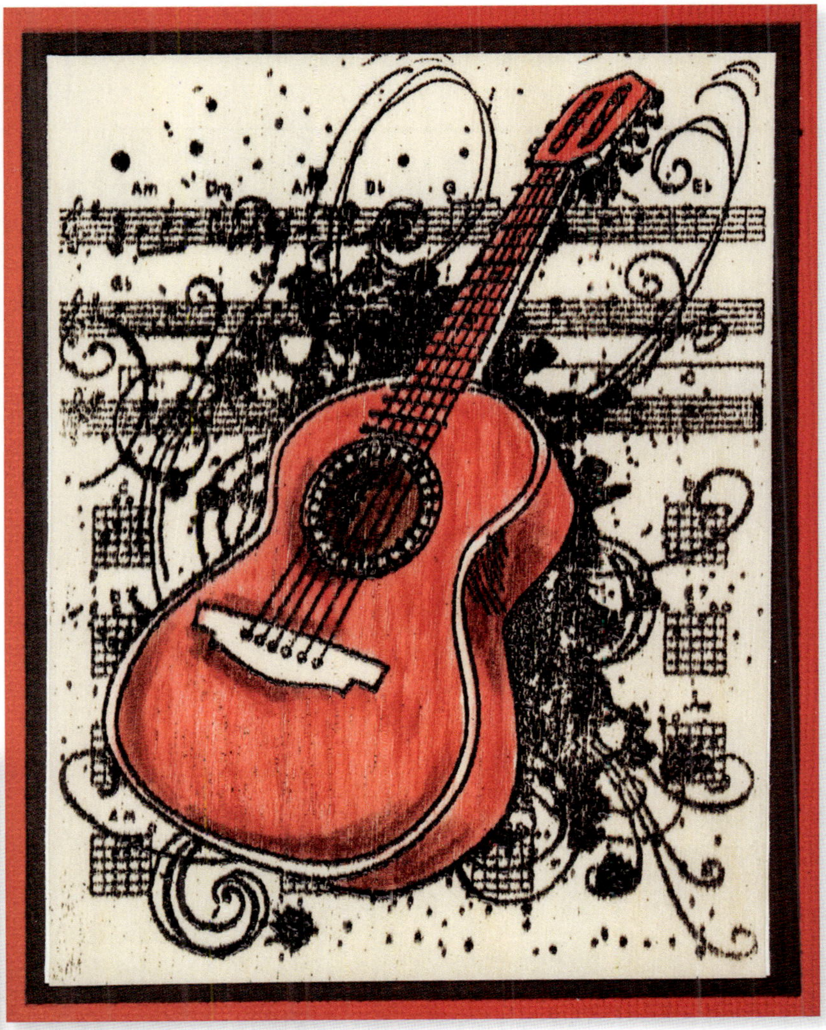

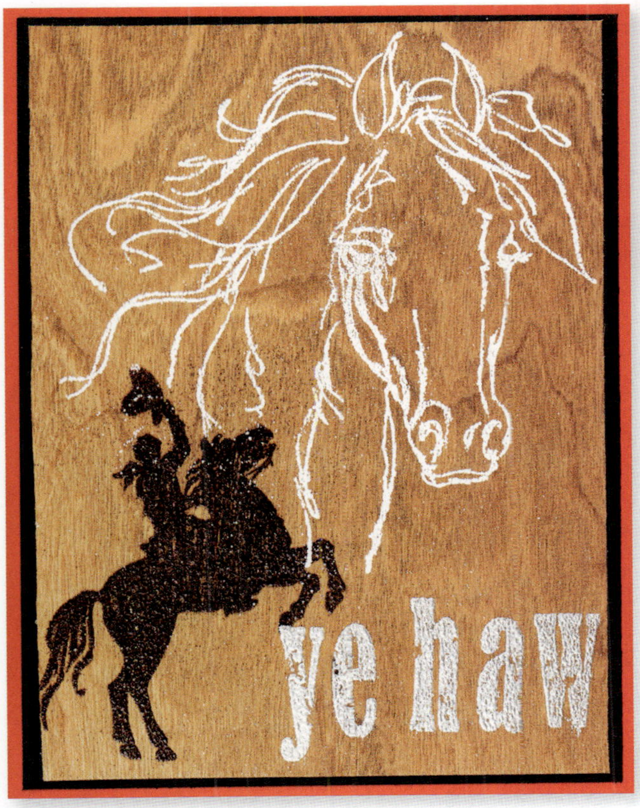

Tip for embossing overlapped images:
Stamp and emboss foreground image first. Stamp background image and dust with Embossing Powder. BEFORE heating, use a clean dry brush to remove unwanted powder that overlaps foreground image. Heat.

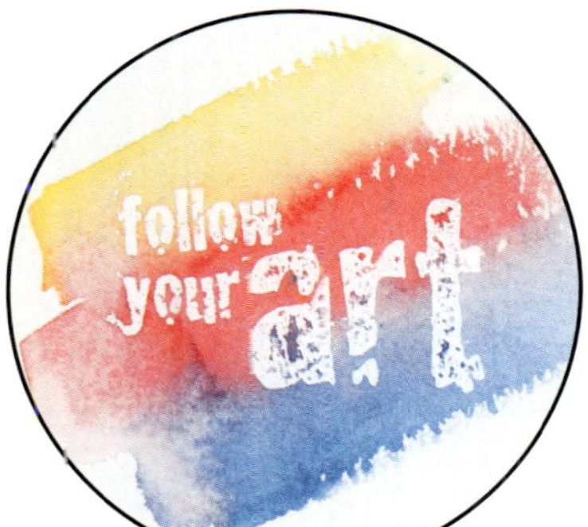

Tip: YUPO® Synthetic Papers are made of recyclable, waterproof and tree-free polypropylene. They have a glossy surface yet work beautifully for watercolor and embossing without warping. Test other synthetic paper options.

Tip: Watercolor papers are available in many weights and textures. Select a smooth surface and detail powders for detailed impressions. Expect a more broken up impression on rough papers.

ENCRUSTED JEWEL TECHNIQUE
WITH SPOONFUL MIXES

S

The Encrusted Jewel Technique relies on the option of heating from underneath. It goes beyond Embossing Powders to include any number of other elements that won't melt, but will be embedded into the molten Embossing Powder. Just spoon it on.

Layers Tip: To avoid warped layers, hold them together, but don't glue them together until after embossing.

STEP-BY-STEP INSTRUCTIONS

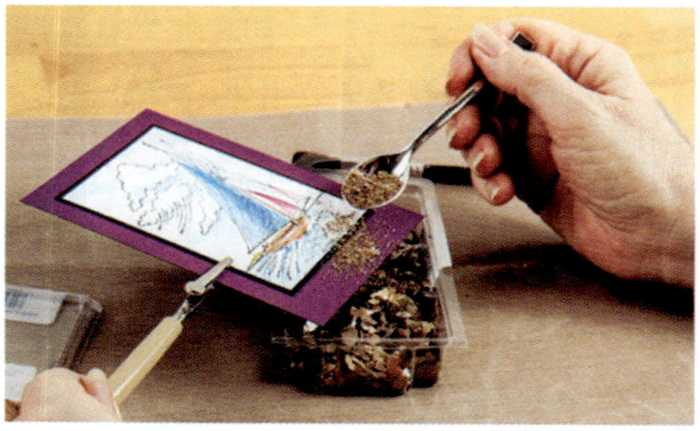

1. Sprinkle a small spoonful of the Gold Dust Mix Embossing Powder on card. NO INK is needed to hold the powders - just gravity. Clip tool will help hold card level.

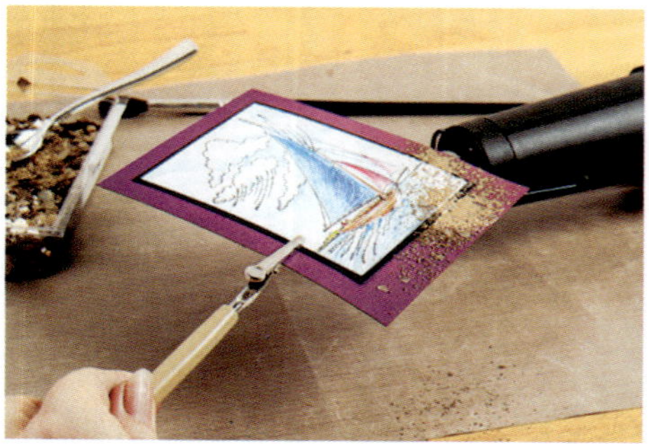

2. Heat it by holding heat tool closely UNDERNEATH paper. Move it from one area to another as needed until powders melt.

Spoonful Mix Kits offer a bag full of unique powders and elements for distinctive looks such as Gold Dust, Confetti, Rust, etc. Other elements may include Mica Flakes, Shaved Ice, Color Fragments, Crushed Glass Glitter, etc. Kits also provide a handy working tray.

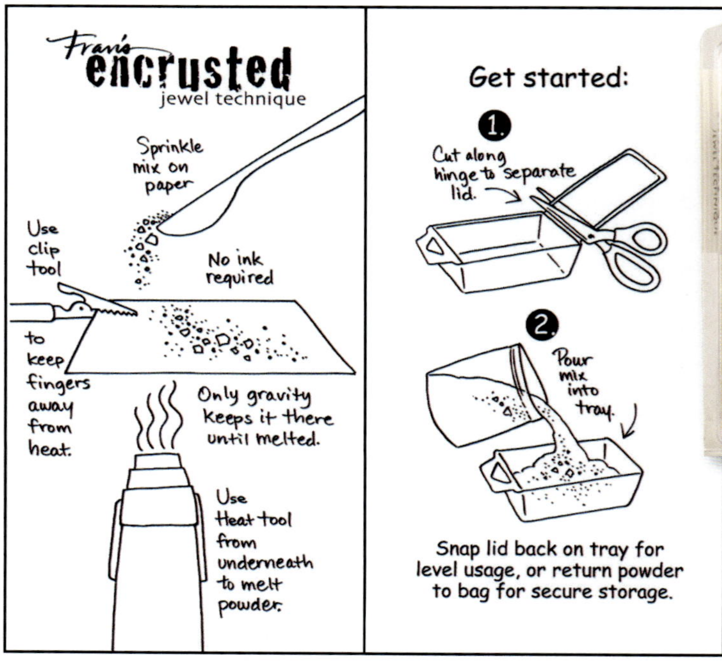

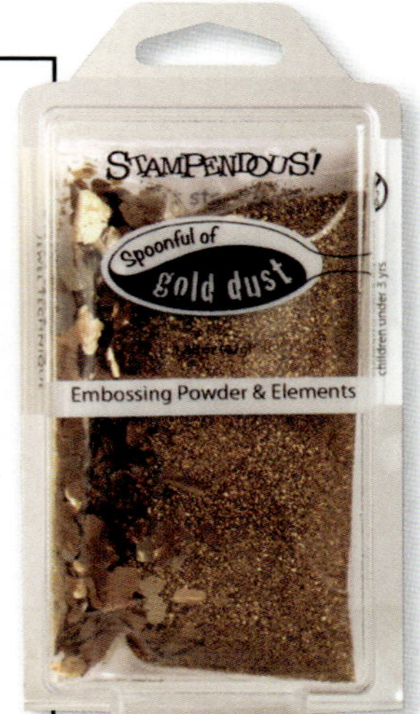

This printed insert comes in the Spoonful Mix. It explains the technique and shows how best to work with the tray which is just big enough for an A2 sized card.

ENCRUSTED JEWEL VARIATIONS

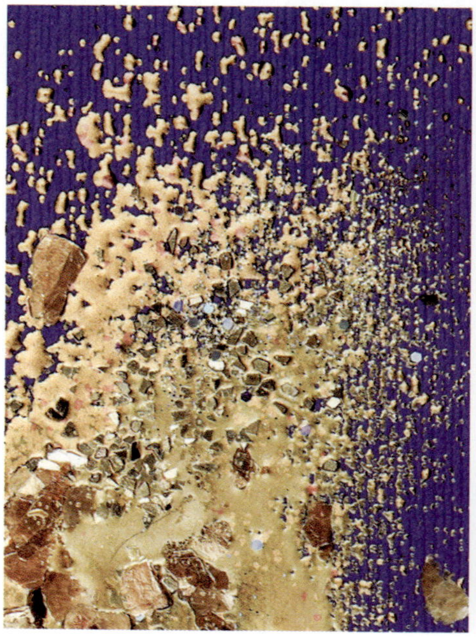

Simply splash a spoonful of Gold Dust on the card and then heat from underneath.

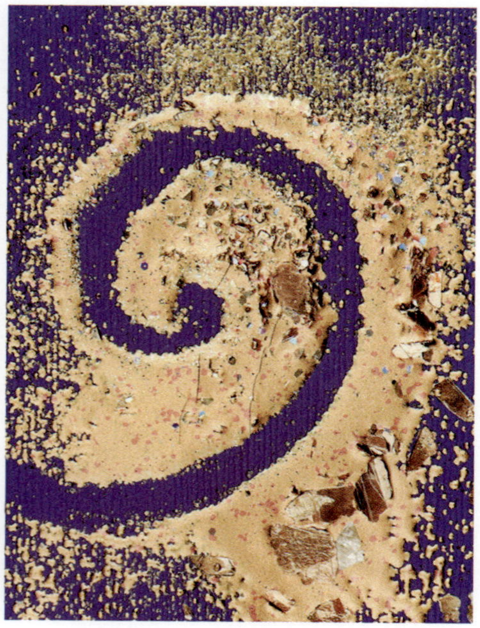

Splash a spoonful of Gold Dust on the card and use a small brush or stylus tool to doodle in it before heating from underneath.

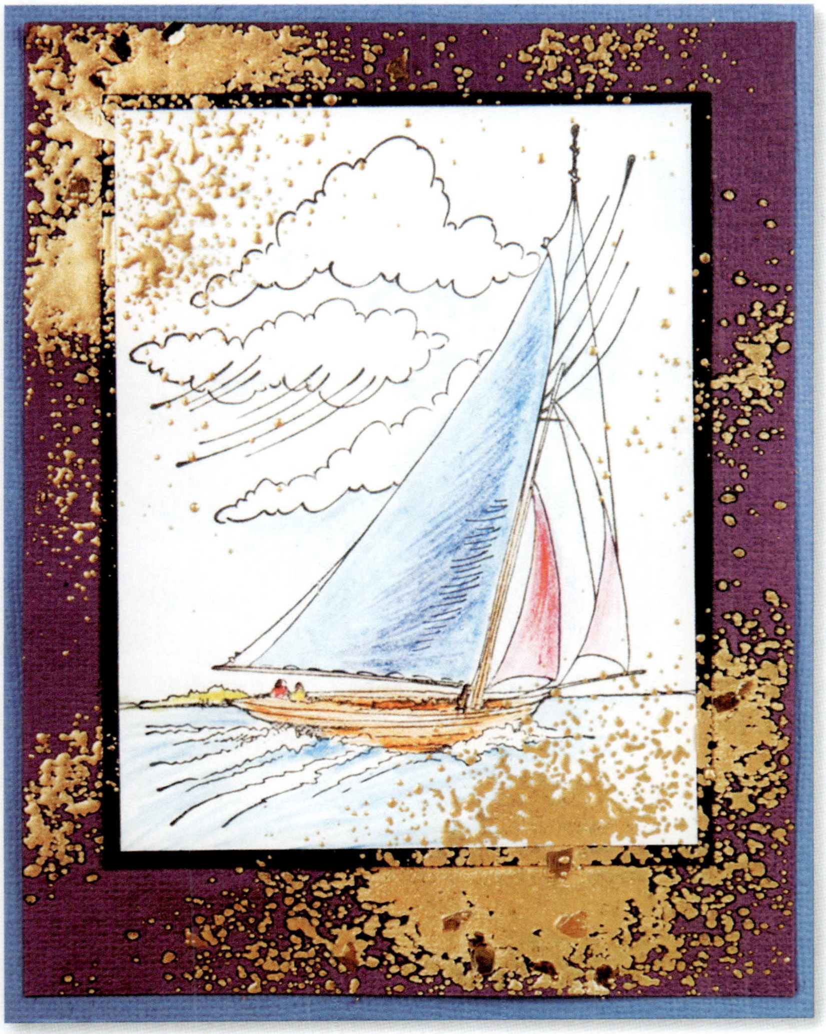

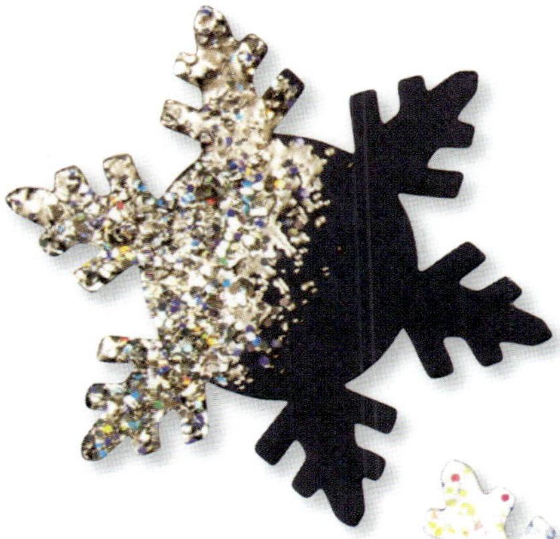

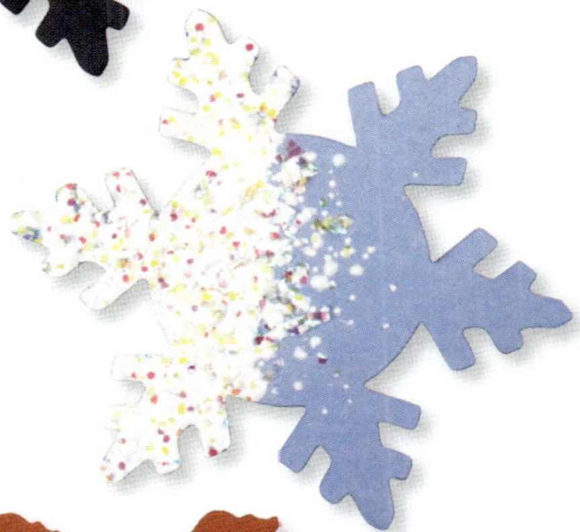

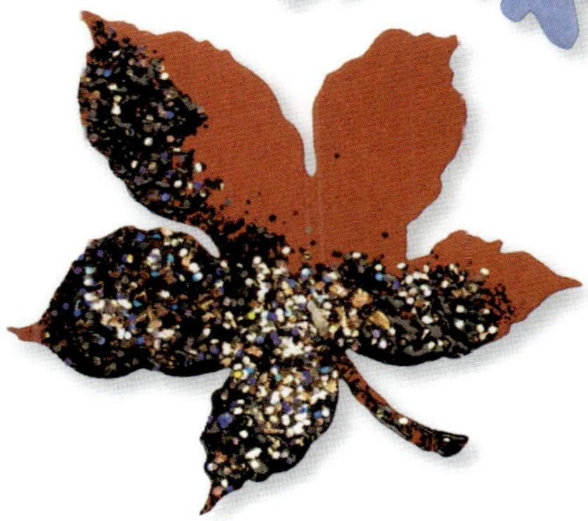

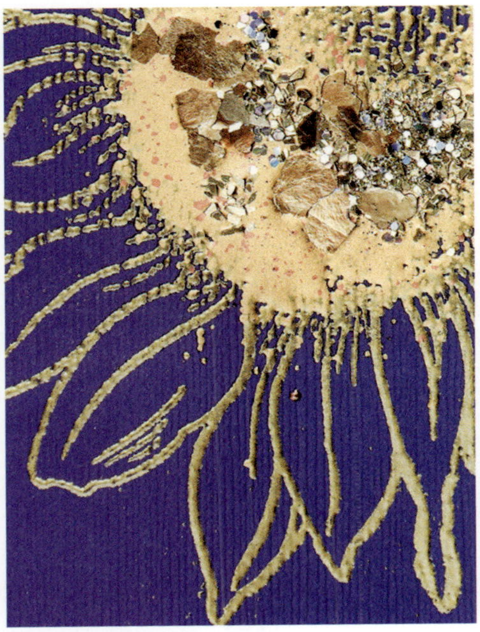

Splash a spoonful of Gold Dust over an embossed image and use a brush to guide powder into place before heating from underneath.

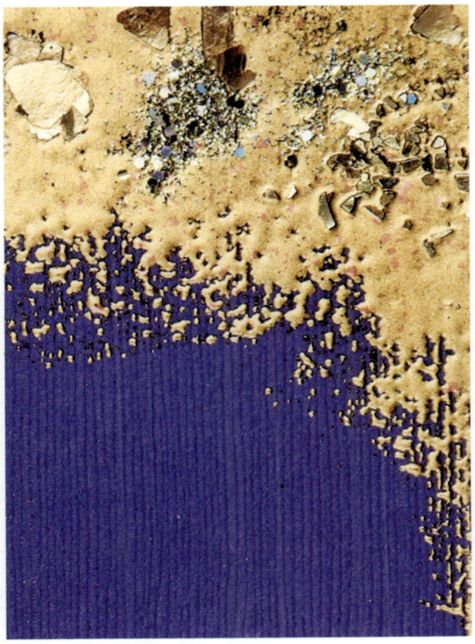

Use VersaMark™ ink along the edge to hold Spoonful Mix in place while heating from underneath.

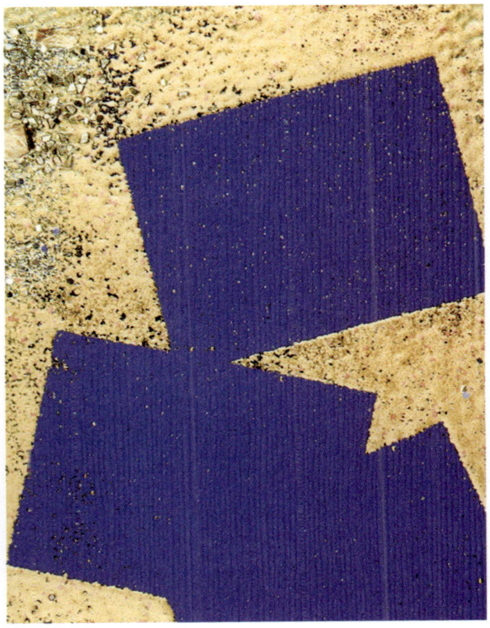

Cover or mask out areas where you don't want powder before using VersaMark™ ink across the surface. Dust and heat from underneath.

ENCRUSTED JEWEL TECHNIQUE
WITH 5 JAR KITS

Besides Spoonful Mixes, you can use 5 Jar Kits or ANY combination of Embossing Powders and elements. Start with Embossing Powder so elements can melt in. Heating from underneath gives you the freedom to splash it on. Gravity does the rest. Inks are not required, just helpful "place holders" to keep powders from flying away on corners.

STEP-BY-STEP INSTRUCTIONS

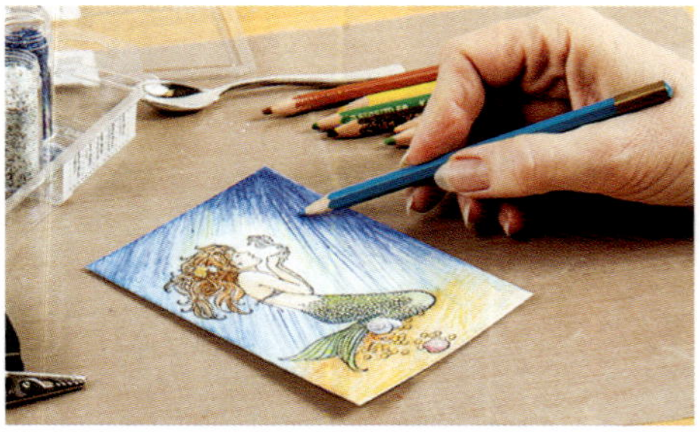

1. Stamp and color image and background with colored pencils, or other media.

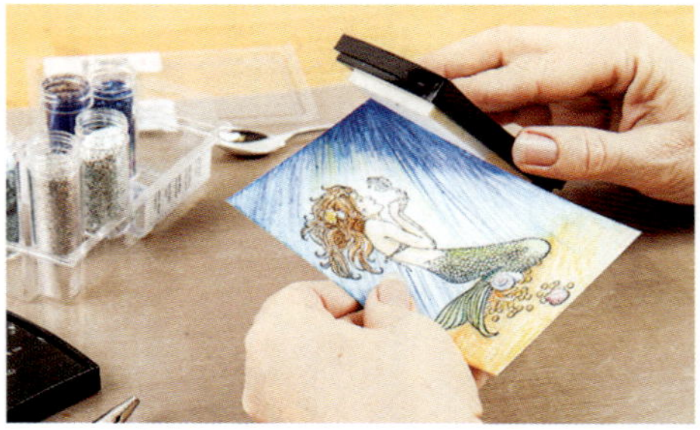

2. Ink edge with VersaMark™ ink to ensure powders will stay in place out to the corner.

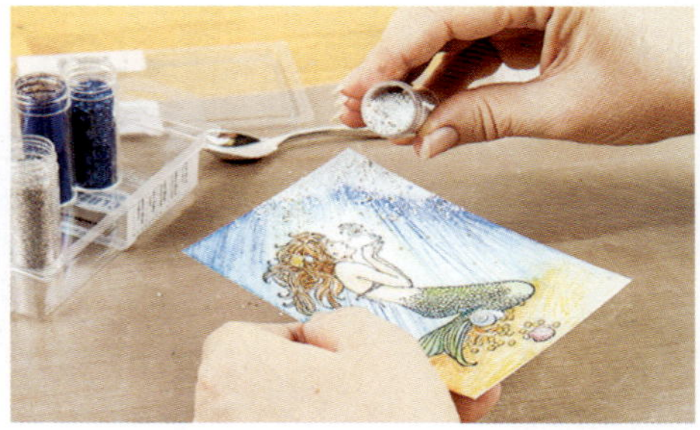

3. Embossing Powder FIRST as a base layer is key to the other elements melting into it.

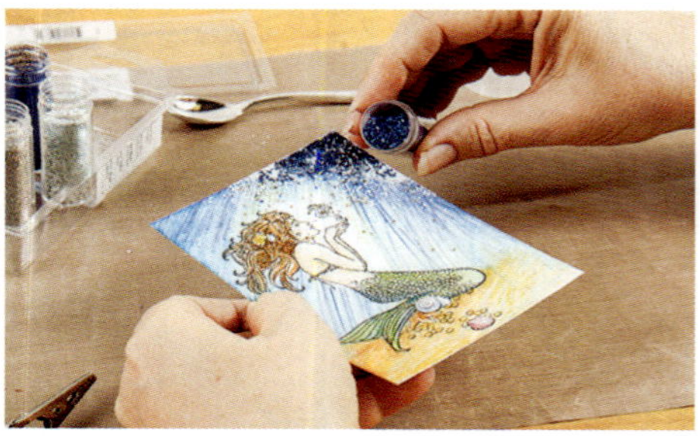

4. Add elements such as Crushed Glass Glitter or more colors of Embossing Powder.

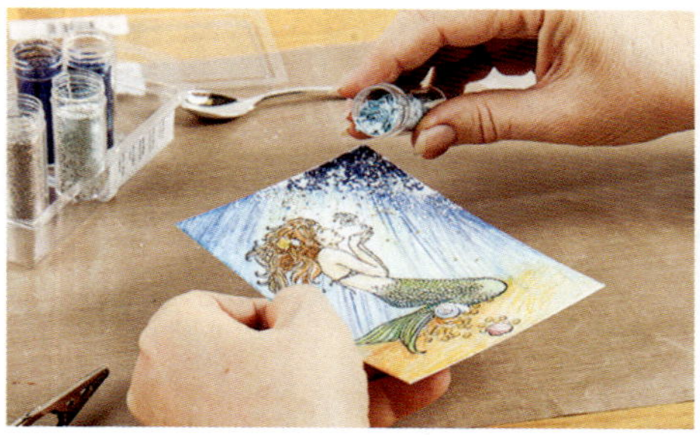

5. Add more elements such as Color Fragments or Mica Flakes with the largest elements last.

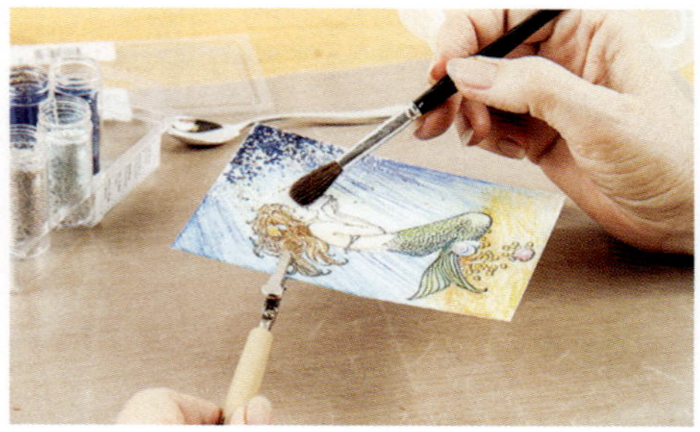

6. Touch up with a dry brush. Now is the time to move it around if needed before you heat it. Clip tool will hold it steady.

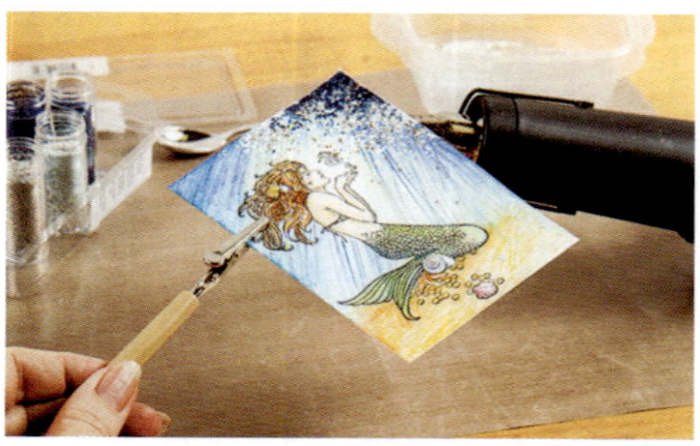

7. Heat it from UNDERNEATH starting at heaviest area. Move heat tool around. Thicker areas need more time.

Smoking Gun Tip: If heat tool starts to smoke, pull it to the side and let it "breathe" then resume heating where needed. Trapped air is usually what causes the smoking.

Seasonings is a mix of chunky metallics and black. A splash can be added to any color to quickly make a Frantage™ mix.

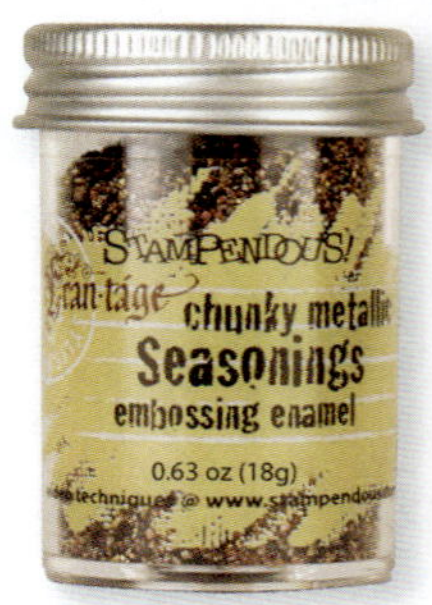

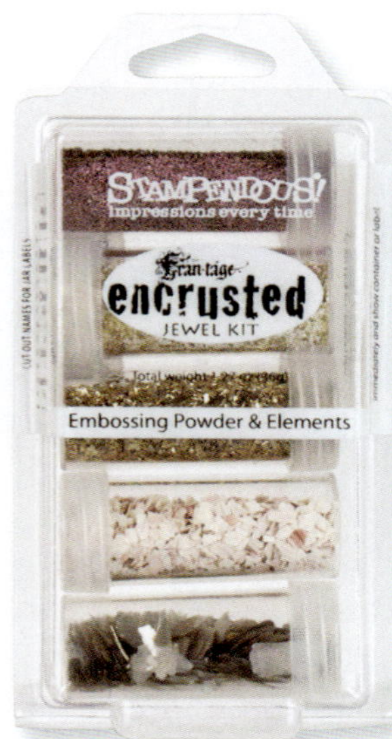

5 Jar Encrusted Jewel Kits are available in many color schemes.

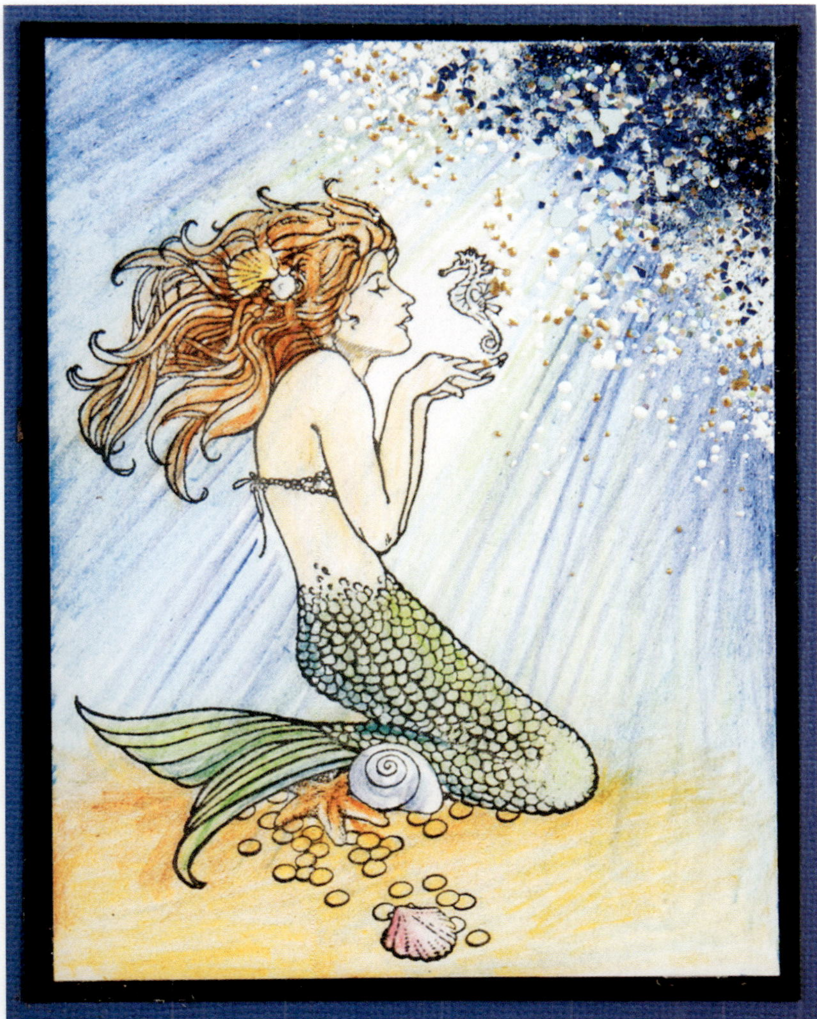

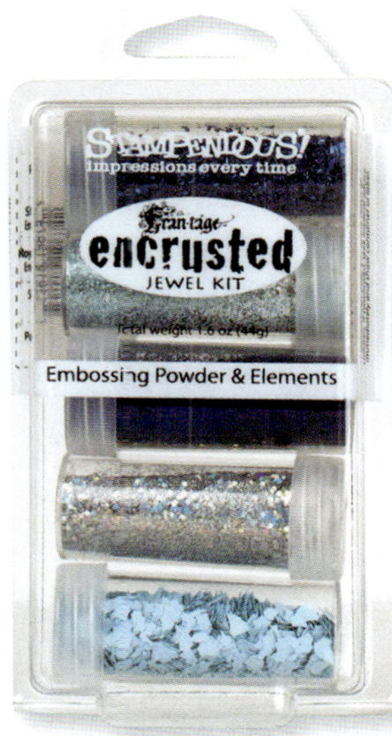

5 Jar Encrusted Jewel Kits are a great value to provide both Embossing Powders and elements in a coordinated color scheme.

Stamp and dust tree with Shabby Blue Embossing Powder. Tap off excess. Then sprinkle more powder on ground and Mica on the leaves. Heat from underneath.

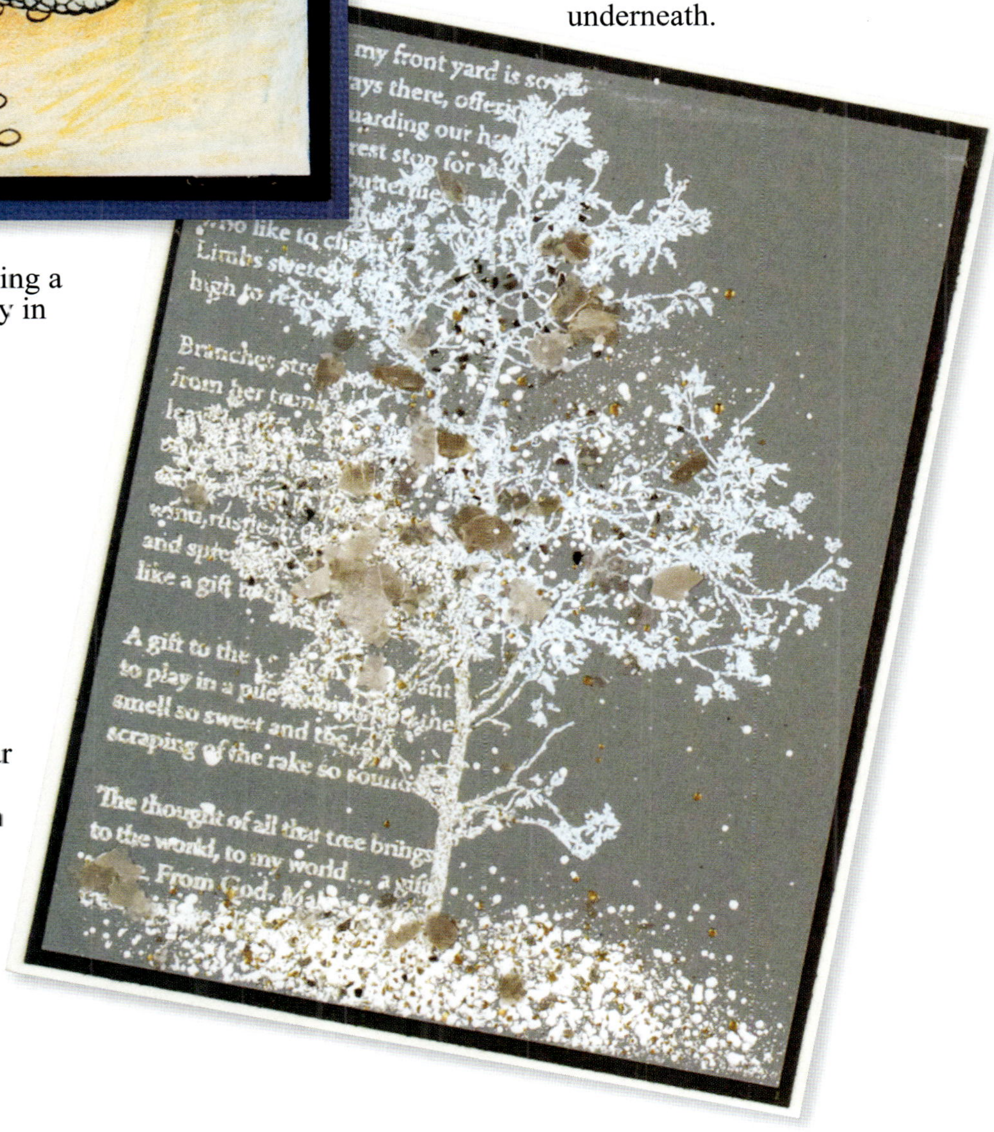

Creative mixes are endless. Premixing a small quantity makes it easy to apply in a splash. Save mixes in empty jars.

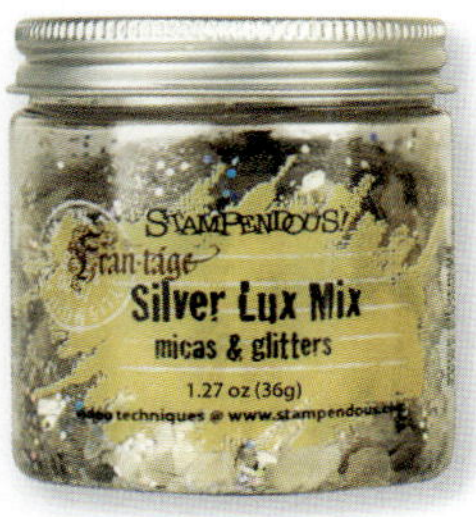

Use **Lux Mixes** of fancy glitter, mica, and elements over any embossing powder.

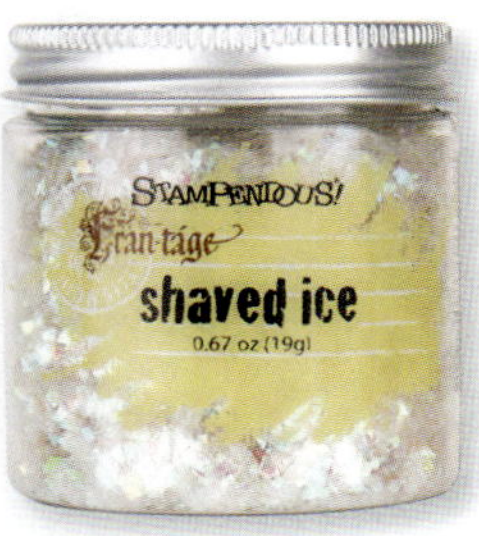

Shaved Ice: Crystal irregular flakes become iridescent when melted.

ENCRUSTED JEWEL TECHNIQUE
FOR MIXED MEDIA TAGS

Create your own mix of Embossing Powders and add Fragments, Crushed Glass Glitter, or Mica, etc. The premixed Spoonful series are a great value. For mixed media tags start with acrylic paint, then add stamps and encrusted embossing accents. Heat from underneath.

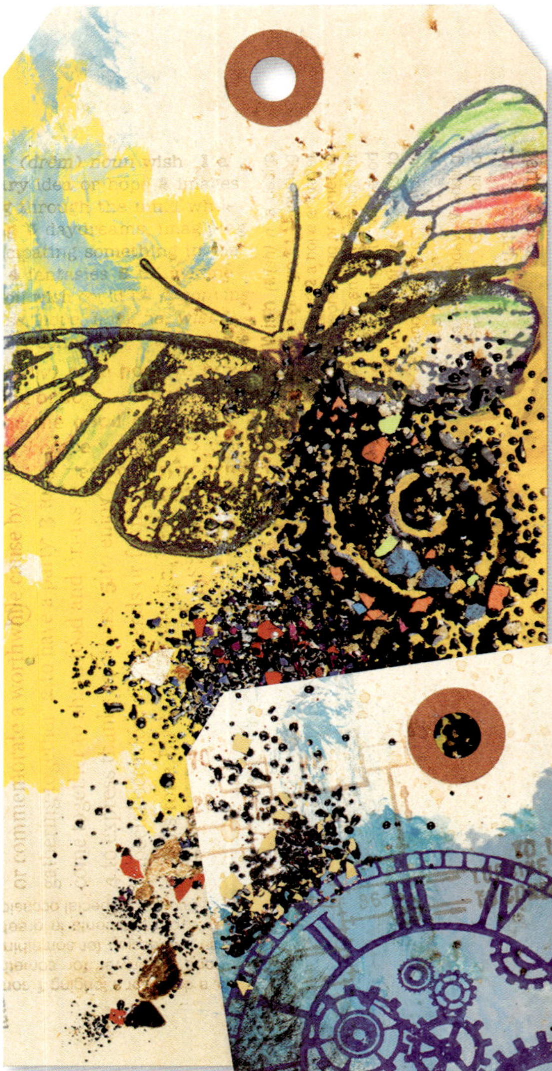

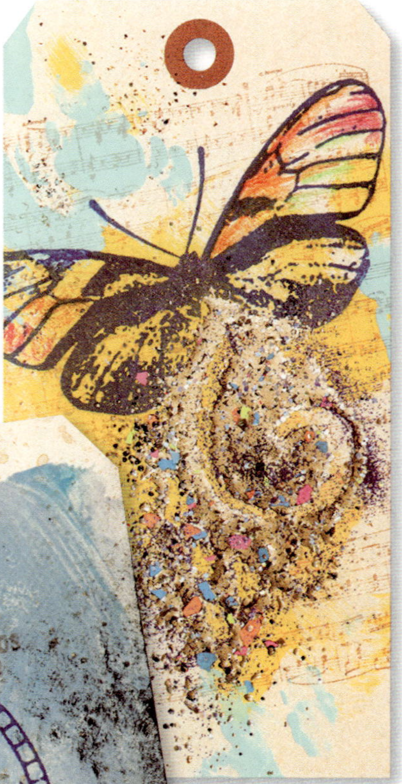

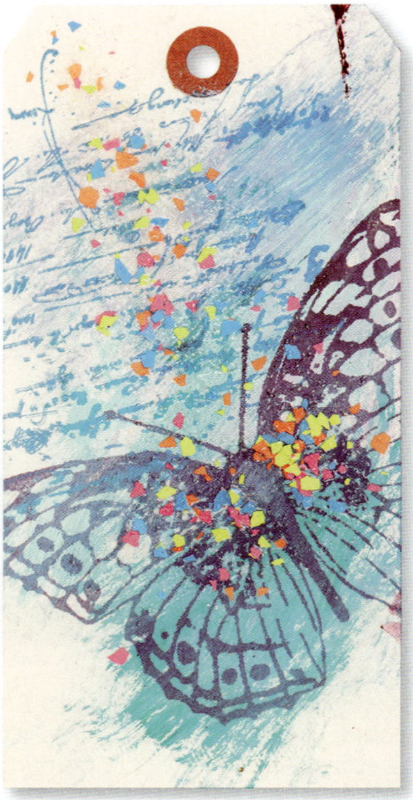

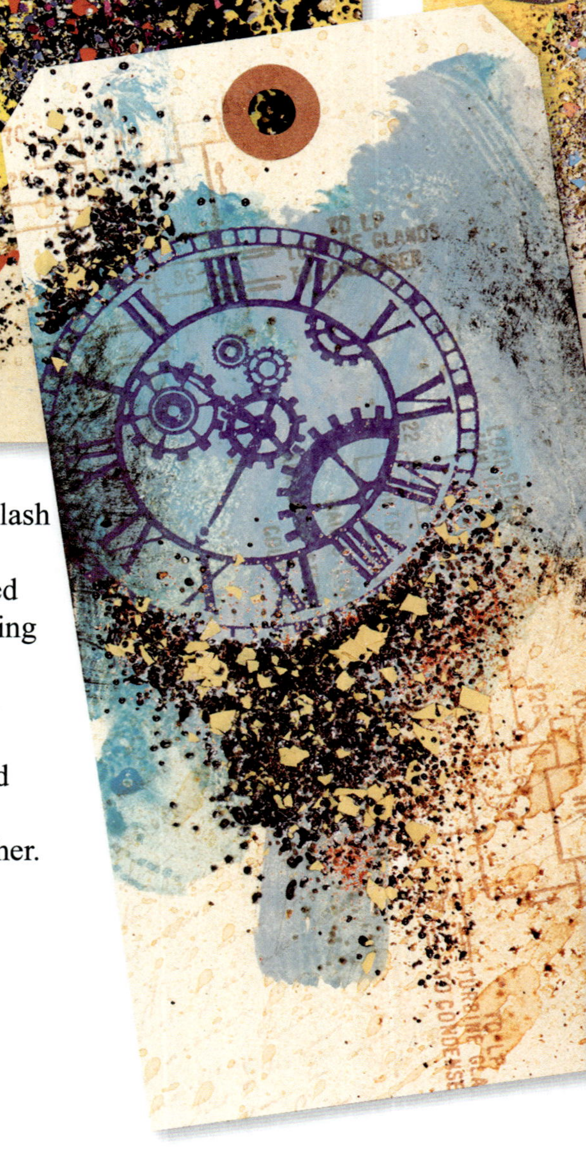

The custom splash mix above has Frantage™ Aged Black Embossing Powder, Gold Crushed Glass Glitter, Party Fragments, and Gold Mica all splashed together.

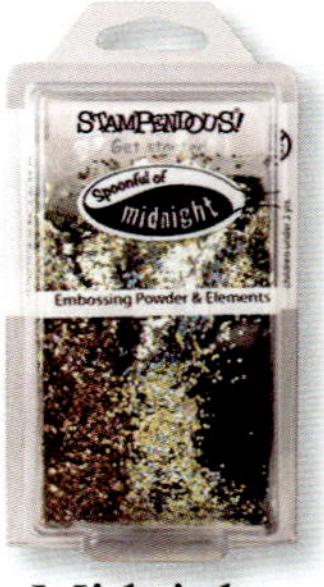

Midnight

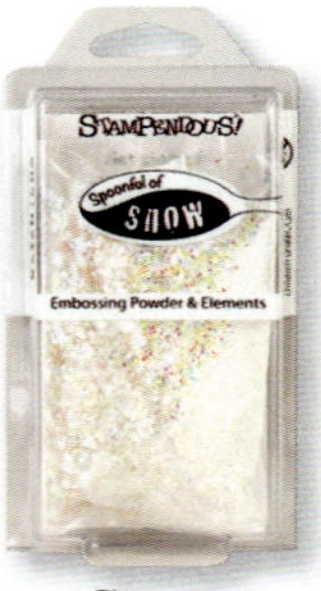

Snow

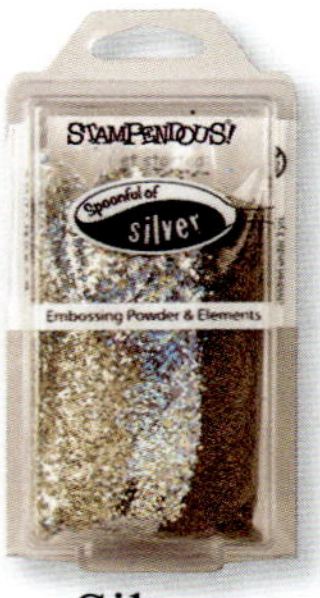

Silver

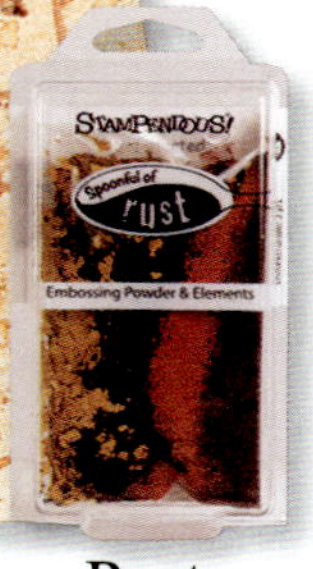

Rust

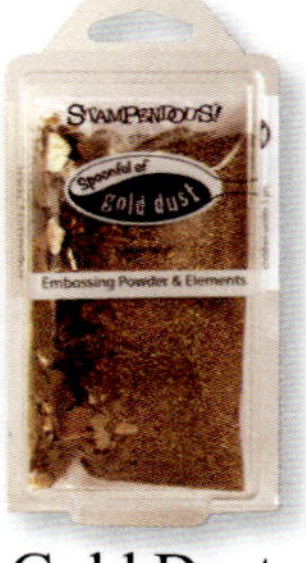

Gold Dust

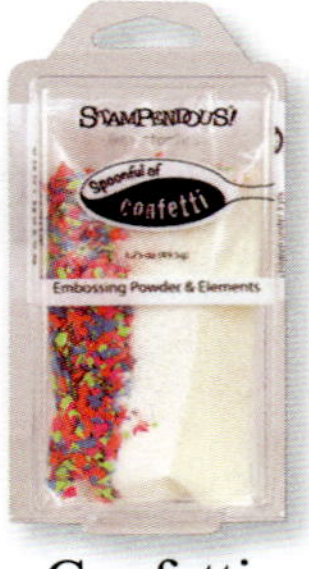

Confetti

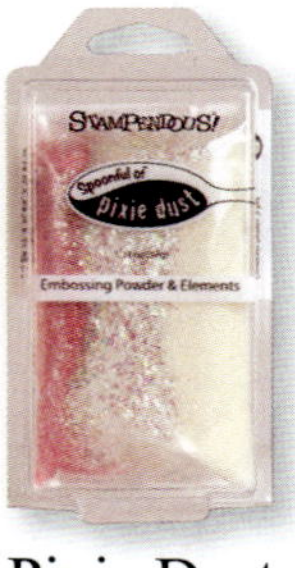

Pixie Dust

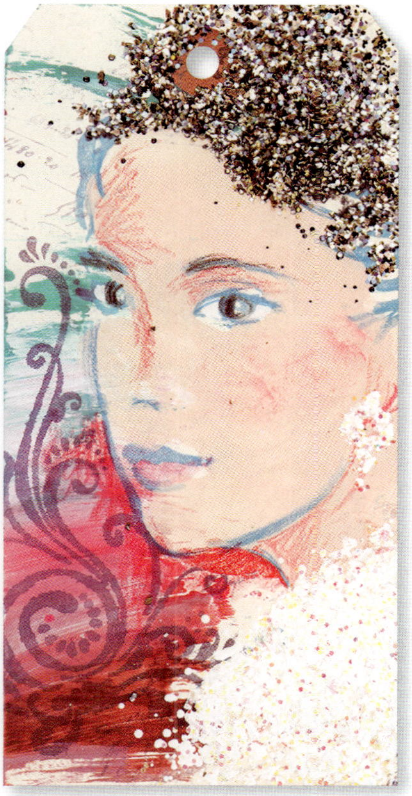
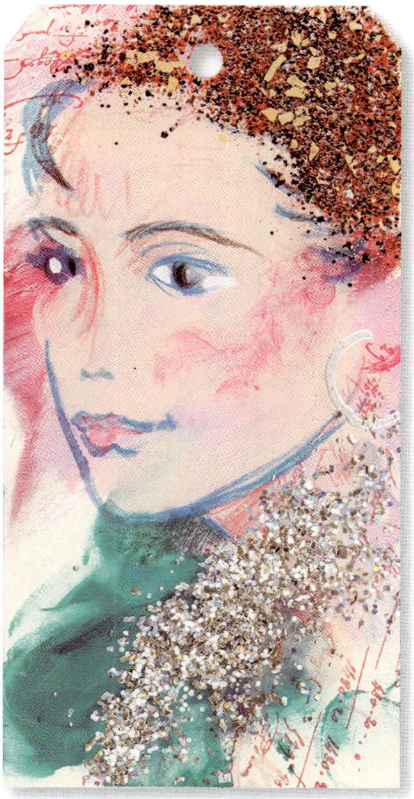
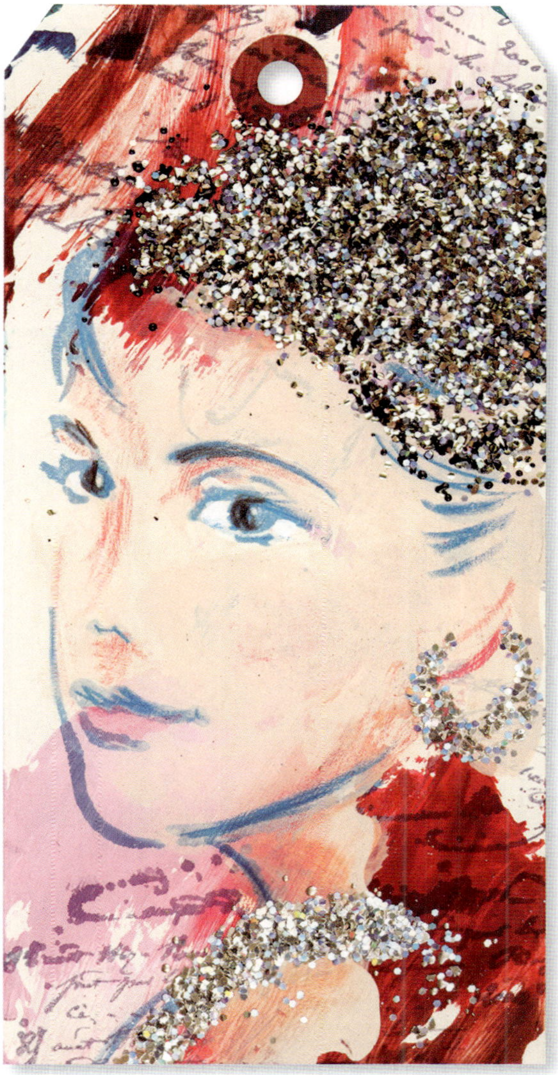
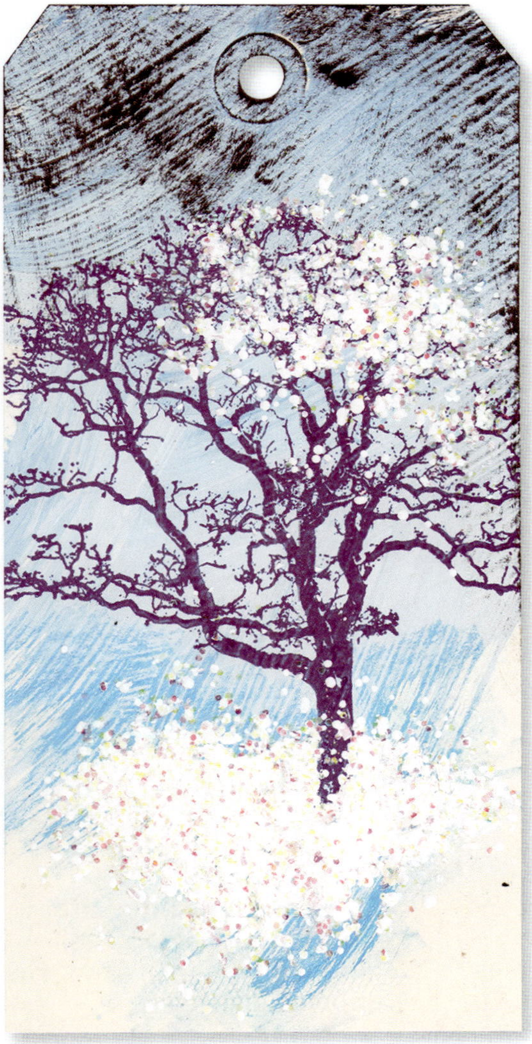
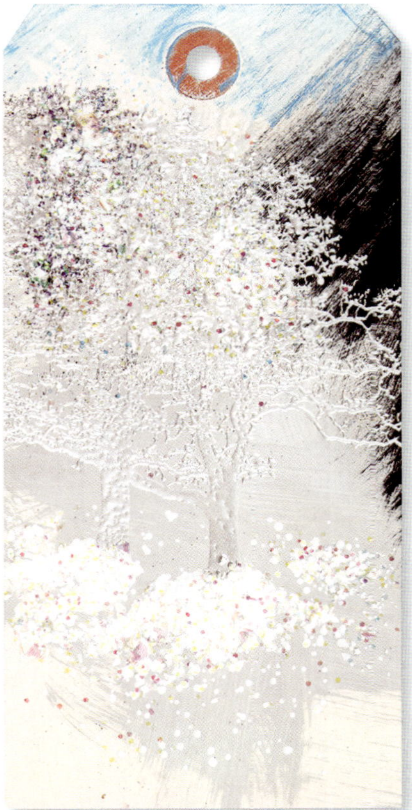
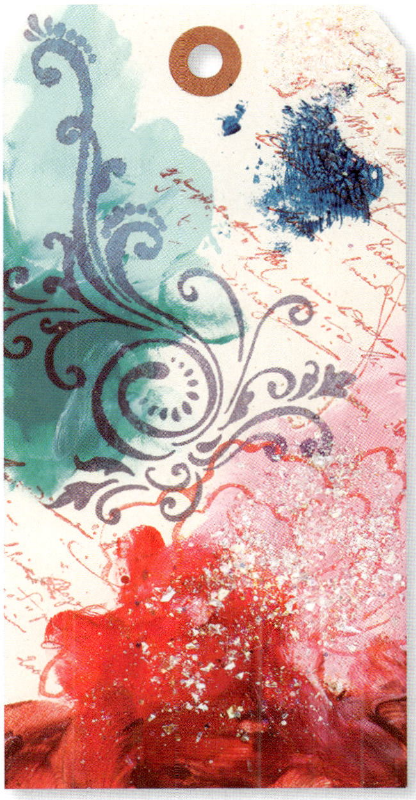

ENCRUSTED ADHESIVE TECHNIQUE
FOR SCRAPBOOK PAGES

There are so many Embossing Powders that make great snow like Crystal, Sparkle Puff, Frantage™ Shabby White, and Shabby Blue. All are used here. Select heavier weight papers. Heat from underneath. If glued layers warp, weigh them down to flatten.

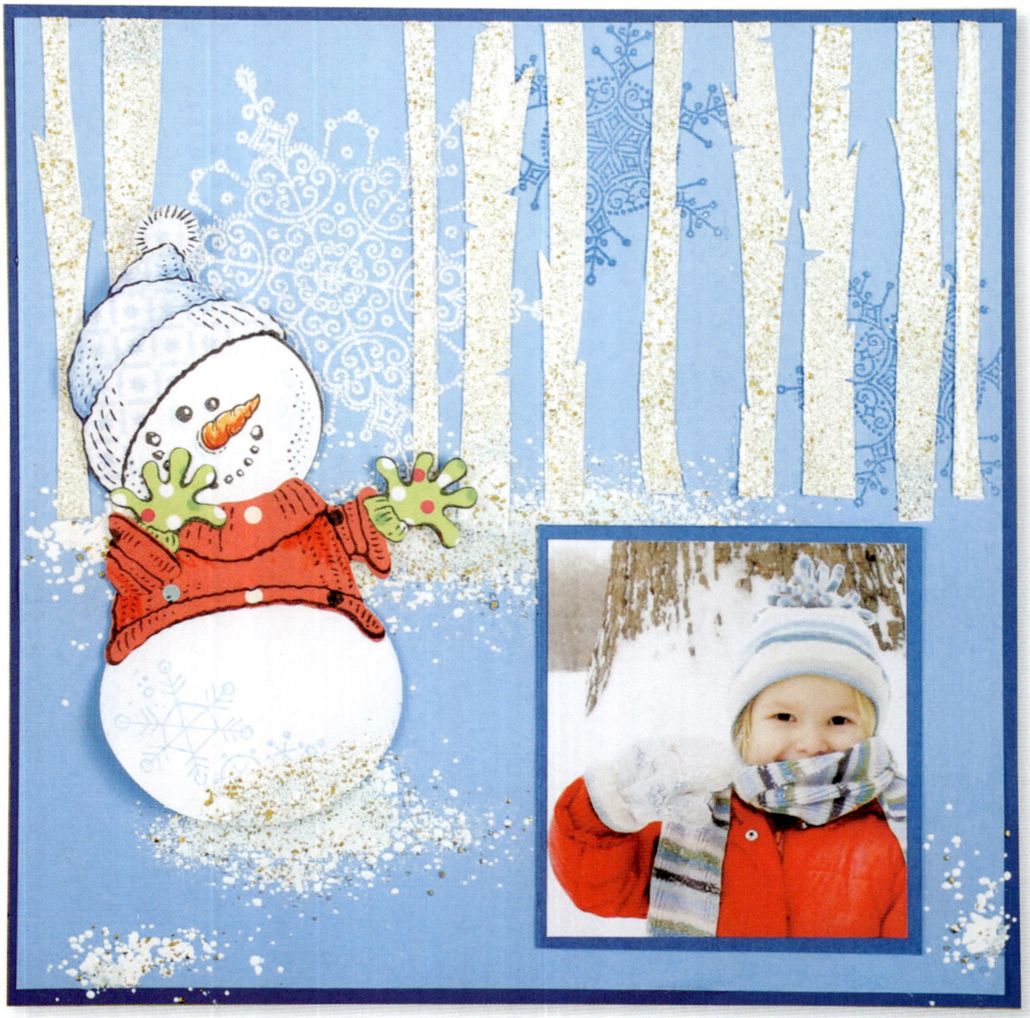

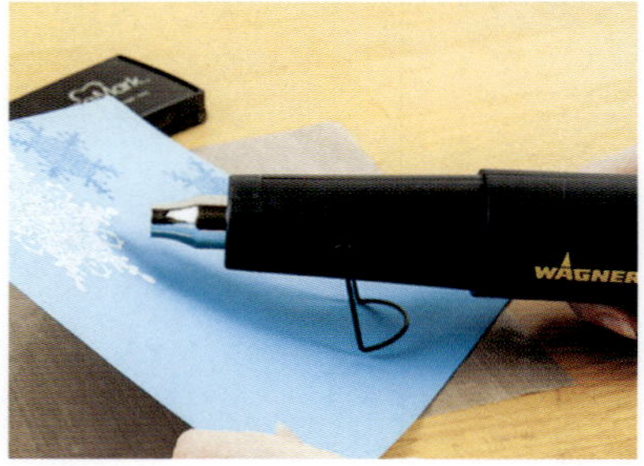

1. Emboss Sparkle Puff and Crystal snowflakes in the background.

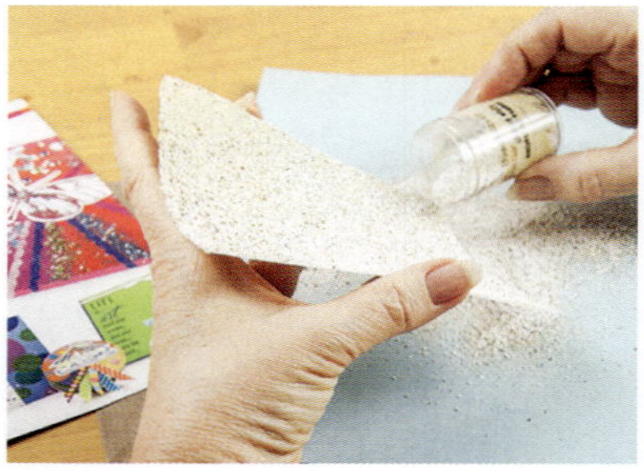

2. Emboss adhesive sheet with a layer of Shabby White Embossing Powder. Heat.

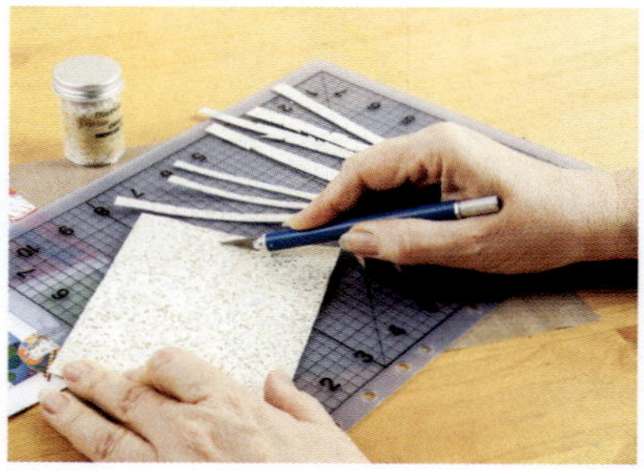

3. Cut strips out of the embossed adhesive panel for sparkly birch trees.

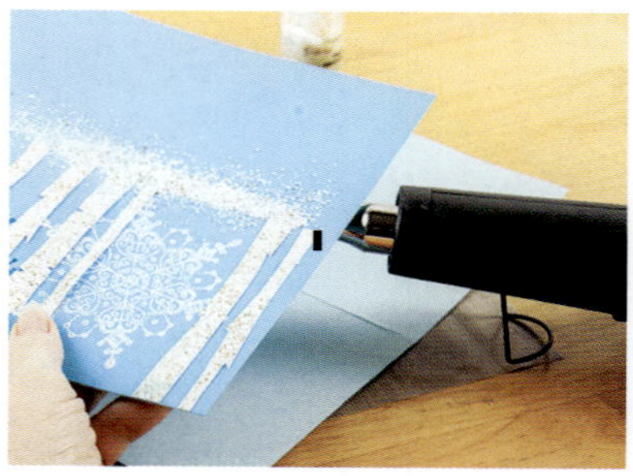

4. Sprinkle Shabby Blue Embossing Powder for a sprinkling of light snow. Heat from underneath.

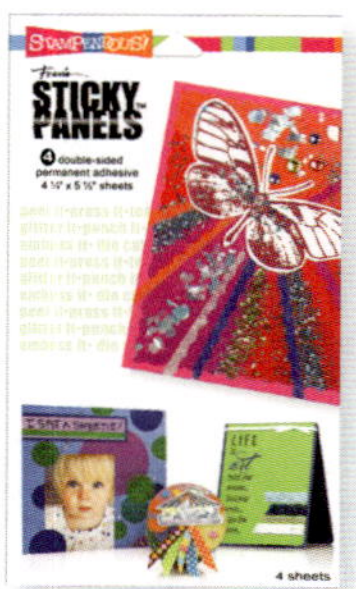

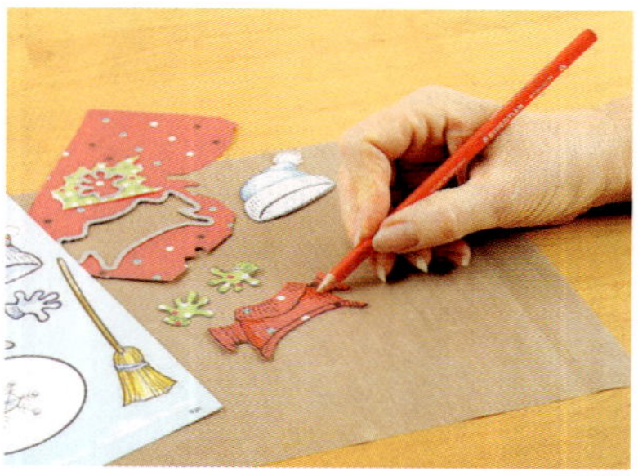

5. Snowman stamps and dies make for quick assembly options. Color in with colored pencils or your favorite markers. Printed papers can be shaded with colored pencils for a finishing touch.

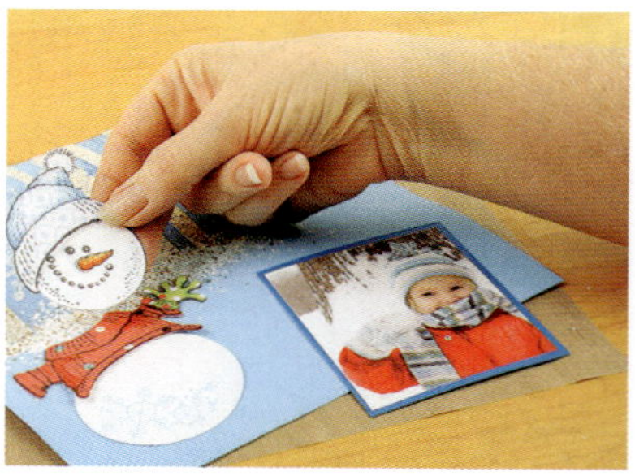

6. Add more snow with Encrusted Shabby Blue powder over the edge of snowman and background BEFORE gluing them together to avoid warping. Secure photos in place last.

EMBOSSING TECHNIQUES
FOR MIXED MEDIA PROJECTS

The mini photo album uses basic, Deckled Edge, Encrusted Jewel, and Deep Impression techniques. The snow canvas uses Deep Impression Technique. Try Dreamweaver® Pastes to add volume and cover with Shaved Ice to air dry, or cover with Embossing Powder and heat. See Table of Contents to find out more about these techniques.

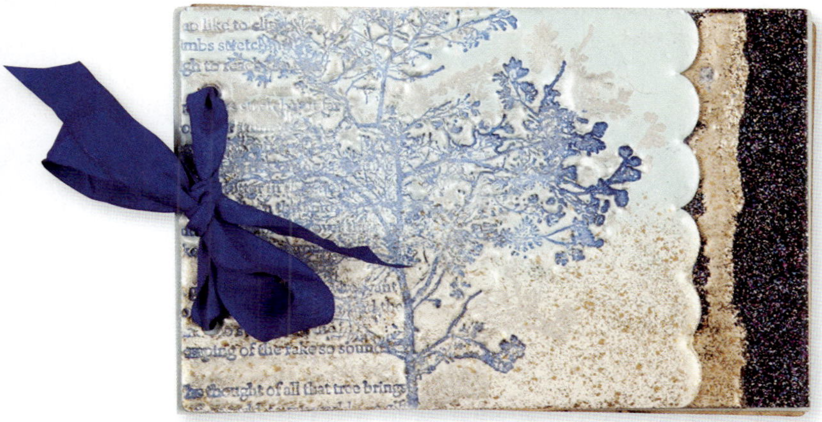

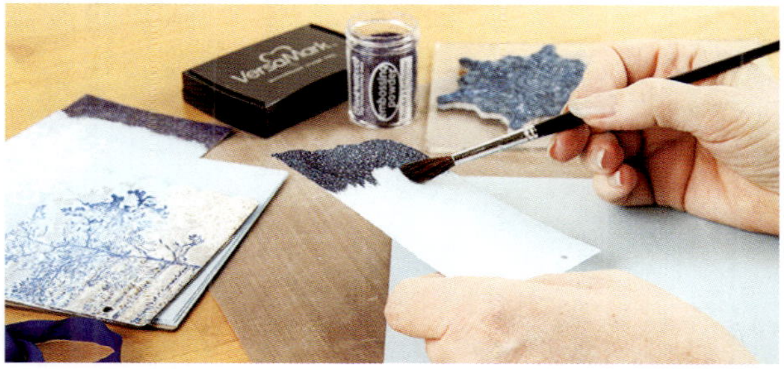

Create deckled edge with Twilight Embossing Powder. If ink pad makes angular edges, use a dry brush to soften edges.

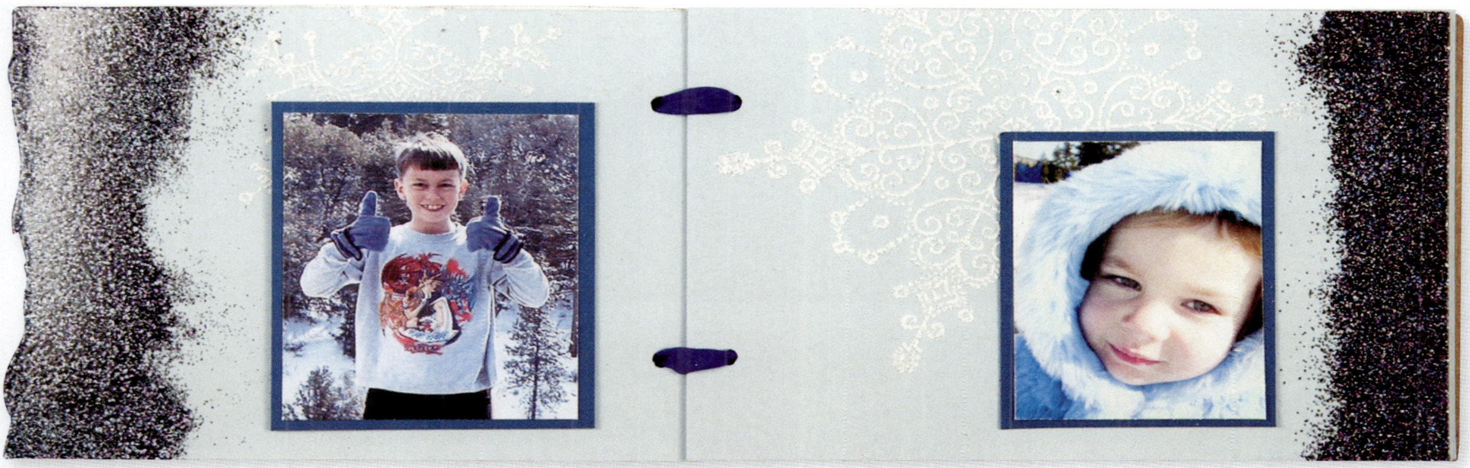

Mini Album Pages have been stamped and embossed with Sparkle Puff, Crystal, Twilight, and Aged Silver. Personalize with photos.

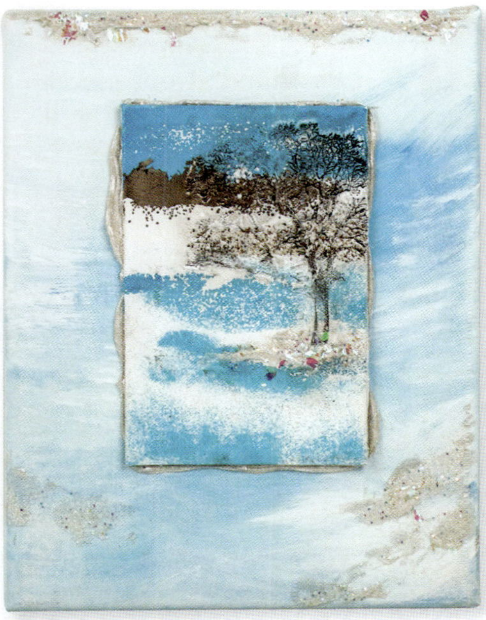

Deep Impression Tile and Frame were melted on pancake griddle. See page 82.

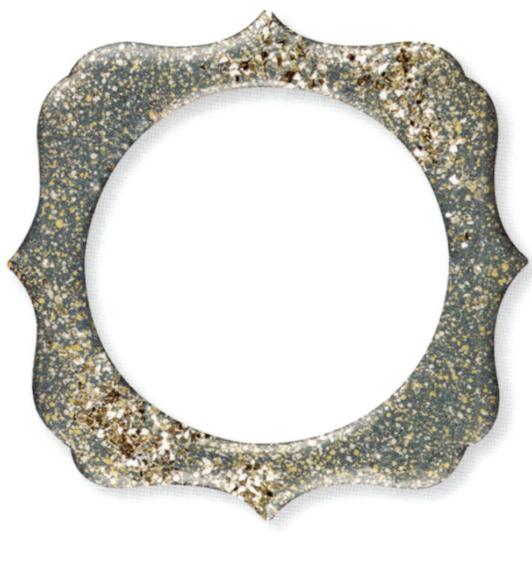

Using Paste as snow is easy with a palette knife on canvas. Embed Shaved Ice or glitters and allow to air dry. Try Matte, White Glossy, Pearlescent, or Silver Pastes. Silver Paste was used on canvas background and dusted with Shaved Ice to air dry.

ENCRUSTED ADHESIVE TECHNIQUE
FOR CARDS OR FRAMEABLE ART

Sticky Panels double-sided adhesive can be dusted with Embossing Powder and heated. It can be cut, torn, and used in a 3D way. Embed ribbons, buttons, cut outs, stickers, etc. Then fill in the remaining sticky areas with glitter and Embossing Powder. Heat.

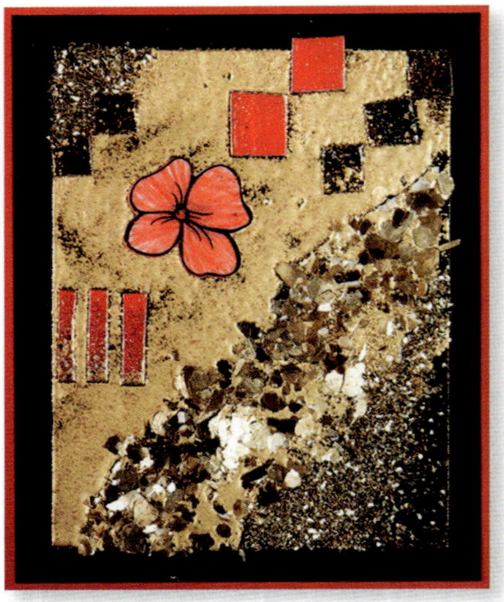

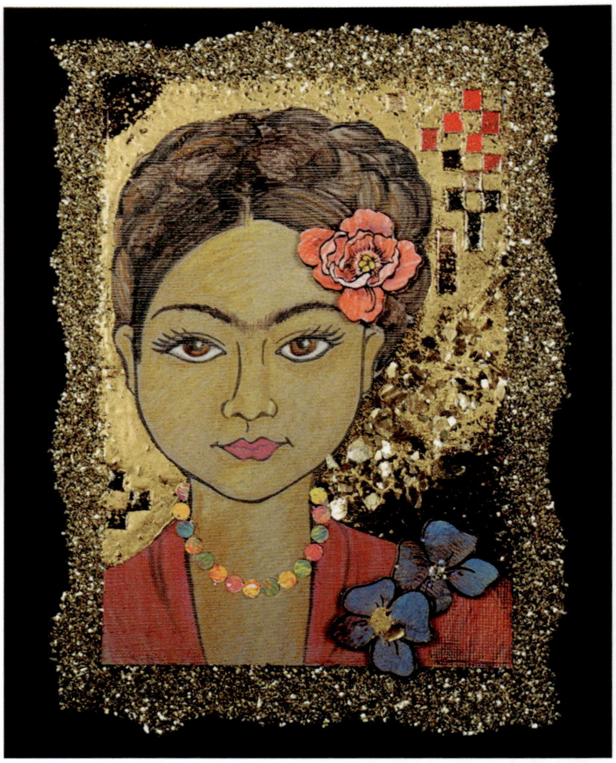

Frida Meets Klimt panel was made in the same way as the small card above.

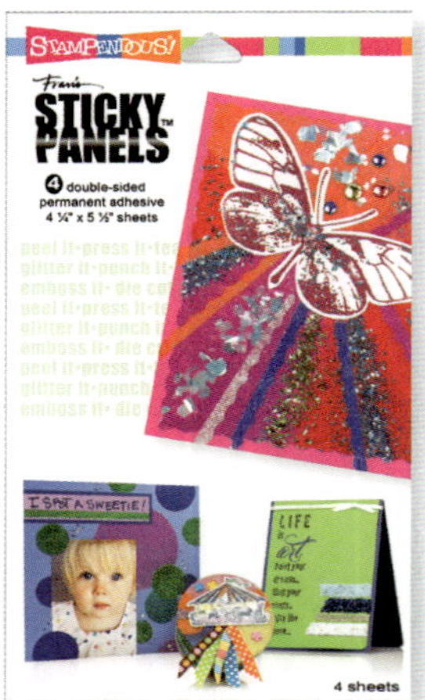

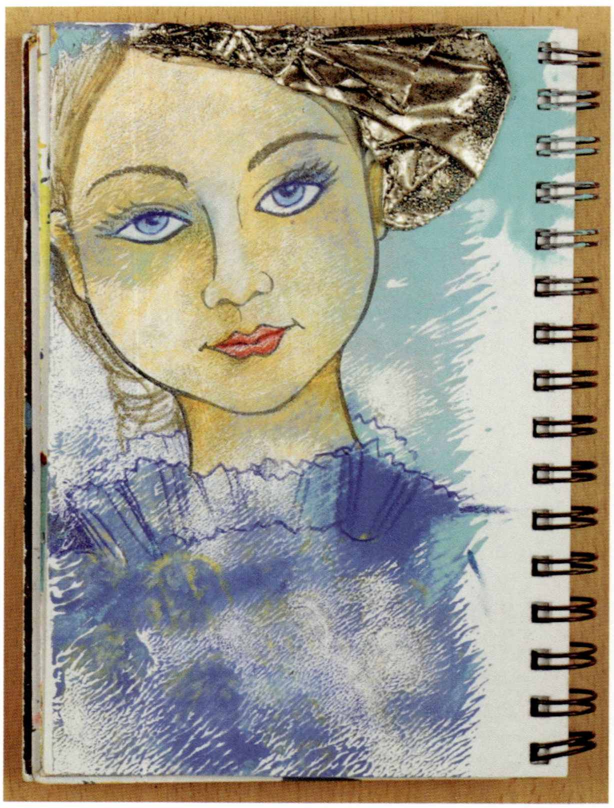

Lady with Turban was made with Sticky Panels which can be shaped and dusted with Embossing Powder. Tap off excess and heat.

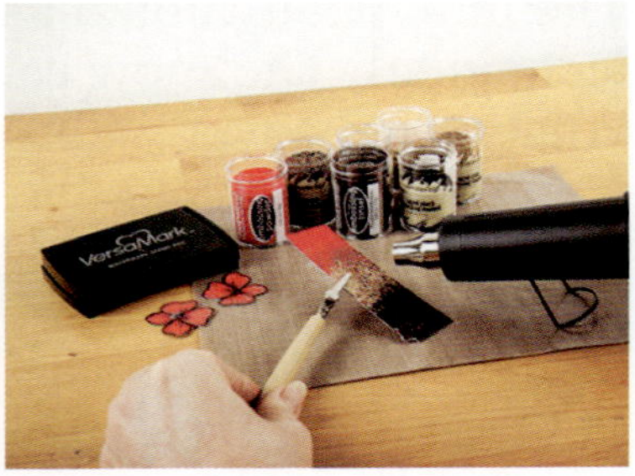

1. Emboss panel with Real Red, Aged Scarlet, Mahogany Tinsel, and Aged Black. Heat.

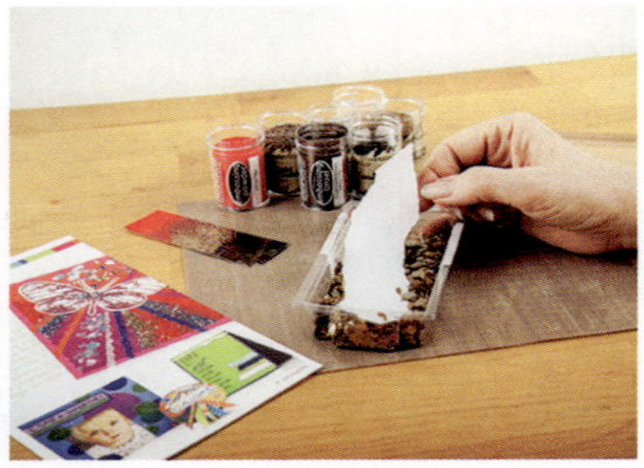

2. Tear adhesive and dip in Spoonful of Gold Dust Mix. Press in for thick coverage.

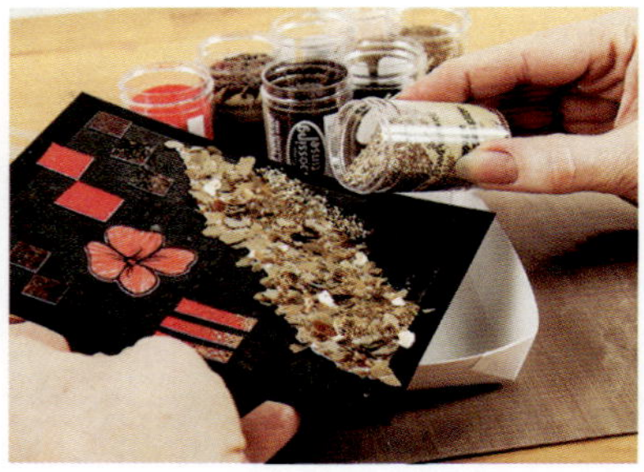

3. Position cut-out pieces onto sticky panel first. Fill in with embossing powder. Cover and press.

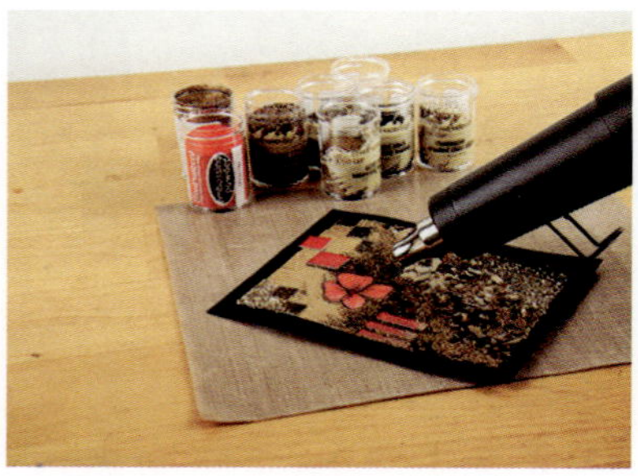

4. Heat Embossing Powder after tapping off the excess.

ENCRUSTED JEWEL ACCENTS
FOR FRAMEABLE ART

This technique applies a heat tool from underneath the paper so that you can sprinkle powders in a random way and add other elements that will get embedded into molten Embossing Powder. Inks can act as "place holders," but are not required for Embossing Powder to bond to paper. Gravity and heat do all the work.

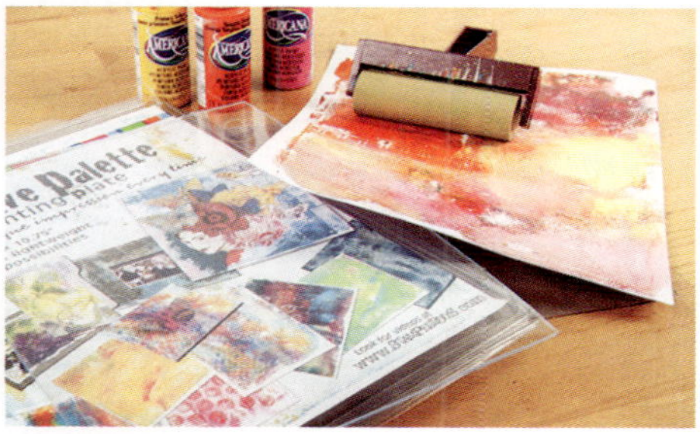

Creative Palette background papers were printed with acrylic paints and brayer.

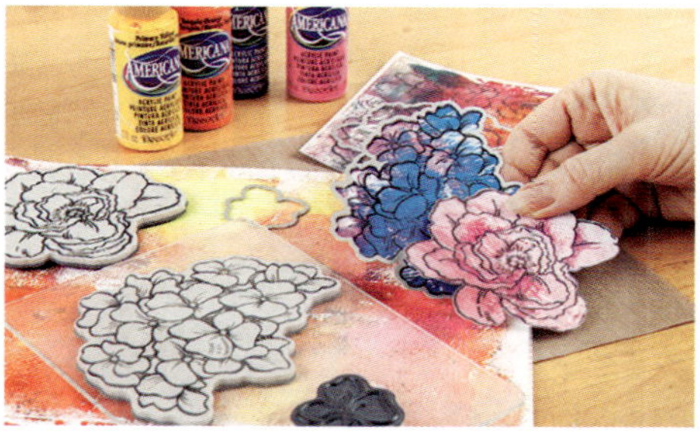

Stamp, emboss, and die cut butterflies and flowers from varied printed papers.

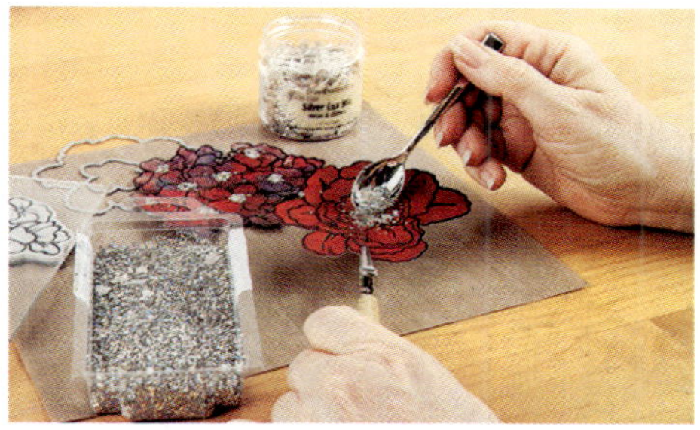

Embellish butterflies and flowers with Silver Spoonful and Silver Lux Mix. Heat from underneath.

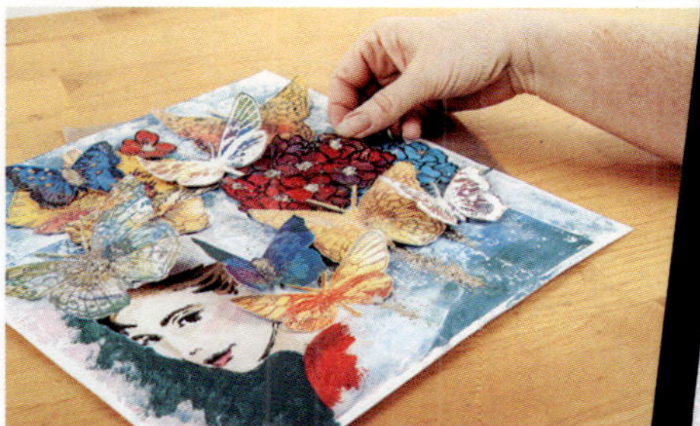

Assemble flowers and butterflies. Drizzle Silver Spoonful and Lux Mix and heat from underneath.

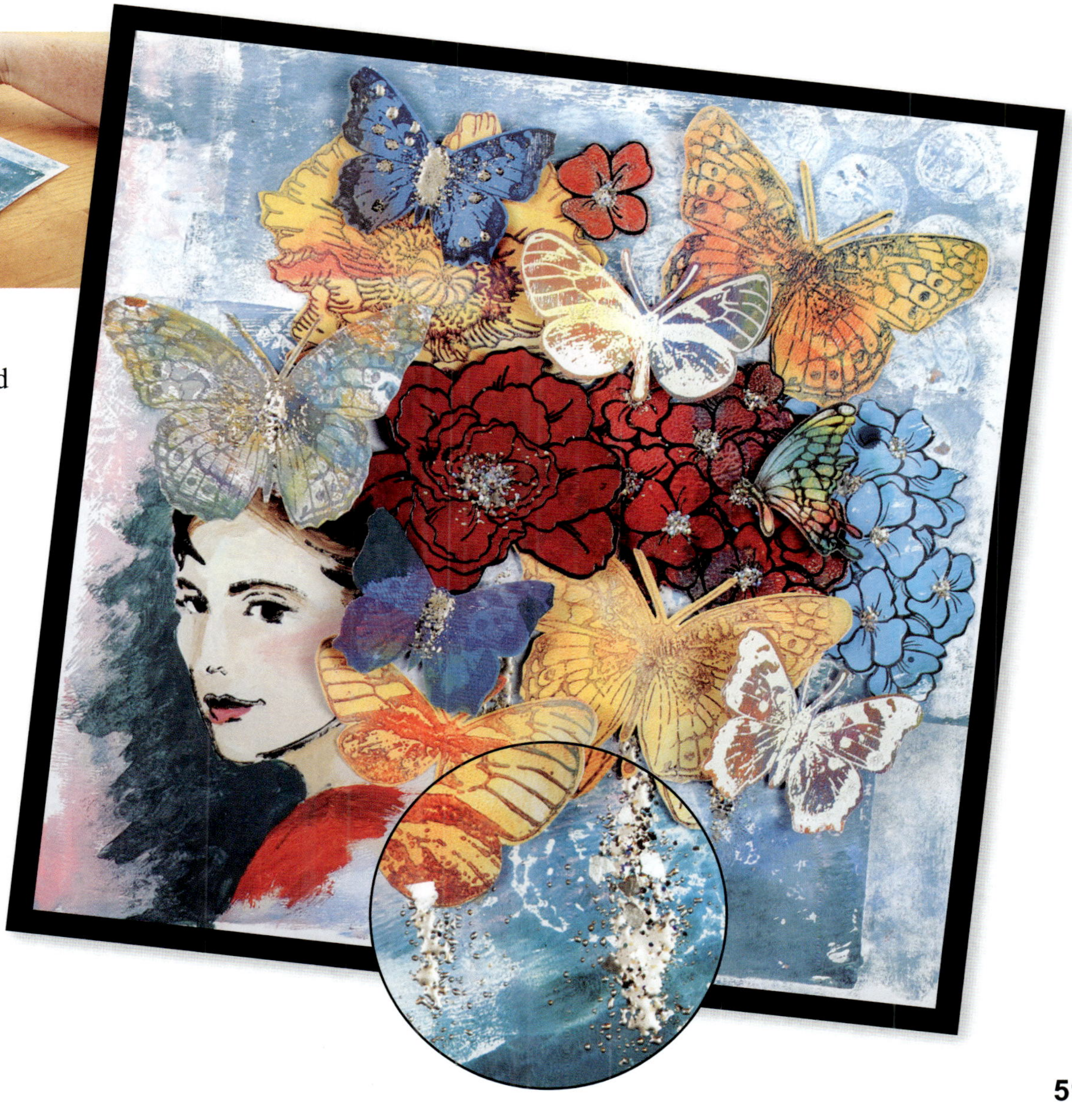

TIPS FOR IRREGULAR SURFACES
TO BE HEAT EMBOSSED

Now that you have seen many embossing techniques, try them on these different surfaces. Remember, if the heat can come through to the surface you can use sprinkling methods. If heat will not come through, you will need to use an ink to get the powder to stay in place for heating from above. Surfaces that are very slick or non-porous such as glazed ceramic mugs will not be durable or washable, and embossing is likely to chip off readily. Glass and metal for decorative applications will be okay. Do your testing on a recycled piece or the bottom or back of an expensive piece. Some surfaces that are NOT suited to embossing would be plastics that will warp, melt, or shrink unevenly or glass that is thin and might shatter with heat application.

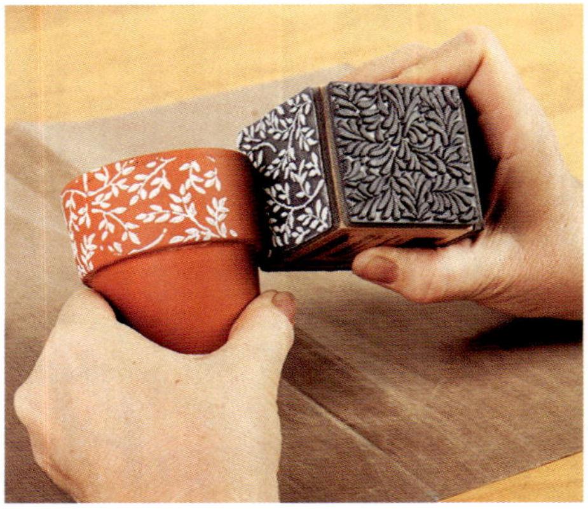

Curved surfaces that are firm are easy to stamp by simply pressing the stamp and rolling around the curve. With a curved paper mache surface, press your fingers from the inner or under side while pressing the stamp from the other.

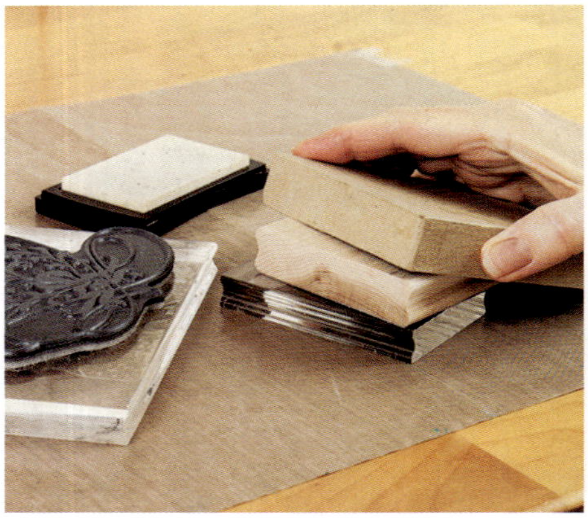

Flimsy surfaces will need some support underneath to get a good impression. Look for handles or blocks that will fit under a lid or inside a gift bag, etc. so that you have a solid surface to press stamp.

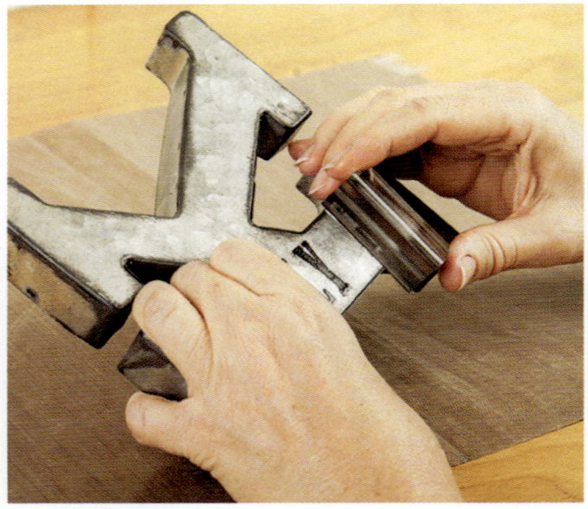

Uneven surfaces make for imperfect impressions. A clear VersaMark™ ink pad may be the most forgiving. Look for repairs you can do BEFORE heating. See more reworking tips on page 60.

SPECIALTY 3D SURFACES
TO BE HEAT EMBOSSED

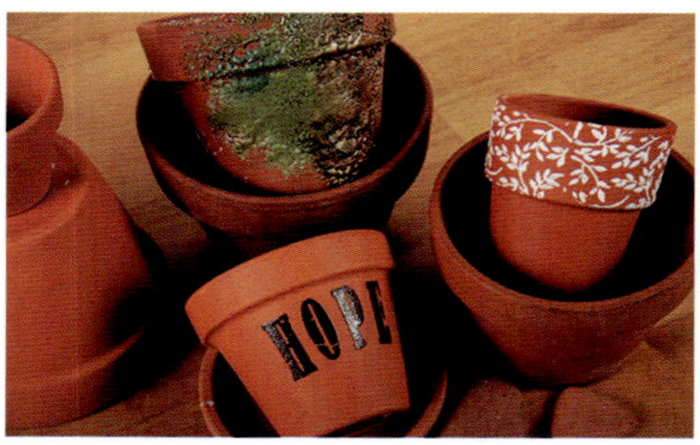

Terracotta pots and tiles are rather porous, but will work well. Try Antique Embossing with chalk paints. Focus heat in one area and melt your way around.

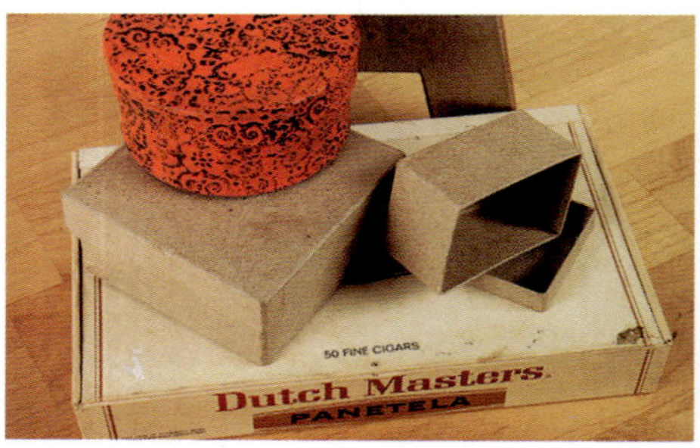

Paper mache boxes or containers will need support from both sides to get a good stamp impression. Look for flat or curved surfaces if you want to stamp on them.

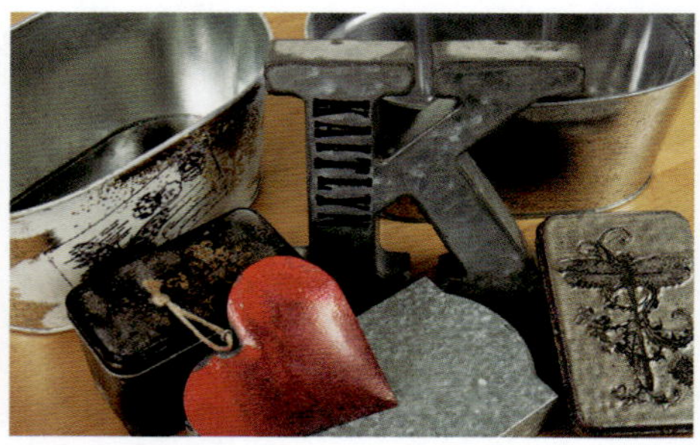

Metal sheets, boxes, or tins will heat very quickly. Work safely with tools, even leather gloves, to avoid burning fingers. Boxes with separate shallow lids are the easiest to emboss.

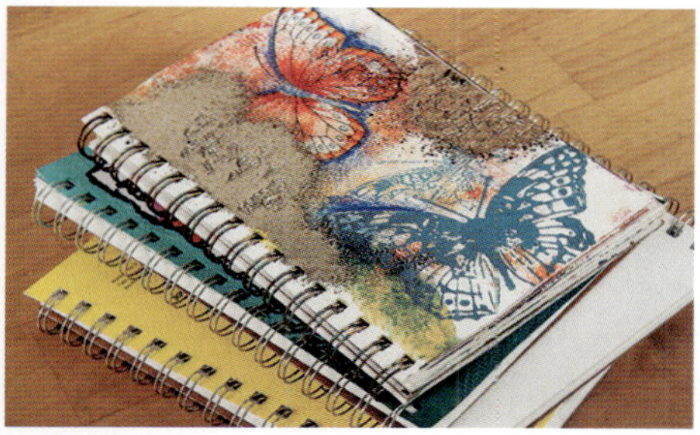

Paper journals with heavier weight papers are the best. Spiral bindings allow you to bend pages to the side for easy access.

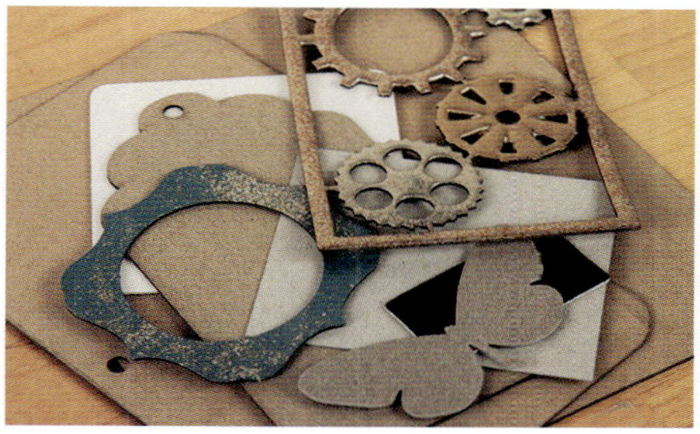

Chipboard comes in many thicknesses. Colors of kraft or grey and die cut shapes are ideal for jewelry, magnets, or ornaments.

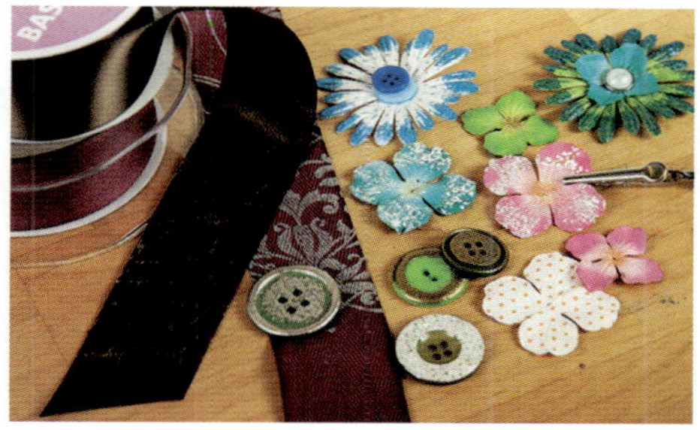

Ribbon embellishments can be embossed for pattern, color, and sparkle. Test ribbons as rayons will melt. Cotton and satin work well.

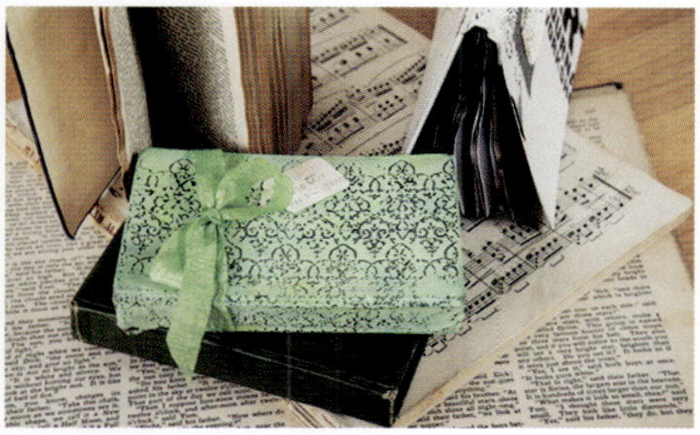

Books that might have been discarded can be re-purposed by embossing on covers or pages.

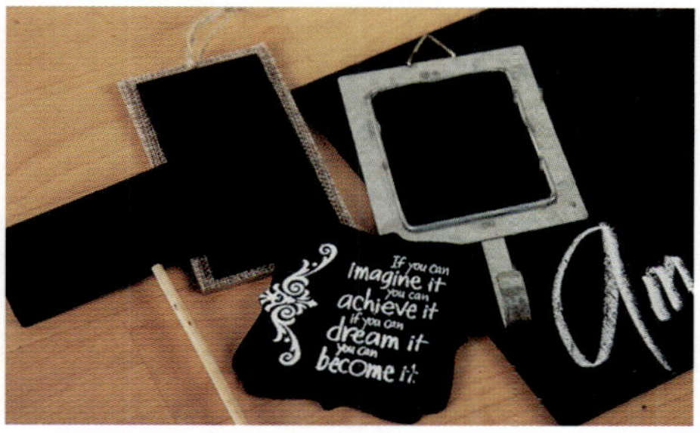

Chalkboard or matte black paint surfaces can be stamped and embossed in white.

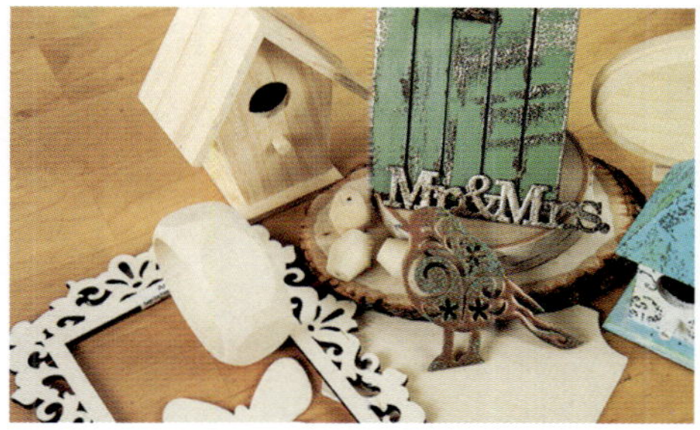

Wood can be unfinished or coated with matte, not glossy, paint. Try many embossing techniques.

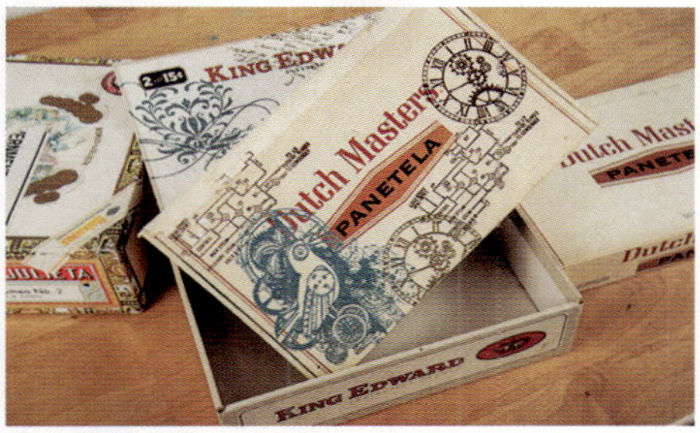

Cigar boxes may be wood or chipboard with paper linings. Flat lids give easy access. Support from both sides as needed.

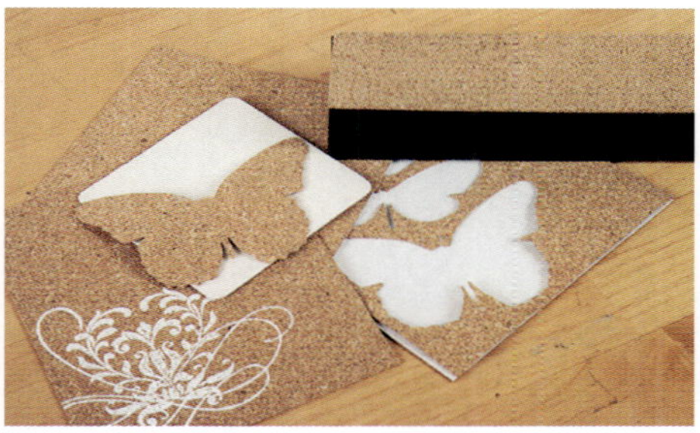

Cork sheets are easy to stamp and heat from the top down. Wafer dies will cut interesting shapes that coordinate with stamps.

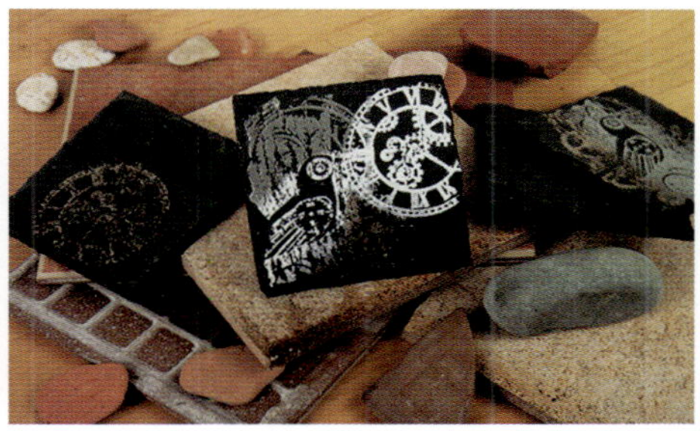

Stone that is porous and smooth is easiest. Try slate slabs, rocks and tiles without a glossy finish.

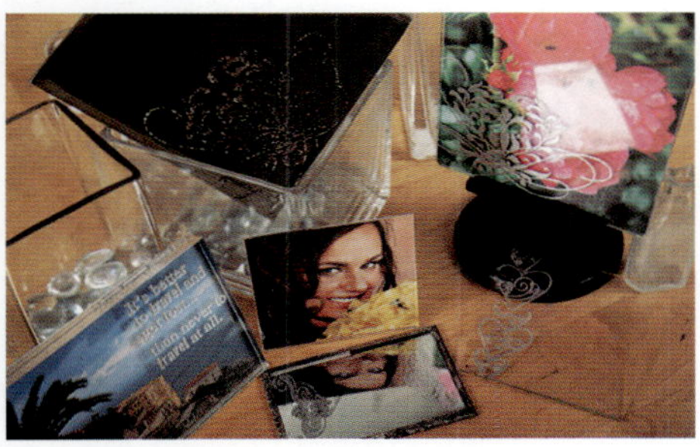

Glass and mirrors need to be thick to withstand the uneven application of heat without shattering. Test and work with care. Surfaces may chip easily and are not dishwasher safe. Emboss on acrylic handles.

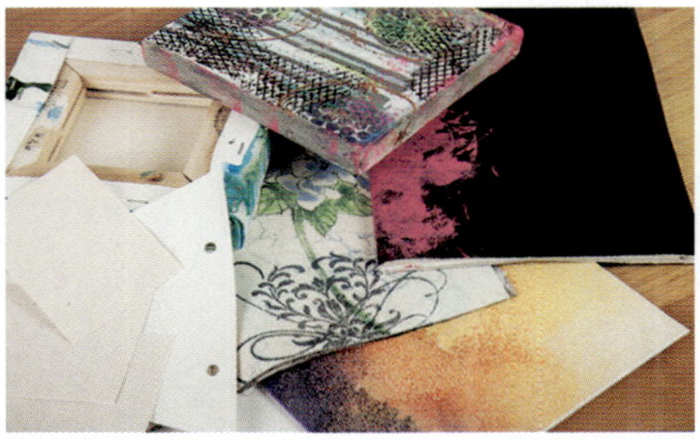

Canvas stretched on frames will need support in the middle, but heat comes through. Clip canvas pieces to something to extend and keep them level. Heat will not come through canvas board so ink is needed.

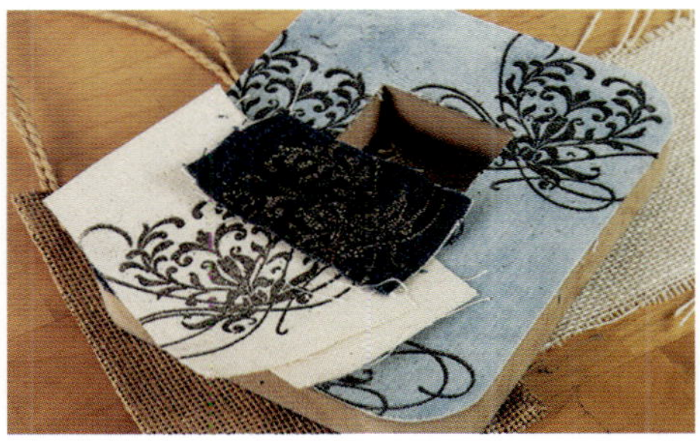

Fabrics such as cotton or muslin can be embossed for decorative uses but are not washable. Burlap is too open a weave for images to show. Stabilize fabric by securing it to cardstock or contact paper before embossing.

CHALKBOARD
EMBOSSING POWDER TECHNIQUE

T

The popular chalkboard look is as easy as white on black with embossed stamp images. Select images that could have been hand written or drawn. Simulate the look with matte black paper or any surface painted with matte black acrylic paint. Special chalkboard paints are available.

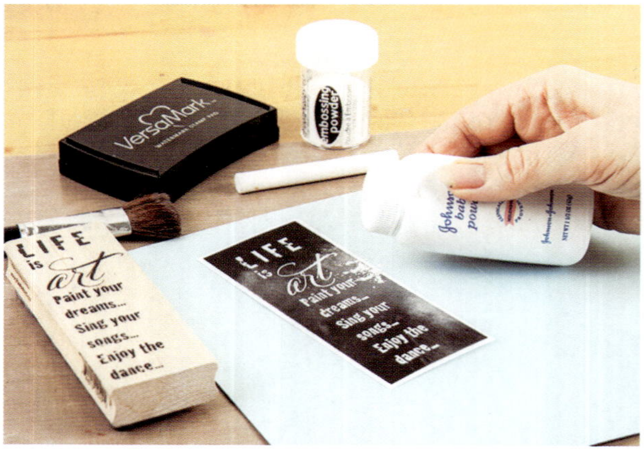

Powder it: Adding a dusting of white chalk or white paint completes the chalkboard illusion regardless of the black and white options underneath.

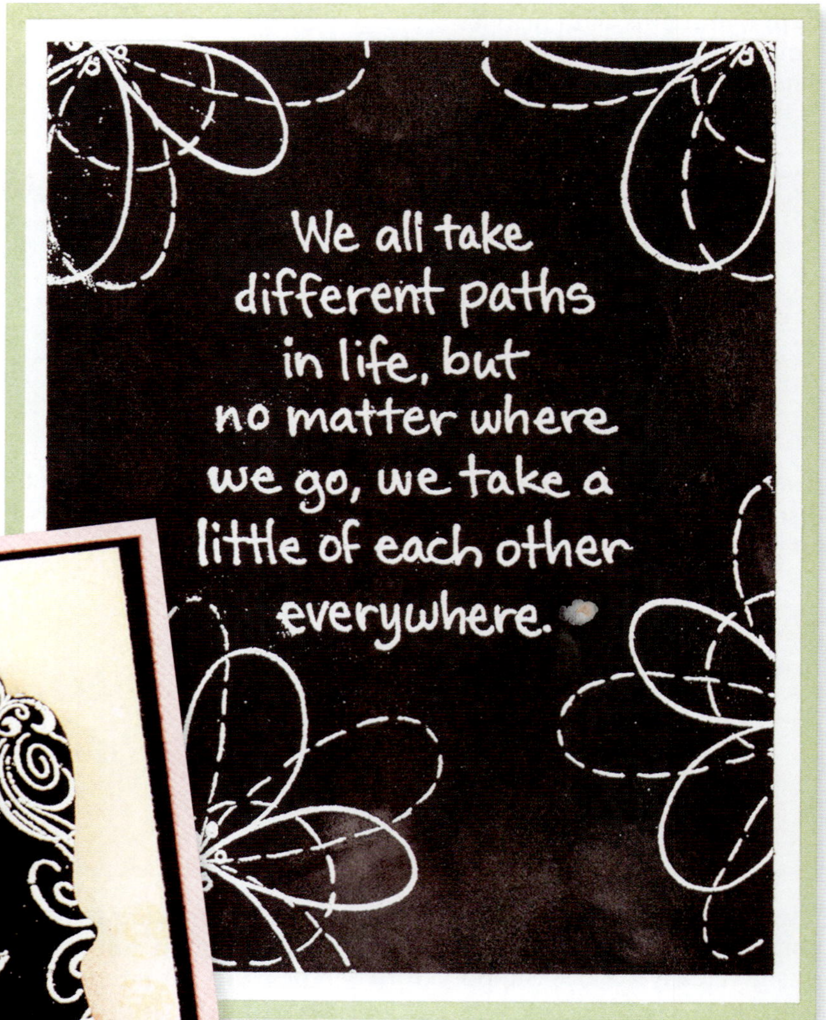

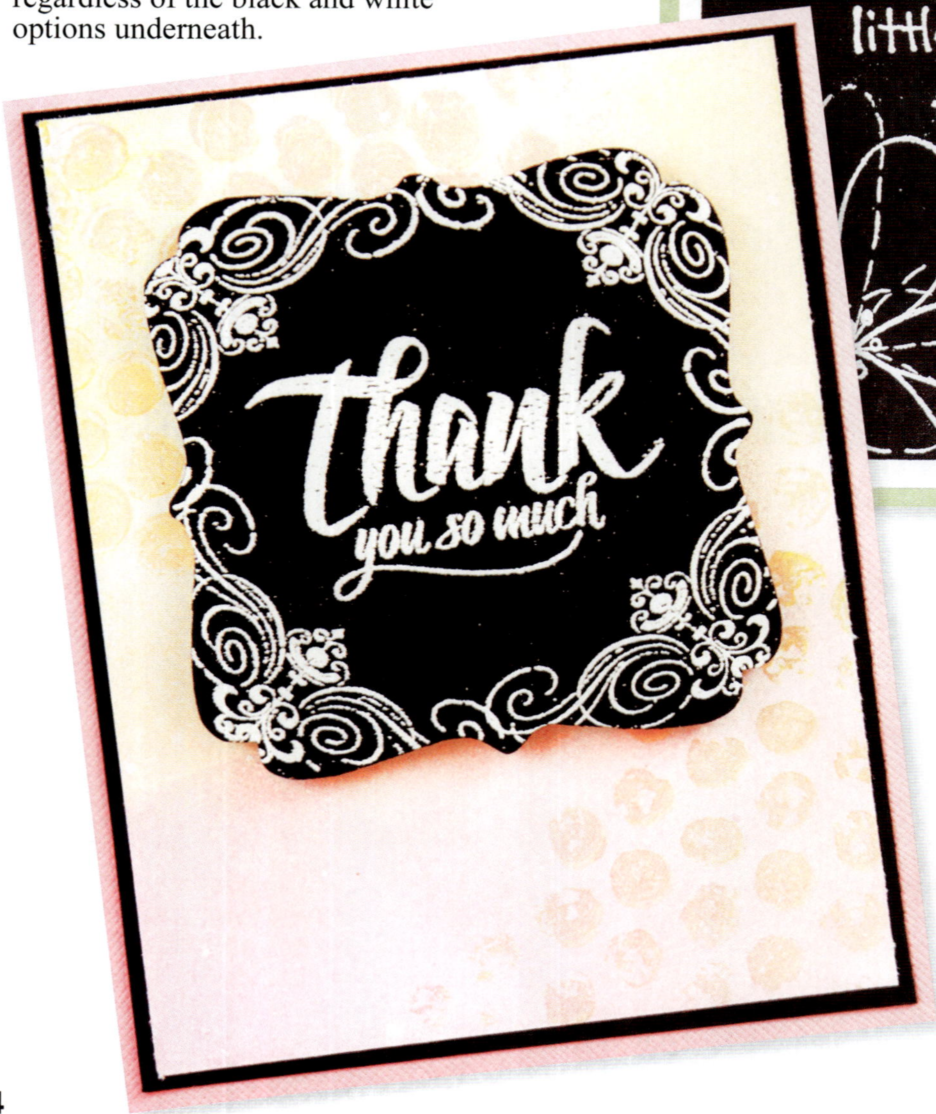

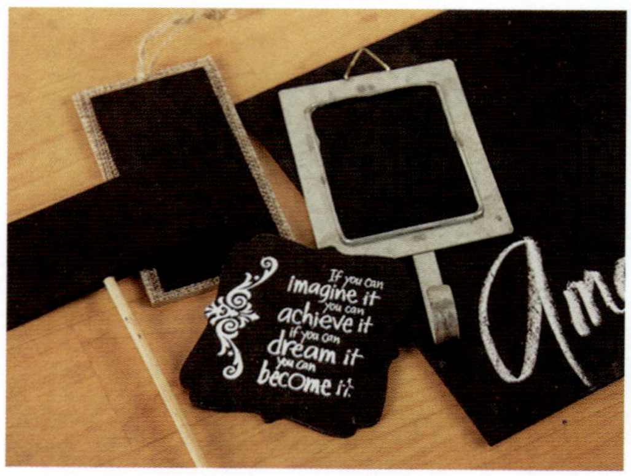

"Before" views are shown here. There are many chalkboard items in craft stores just begging for some stamping and embossing.

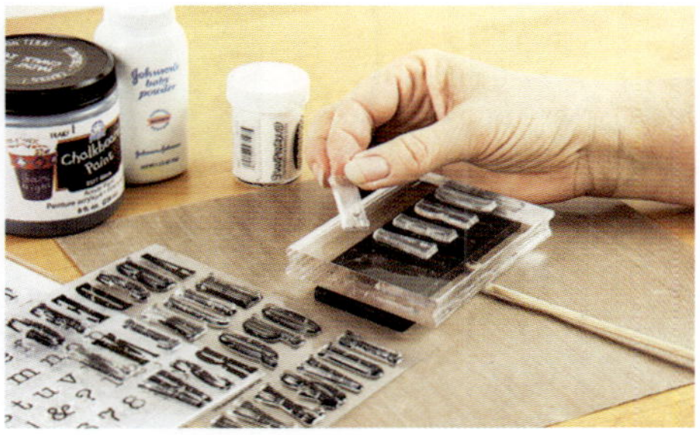

Alphabet letters can be placed on a clear, acrylic block positioned over the sign to work out best spacing. Stamp and emboss all in one.

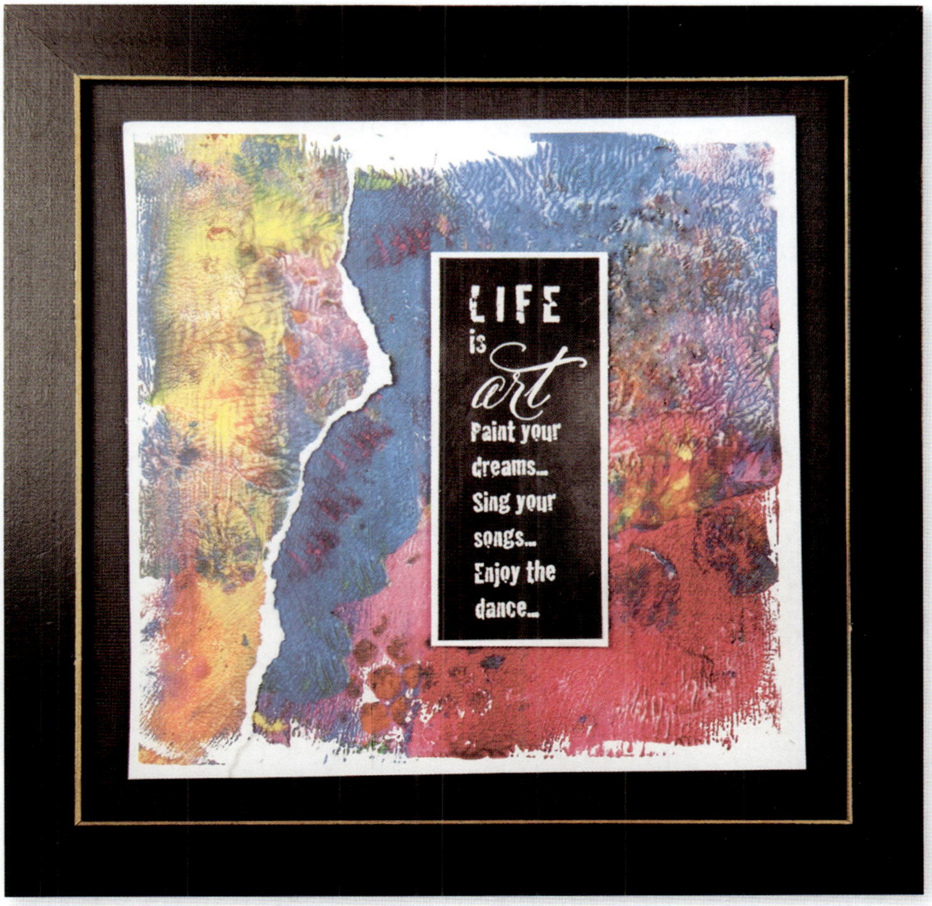

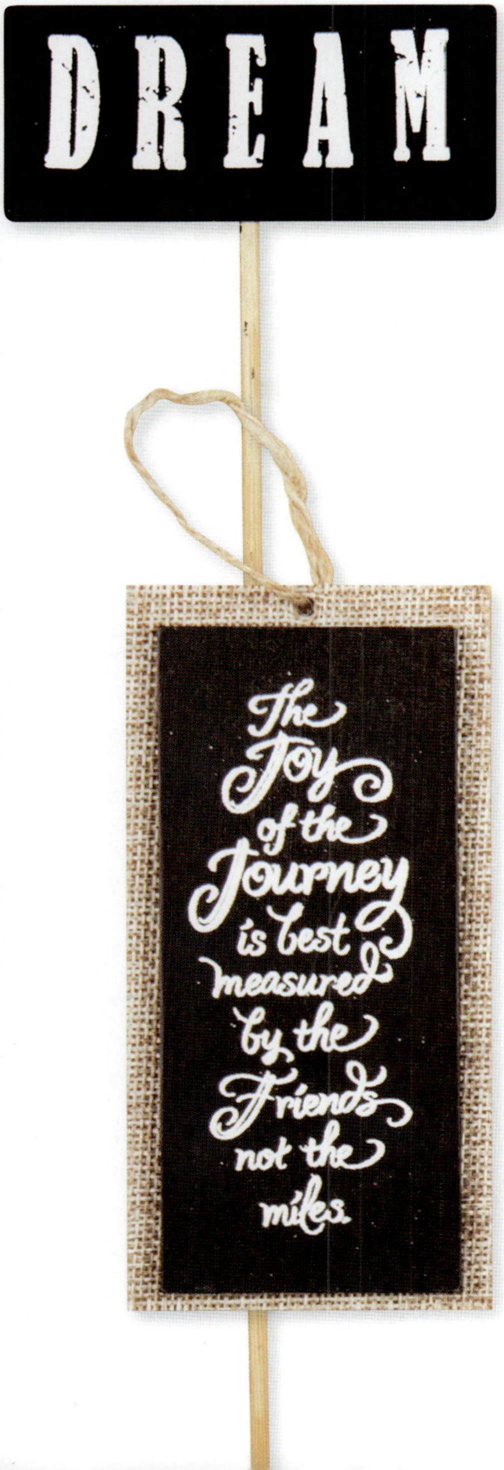

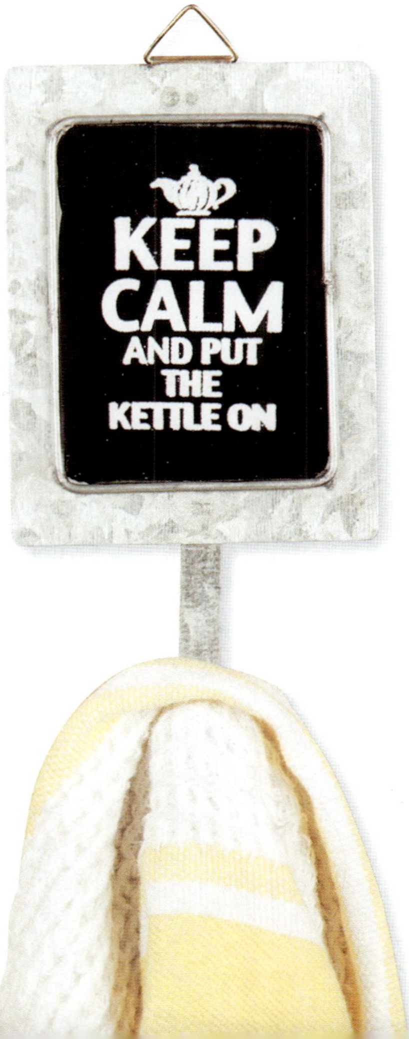

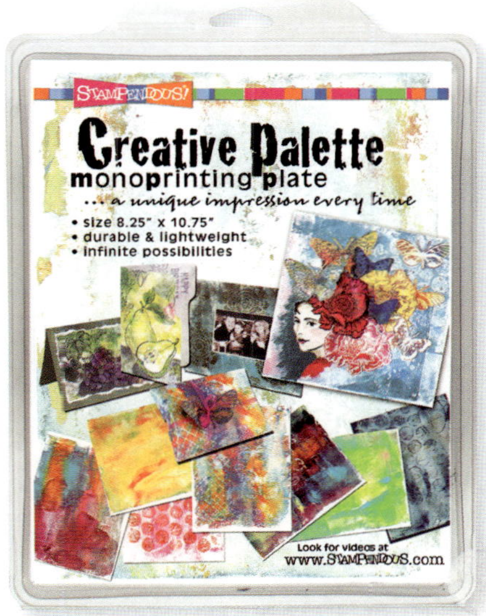

Creative Palette, acrylic paint, and brayer were used to make monoprint used in the background of the framed artwork above.

FILIGREE & LASER CUT-OUTS
EMBOSSING POWDER TECHNIQUE

Cut-away shapes of paper, chipboard, wood, or metal are incredibly fun and easy to emboss. Inexpensive surfaces look like metal. Flat layers become quite 3D with added layers. Simple surfaces are transformed with sparkle and lustre. Excess powders simply fall away through holes.

PAPER

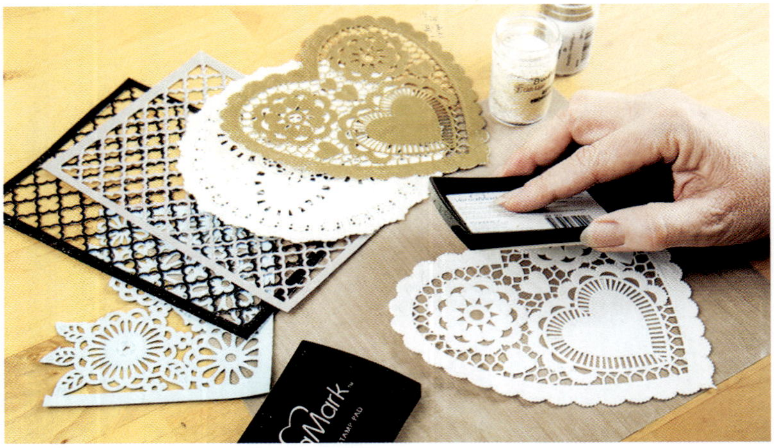

Laser cut papers and doilies with intricate cuts and filigree are inexpensive, plentiful and very easy to enhance with Embossing Powders. Ink and emboss surface using VersaMark™ to completely cover the surface. Embossing Powders will spill through the cut-away openings. Try Metallics or Aged Ivory for a gloss rich finish.

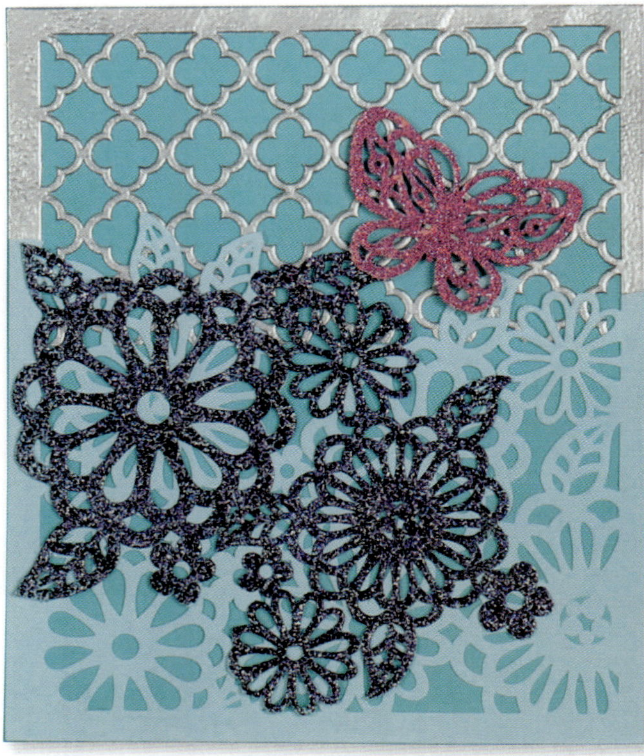

Frantage™ Aged Gold has chunky particles in the mix. Each melting is unique.

Wood Cut-Outs: Ink and emboss surface using VersaMark™ to completely cover the surface. Embossing Powders will spill through the cut-away openings. Try Chunky Aged Silver for a vintage elegant lustre. Make a batch for a wedding. With Aged Silver no two will be alike.

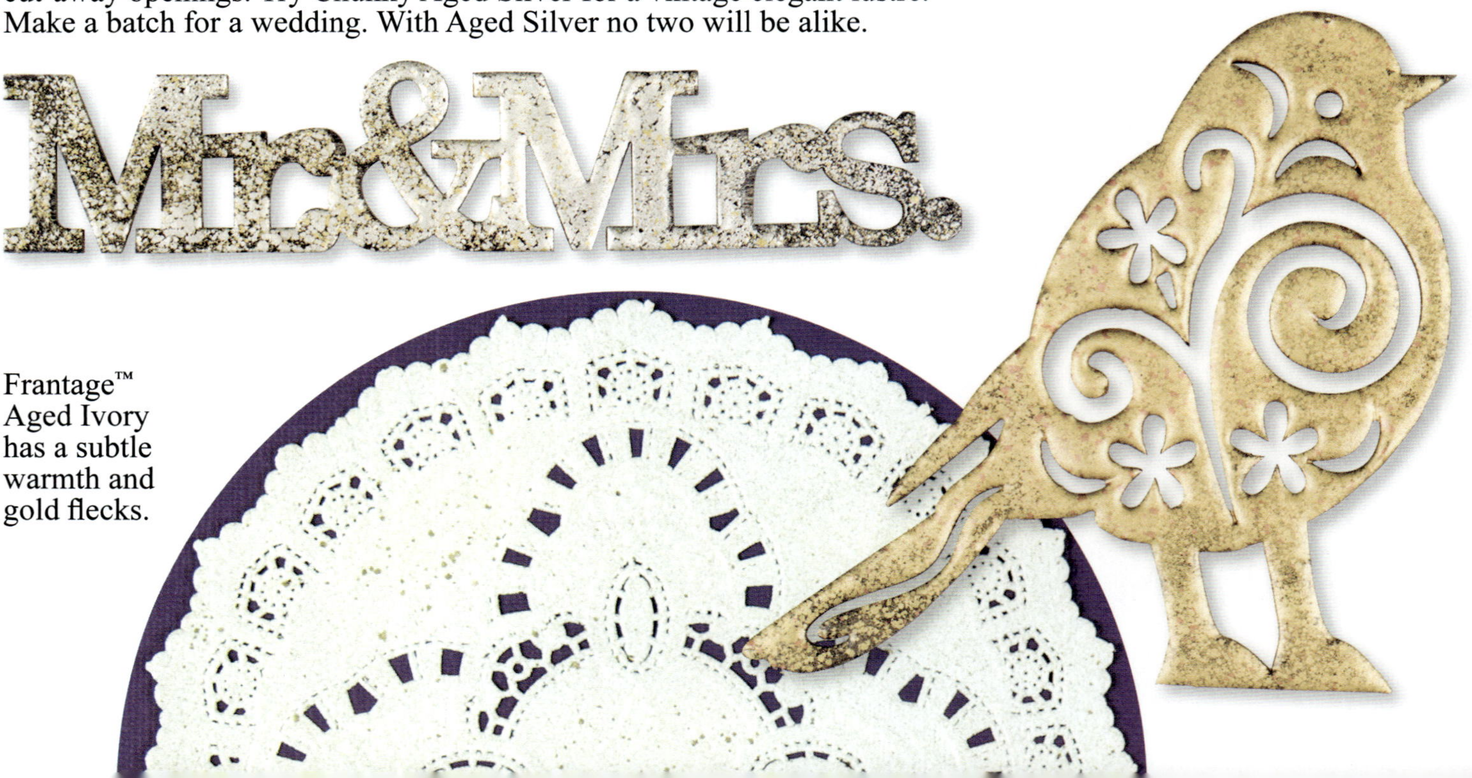

Frantage™ Aged Ivory has a subtle warmth and gold flecks.

CHIPBOARD

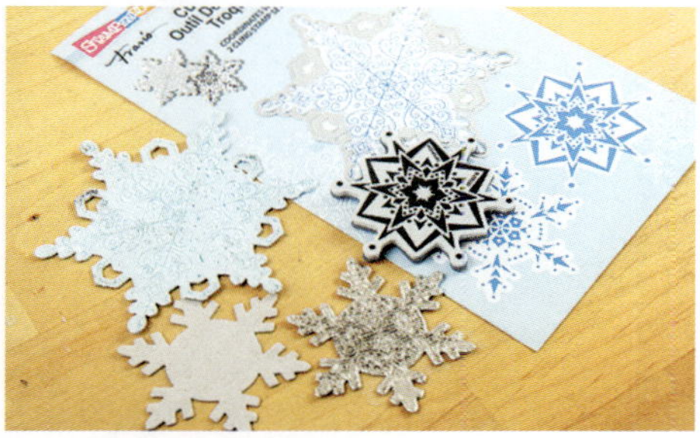

Chipboard can be die cut or laser cut in many beautiful patterns. Look for stamps with matching wafer dies.

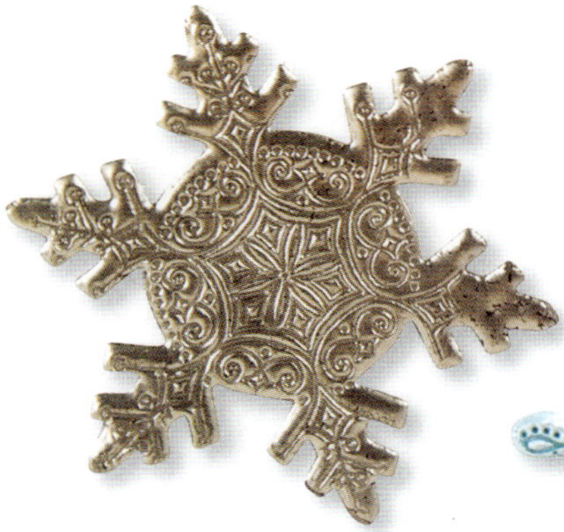

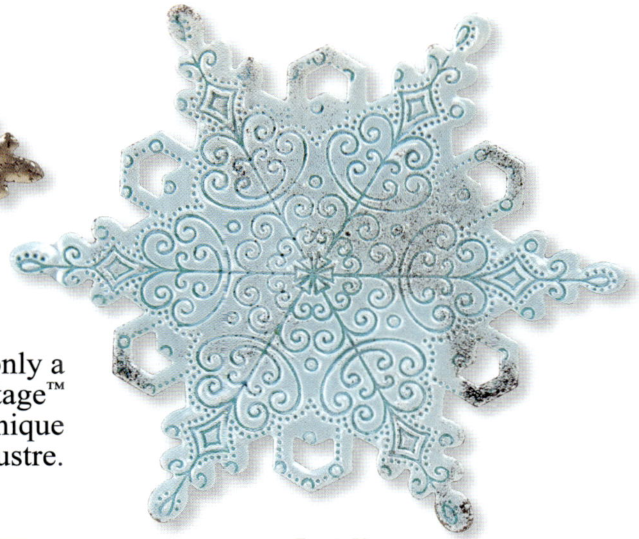

Snowflakes have only a thin layer of Frantage™ Ice Blue with its unique opaque lustre.

WOOD

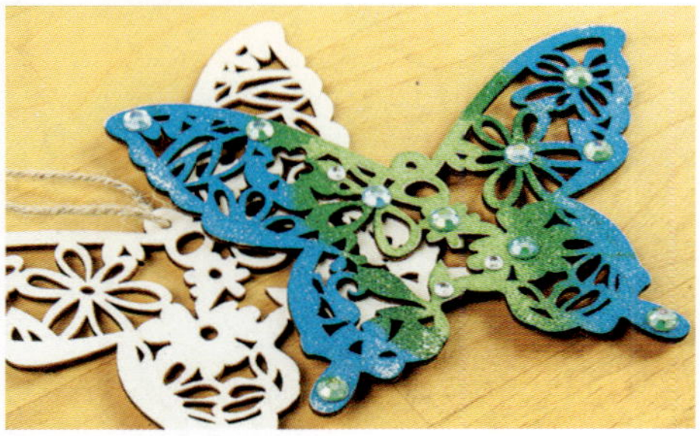

Flat surfaces are easy to ink with ink pad. Dust with multiple color powders and heat all at once. Glue on rhinestones.

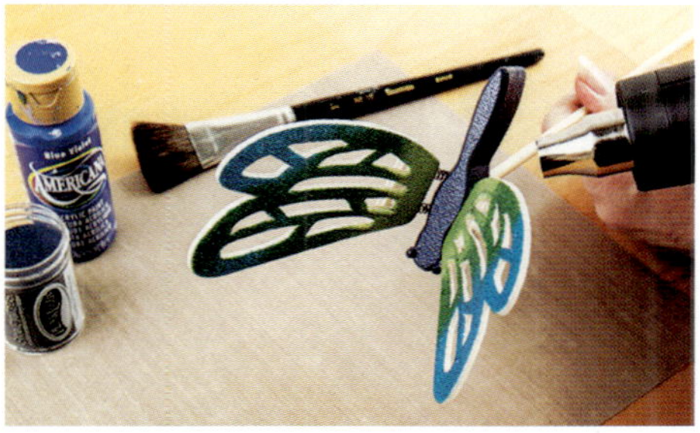

Paint can be applied with a brush to get into tight spots an ink pad wouldn't reach. Dust with Embossing Powder while paint is still wet, and you are ready to heat.

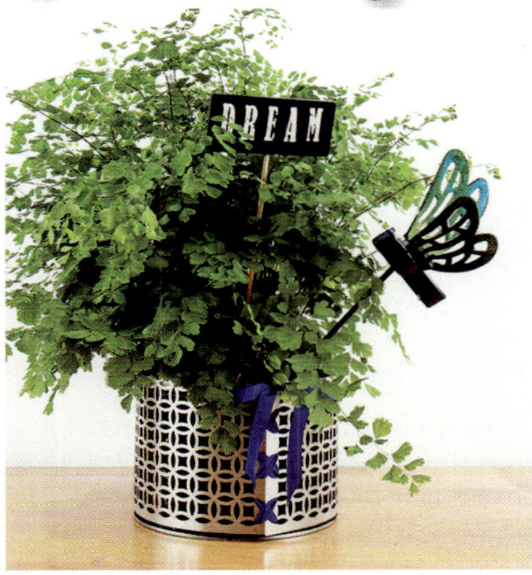

Frantage™ Aged Copper has chunky particles and Verdigris mix. Each melting is unique.

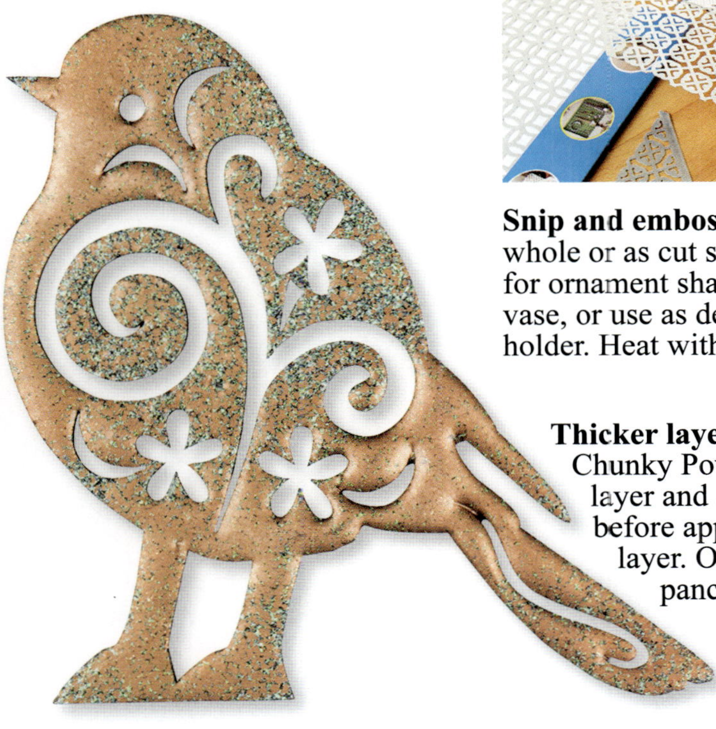

METAL

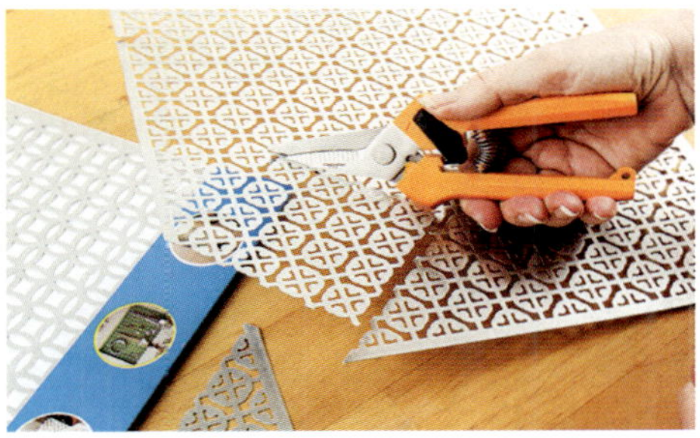

Snip and emboss metal sheets as a whole or as cut segments. Emboss for ornament shapes, wrap around vase, or use as decorative earring holder. Heat with care.

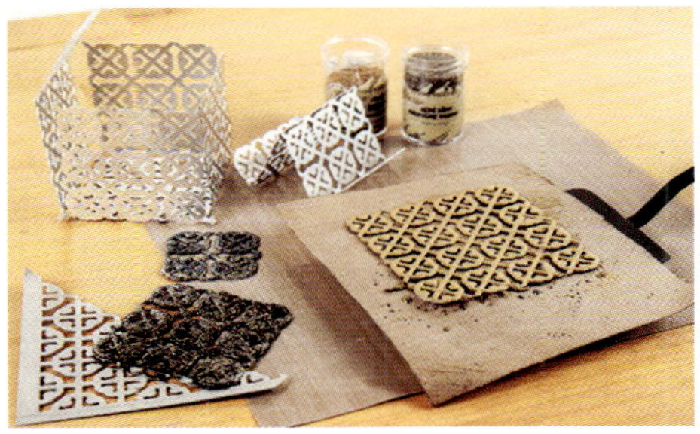

Heat on griddle over craft sheet. See page 82.

Thicker layers are quick with Chunky Powders. Melt first layer and allow it to cool before applying ink for next layer. OR melt layers on pancake griddle.

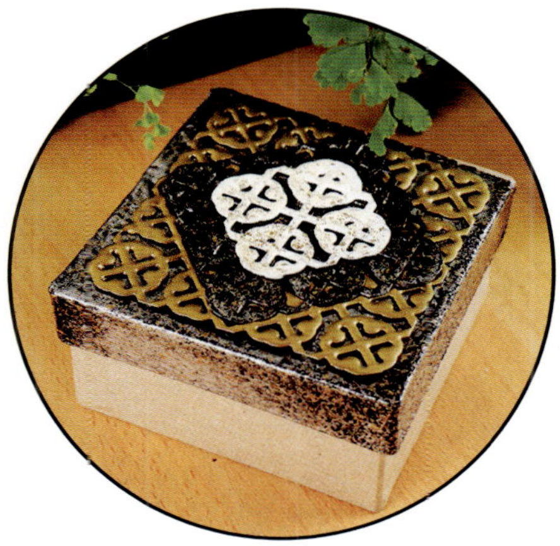

PAPER JEWELRY
EMBOSSING POWDER TECHNIQUE

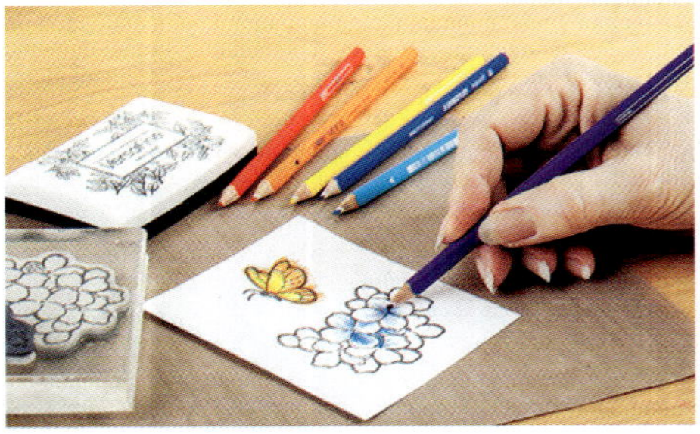

1. Stamp and color images with colored pencils, inks, or watercolor.

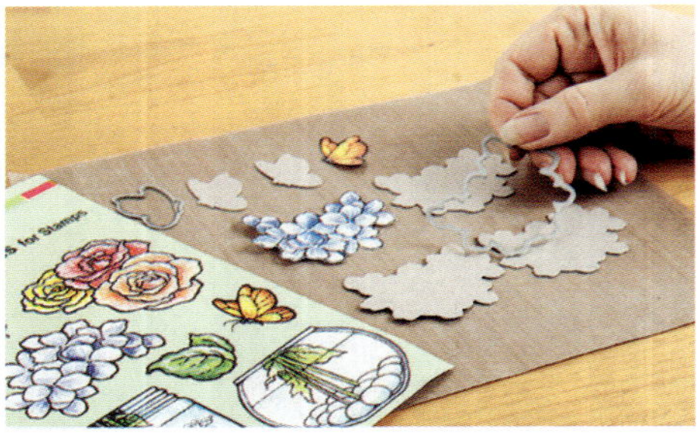

2. Die-cut images using matching wafer dies. Cut two chipboard layers for butterfly and three chipboard layers for flowers.

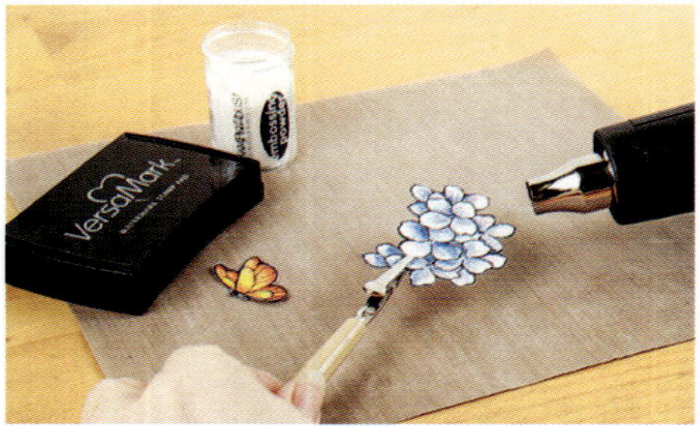

3. Emboss a layer of Clear or Crystal Embossing Powder to seal top color surfaces.

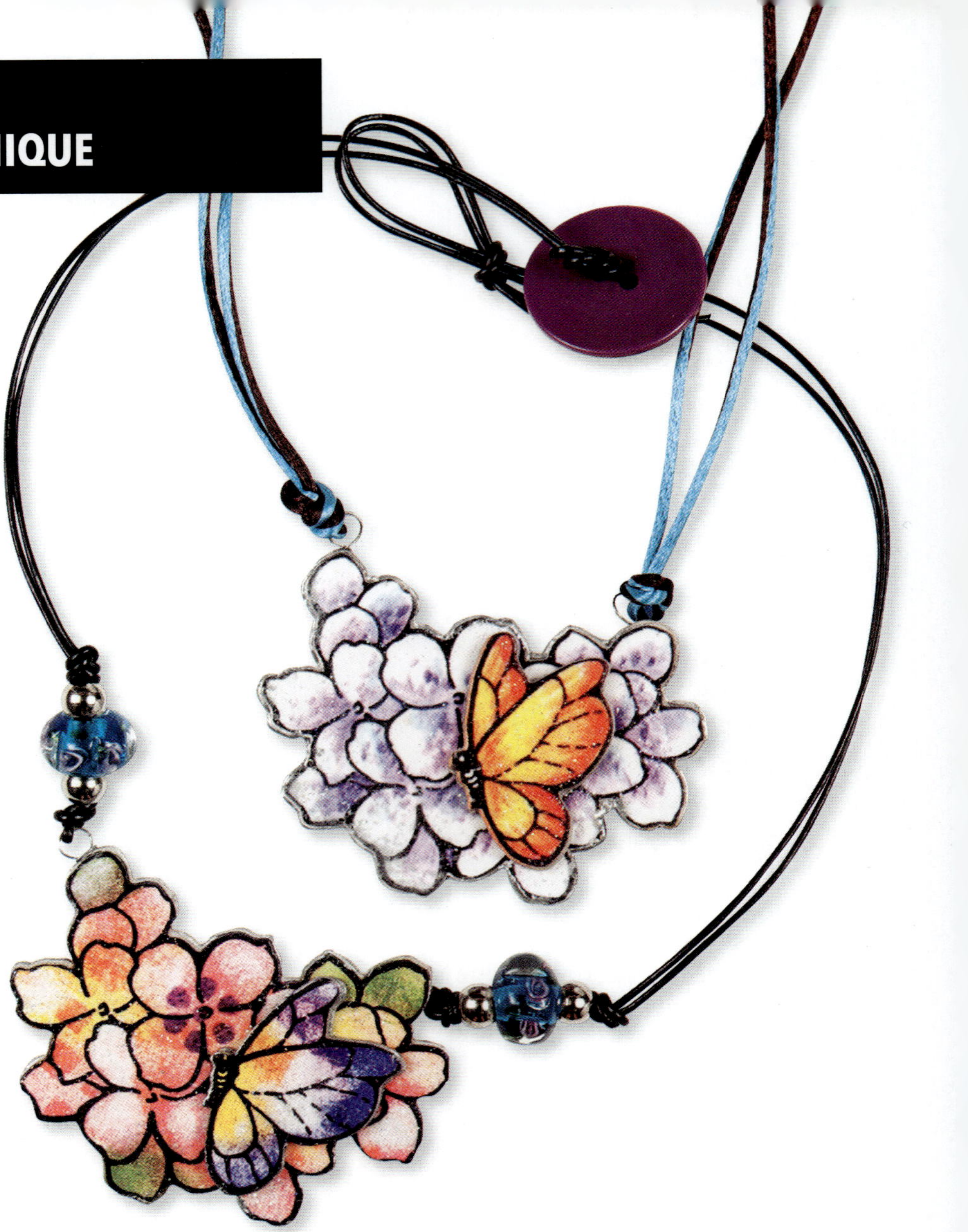

Clear or Crystal Embossing Powders create a durable seal for paper jewelry. Look for stamps with matching wafer dies. Edges and backing can be sealed with Aged Silver or Opaque Embossing Powders. Metallic pens can be used on the edges. Finish the look with chain, beads, and metal findings.

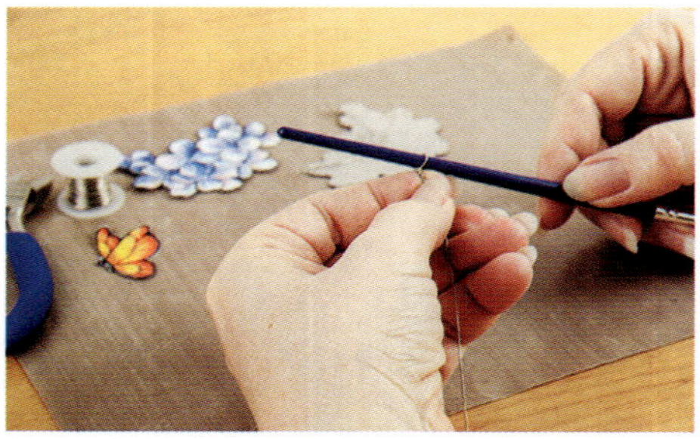

4. Wire rings can be formed around a dowel to create double-ended jump rings that can be secured between layers.

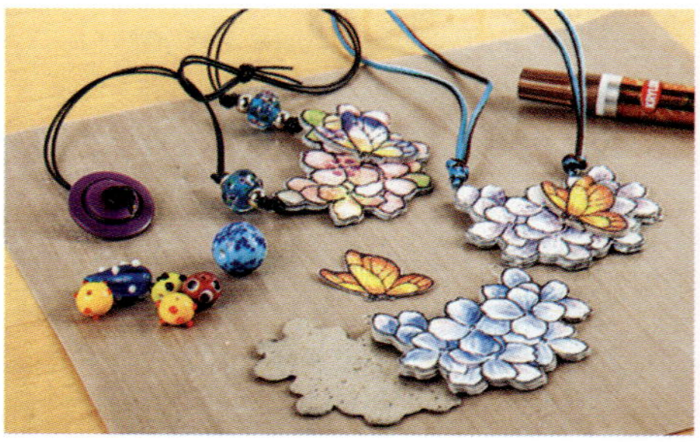

5. Assemble layers with glue, add beads and cording, and create button clasp ties.

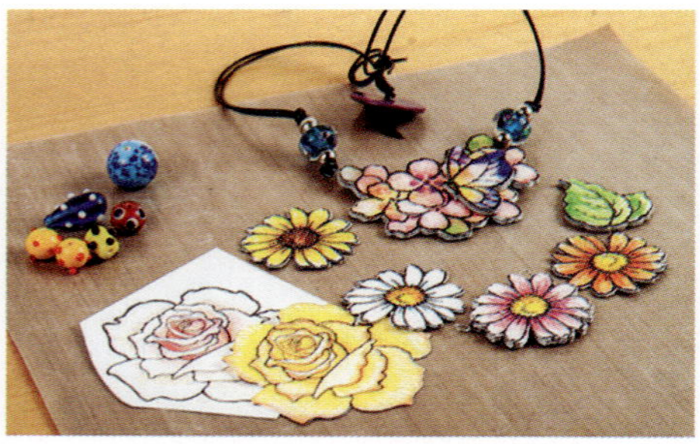

Variations can be made with any number of flower combinations.

WOOD JEWELRY
EMBOSSING POWDER TECHNIQUE

Relatively lightweight and inexpensive wood bracelets and beads can be embossed and stamped to add a unique look of sparkle and lustre. Frantage™ Aged Embossing Powders were used here for a dimensional look.

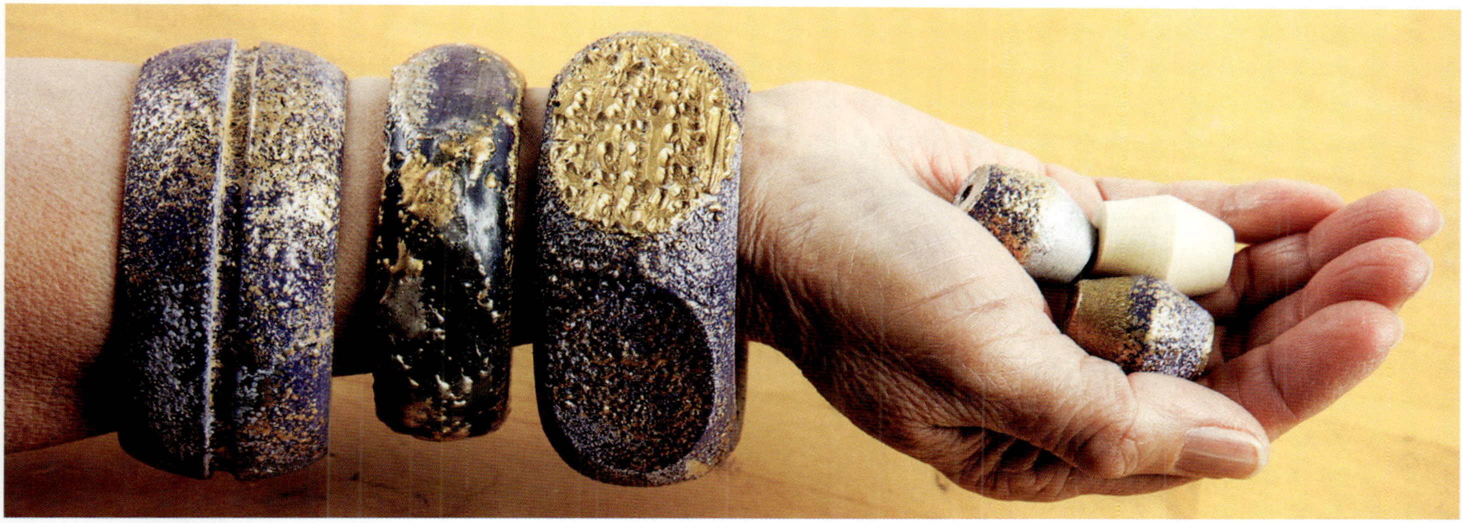

BRACELET TIPS

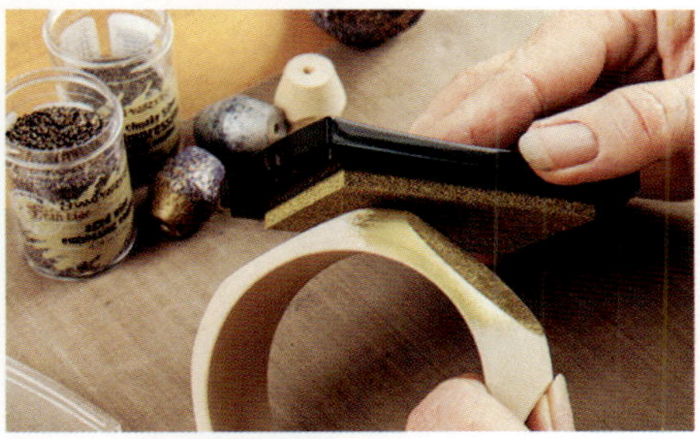

Ink wood bracelet with pigment ink and work in small sections if needed to keep it wet for powders.

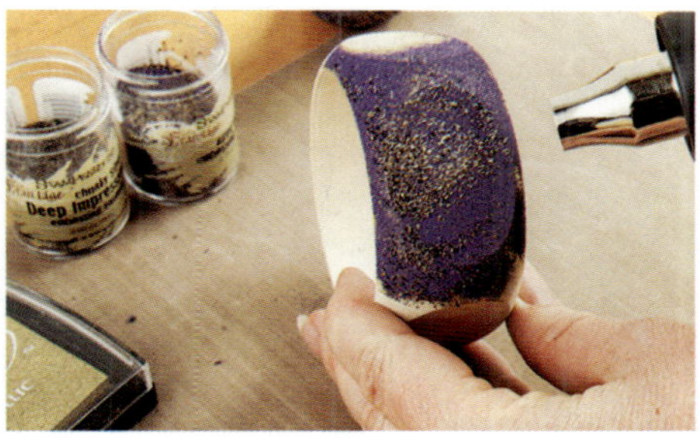

Dust and heat with Frantage™ Embossing Powders for a textured, dimensional look.

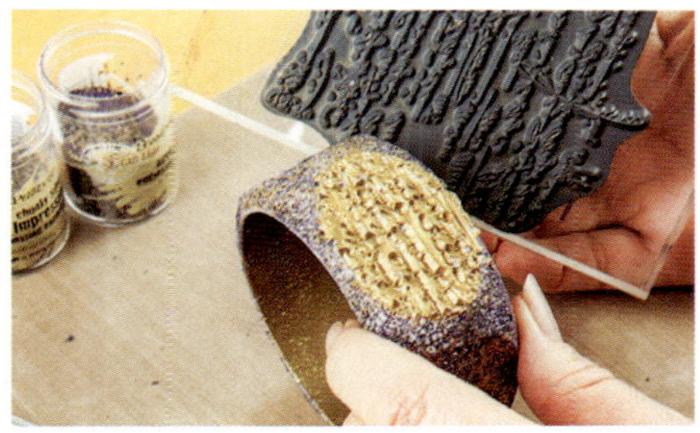

Add layer of Chunky Embossing Powder and quickly stamp into it when molten for deep impression.

BEAD TIPS

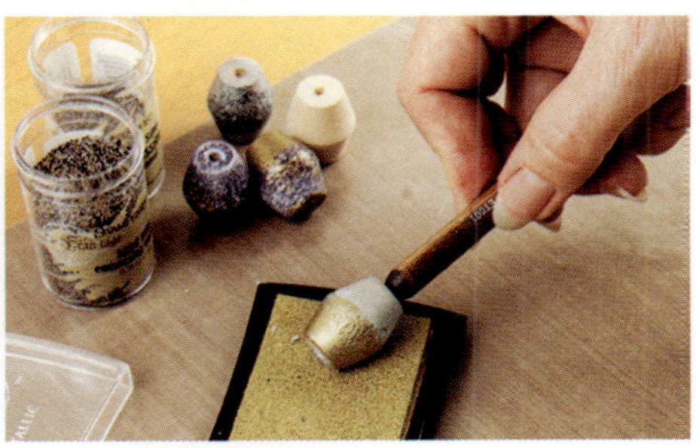

Ink it: Use stencil tool to hold bead steady and roll onto ink pad.

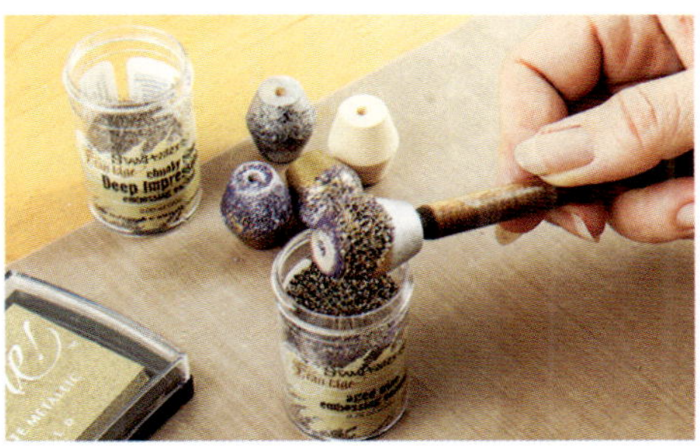

Dust it: Use stencil tool to dip bead into embossing powder.

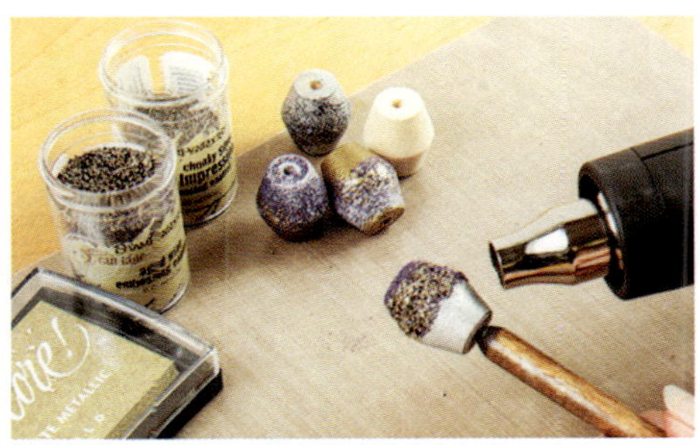

Heat it: Warm bead from a distance and then move closer to melt chunky particles.

METAL CRAFTS
WITH EMBOSSING POWDER

There are many embossing techniques you can use to decorate a metal surface. Remember metal will get very hot, so handle with care and tools as needed. The more expensive the piece, the more valuable these repair tips will be. Recycling inexpensive metal pieces is a great place to start with paint as a first layer such as the Antique Embossing Technique.

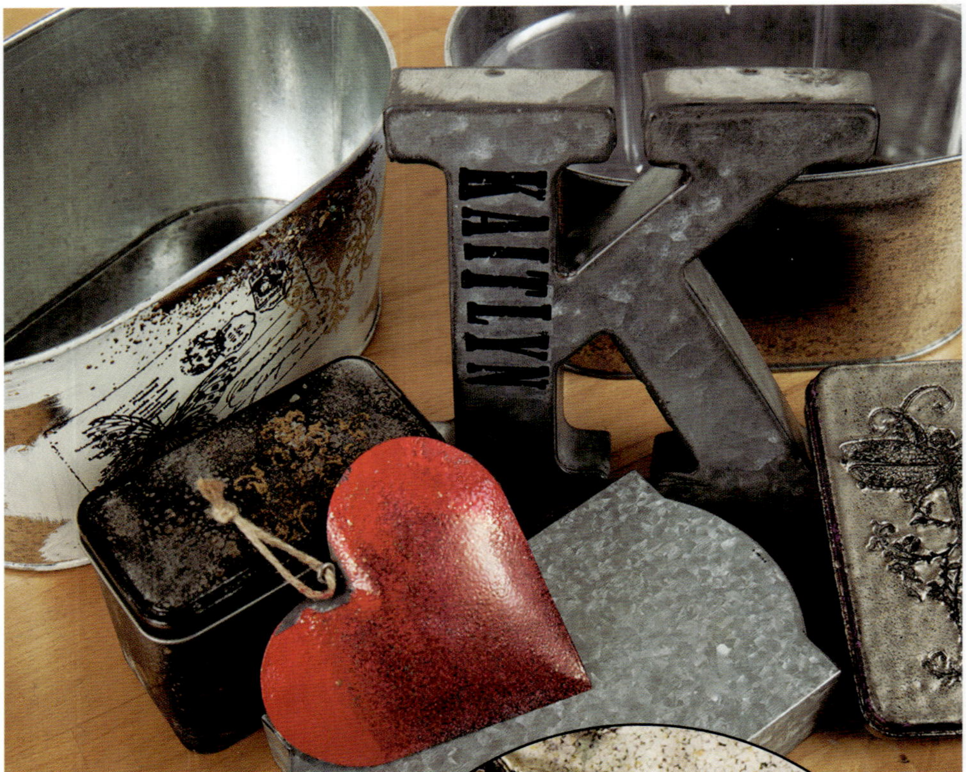

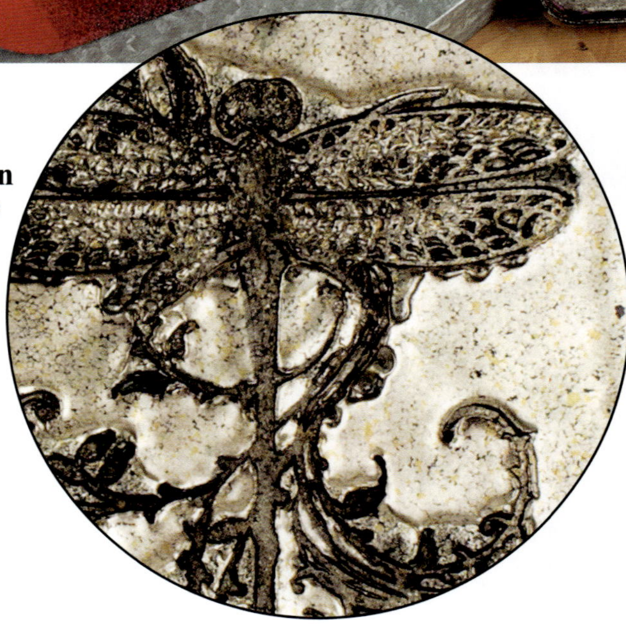

Deep Impression stamping can be done with a heat tool. See more on page 81.

REWORKING TIPS

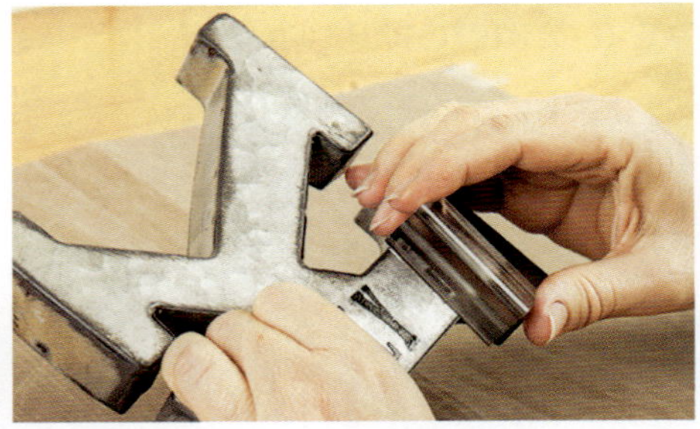

Single impressions: Start with a clean surface. In case it is uneven, it will be most forgiving to stamp one letter at a time.

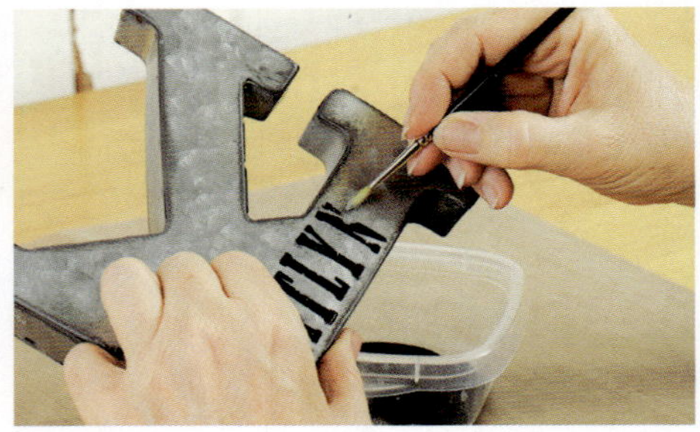

Touch up excess powder with a dry brush BEFORE heating.

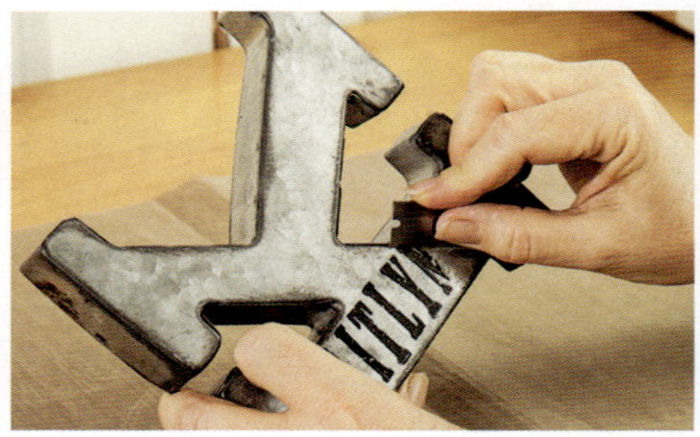

Remove with a flat-edged razor after heating.

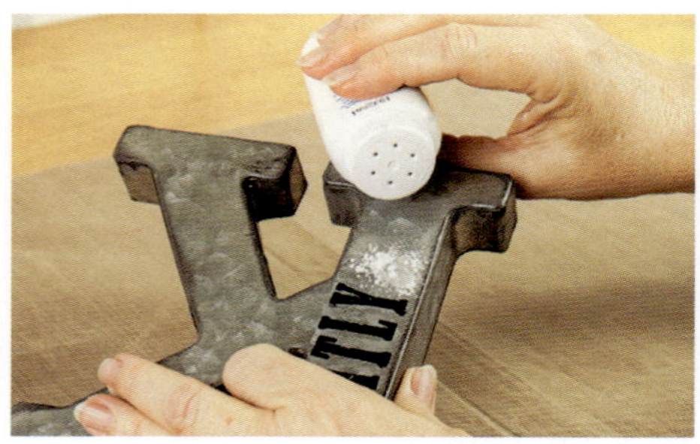

Wet wipe and talcum powder may be needed to completely remove any remains of sticky ink so that you can start all over again.

RECYCLED METAL

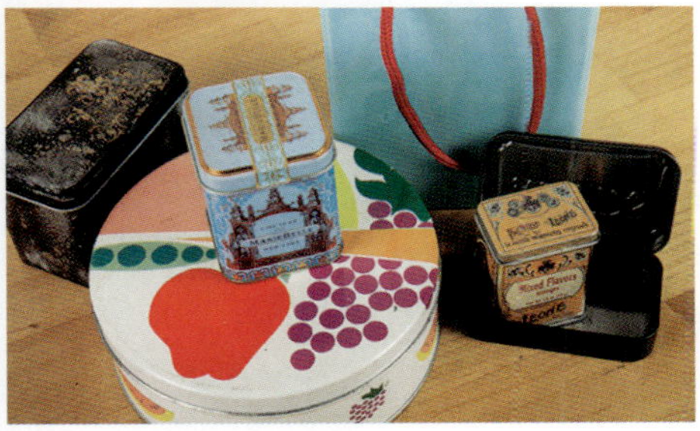

Recycle tins: The uglier the tin, the cheaper you can get them. Remember some old tins are very valuable as is. Look for flat or curved, but not embossed surfaces. Painted bases make lids hard to fit back on. Sand down if need be. Start with a layer of matte black acrylic paint and emboss over it.

BLACKENING

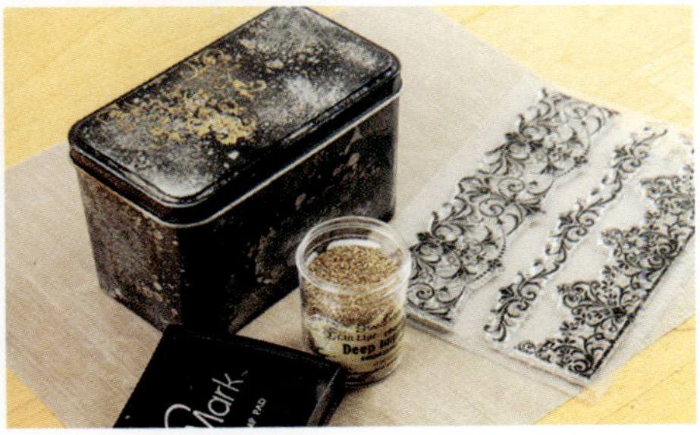

Blacken tins by placing them in BBQ or blacken with a blow torch for an aged look. Add stamped and embossed patterns.

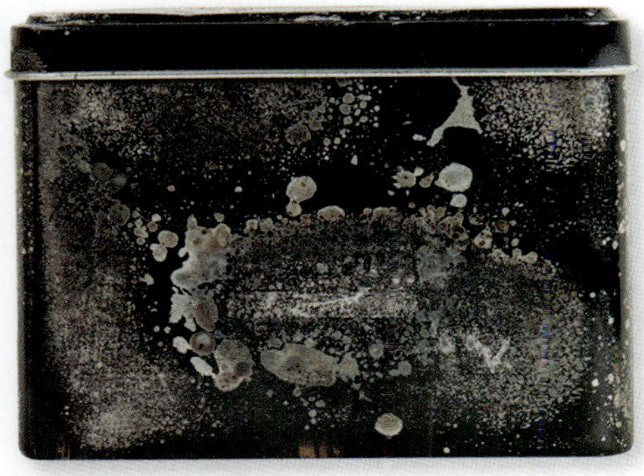

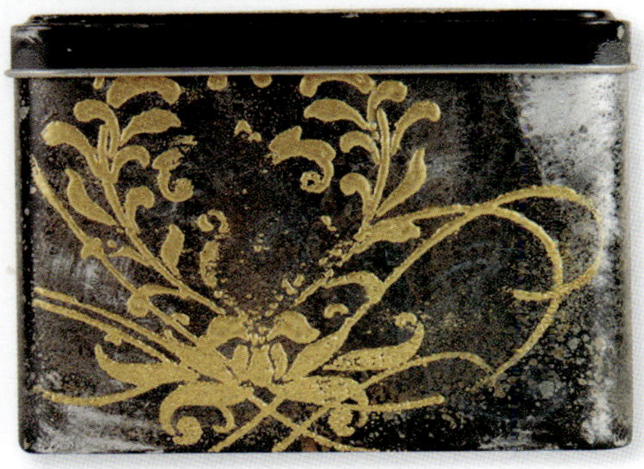

ENAMELING

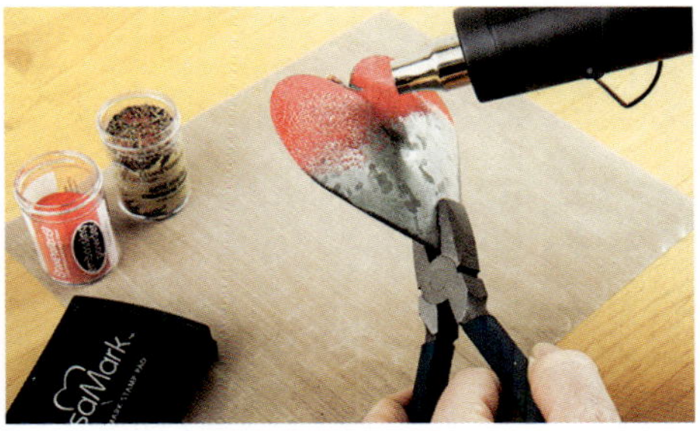

Ink and emboss: Look for flat or curved metal items like this ornament. Hold firmly with pliers.

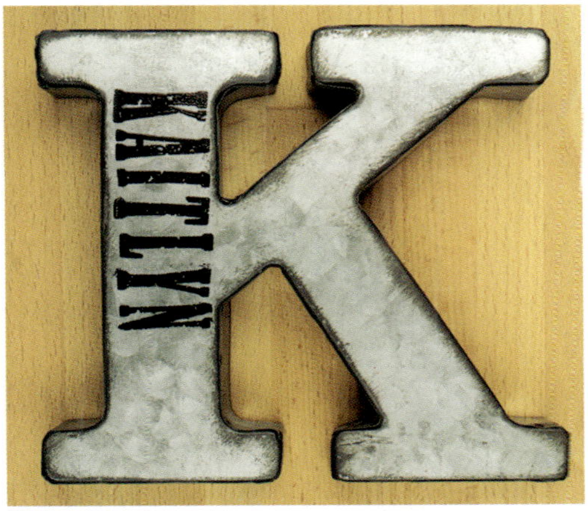

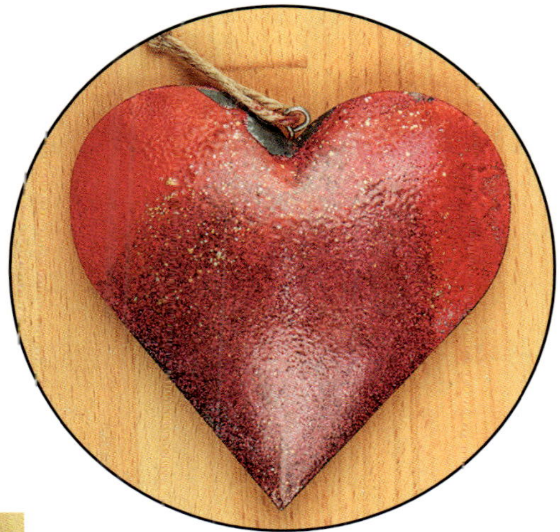

Heart Ornament was enameled with a coating of VersaMark™ ink to catch a blend of embossing powders.

Metal Planter has a layer of acrylic paint, embossed stamp image, and a spoonful of Gold Dust Mix melted on by heating from underneath. Pre-warm metal from inside to start.

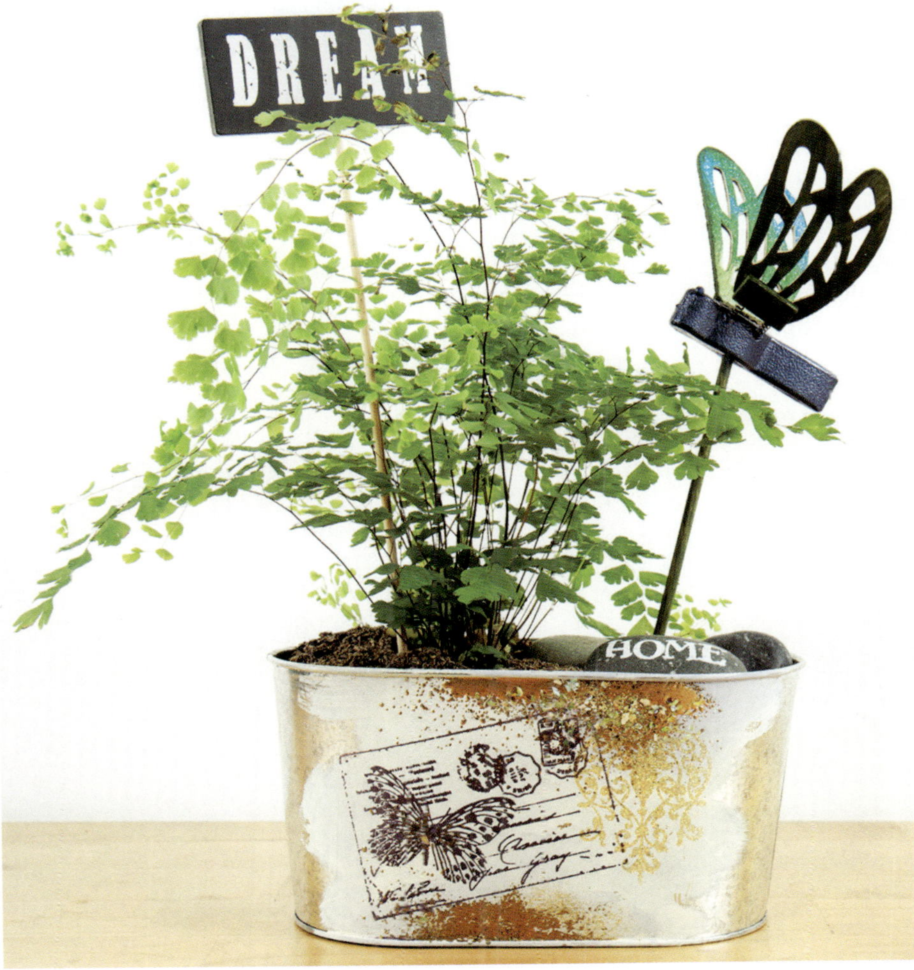

TIPS FOR GLASS, MIRROR, & ACRYLIC
EMBOSSING POWDER TECHNIQUES

V

Stamping and embossing on non-porous surfaces takes a lot of patience if you have to have it perfect. Start clean and dry. If you have problems, wipe it clean, dry, and start again. Blow away excess powder. Heat only when you are satisfied.

JUMBO HANDLES

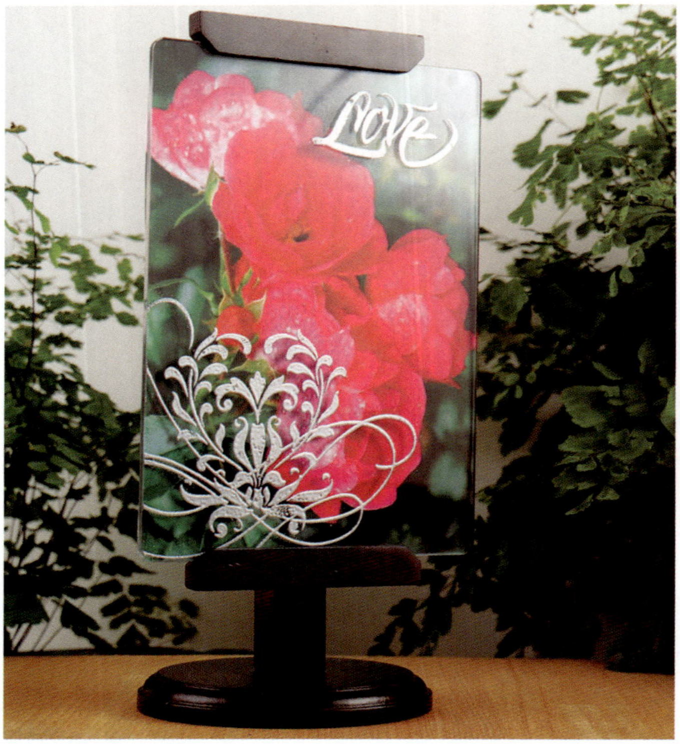

Ink, stamp, and emboss message or design on front of clean and dry glass or jumbo handle to fit frame. Plan design to work with photo or stamped art to be inserted or changed out from behind. Silver Embossing Powder was used.

ACRYLIC BLOCKS

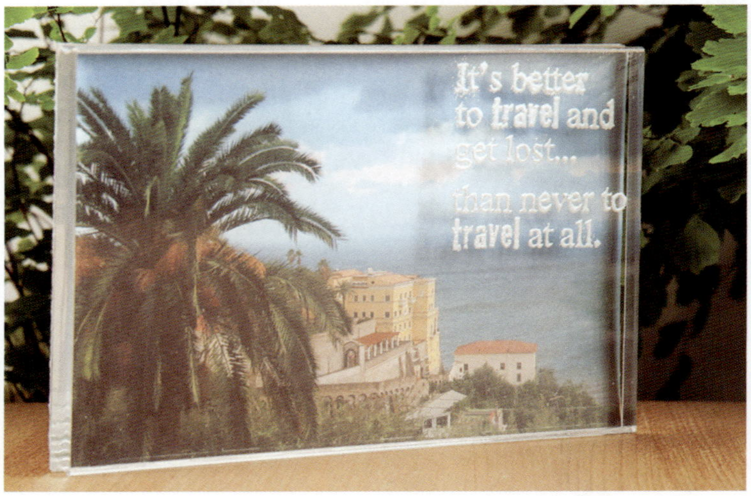

Ink, stamp, and emboss message on front of clean and dry acrylic block. Plan design to work with photo or stamped art to be taped in place from behind. Silver Embossing Powder was used.

MIRROR

Ink, stamp, and emboss using VersaMark™ ink and Aged Silver Embossing Powder.

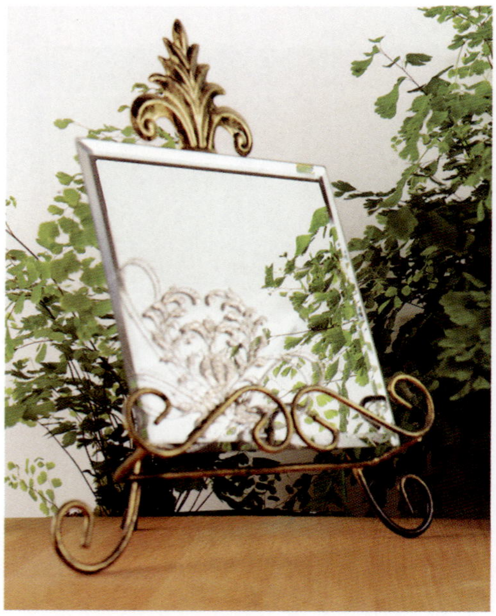

CERAMIC

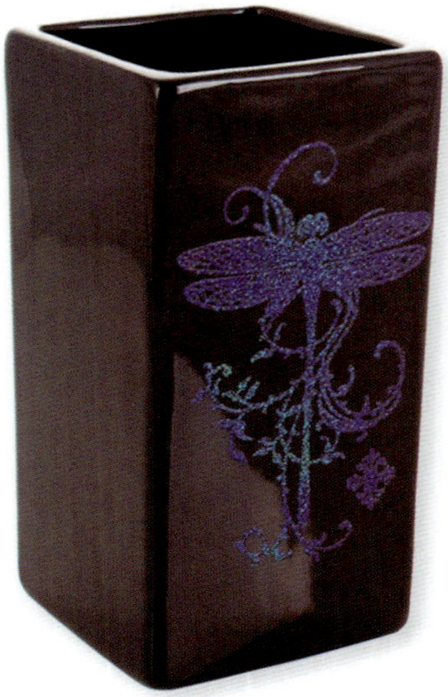

Ink, stamp, and emboss using VersaMark™ Ink and Kaleidoscope Embossing Powder over black surface. Powder is heat sensitive with changing colors according to amount of heat applied. See page 22.

GLASS

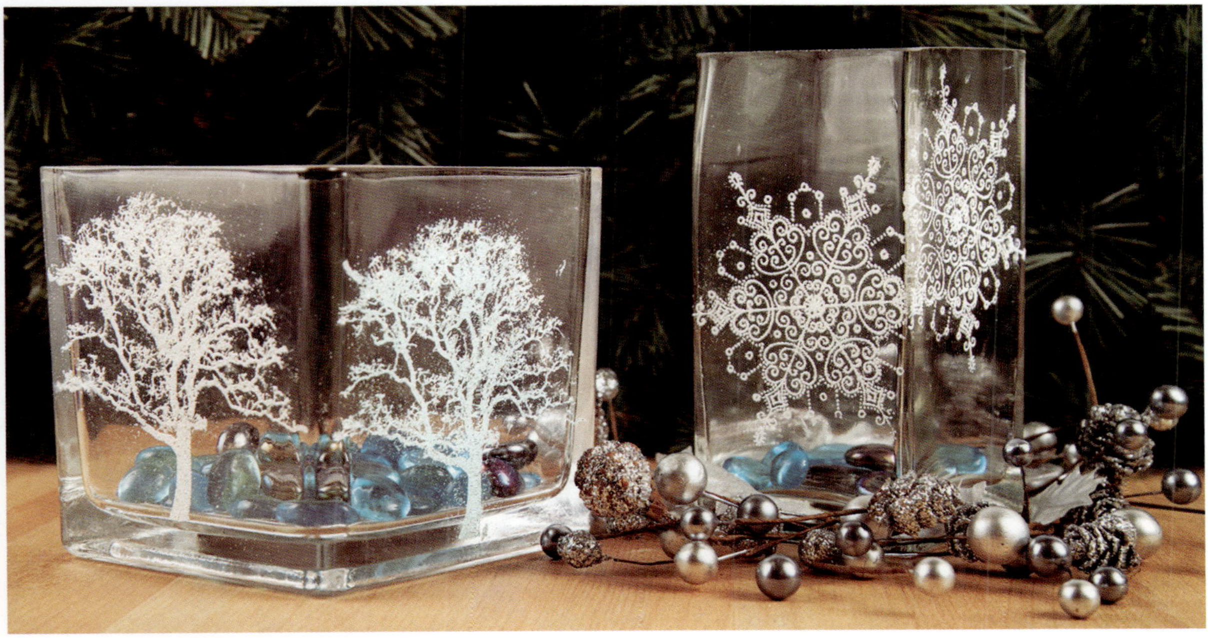

Best Powders for snow are Sparkle Puff, Shabby White, Shabby Blue, Shabby Pink or Shabby Green. Detail powders have too much static to work easily on glass.

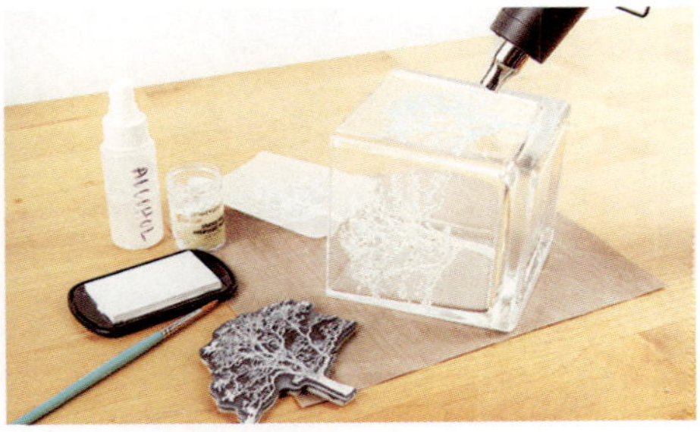

Glass vases: Select flat-sided vases that are thick enough to withstand uneven heating without shattering. The flat surface is usually deceptively uneven. A smooth, curved surface will work as well.

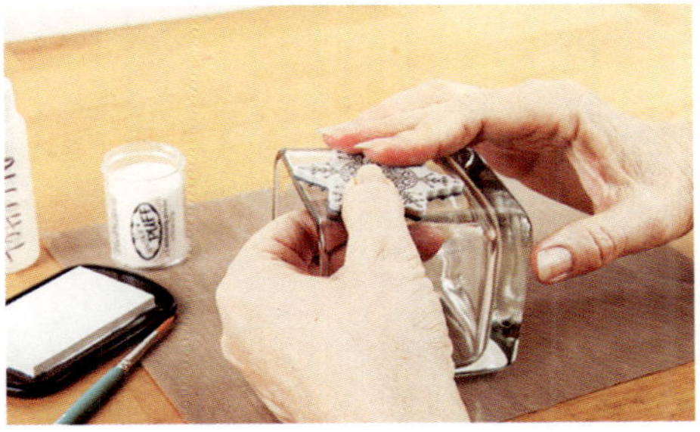

Cling stamps in hand instead of on a block handle work best if you place it, hold it and then press around edges. This works for curved surfaces, too.

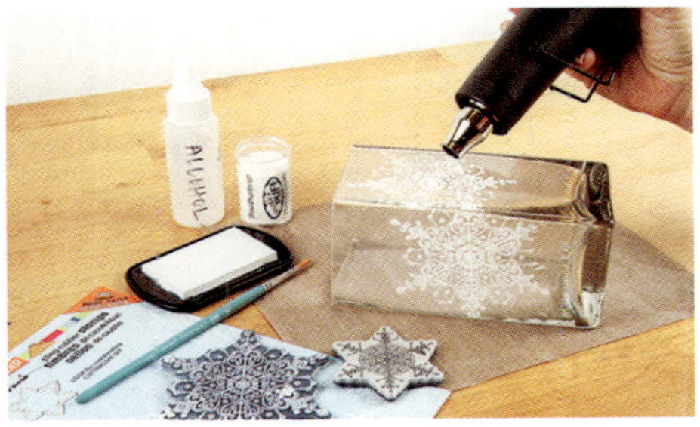

Ink and emboss: A white ink pad will confirm if you have a good impression. If not, wipe clean, dry, and try again. Alcohol is ideal to clean between attempts. Dust with Embossing Powder. Blow away excess powder or remove with dry brush before heating.

ACRYLIC BLOCKS

Tip: Start heating from a distance. Alternate heating inside and outside to keep glass temperature even.

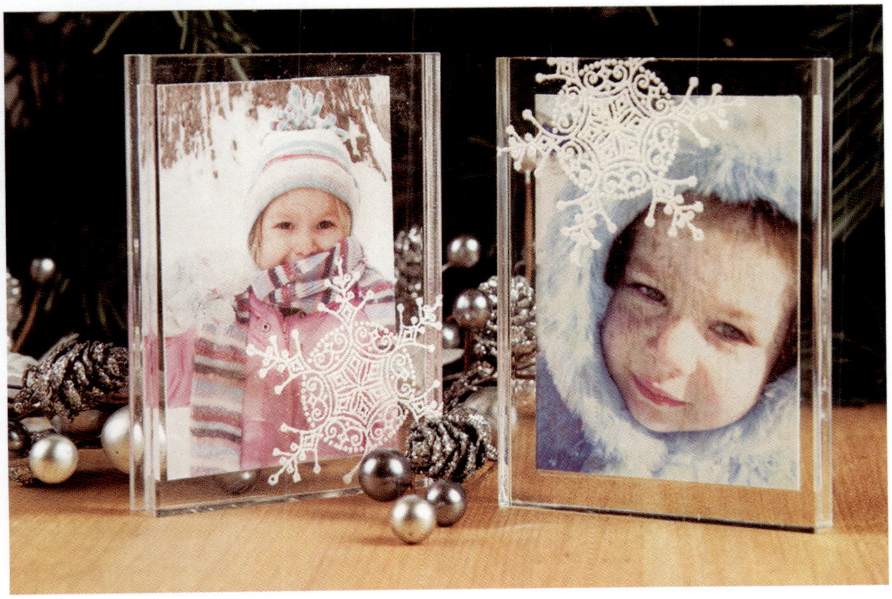

Ink, stamp, and emboss using Sparkle Puff Embossing Powder. Trim Sticky Panel adhesive to size of photo and press in place from the back.

STEAMPUNK
EMBOSSING POWDER TECHNIQUE

Embossing Powders can help you create a Steampunk look on any number of surfaces in ways that will instantly give you that vintage look. Select stamp images of gears or clocks, etc. Any of the Aged Embossing Powder mixes are especially interesting. Aged Silver is an all time favorite.

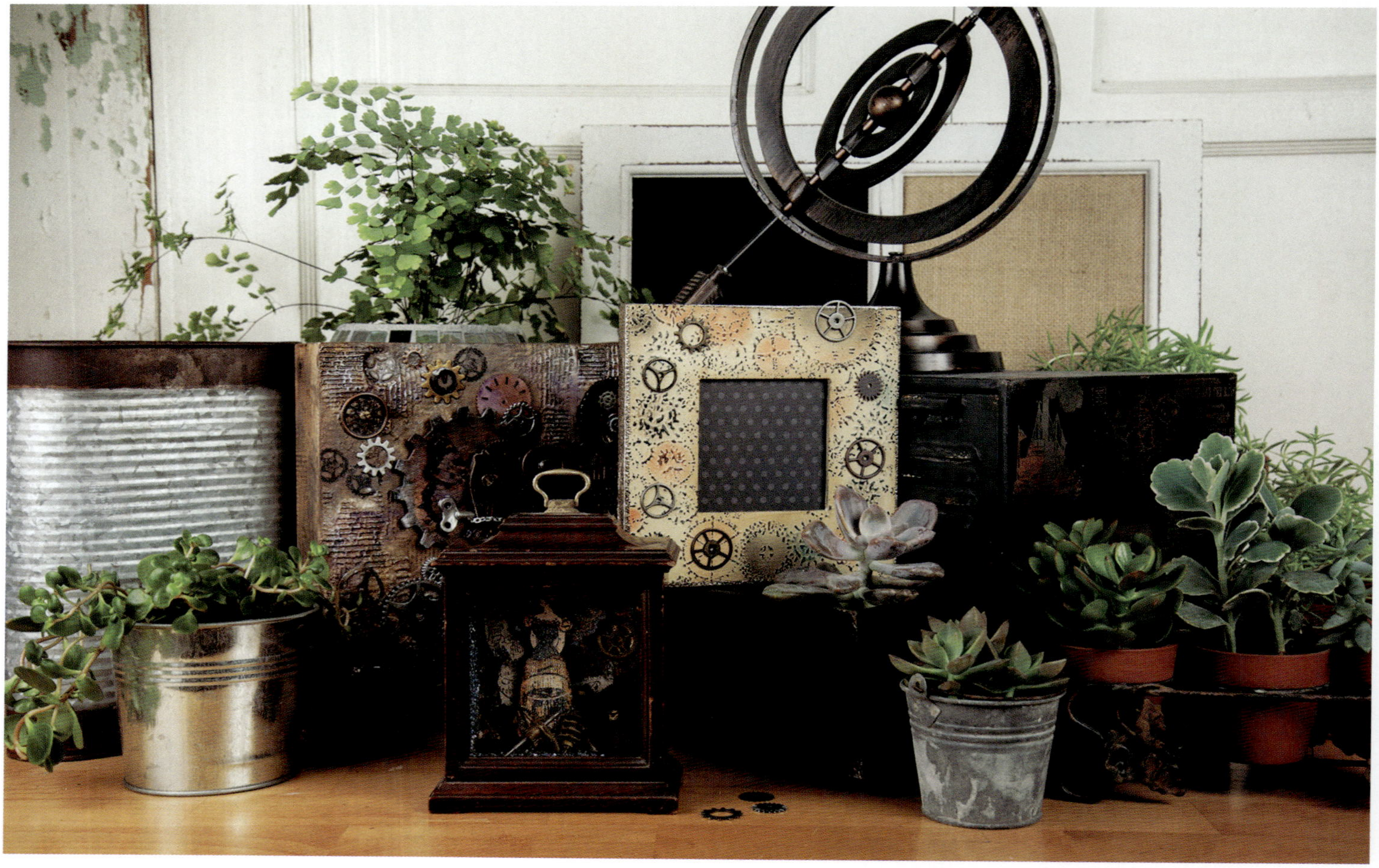

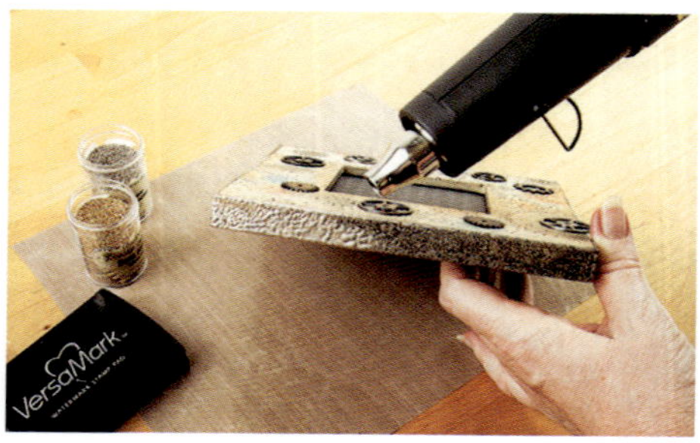

Emboss edge: Apply ink and dust with Embossing Powder for metallic finish.

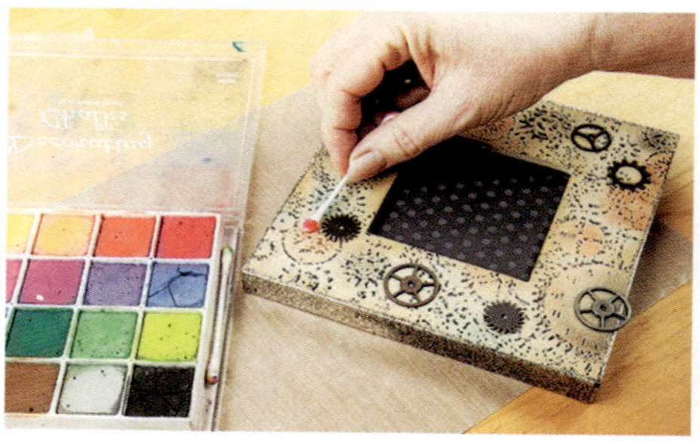

Chalk it: Apply chalk over paint for subtle color changes. Add metal gear embellishments.

FRAMES

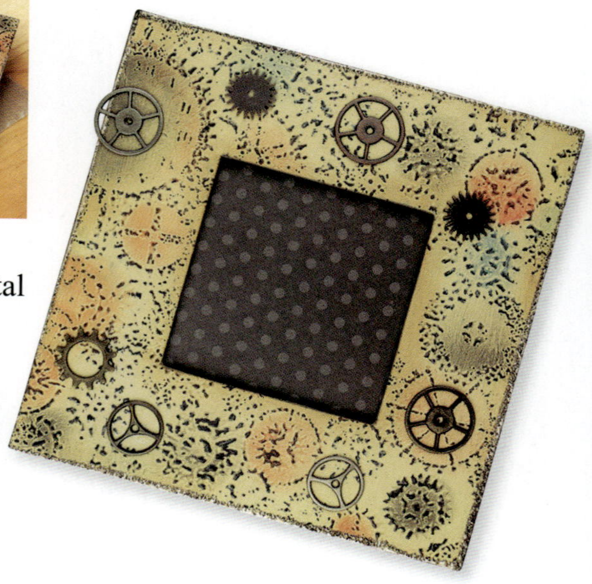

Antique Embossing Technique and Gears Stencil were used to create this frame.

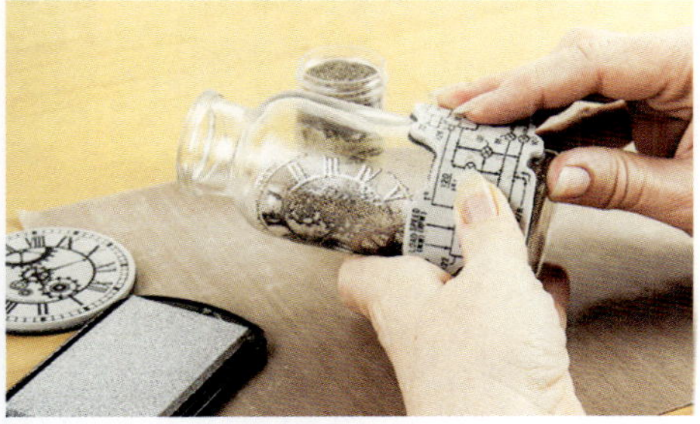

Stamp curved surface: Unmounted stamp can be held in place and then pressed around.

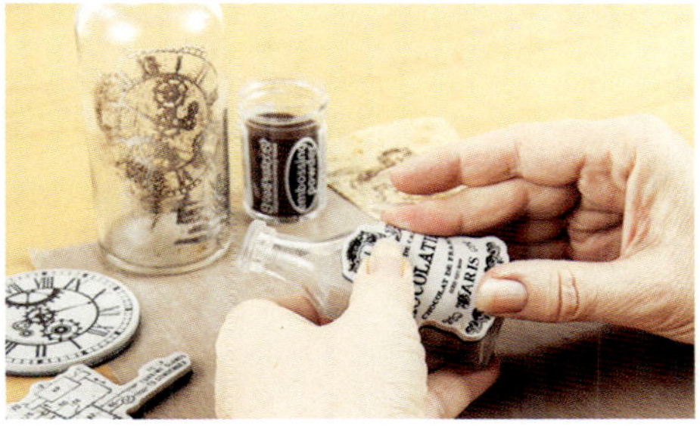

Stamp on bottle: Stamp around curve of bottle. Stamp with an ink you can see to be sure you have a good impression.

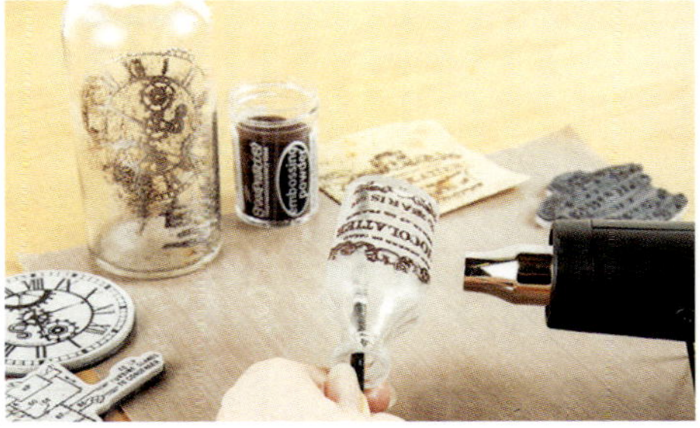

Dust and emboss with Clear Bark or Chocolate Brown. Brush handle will suspend bottle for heating.

BOTTLES

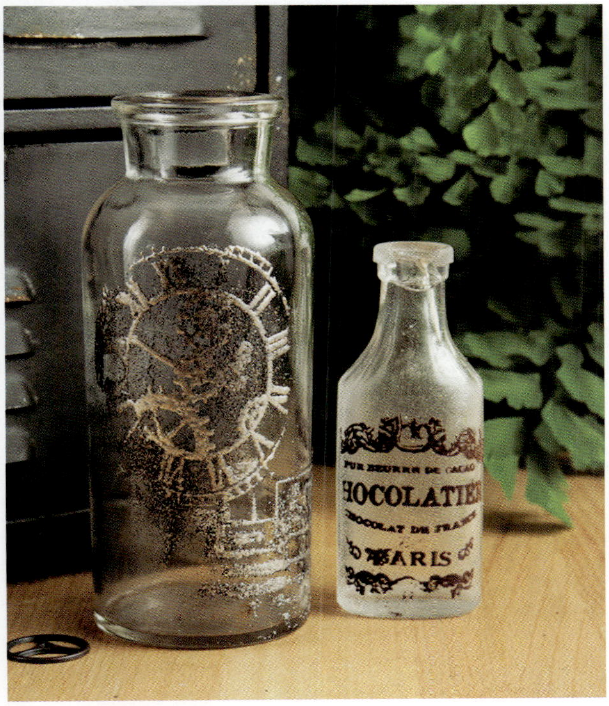

Old bottles stamped and embossed with Aged Silver have a tarnished look. Imperfect impressions will look more worn.

BOOK COVERS

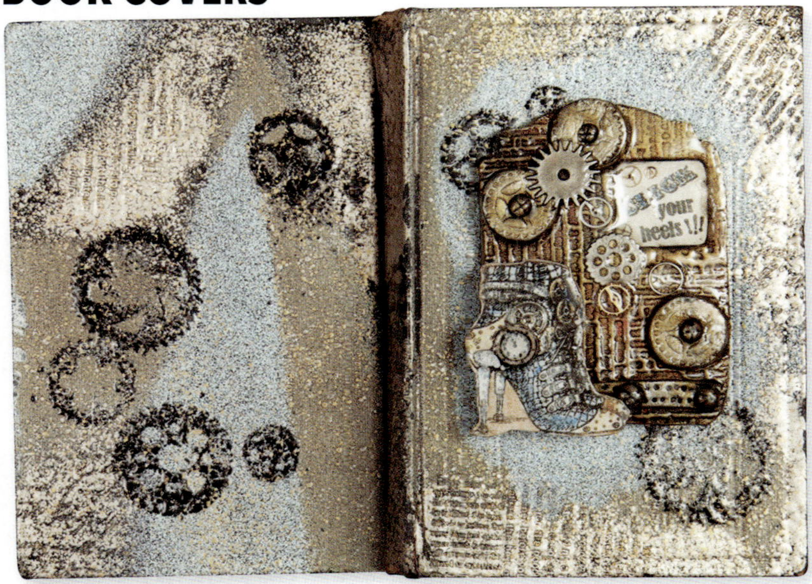

Book Cover was embossed with Aged Aqua, Aged Taupe, Aged Silver, and Aged Black. Ink surface and pour multiple colors of powder. Heat.

SLATE COASTERS

Coasters were stamped and embossed with multiple pours of Metallic Silver, Aged Silver, Aged Black, and White.

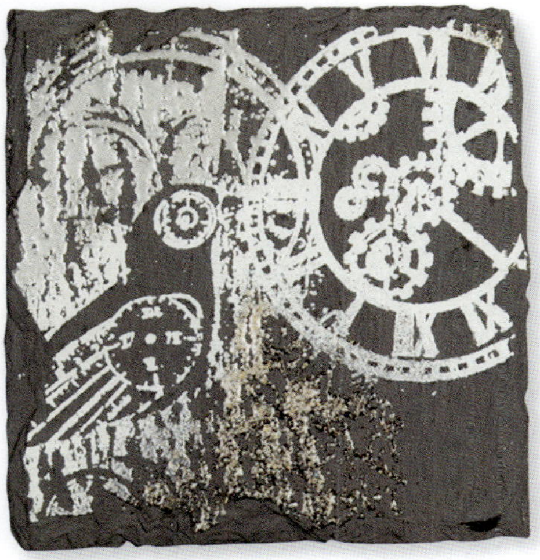

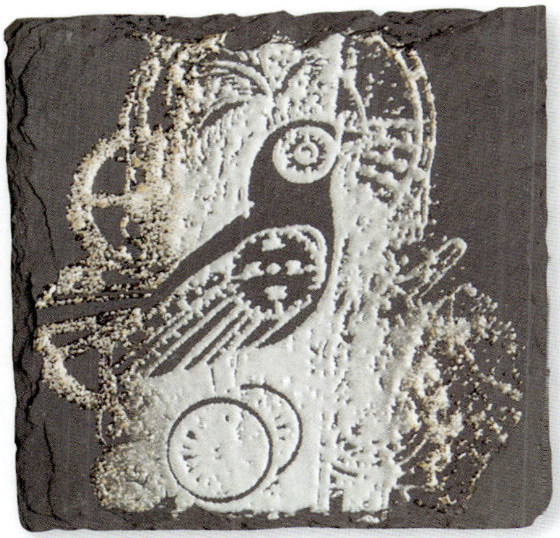

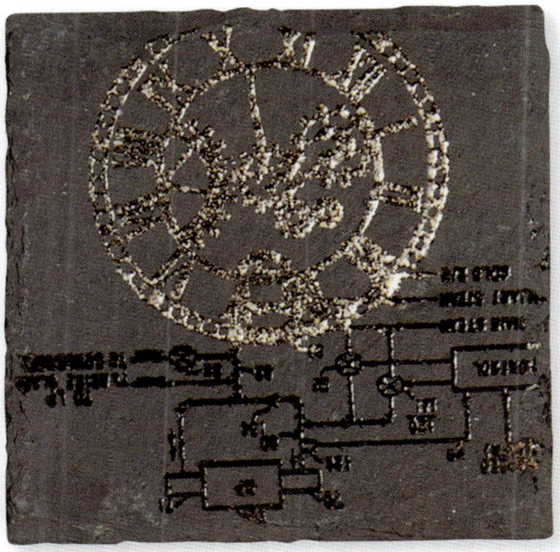

NATURAL OBJECTS
TO BE EMBOSSED

Many natural objects can be enhanced or personalized with Embossing Powder. Test leaves, barks, sea shells, pebbles, feathers, or slate.

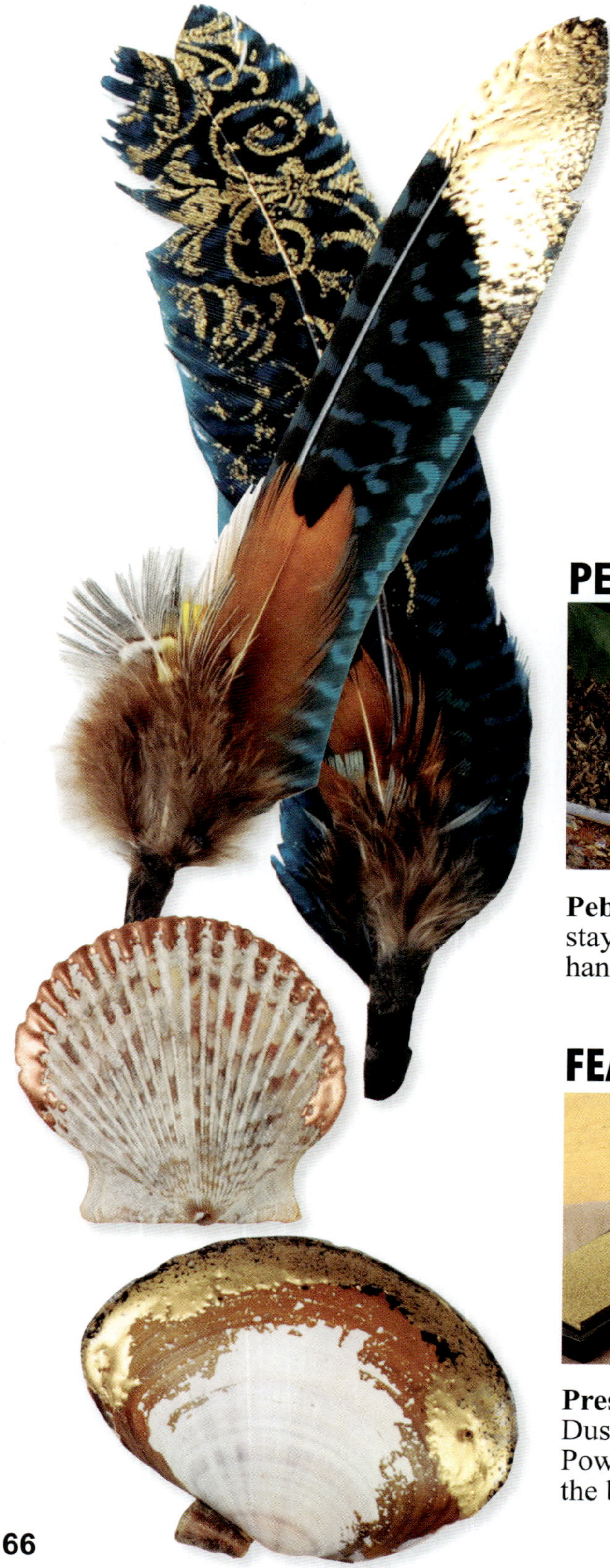

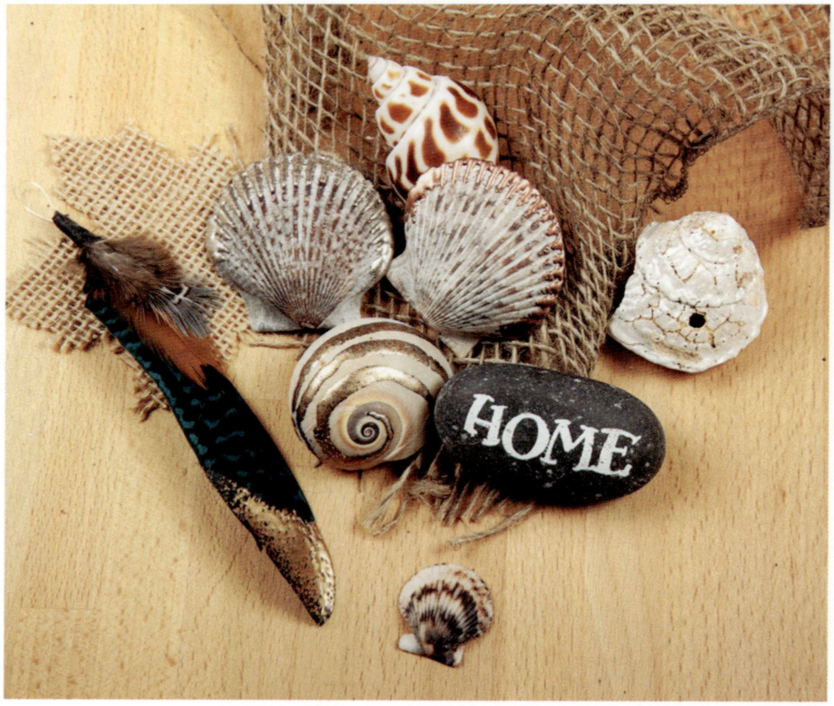

PEBBLES

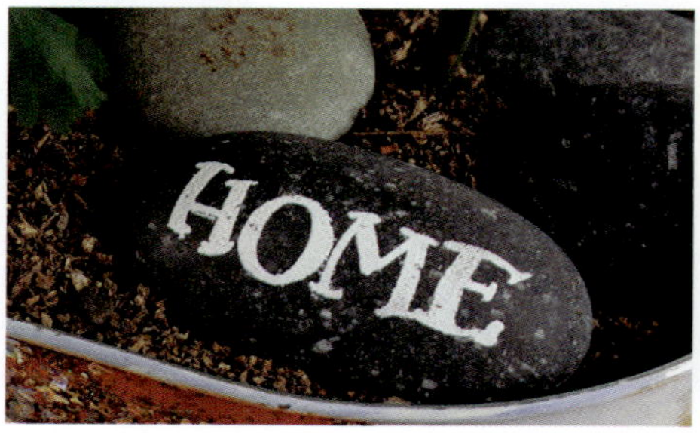

Pebbles take a while to heat up and stay hot for a while, be patient and handle with care.

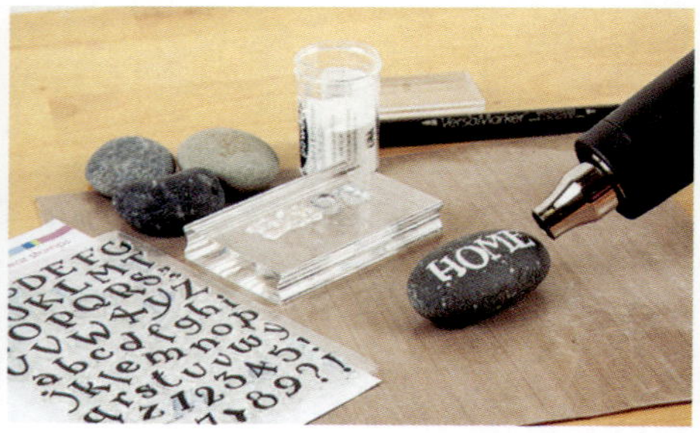

Alphabet stamps on pebbles are fun. Position letters together on block or use one by one. Touch up with VersaMarker™ if need.

FEATHERS

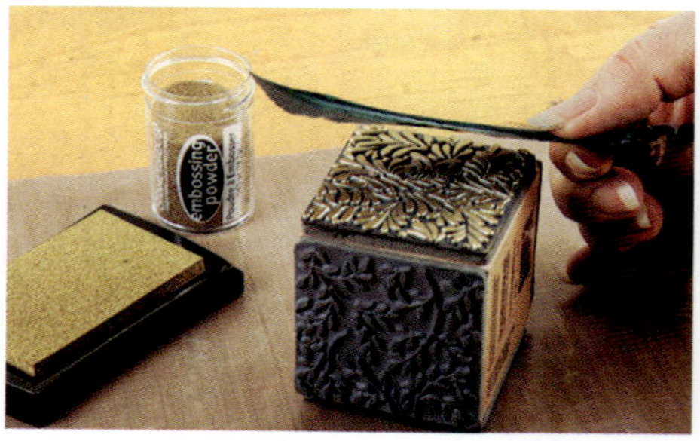

Press feather to inked stamp. Dust with Aged Gold Embossing Powder and heat from the top or the bottom.

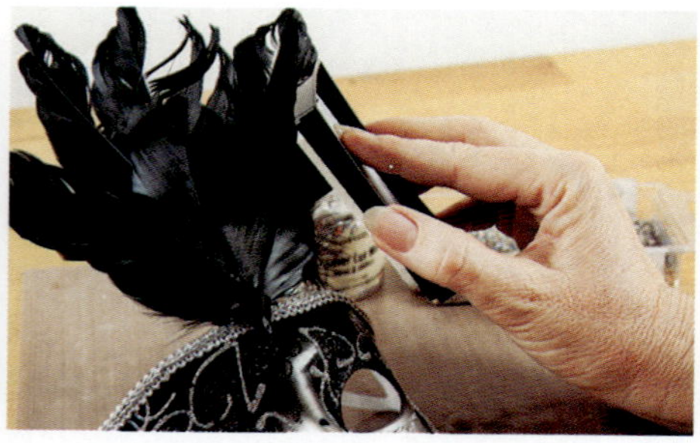

Apply ink to tips of feathers. Dust with Silver Embossing Powder and heat from top or bottom.

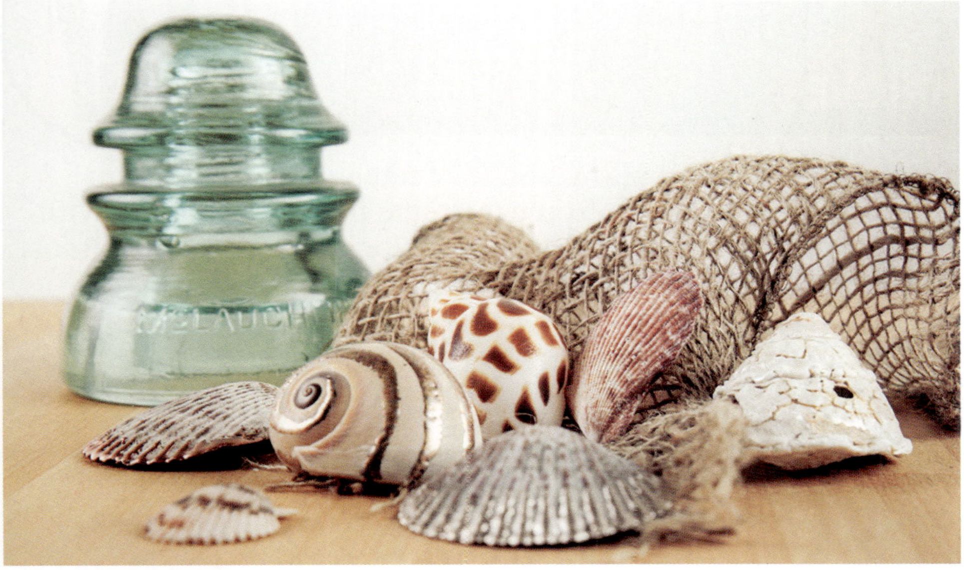

SEA SHELLS

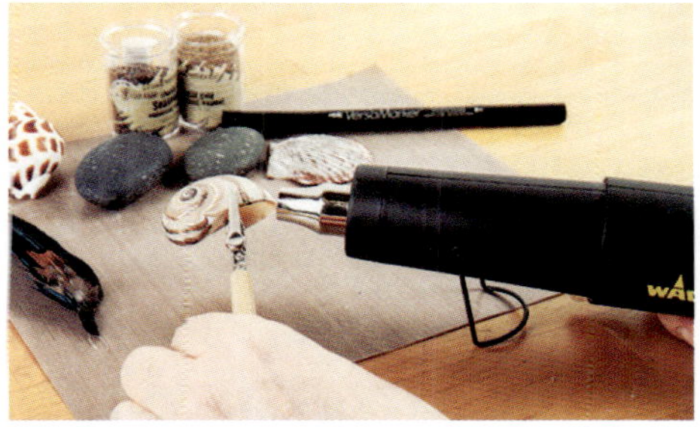

Emboss pattern on shells using VersaMarker™. Dust with Copper Embossing Powder. Hold with clip tool and heat to melt powder.

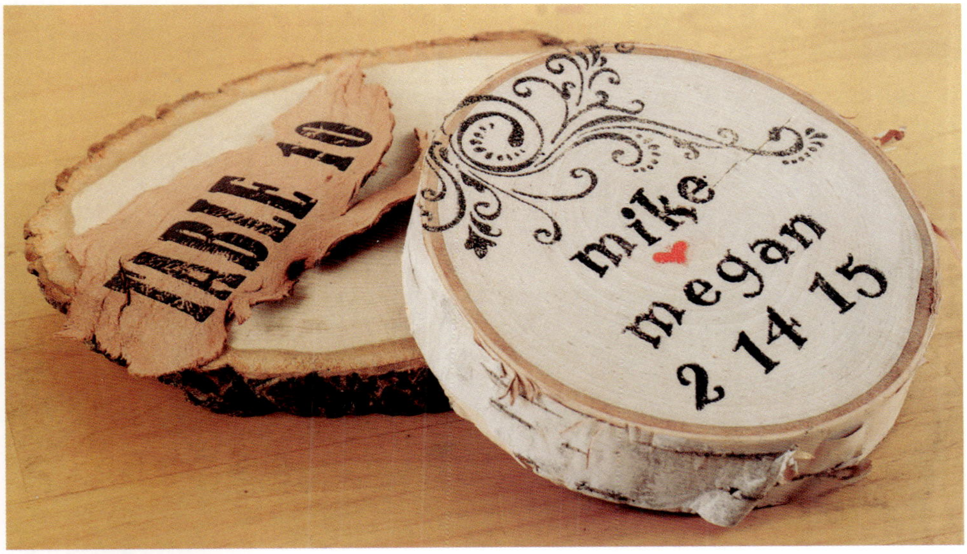

Bark may need to be flattened to stamp on it. Look for birch or eucalyptus bark. Tree branch slices can be sanded if needed.

BARK or WOOD

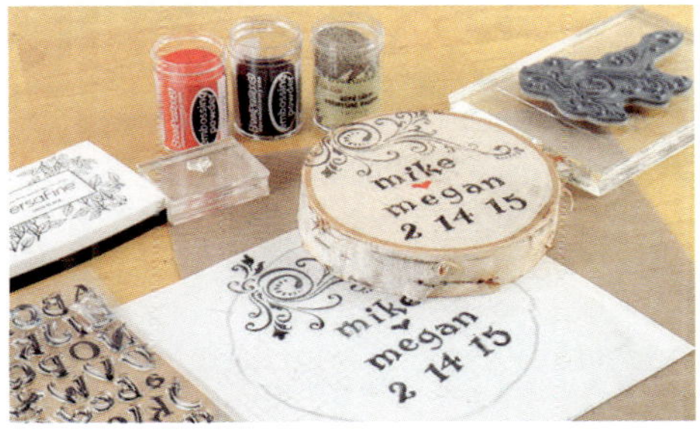

Plan wording on grid paper and tracing paper for ideal fit. Dust with Black, Red, and Aged Silver Embossing Powders. Heat all at once to avoid overheating.

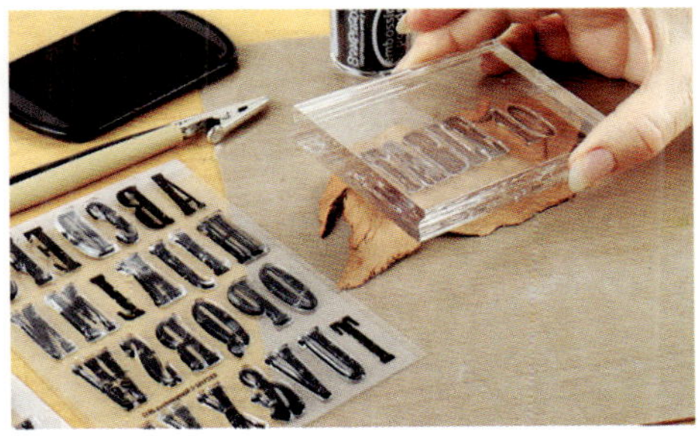

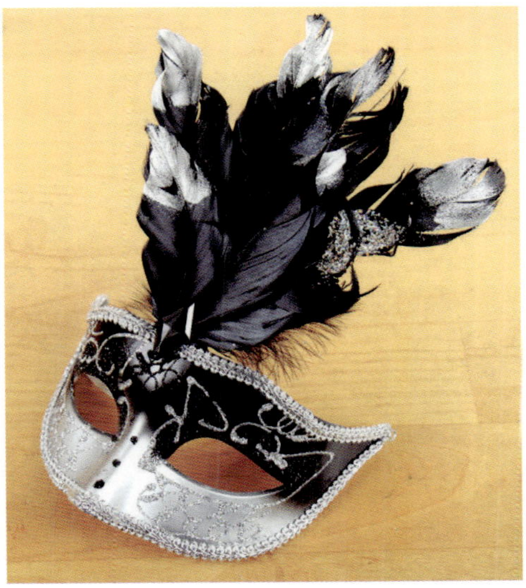

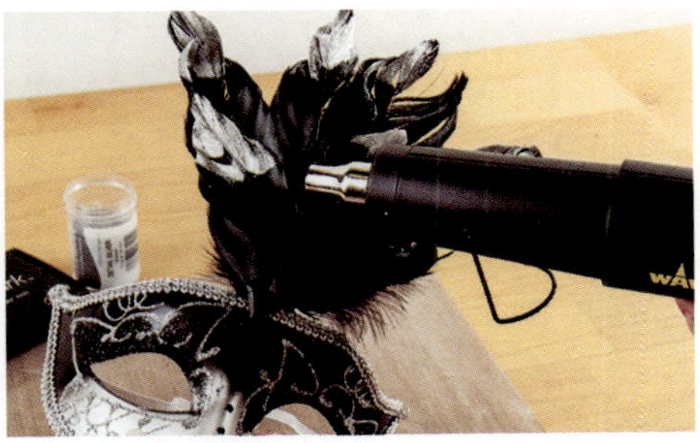

Test: Elements like glass glitter may become too hot and burn feathers. Try on a small area first.

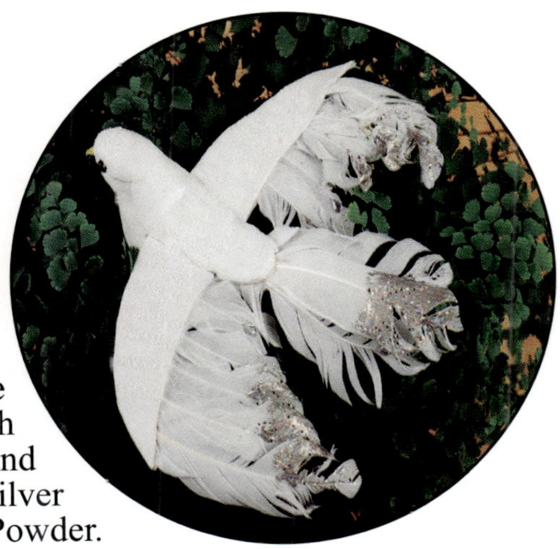

Feathered Dove was tipped with VersaMark™ ink and embossed with Silver Embossing Powder.

ANTIQUE
EMBOSSING POWDER TECHNIQUE

W

Antique Embossing is a wonderful technique that will allow you to create the look of old tin ceiling tiles. Select bold patterned stamps for best results. You can create this instant aging with stamps, Embossing Powder, and acrylic paint. You can do this on cardstock, wood, metal, almost any surface. Select the color and patina. This is a great technique for recycled 3D items.

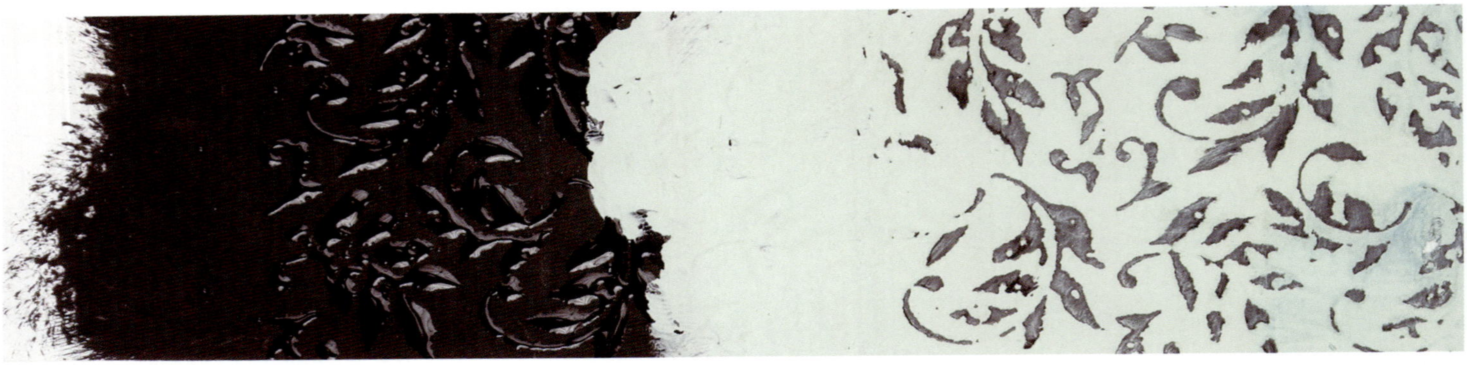

Black base is most forgiving. It can be glossy black card stock or matte black acrylic paint on cardstock or a 3D surface.

Stamp and emboss in Chunky Clear Deep Impression Embossing Powder. Extra heat will give it the most relief.

Paint over it with water-based acrylic paint. For best results, allow it to mostly dry but not set entirely. Do not heat to dry as paint will blister.

Scrub it with a terry cloth rag. Start with a gentle circular motion to remove paint over the raised black impression.

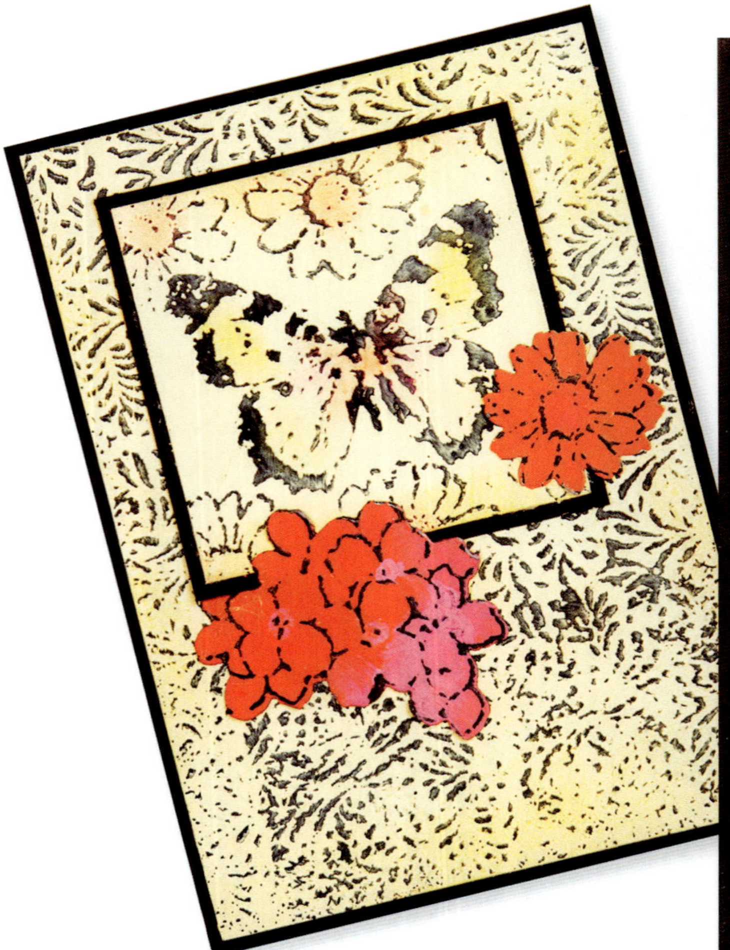

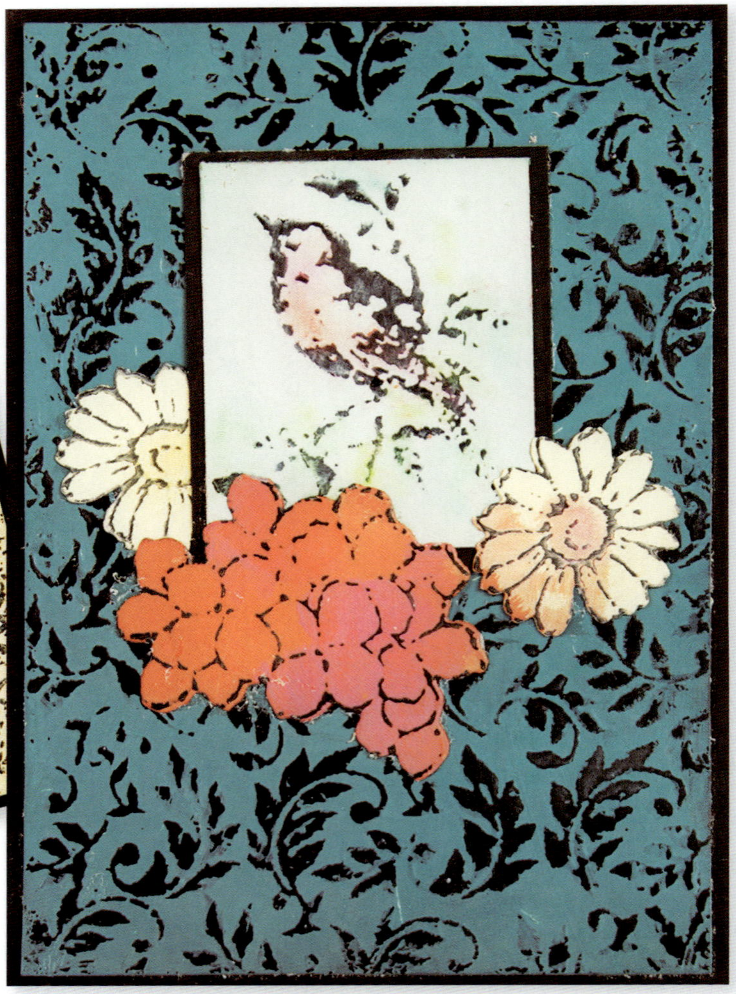

ANTIQUE EMBOSSING PAINT VARIATIONS

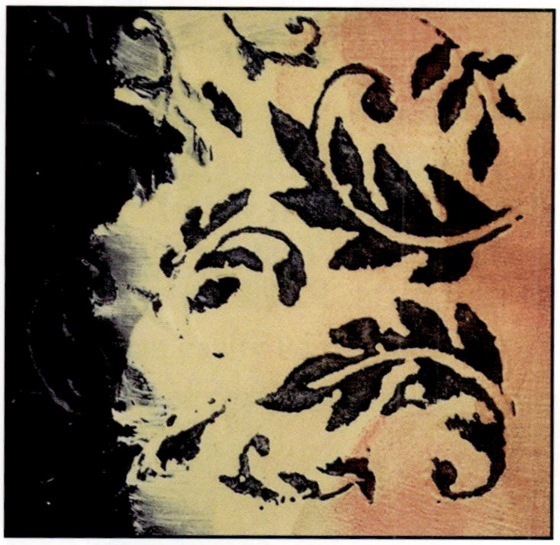

Shabby pastel colors fit this look well. Stick to one color paint and tint with powdery chalks when dry. Otherwise patching is tricky.

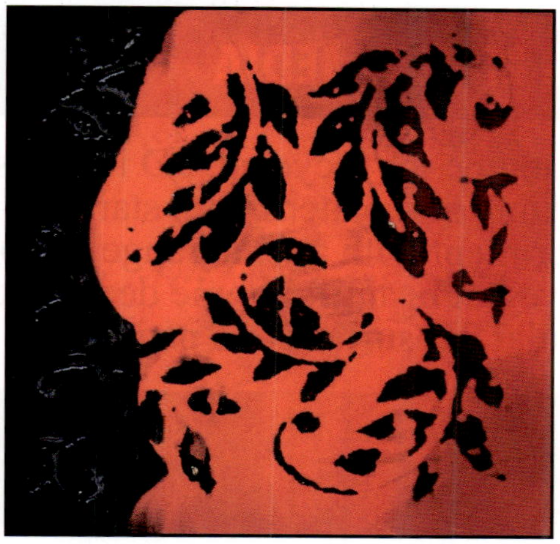

Deep colors work over black with equal success. When dry, finger paint highlights with metallic pastes for a bit of sheen.

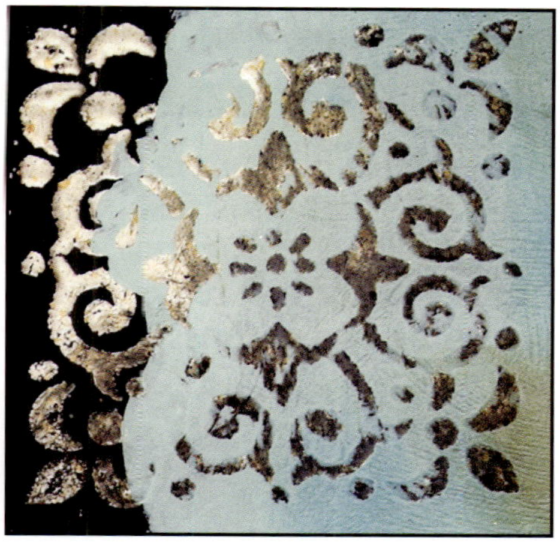

Metallic Chunky Embossing Powders will look like tin ceiling panels. Metallic ink pad will help align impressions as you go.

BASE COLOR VARIATIONS

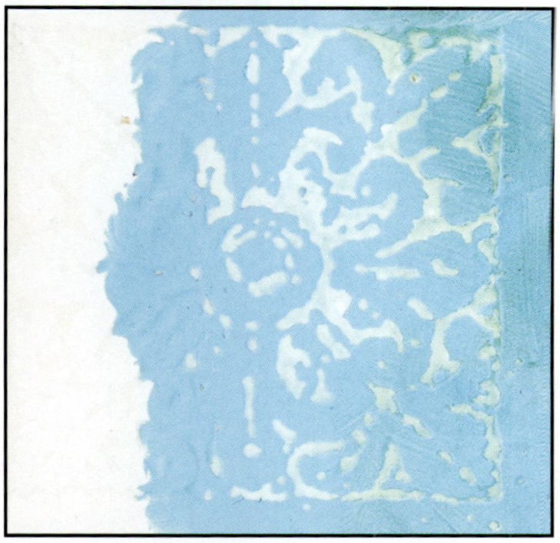

Light base white paint under Clear Chunky Embossing Powder with blue paint, and green chalk.

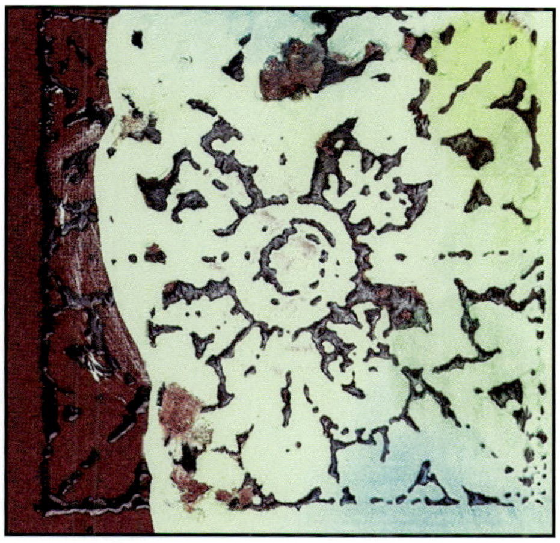

Add foil leafing after scrubbing. Use heat tool to reheat sections and immediately press foil. Press with craft sheet, and block. It gets hot!

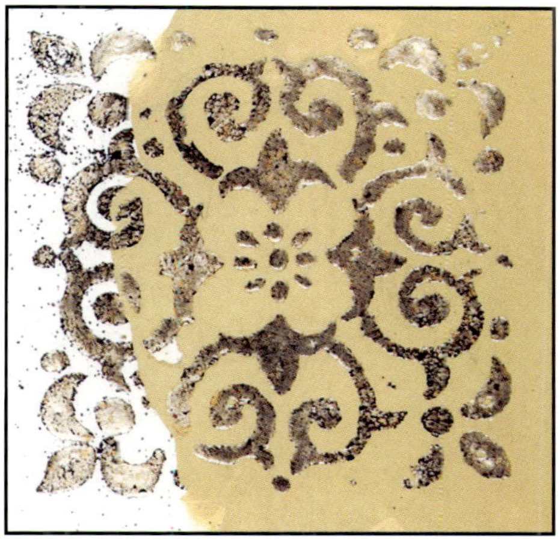

Metal sheet painted white, embossed with Aged Silver and painted with tan acrylic. Use clip tool to hold. It heats quickly.

SURFACE VARIATION

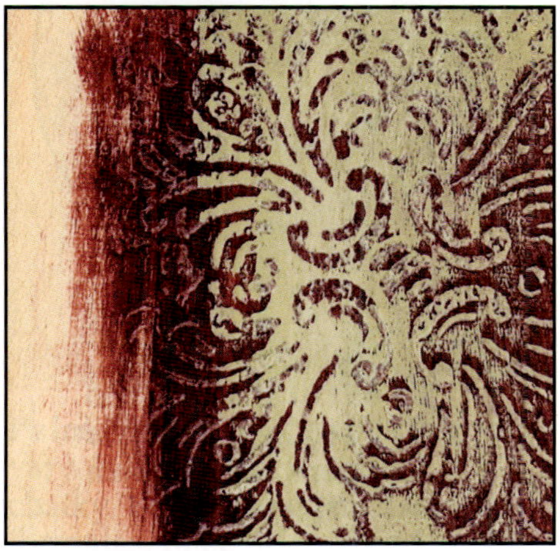

Wood base with stain, Chunky Clear powder, and green paint.

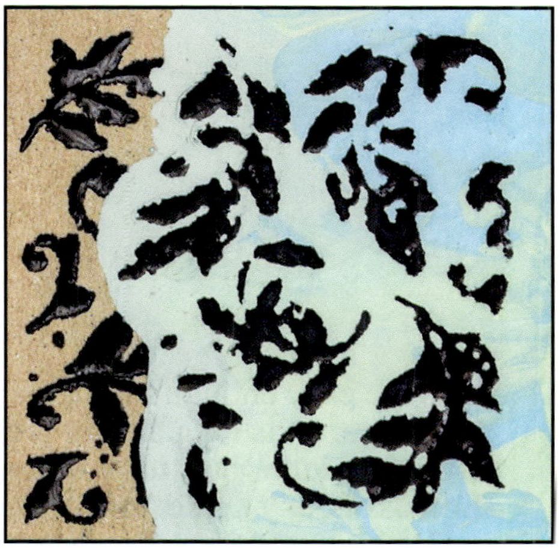

Paper mache kraft unpainted, Chunky Black, blue green paint.

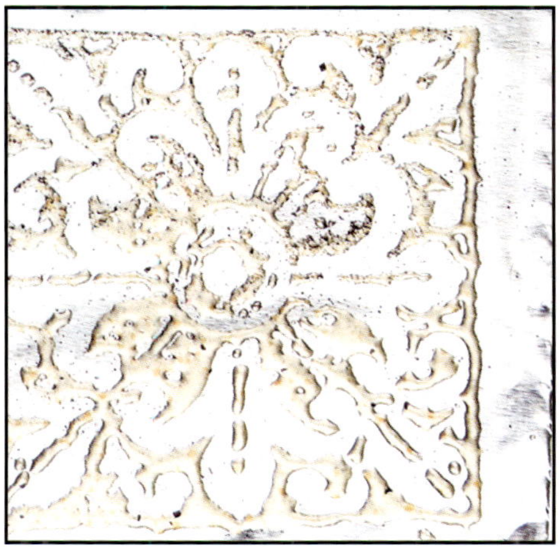

Metal sheet with Chunky Aged Silver. Use clip tool.

PAINTING WITH POWDER BACKGROUND
EMBOSSING POWDER TECHNIQUE

X

This technique can be as simple as pouring colors in stripes or random patterns. It is all about the colors and layers you can create with Embossing Powders. This technique showcases the beauty of the mixes. You can work quickly between colors if you have a large shallow container open for each color and a spoon to recapture powders.

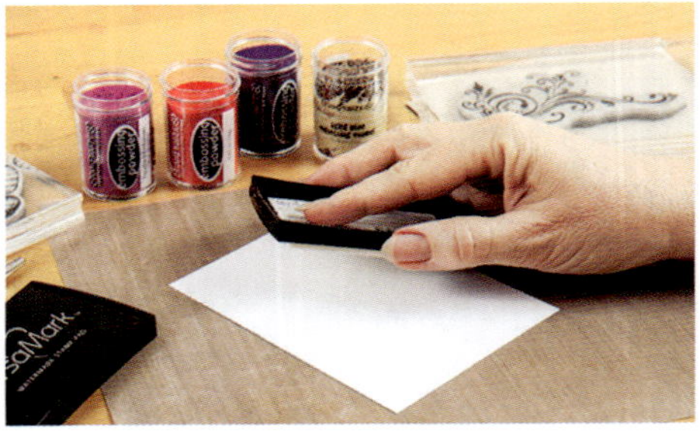

1. Ink it: Apply clear VersaMark™ ink over entire surface of pre-trimmed card panel.

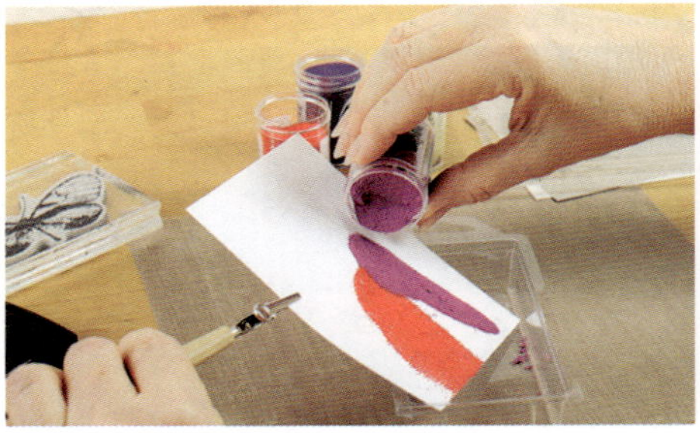

2. Dust with one or more colors of opaque embossing powders. Pour powders off at angles. Add more colors until entire wet ink area is covered by powders.

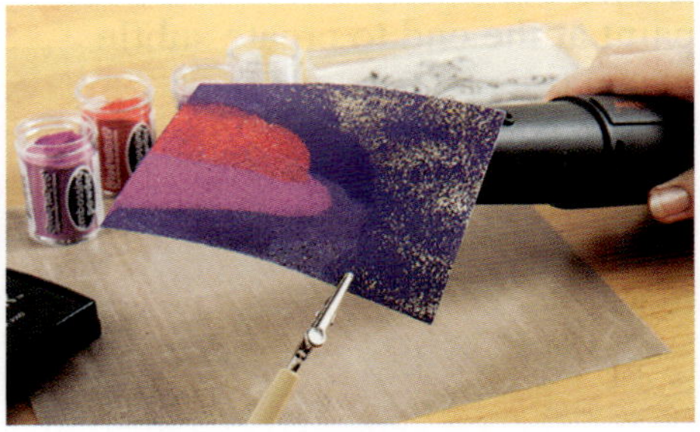

3. Heat it: Hold panel at edges or with a clip tool so as not to disturb powder until melted. Heat from underneath to retain the chunky particles.

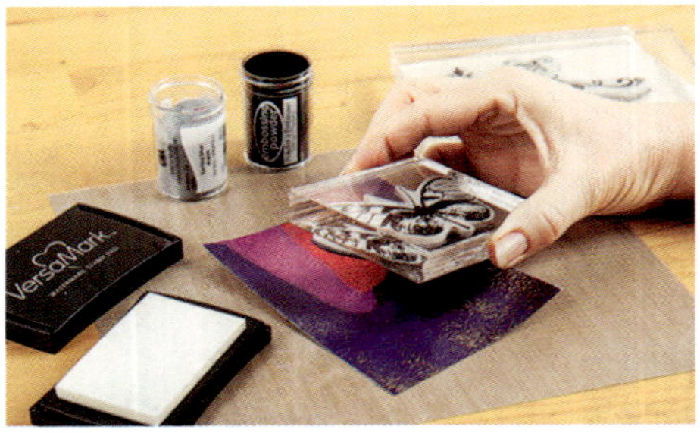

4. Stamp over it: Press with care, embossed surface is slick.

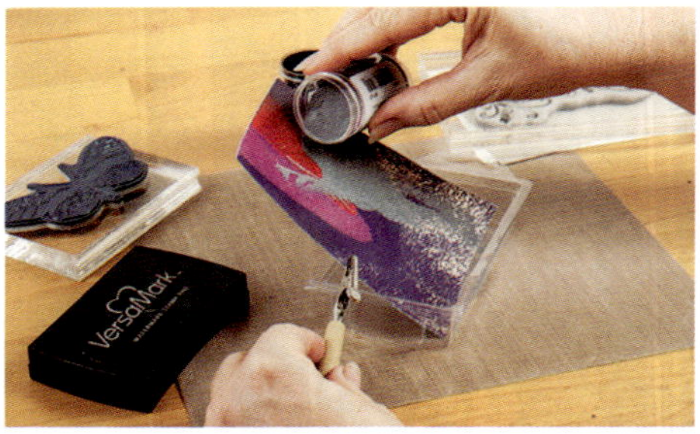

5. Dust it with a clear color or metallic powder.

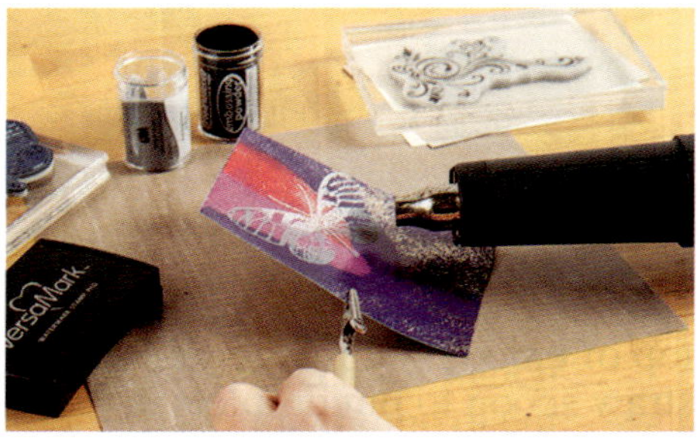

6. Heat it from the top. Add more impressions as you like.

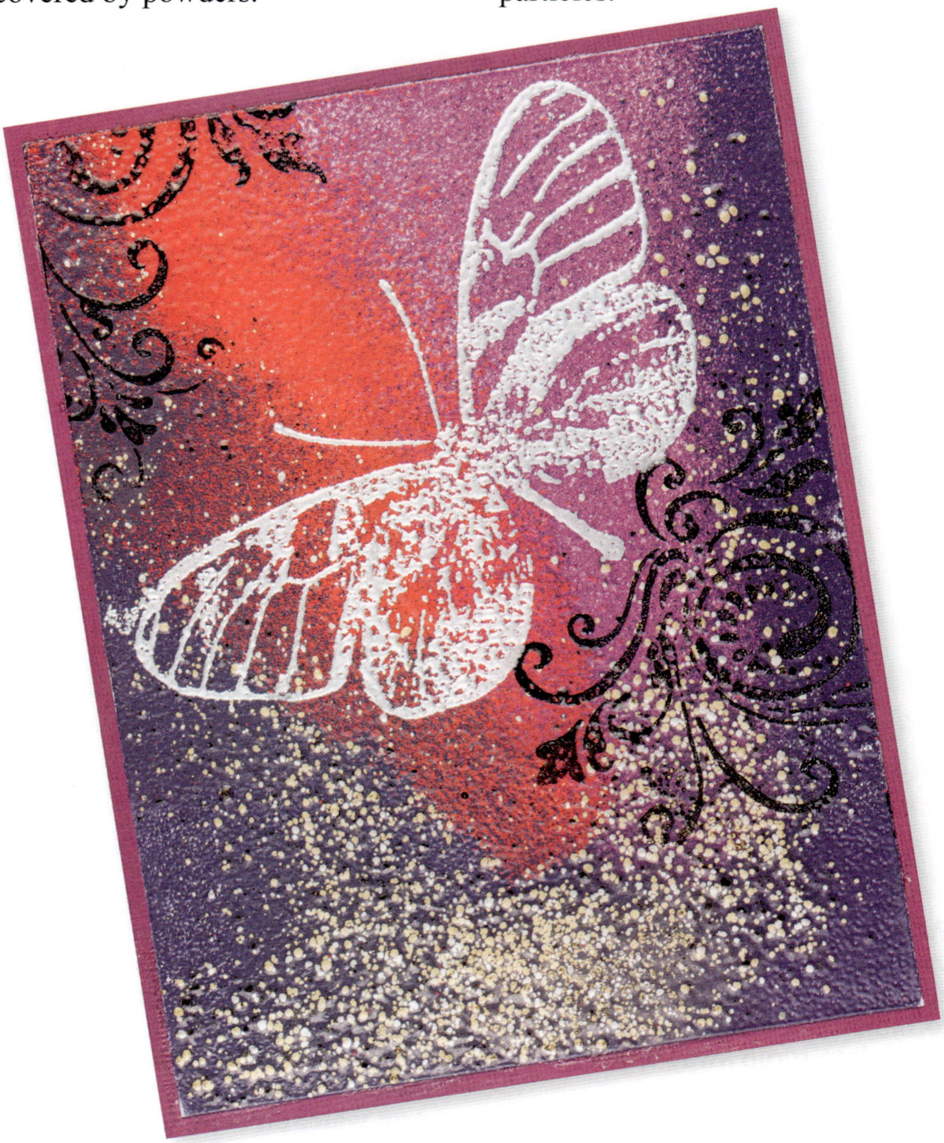

VARIATIONS: Try any combination of stamping and inking for multiple layers on cards, scrapbook pages, or mixed media journals. See more variations on the next pages.

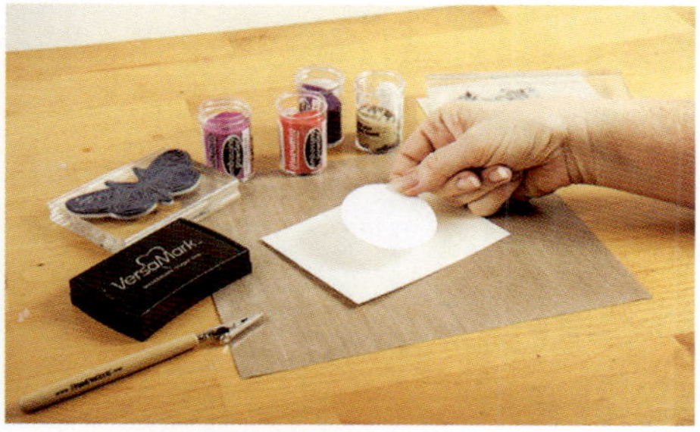

Masked shapes can be placed on card to preserve a negative space.

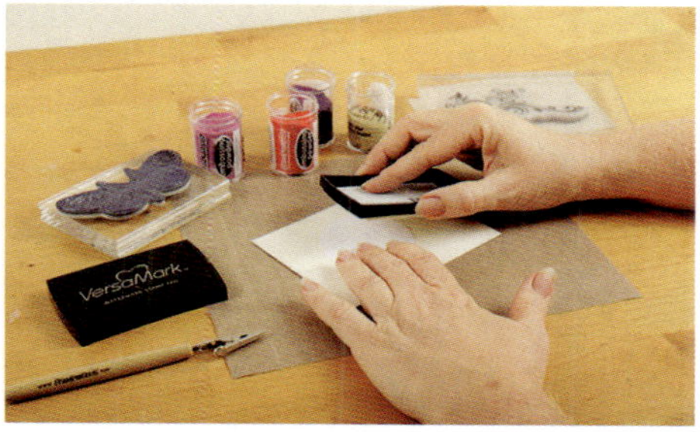

Ink background while holding mask shape in place.

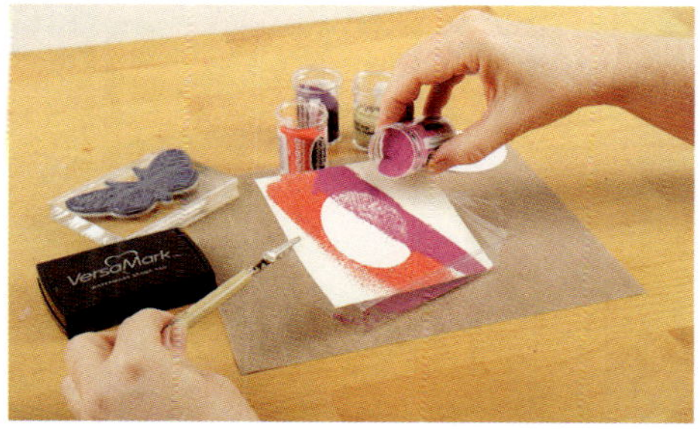

Dust sticky areas with any variety of Embossing Powders.

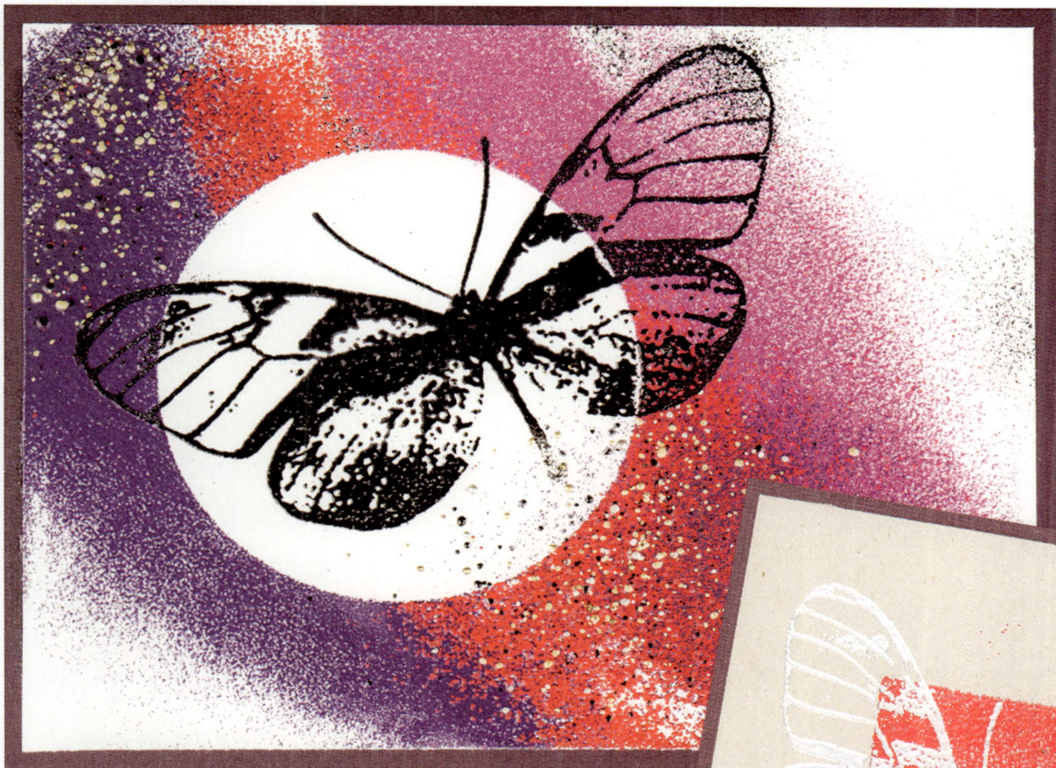

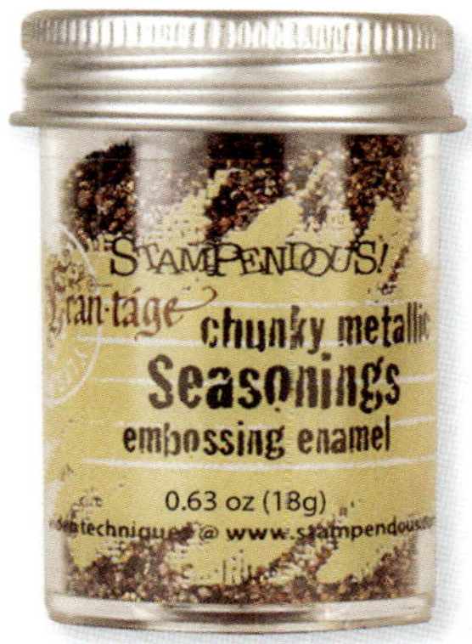

Seasonings is a mix of Chunky Metallic Powders that can be added to any color for a Frantage™ look.

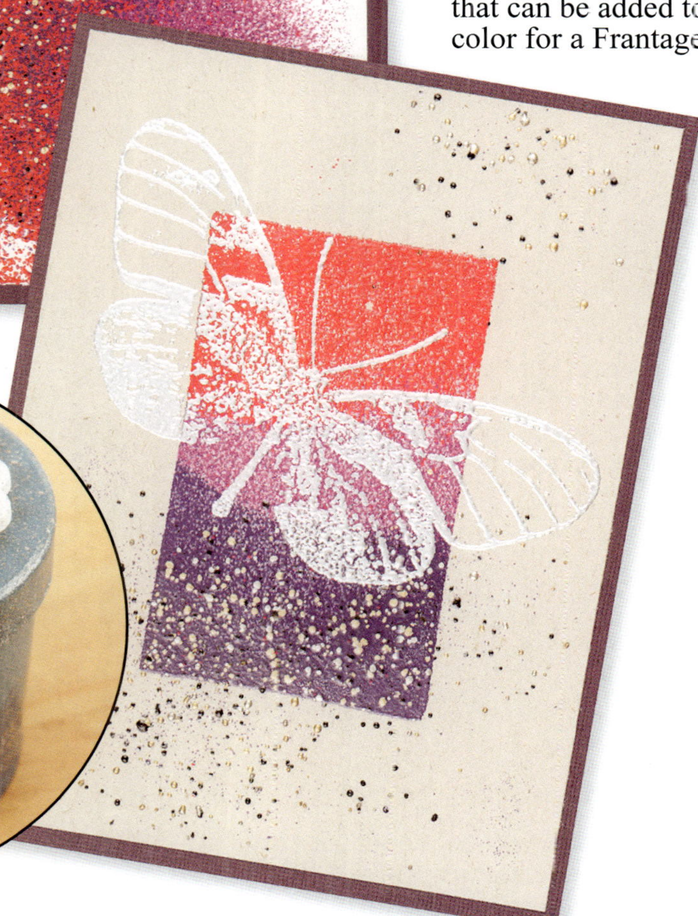

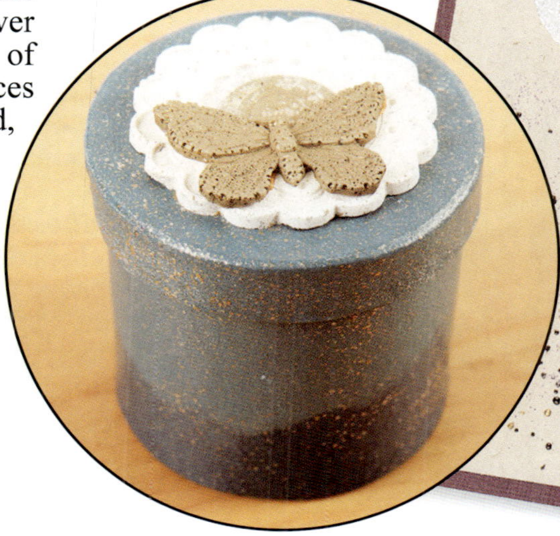

3D Tip: Use this technique to cover entire surfaces of flat or 3D surfaces such as wood, paper mache or metal. See tips for specialty surfaces on page 52.

PAINTING WITH POWDER SCENES
EMBOSSING POWDER TECHNIQUE

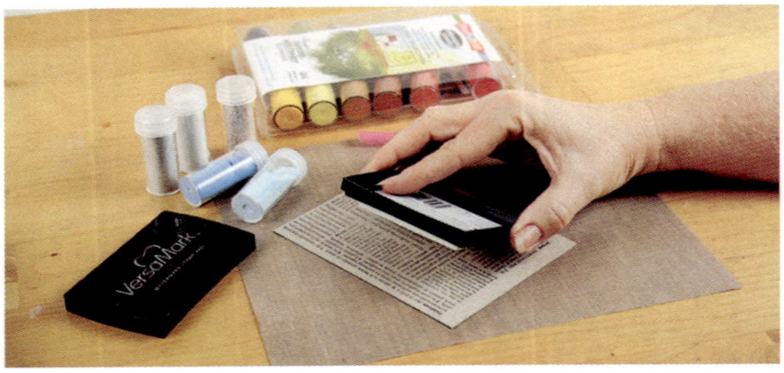

1. Stamp it: First stamp background pattern. Then make a wet impression with the entire VersaMark™ ink pad. Select Embossing Powder - have a separate container or folded scrap paper to catch excess of each color.

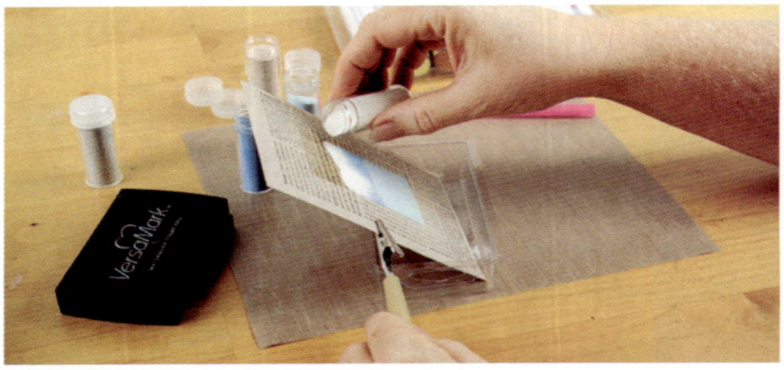

2. Dust it: Begin at the top and dust a stripe of one color after another to cover wet ink.

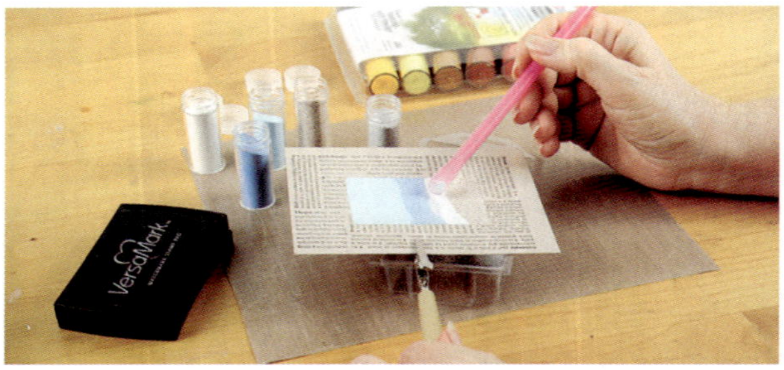

3. Add elements: Stardust Embossing Powder is a clear sparkly mix which comes in the 14 Jar Kit. Use straw scoop in kit to add Stardust on top of other opaque powders.

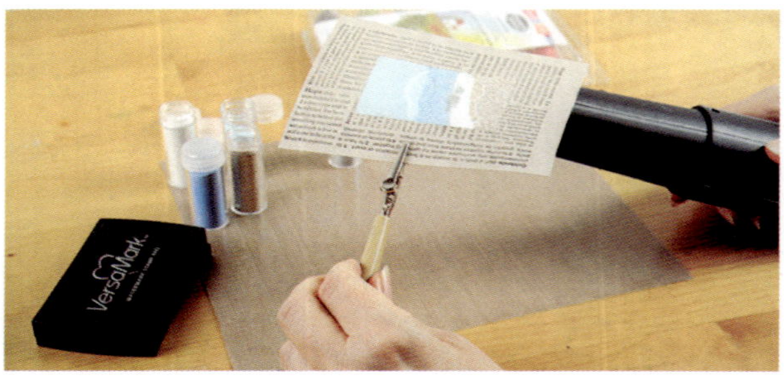

4. Heat it: Clip tool will help hold card level while heating from underneath.

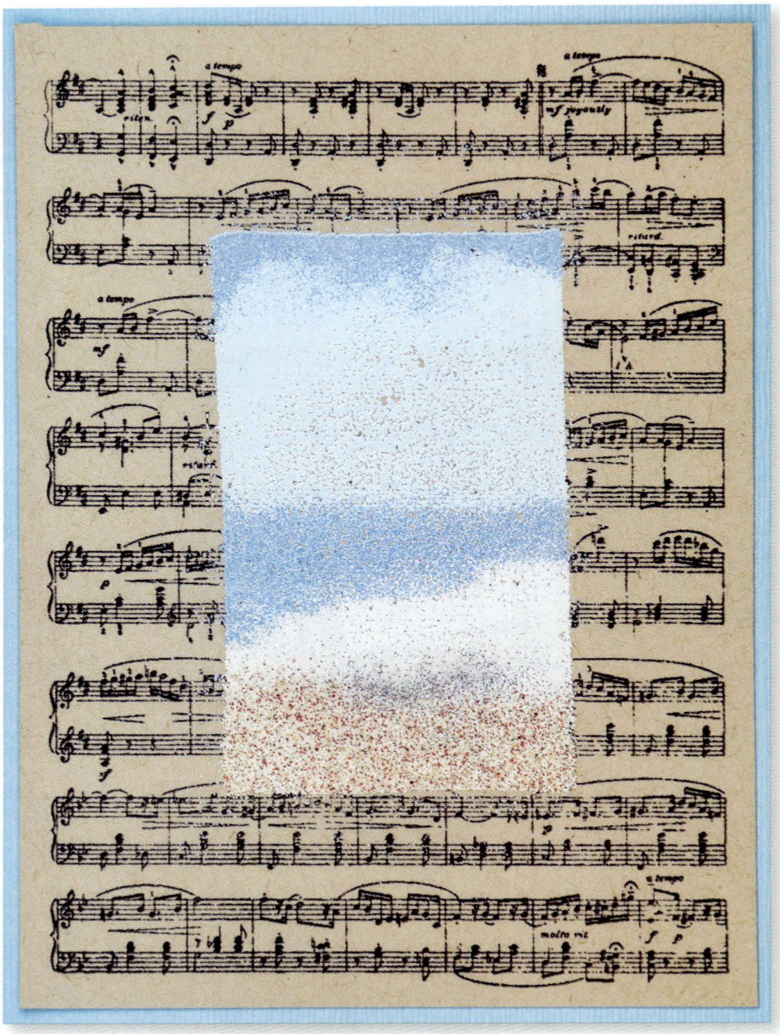

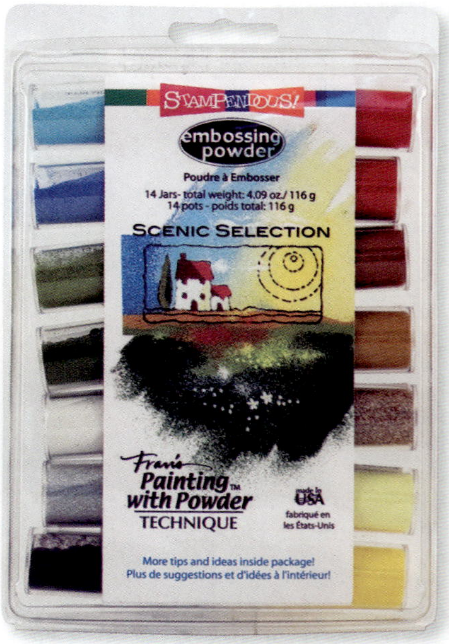

Tip: 14 Jar Embossing Powder Kit is a great value with a wide variety of colors ideal for any regional scenes. A small jar goes a long way for making many projects. Kit includes some step by step instructions and two straw style mini-scoops.

Embossing Powder Colors included in 14 Jar Kit:
Opaque Colors: Red, Chinese Red, Paprika, Honey, Lettuce, Olive, Sky Blue, Aqua, White, Lemon Yellow

Clear colors: Lemon, Bark

Mixes: Golden Sand, Stardust

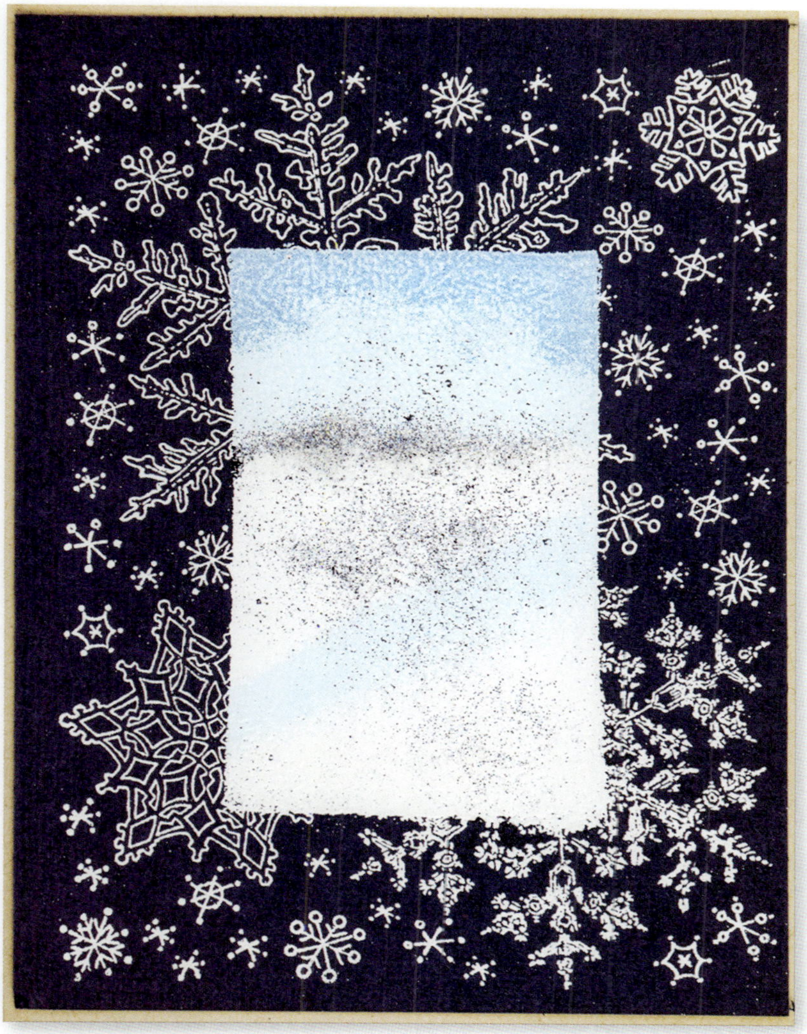

Layer Tip: Embossed patterns on the background layer will be covered by the additional layers of Embossing Powders.

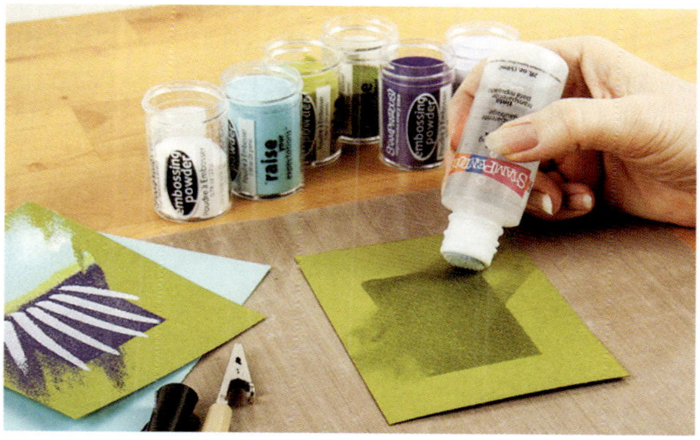

Embossing ink bottle offers a brushed edge to go beyond the ink pad. Dust with many powders and heat.

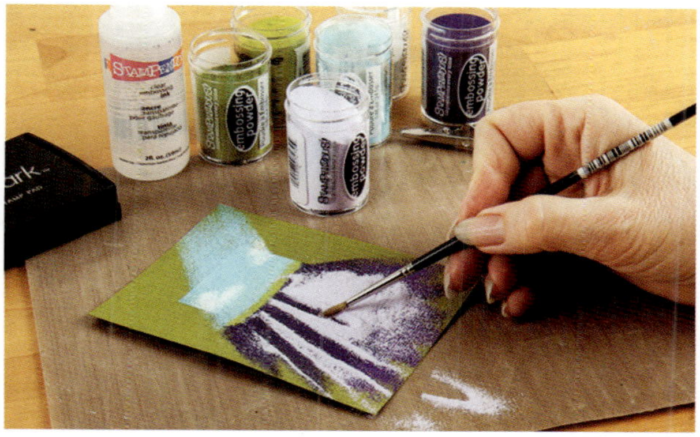

Second layer of lavender powder can be sprinkled on and partially brushed away with a small dry brush. Hold level and heat again from underneath.

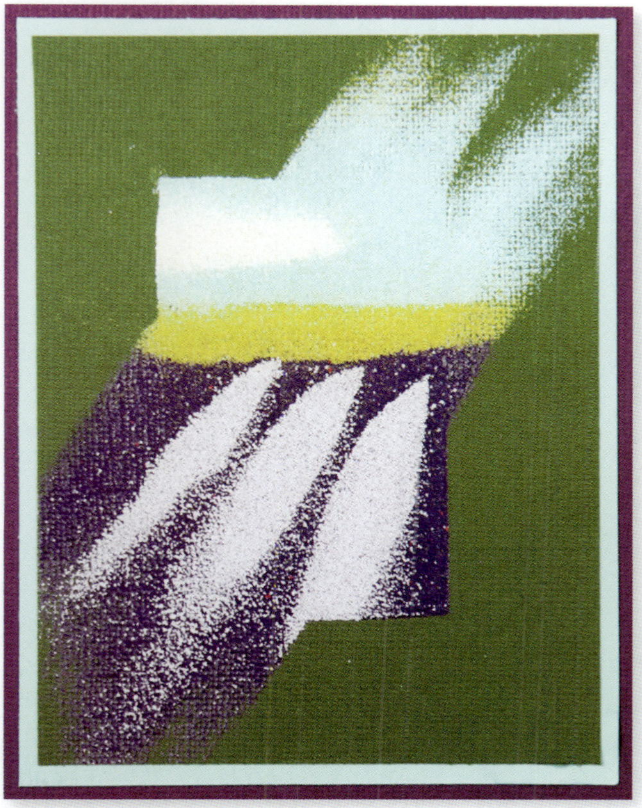

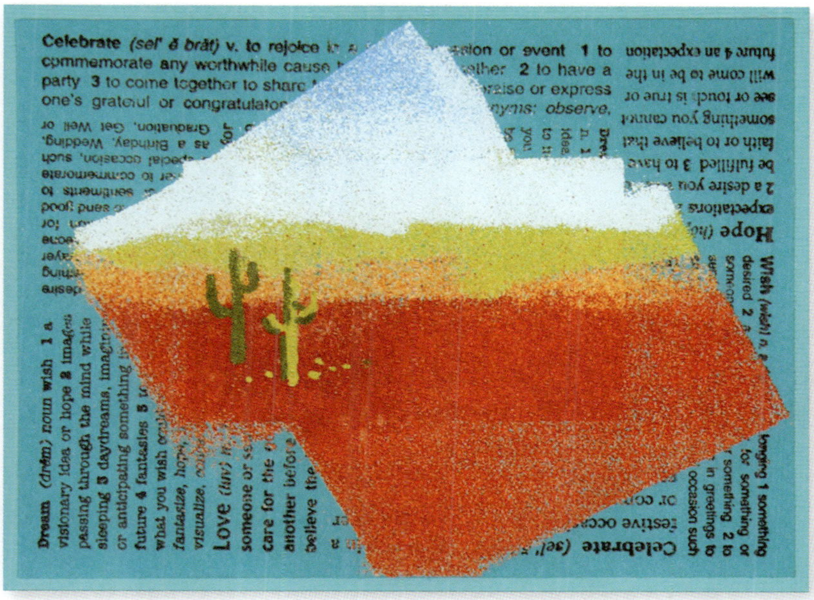

PAINTING WITH POWDER ADVANCED
EMBOSSING POWDER TECHNIQUES

Try your hand at doodling or stamping other images over your abstract color scenes. This technique can be done on many surfaces. Try it on chipboard, wood, paper mache, canvas, etc. Metal will heat quickly so hold carefully with clip tool.

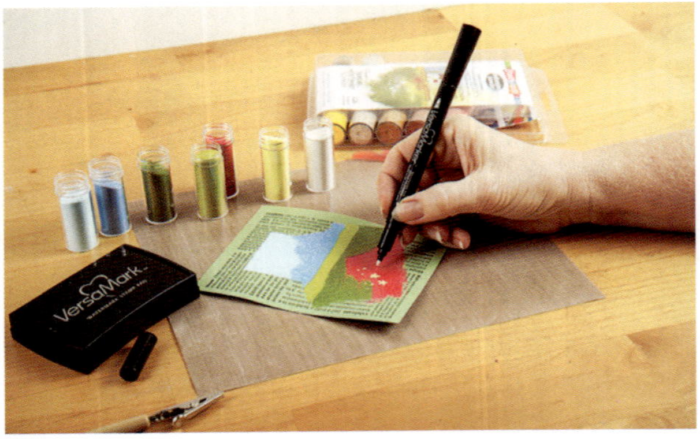

Marker Tip Flowers: After heating the background colors, use a VersaMarker™ to make 5-dot flowers to emboss in contrasting colors of Embossing Powder. Heat.

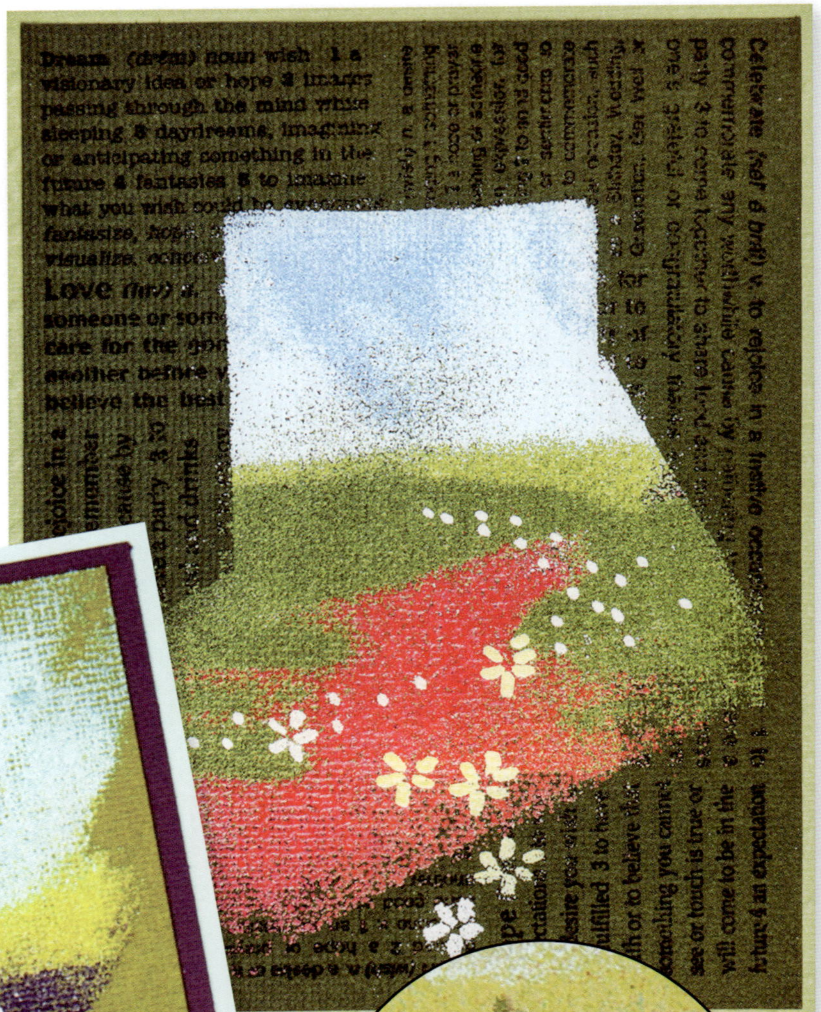

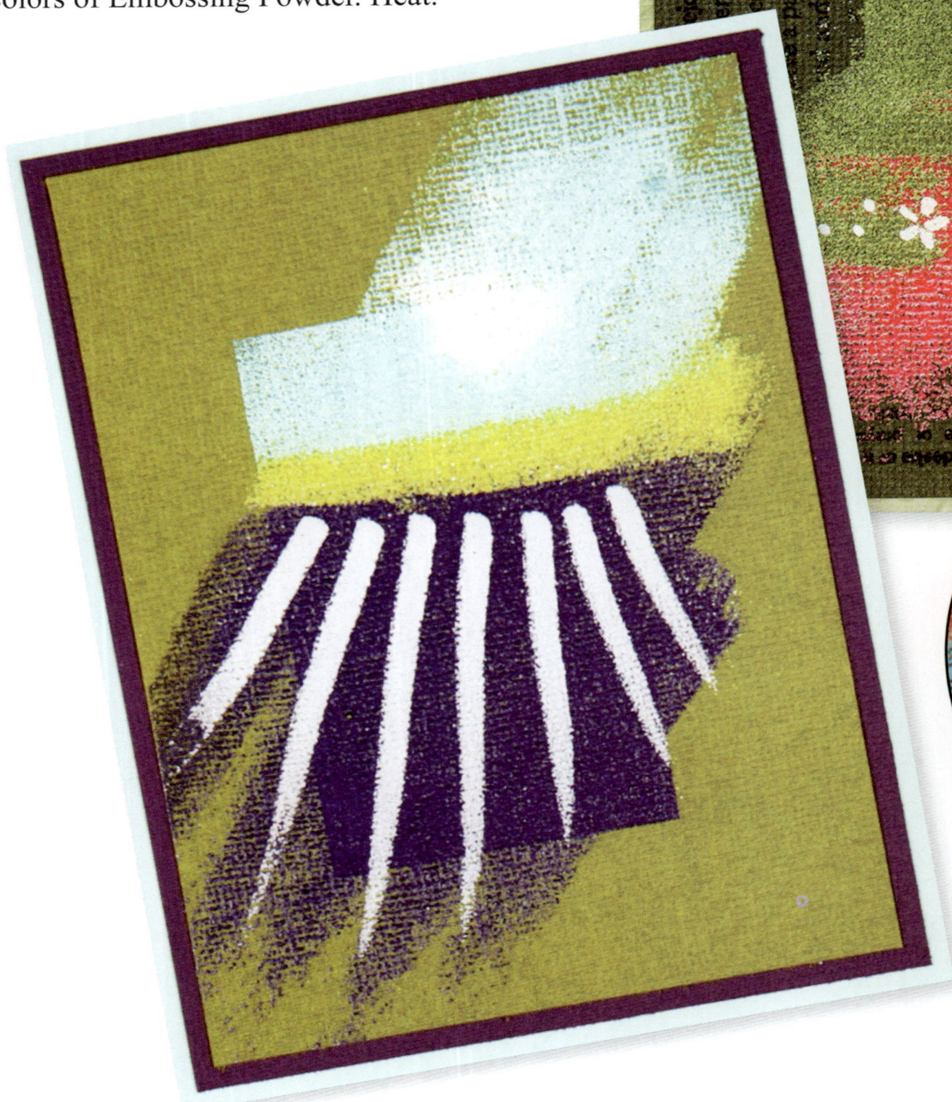

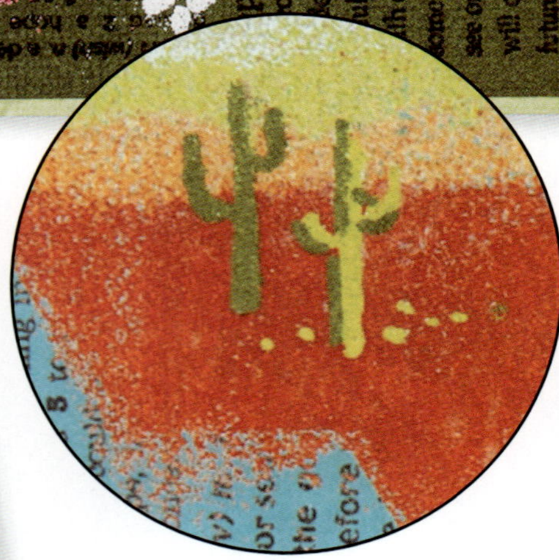

Marker details such as rows of lavender or stripes of small cacti can be added as a second layer.

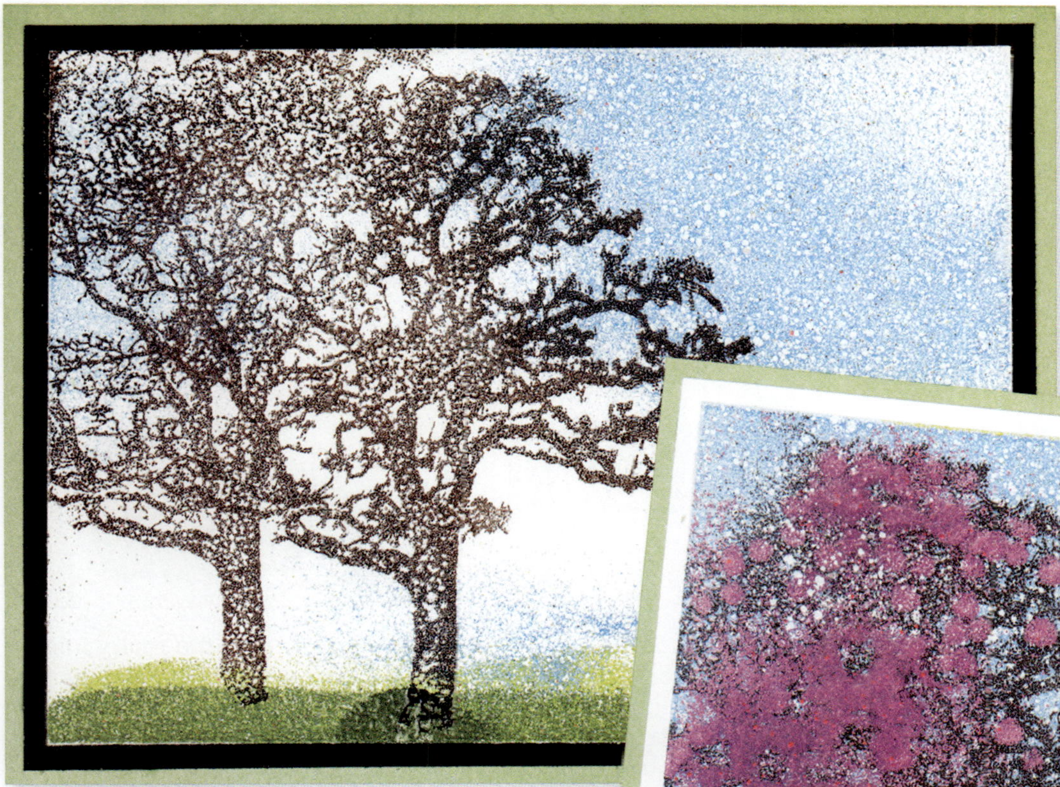

Overstamping Tip: Press stamp carefully; embossed background will be slick.

Melting Tip: Clear or metallic powders melt more readily and hold detail when stamped over opaque colors.

Sprinkling Tip: Green Embossing Powders or mixes can be sprinkled on and heated from underneath to quickly add foliage colors.

Marker Tip: Choice of Embossing Powder color and VersaMarker™ dots is all it takes for blossoms.

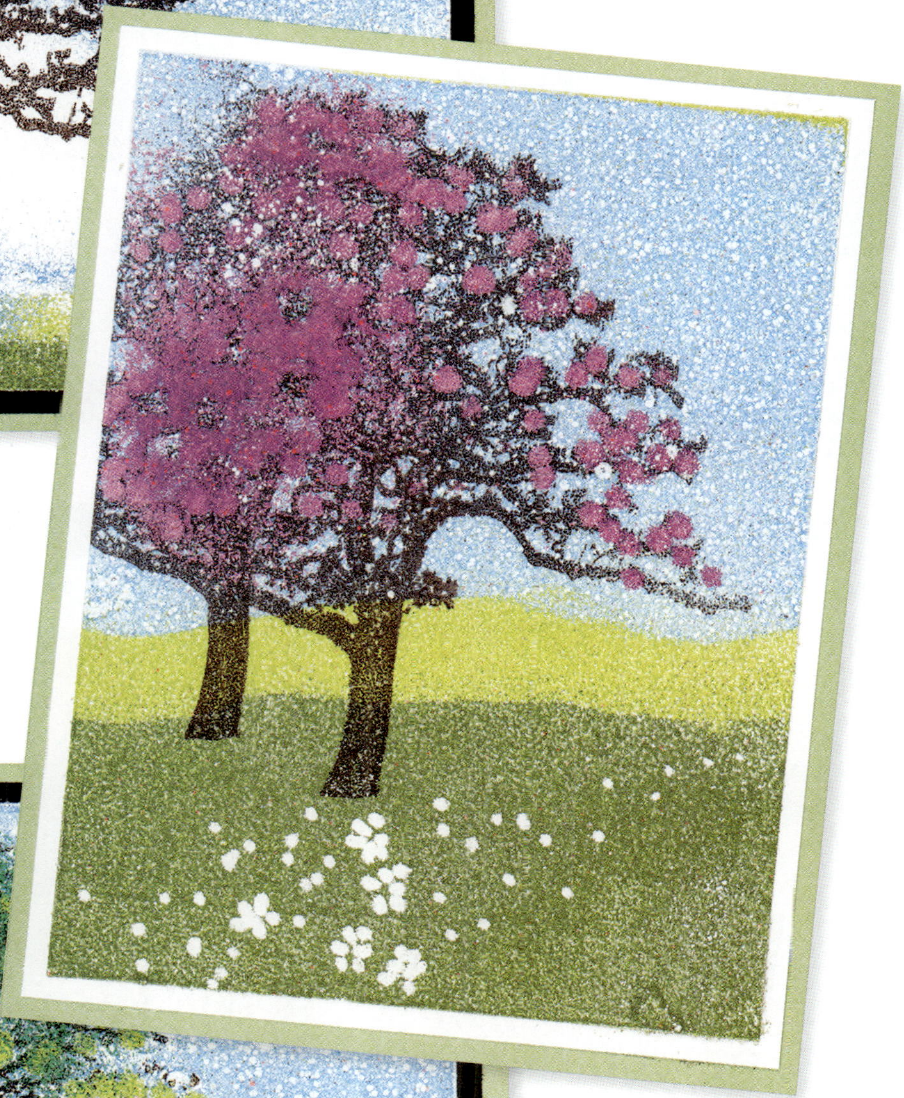

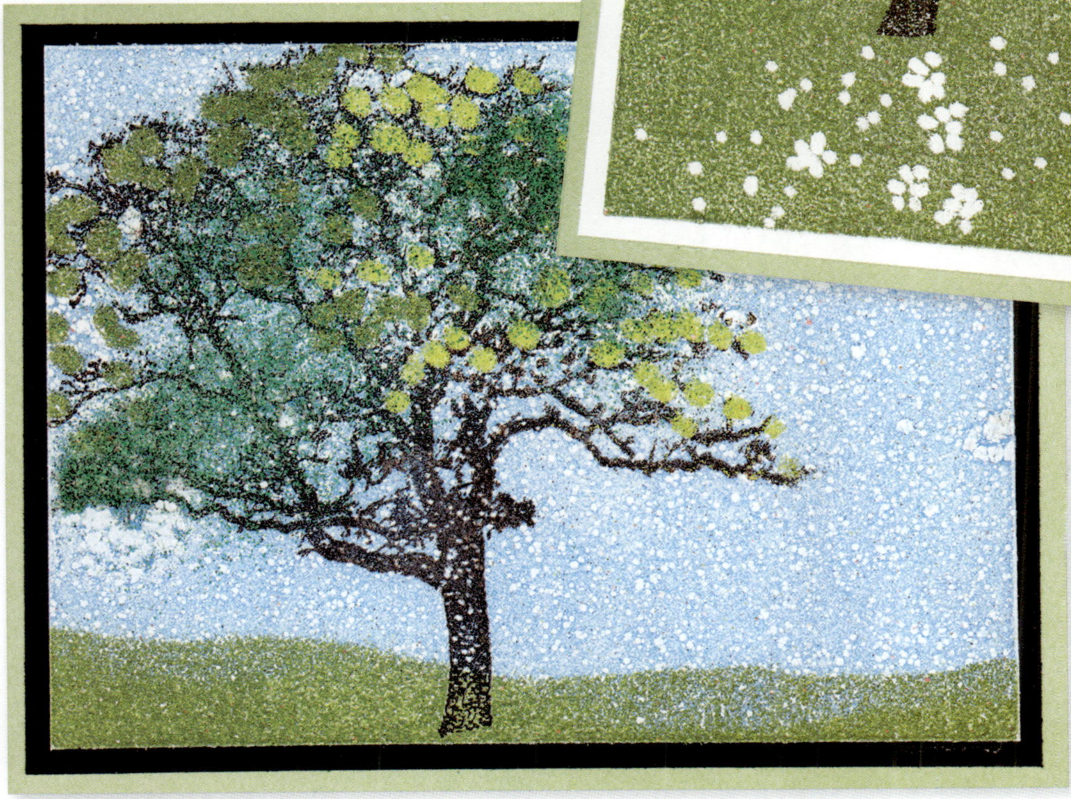

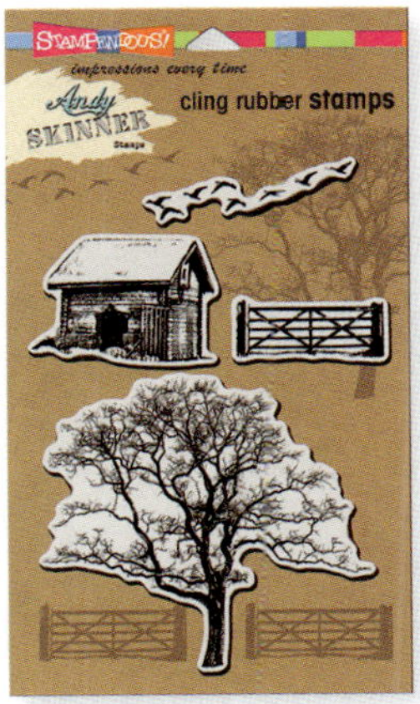

DEEP IMPRESSION CARDS
EMBOSSING POWDER TECHNIQUE

Y

This technique takes advantage of the fact that Chunky Deep Impression Enamel Powders build up a thick layer that can be stamped into while still molten for a very 3D relief pattern. You can build up many layers with regular Embossing Powder or add a top layer of regular powder over a layer of Chunky Clear.

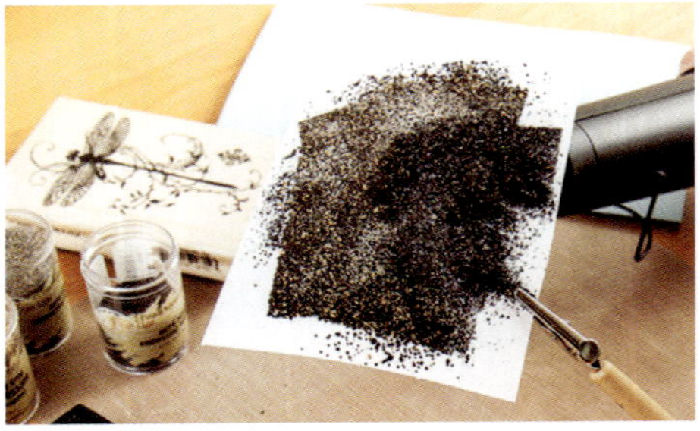

Emboss first layer: Apply VersaMark™ ink pad several times and sprinkle additional chunky powder on card. Hold it level with a clip tool and heat from underneath. Allow to cool.

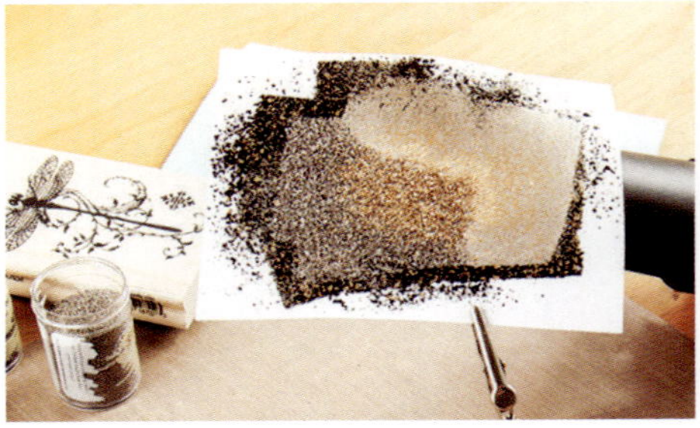

Emboss second layer: Allow surface to cool and repeat the process with another chunky powder for deeper impression. Remove clip tool and reheat flat to be ready to stamp.

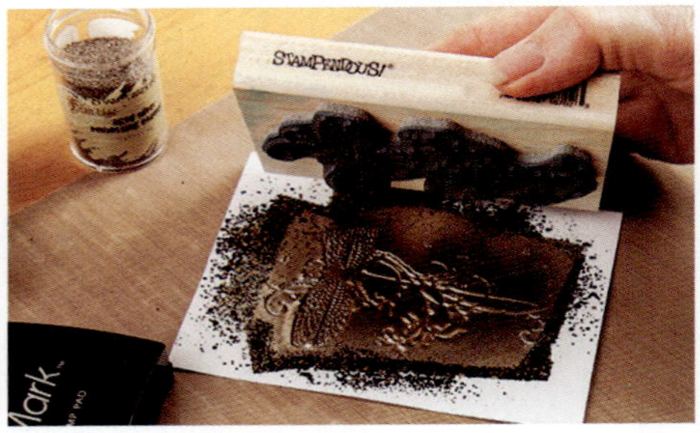

Stamp it: Have stamp ready and inked if you want a contrasting color. Ink is not required. Press stamp into molten surface. It's hot!

Warning: Pressing your ink pad into molten Embossing Powder may ruin both pad and card.

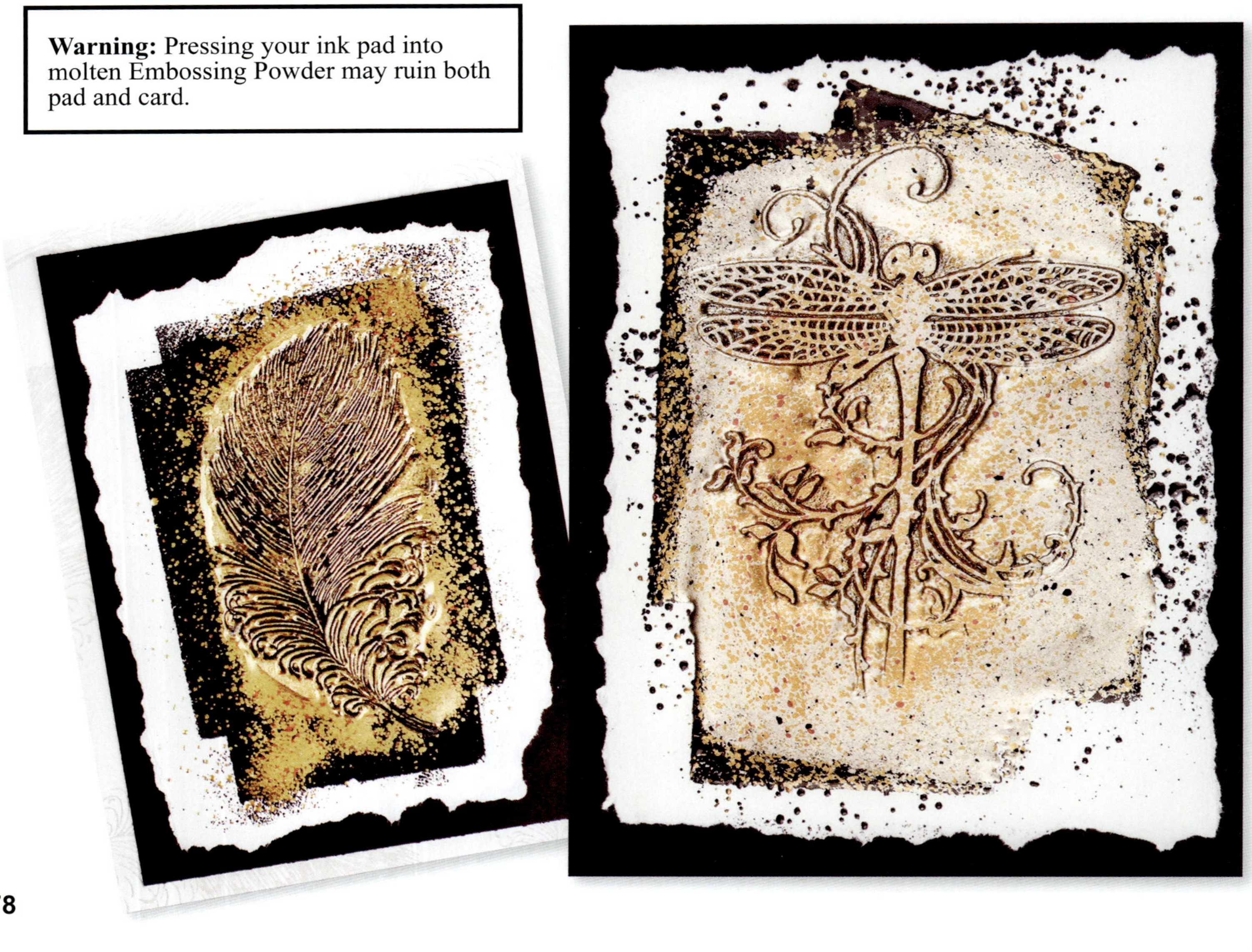

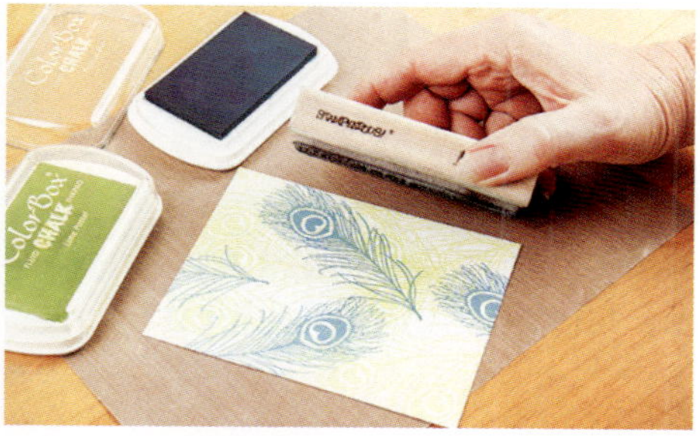

Stamp background with peacock feather in lime and turquoise.

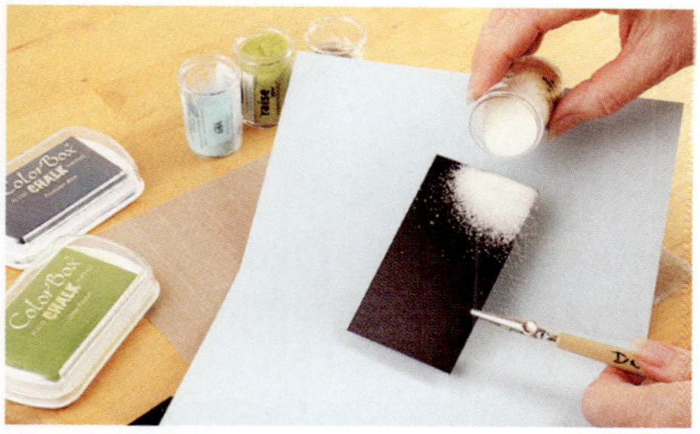

Ink and emboss first layer of Deep Impression Chunky Clear over black paper with VersaMark™ ink. Heat to melt powder.

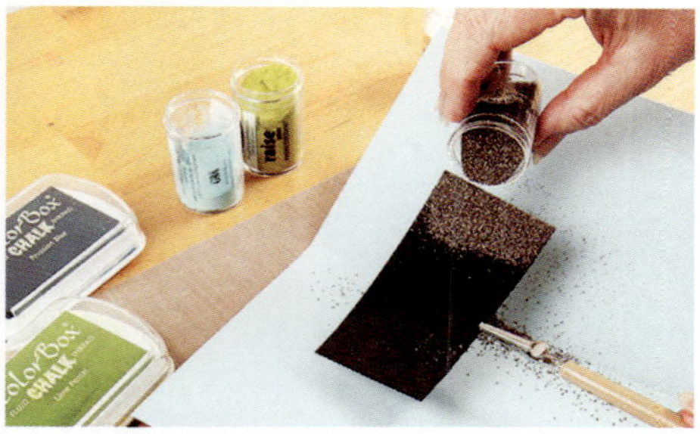

Cool and repeat with a second thick layer of Aged Silver Embossing Powder. Heat.

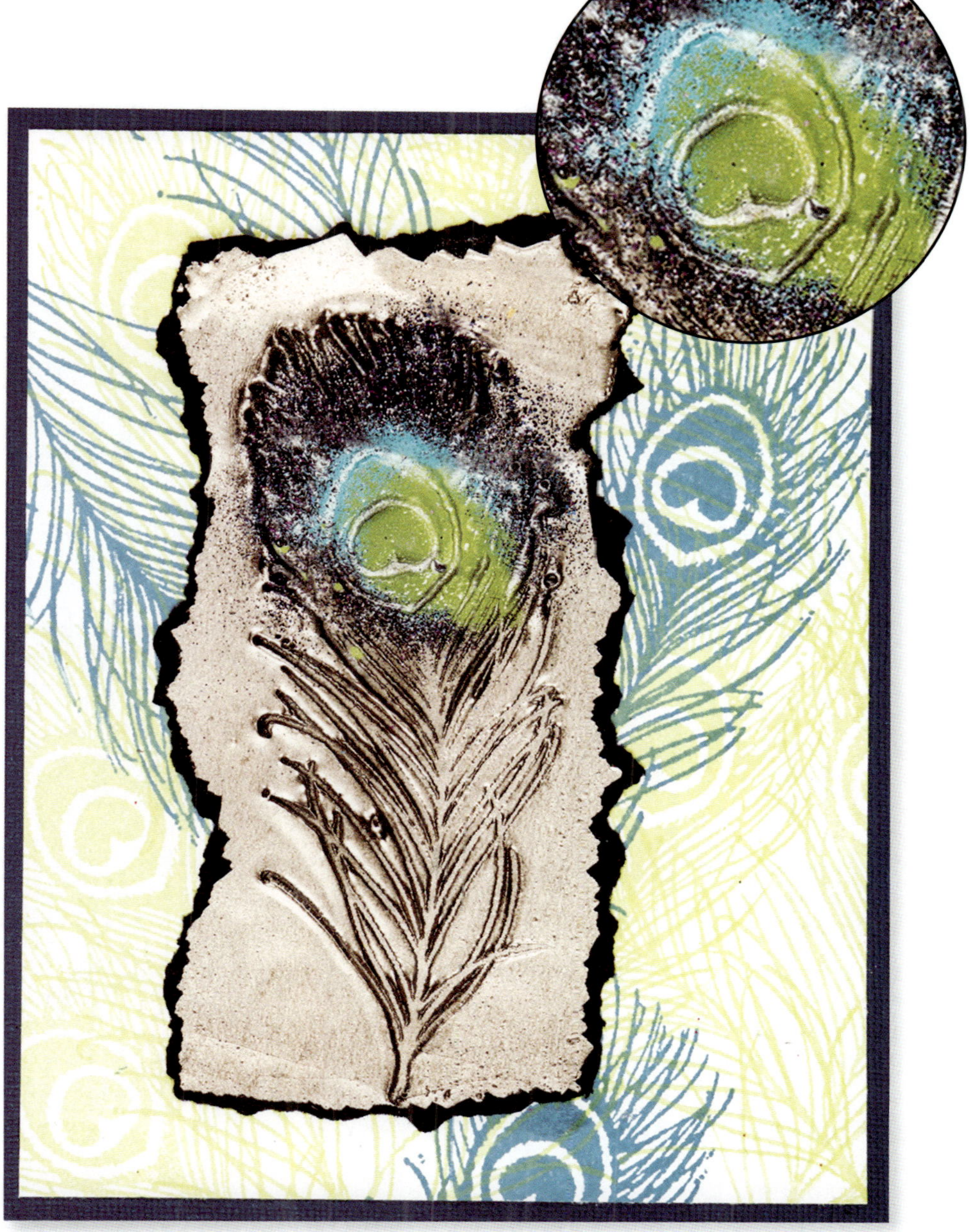

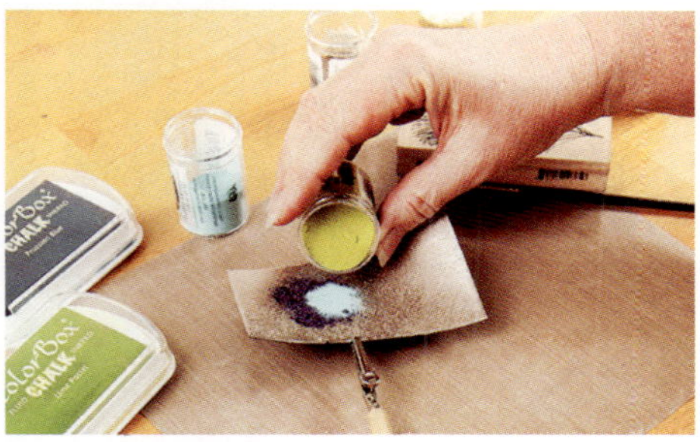

Add powders Twilight, Baby Blue, and Lettuce. Hold with clip tool and heat first from underneath.

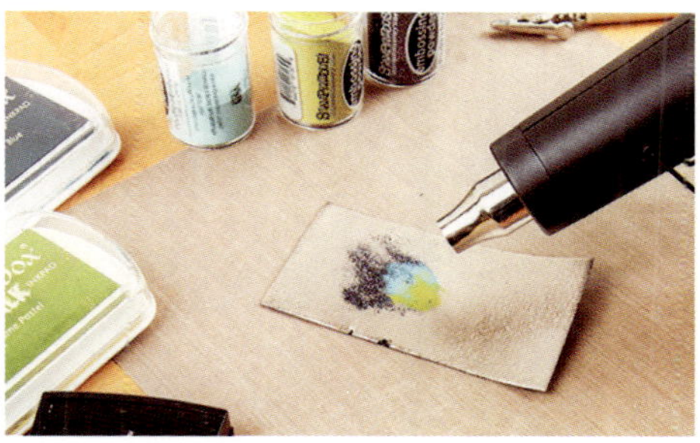

Reheat panel from top down on flat surface. Heat until powder is molten again which needs to be flowing on the surface. The larger the image the more difficult it is to get it all hot enough. A piece of metal underneath may help.

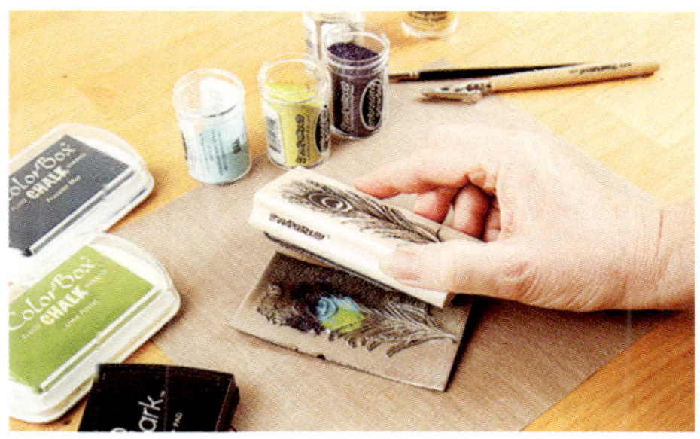

Make deep impression into molten surface. Have stamp ready with ink if you wish because it needs to be stamped immediately.

RECYCLED METAL CRAFTS
WITH EMBOSSING POWDER

Recycling aluminum cans can be fun for the colorful patterns or to cover with Embossing Powders. Try simple embossing, Encrusted Jewel Technique, Antique Embossing, or Deep Impression Techniques.

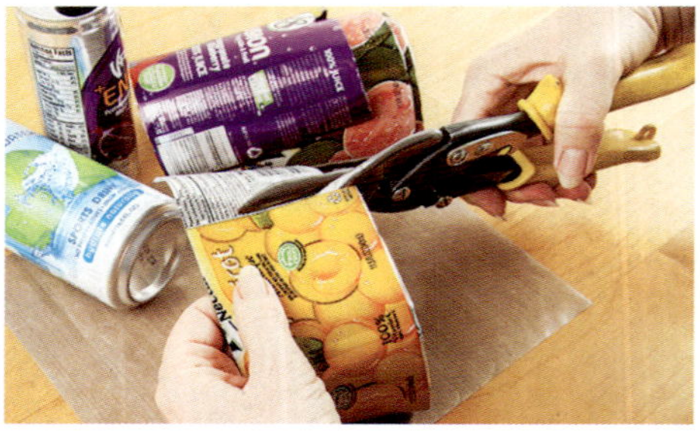

Snip aluminum cans: Cut away top and bottom pieces. Metal sheets are available in varied colors and thicknesses.

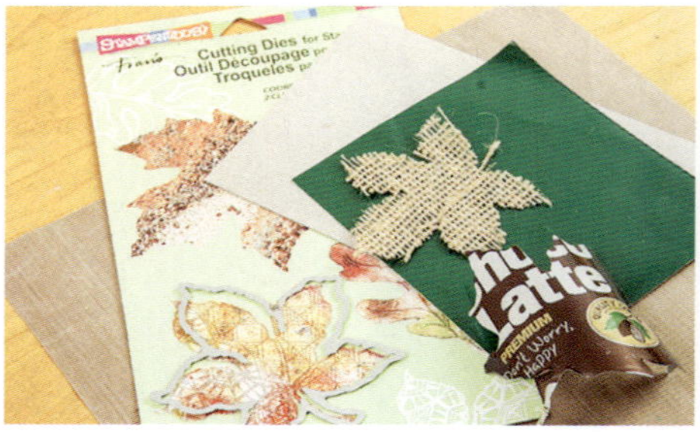

Die cut shapes: Look for wafer dies that have matching stamps.

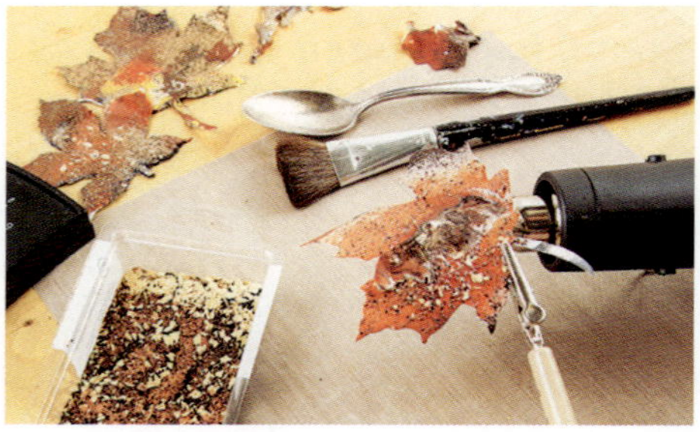

Emboss it: Spoonful of Rust Mix is ideal. Add melted puddles.

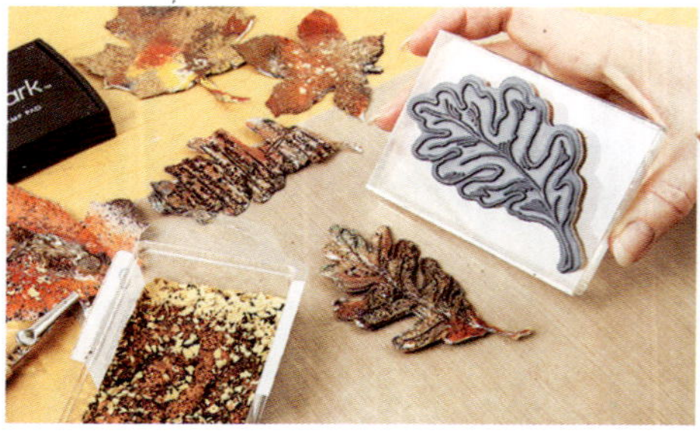

Stamp it: Have stamp ready and inked if you want a contrasting color. Ink is not required. Press stamp into molten surface.

Deep Impression stamping can be done on a griddle with heat from underneath. Puddles are easy to remelt. See more on page 84.

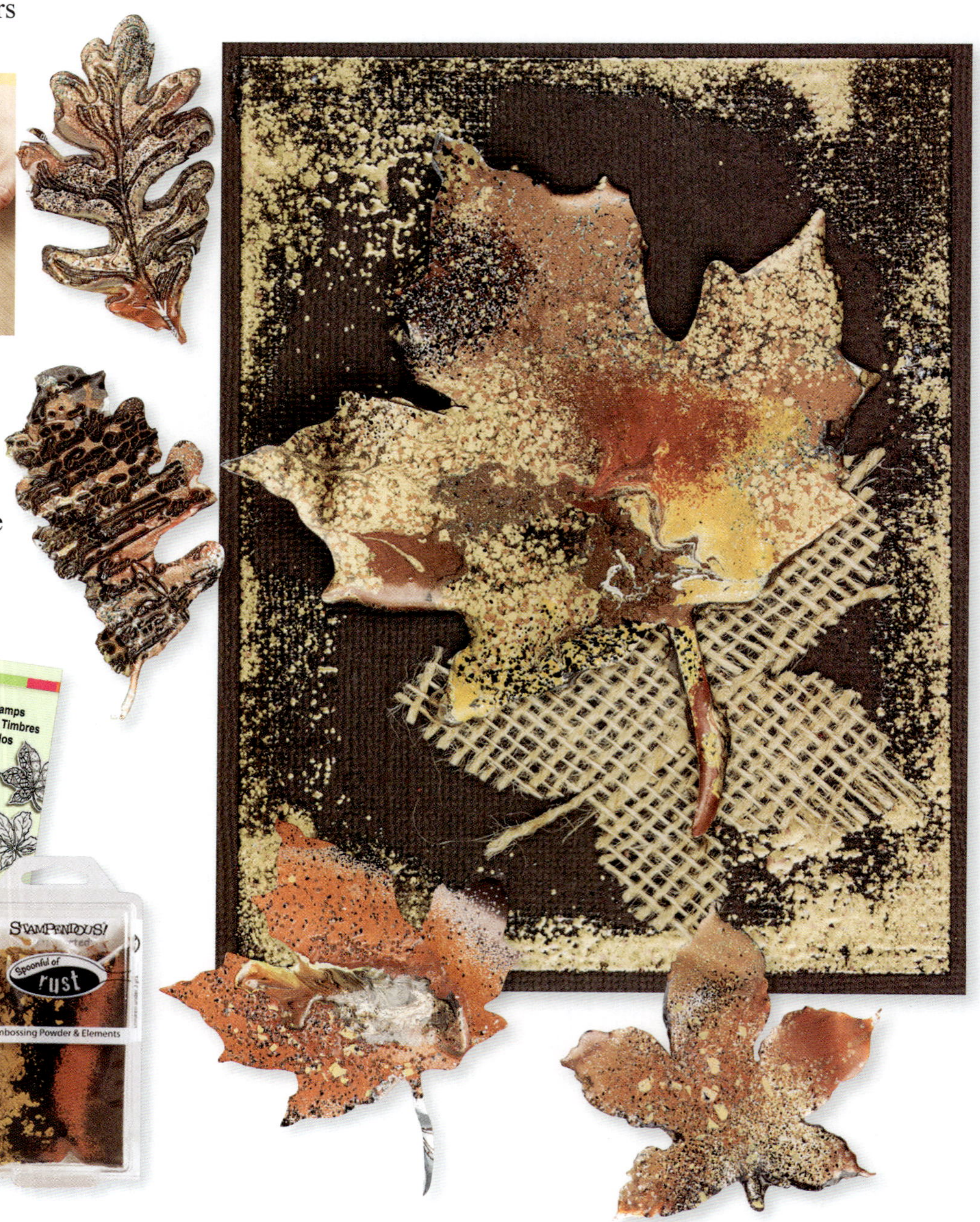

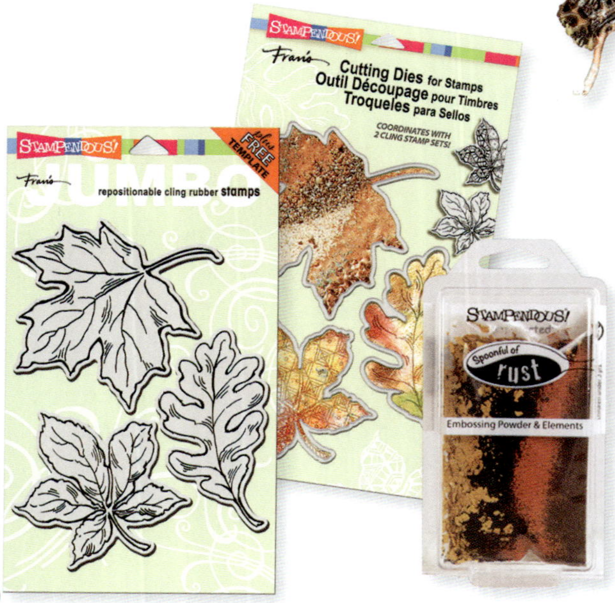

DEEP IMPRESSION TIN
EMBOSSING POWDER TECHNIQUE

This technique can be done on many surfaces including a metal tin. Select a shallow lid that can be stamped on separately from the base. Work very carefully to not burn fingers as metal conducts heat quickly and molten Embossing Powder can burn fingers as well. This technique will be quite messy, but the results are spectacular.

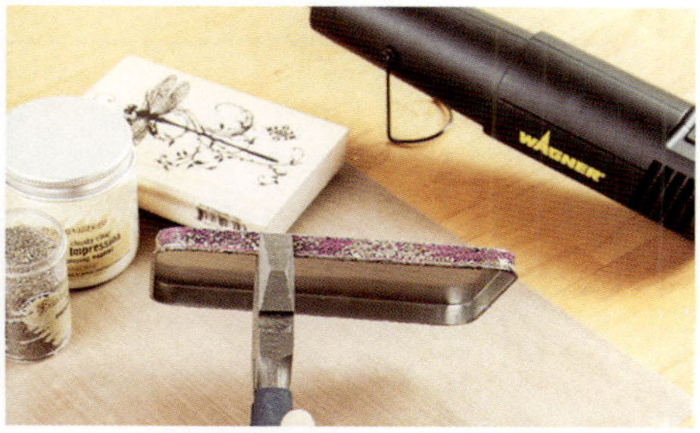

Hold it with sturdy pliers and heat first Chunky layer from underneath. Let it cool. Repeat for a second chunky layer.

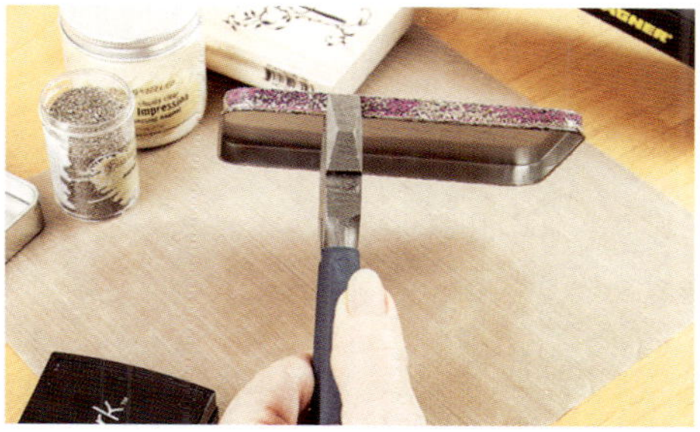

Support it: Even a shallow lid will cave in without solid support. Reheat it flat on block until molten once you have stamp ready.

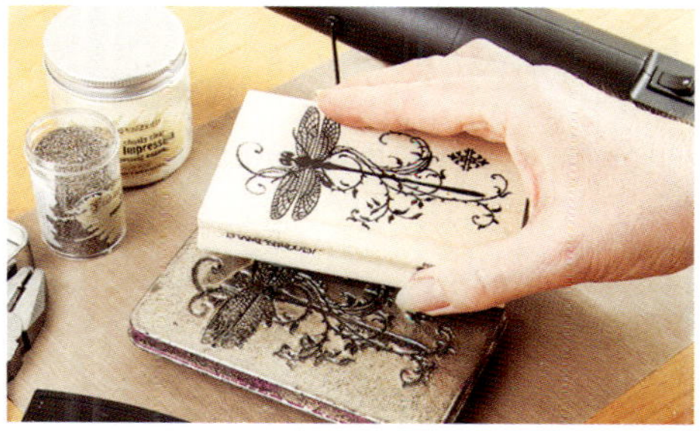

Stamp it: Pre-ink stamp with pigment and have it ready. The trick is to keep the powder molten, and be ready to stamp immediately.

Look for the Stampendous YouTube video titled Deep Impression Embossed Tins.

Step by step: Ink lid and dust with Chunky Powder. Hold with pliers and heat from underneath. Let cool. Repeat for a second thick layer. If you want a contrasting impression, use pigment ink and have inked stamp ready. Position tin on a block and reheat top down until surface is molten again, almost flowing. Stamp quickly. Allow stamp to cool before releasing.

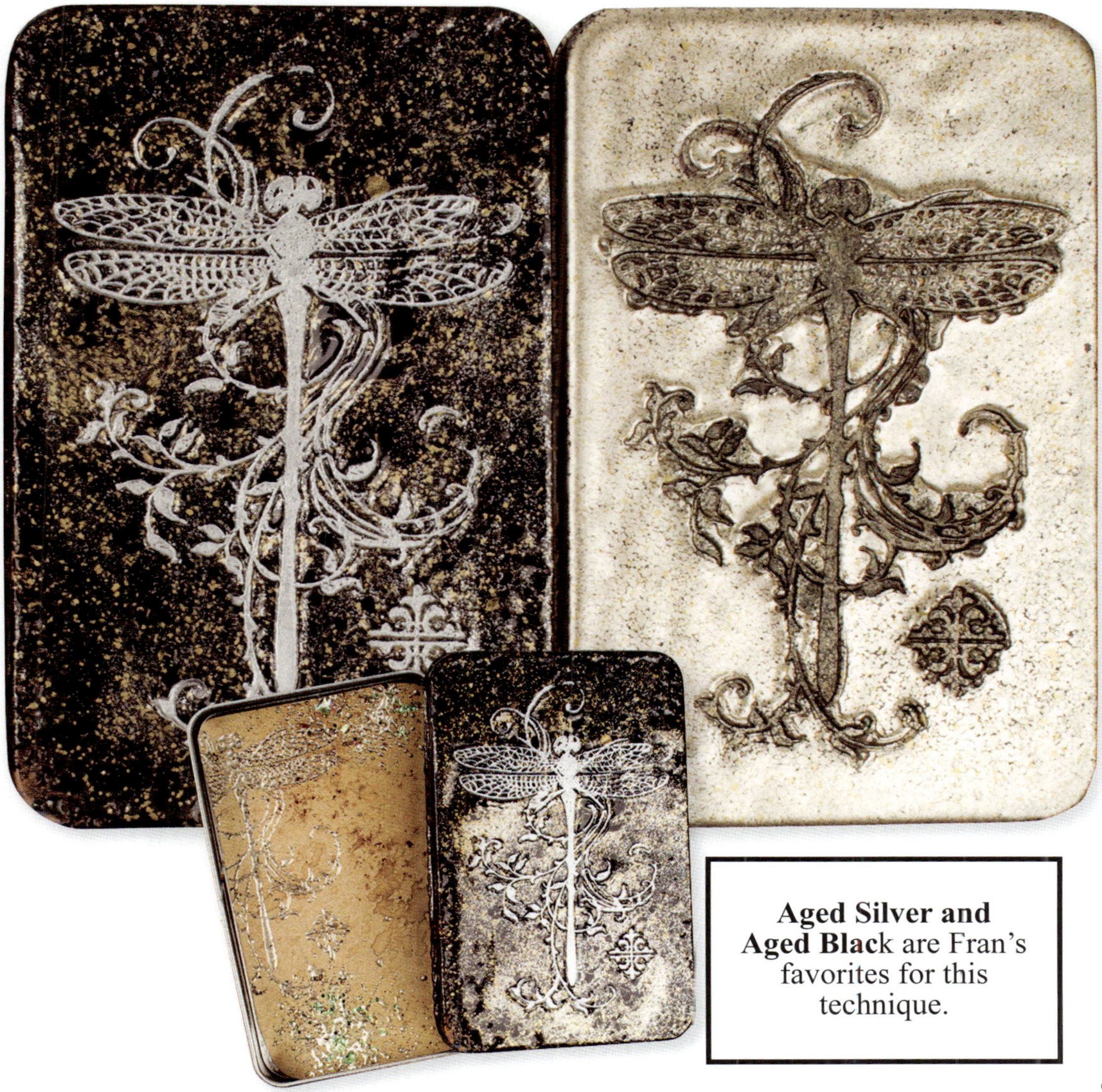

Aged Silver and Aged Black are Fran's favorites for this technique.

DEEP IMPRESSION BASICS WITH GRIDDLE
EMBOSSING POWDER TECHNIQUE

The Deep Impression Technique works best with a flat heat source underneath. The key to the pancake griddle is that heat is constant and always underneath so you can work hands-free. NO more ink pads or waiting for it to cool for next application. It melts quickly. If you follow these directions you can work safely and create spectacular, miniature works of art.

Butterflies: Look for stamps with matching wafer dies that will cut thinner chipboard layers.

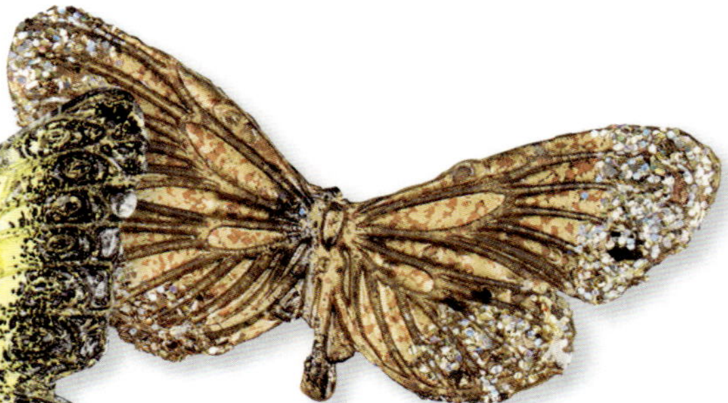

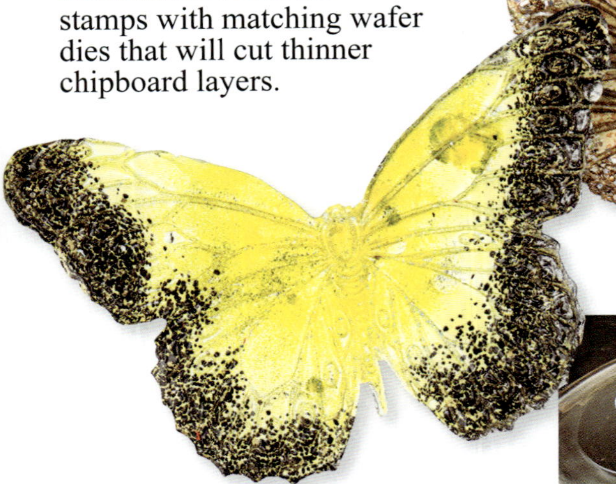

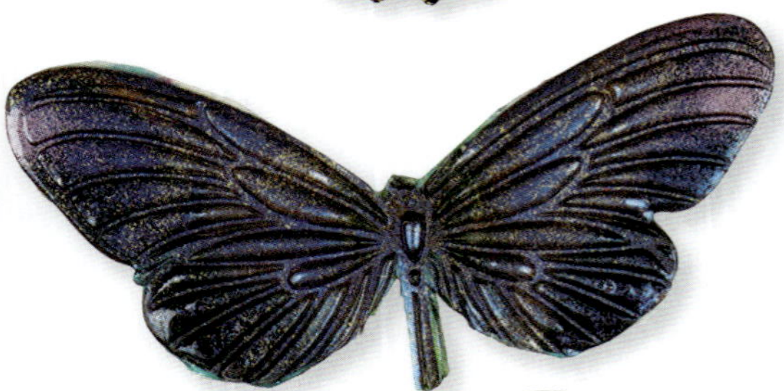

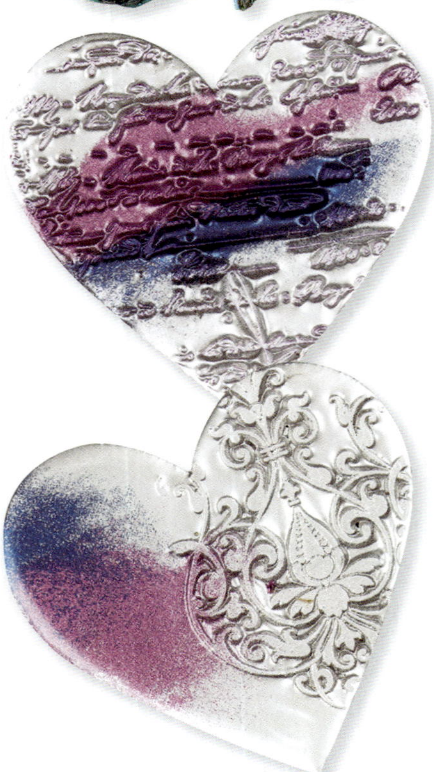

Warning: Do not touch molten Embossing Powder. It will burn your fingers.

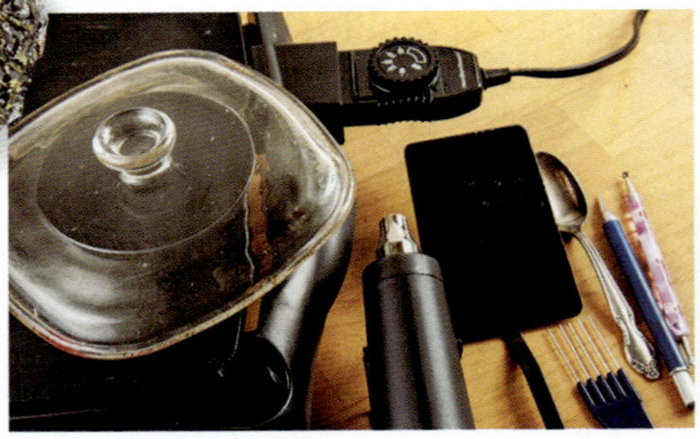

Heat source: Needs to be a flat, smooth surface preferably with a heat control. This could be an old pancake griddle or an electric skillet. A clear glass lid helps.

Tools: flat metal spatula, heat tool, craft knife, stencil tools as "extra hands", metal spoon to scoop, and a hair pick with no plastic tips to swirl patterns. Teflon type craft sheet that can take the heat and clean up easily. Use one to protect work table. Cut another one into manageable size squares to place on and off skillet.

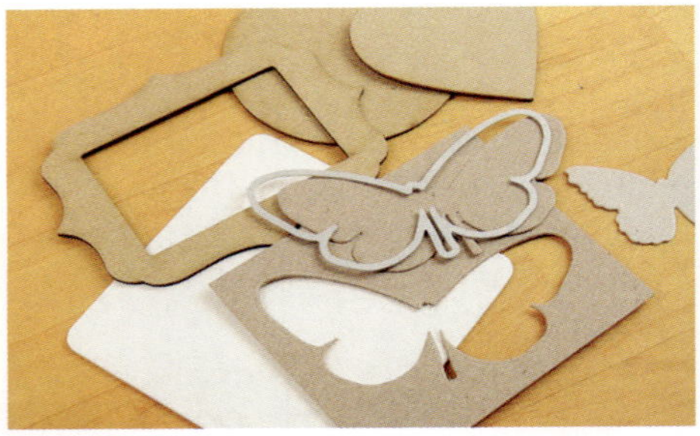

Surfaces: Heavier weight chipboard shapes are ideal. Wafer dies will cut thinner chipboard.

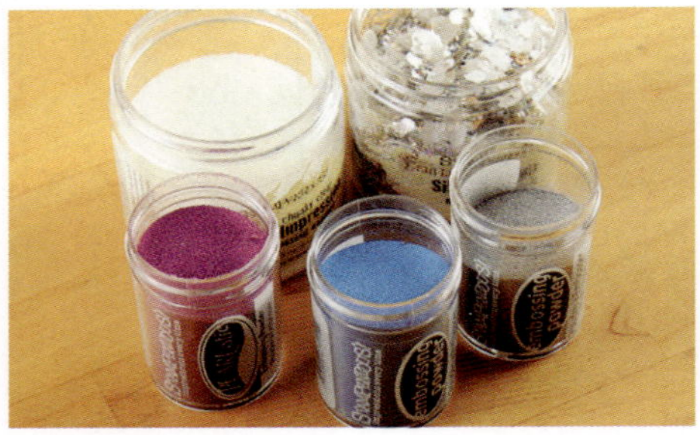

Embossing Powders plus: Any types of powder can be used. With a first layer of Chunky Clear, even Detail Powders will melt beautifully on the surface. Besides powders, you can add elements like Lux Mixes, Mica, etc.

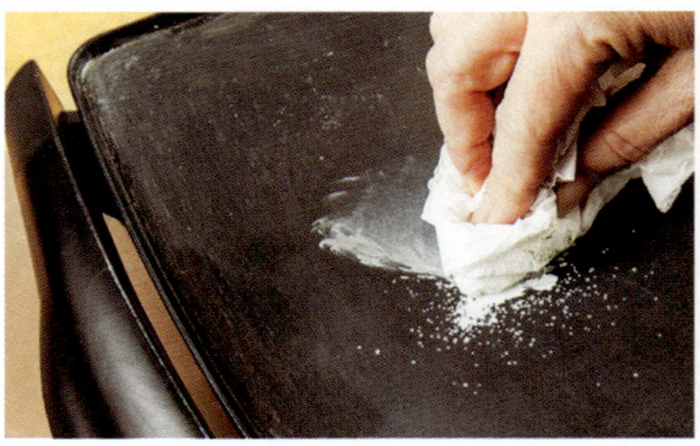

Clean up: Use paper towels on hot griddle to wipe up any spills that will cause craft sheet to stick.

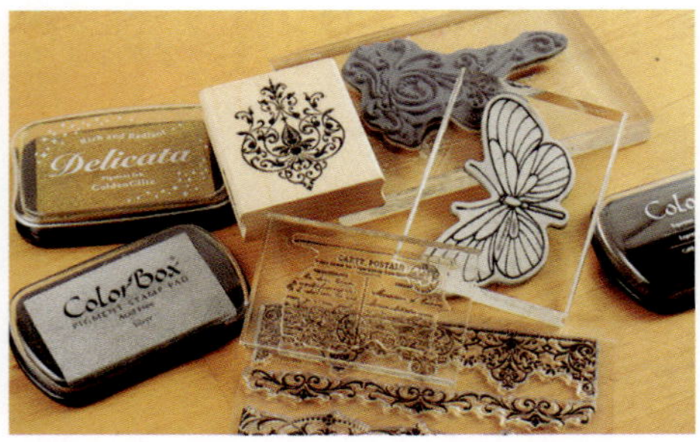

Stamps and inks include wood mounted and cling rubber stamps as well as clear stamps.

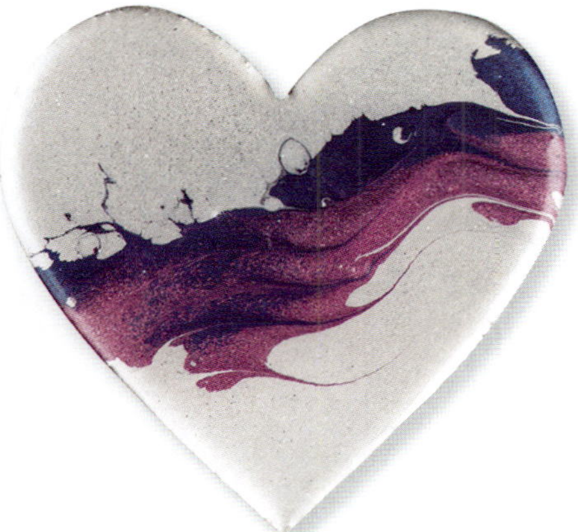

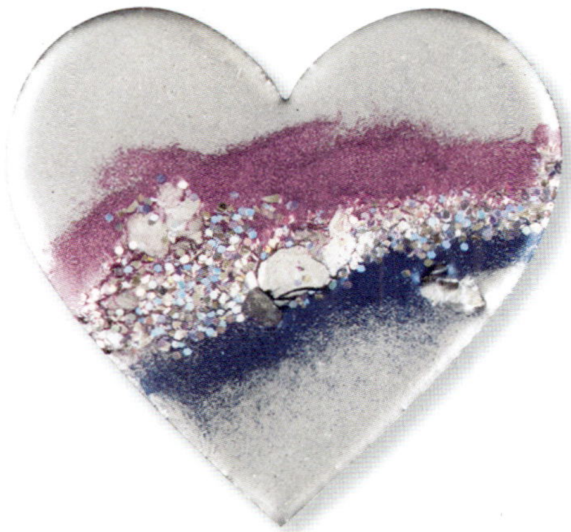

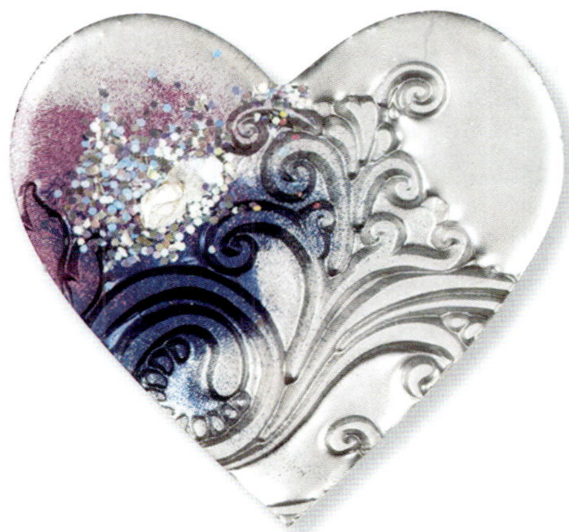

STEP-BY-STEP INSTRUCTIONS

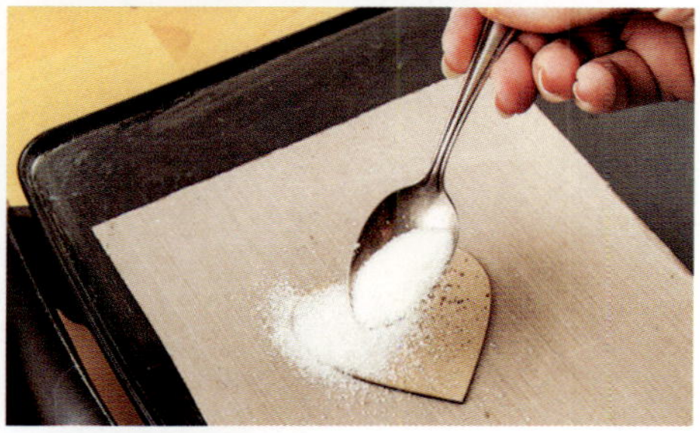

1. Heat it up: Set heat to about 300 degrees. Once melting begins, if it bubbles, lower heat. Some appliances shut off periodically and you may need to turn it back up.

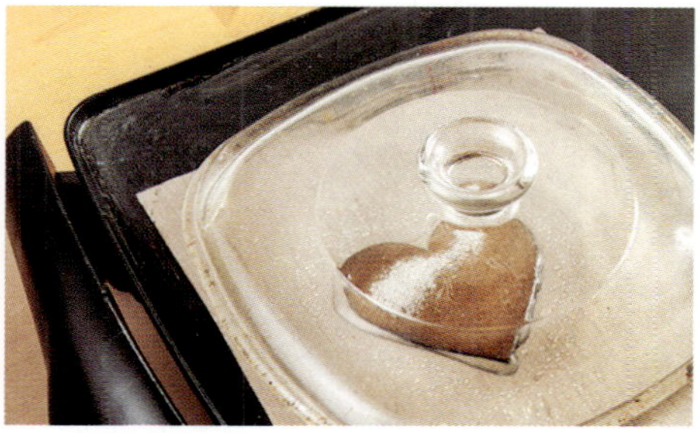

2. Layer it up: Place craft square down first so you are not making a sticky mess of the heating surface. Add chipboard tile. Spoon on a layer of Chunky Clear and put a lid on it until it melts.

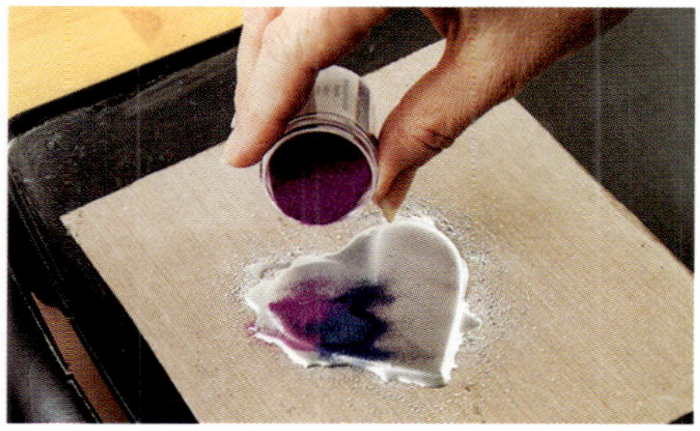

3. Add powders or any other type of color. These will melt quickly on the surface. Once it starts melting you can use heat tool from the top as well.

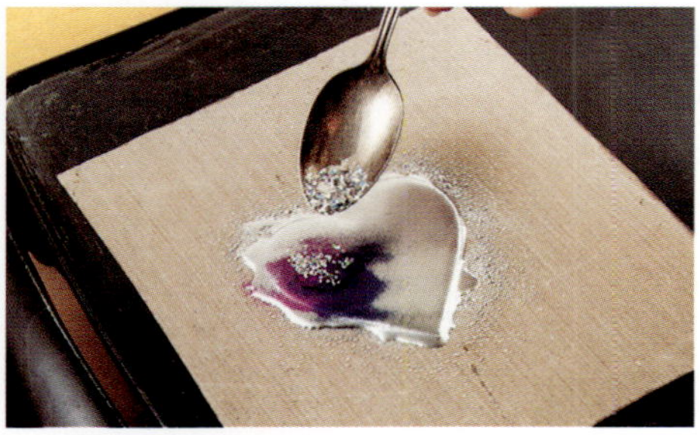

4. Add elements such as Lux Mix and puddle left overs from other projects. Swirl molten powders with hair pick or other tools.

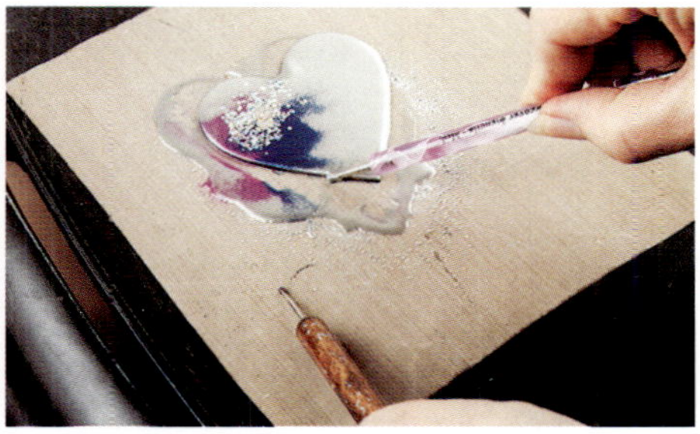

5. Clear edges: Use 2 tools to slide tile out of puddles to clean edges just before removing from heat.

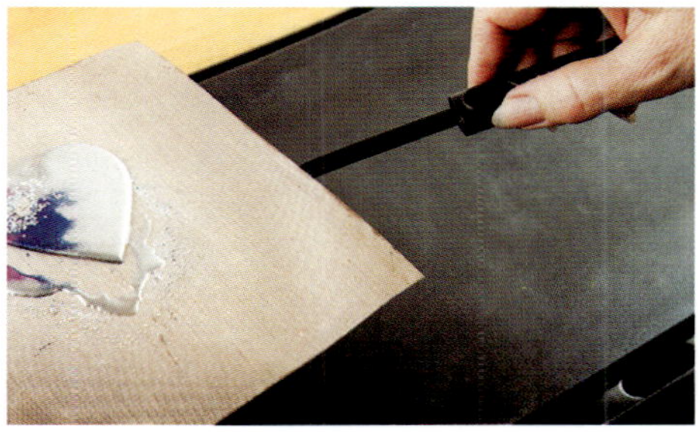

6. Remove from heat by using spatula under the craft sheet keeping tile level. Place flat on table protected by craft sheet.

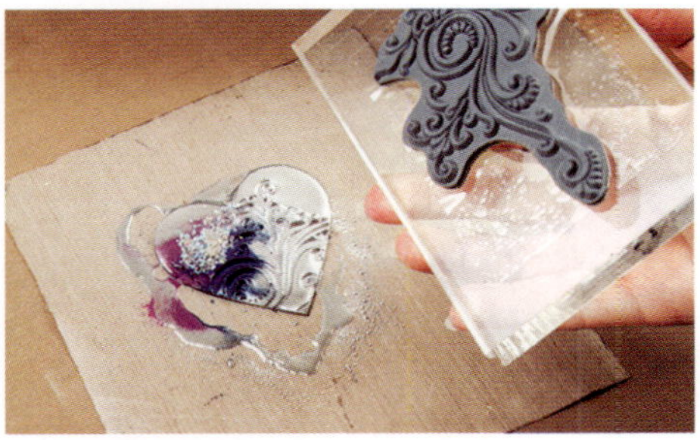

7. Stamp into it: Have stamp ready and inked with a pigment ink if you want a contrasting color. Stamp into molten Embossing Powder. Allow to cool and stamp will pop out.

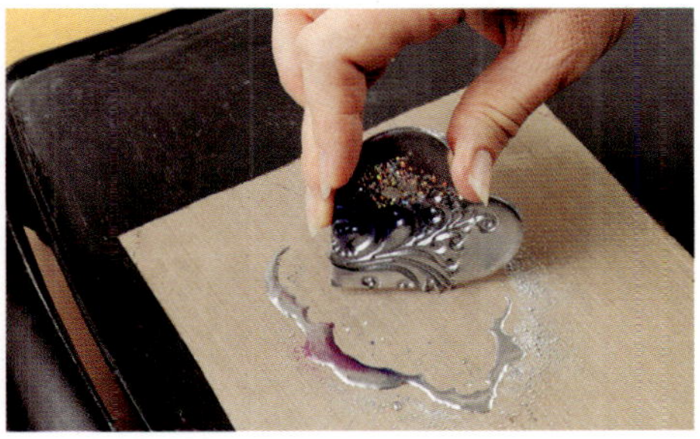

8. Melt edges: Stand tile on edge back on craft sheet on hot surface to melt away a rough edge.

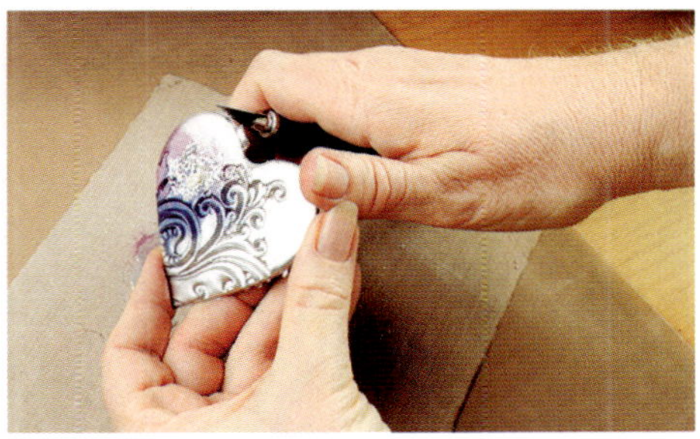

9. Refine edges: You can cut away edges while warm. When cool you can sand edges.

DEEP IMPRESSION TECHNIQUES
WITH EMBOSSING POWDERS

These Deep Impression Techniques started by accident. Puddles are the melted bits left on the craft sheet. They are often too pretty to throw out. They have fluid patterns different than sprinkled patterns. So drop them back in and remelt for serendipitous results.

PUDDLE LEFTOVERS

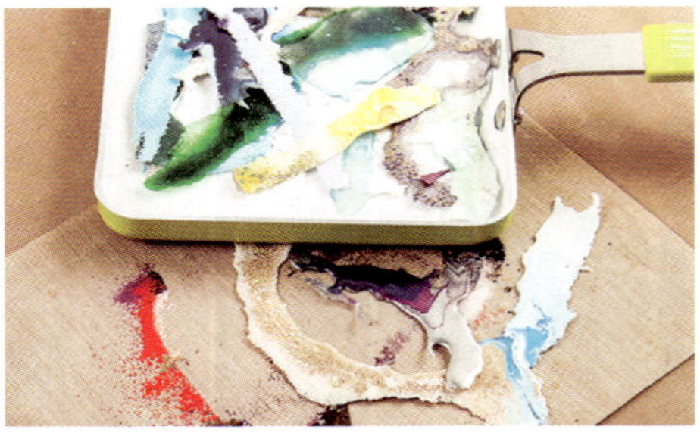

Puddle leftovers need not be thrown out. Save the larger, more interesting, abstract puddles to throw back into the next melting. Use spatula to clean remaining tidbits from craft sheet.

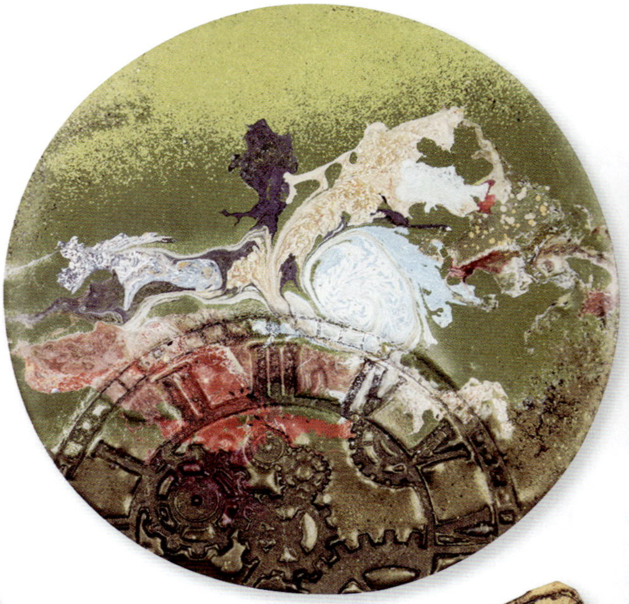

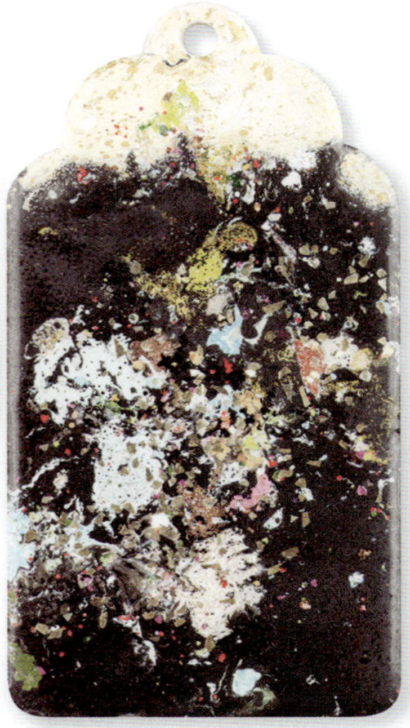

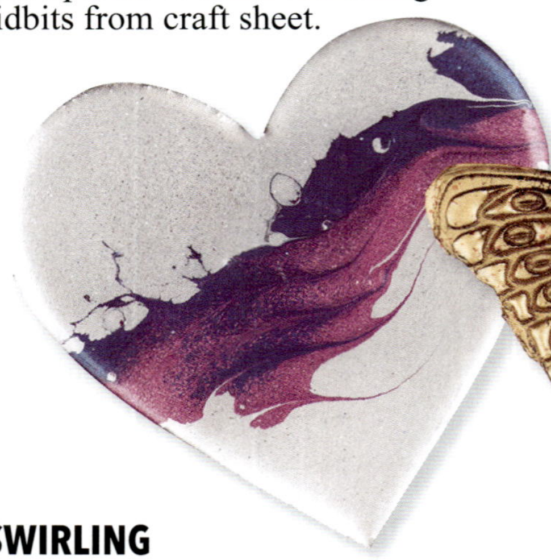

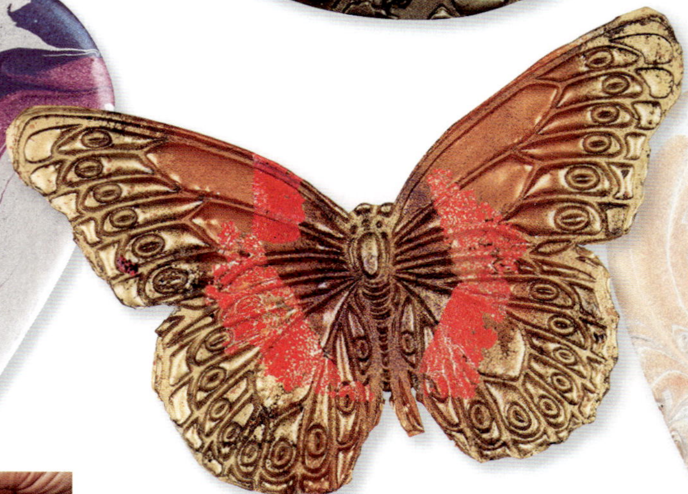

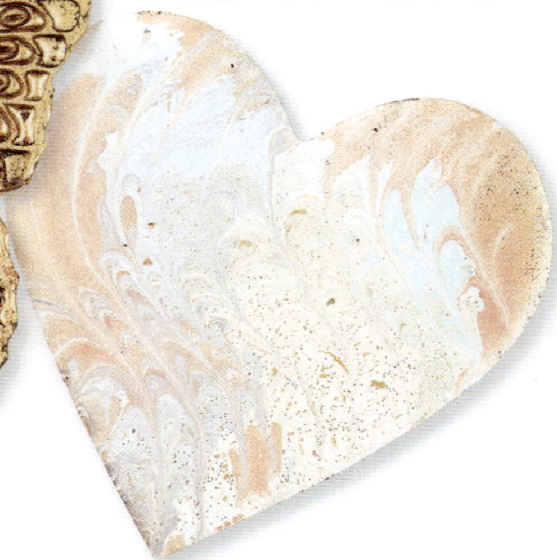

SWIRLING

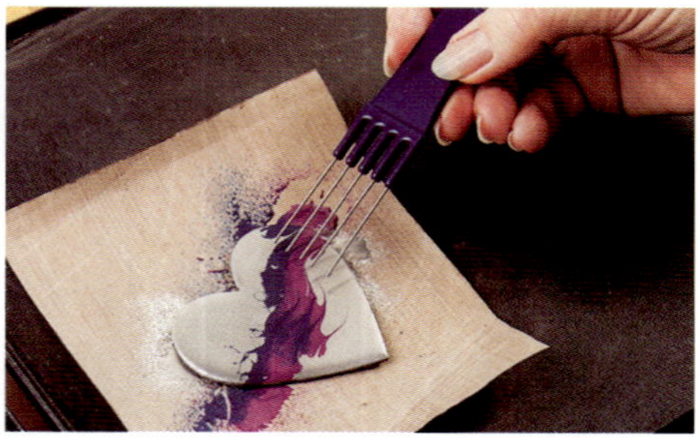

Marbling patterns can be made by swirling a multi-prong hair pick in molten Embossing Powder. Look for hair pick with no plastic tips. Puddle leftovers offer a quick supply of colors. Patterns remelt quickly and smooth out.

MARBLING

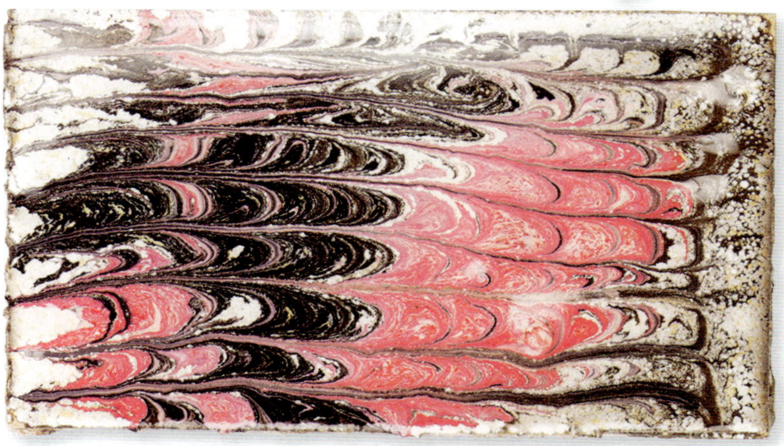

DEEP IMPRESSION

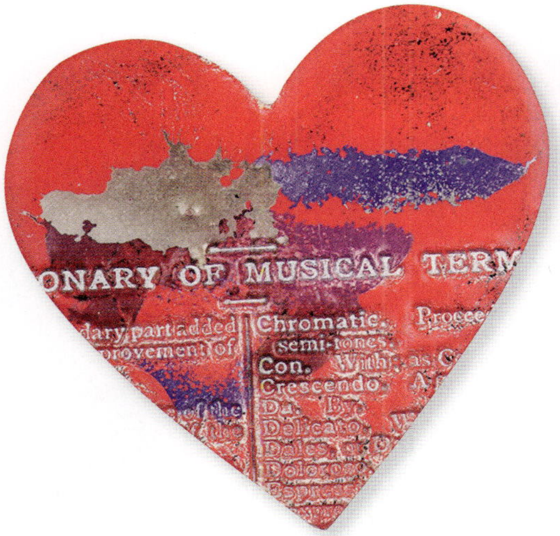

Deep impression: This heart had puddles over reds and purple and then was stamped with silver pigment ink.

PEARLustre™ Embossing Powders are beautifully reflective metallic colors.

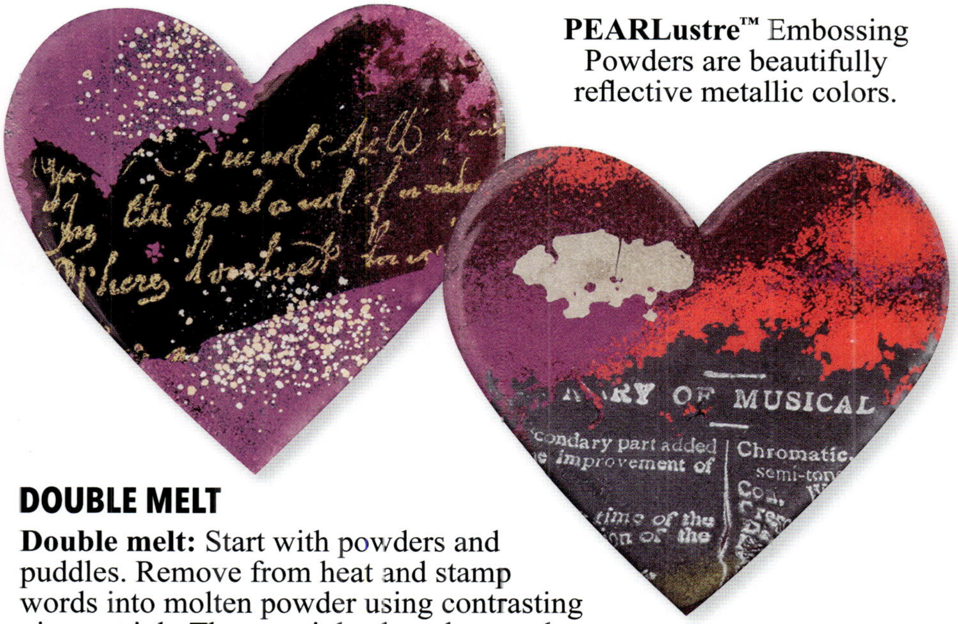

DOUBLE MELT

Double melt: Start with powders and puddles. Remove from heat and stamp words into molten powder using contrasting pigment ink. Then put it back on heat and remelt until smooth.

PUDDLE STAMPING

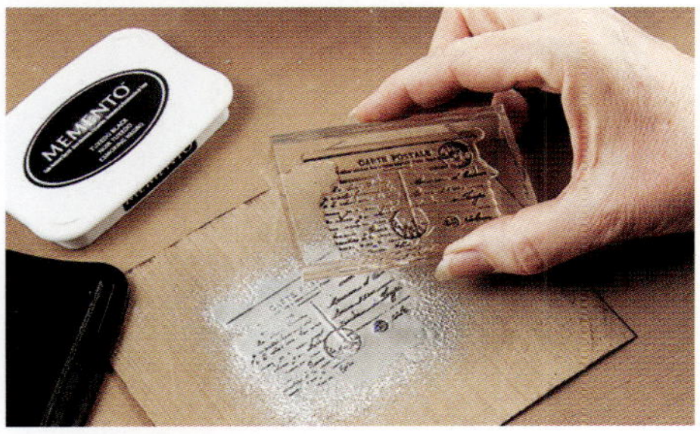

Puddle stamping: Melt a puddle, remove from heat and stamp into it. When cool, lift carefully and drop into molten powder. Design will be flat but hold the detail.

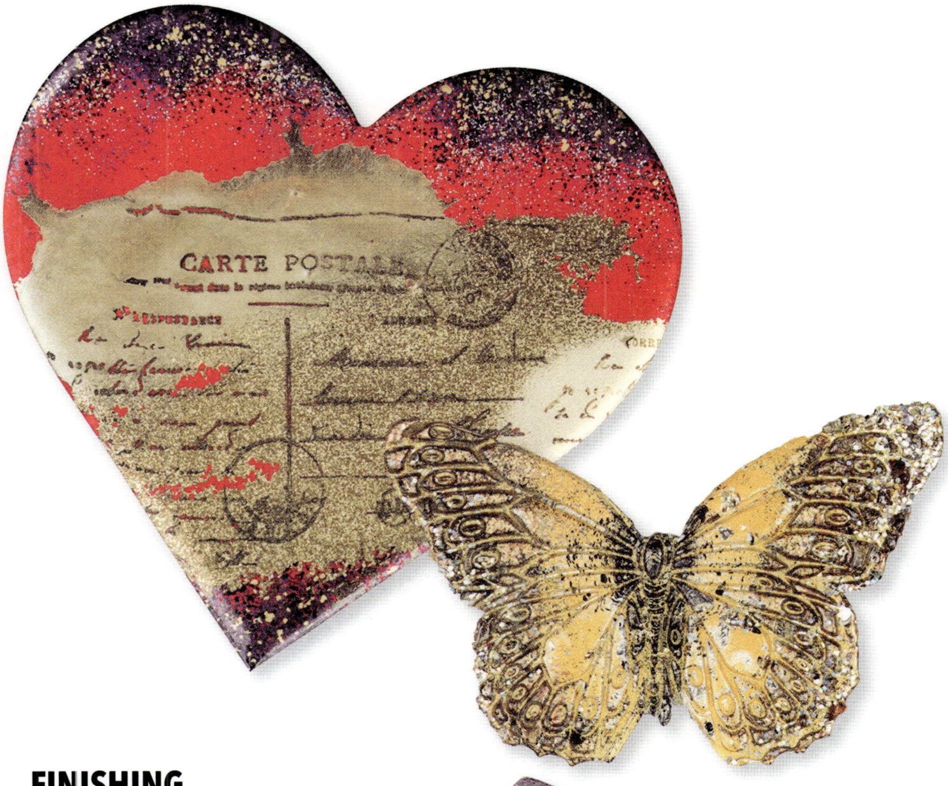

PUDDLE SWIRLING

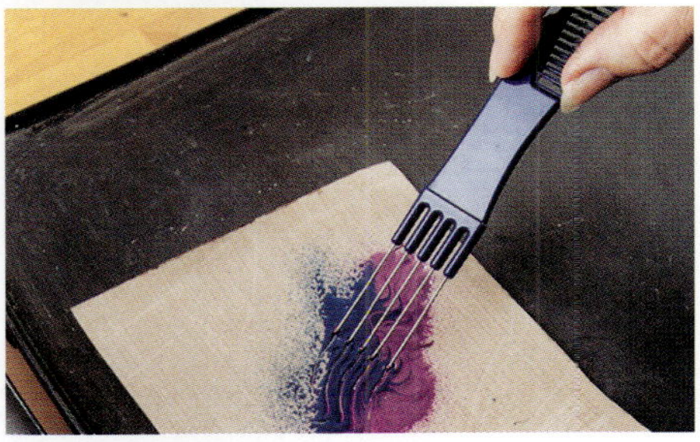

Puddle swirling: Melt a puddle, and use hair pick to swirl puddle colors. Let cool and drop into molten powder.

FINISHING

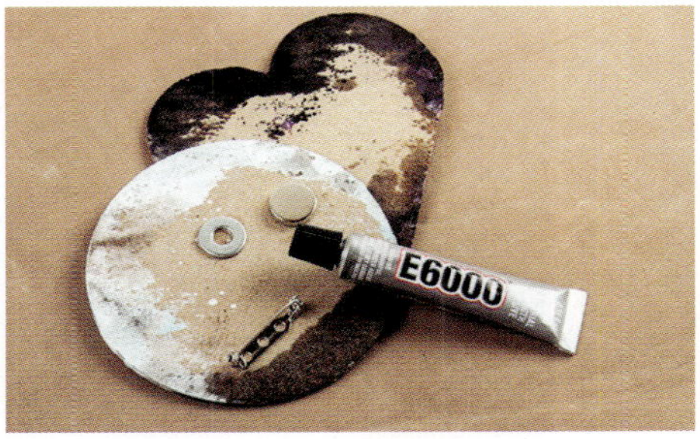

Pin or magnet backings: Jewelry glue will be needed to secure backings. Kraft area will adhere better than a slick embossed area.

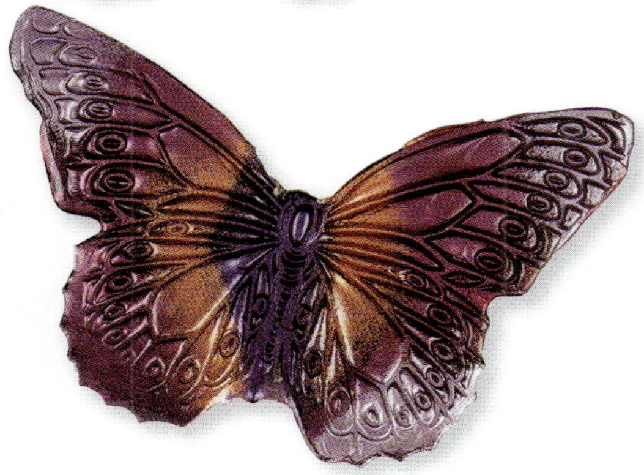

DEEP IMPRESSION ABSTRACT TILES
ADVANCED EMBOSSING POWDER TECHNIQUE

Dreamweaver® Pastes have been used on many of these canvases. Available in matte, glossy, colors, metallics, and crackle options. They are all of fine quality. They remain flexible and durable on canvases.

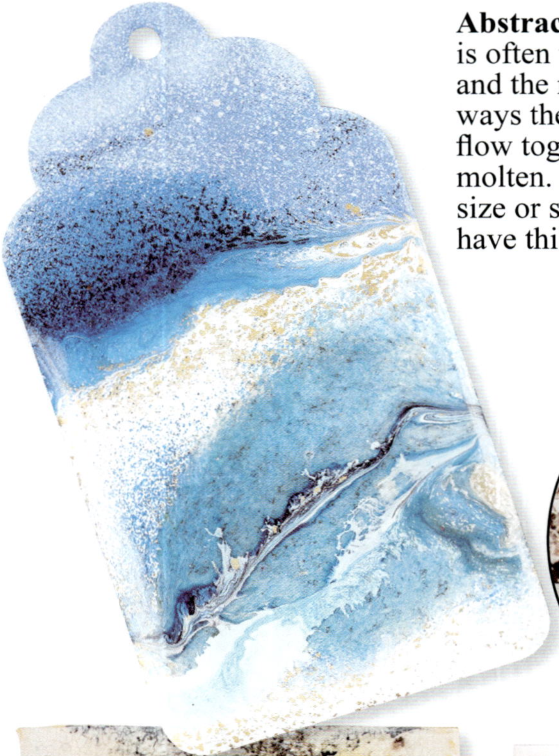

Abstract beauty is often the colors and the random ways they mix and flow together when molten. Work in any size or scale. Puddles have this fluid look.

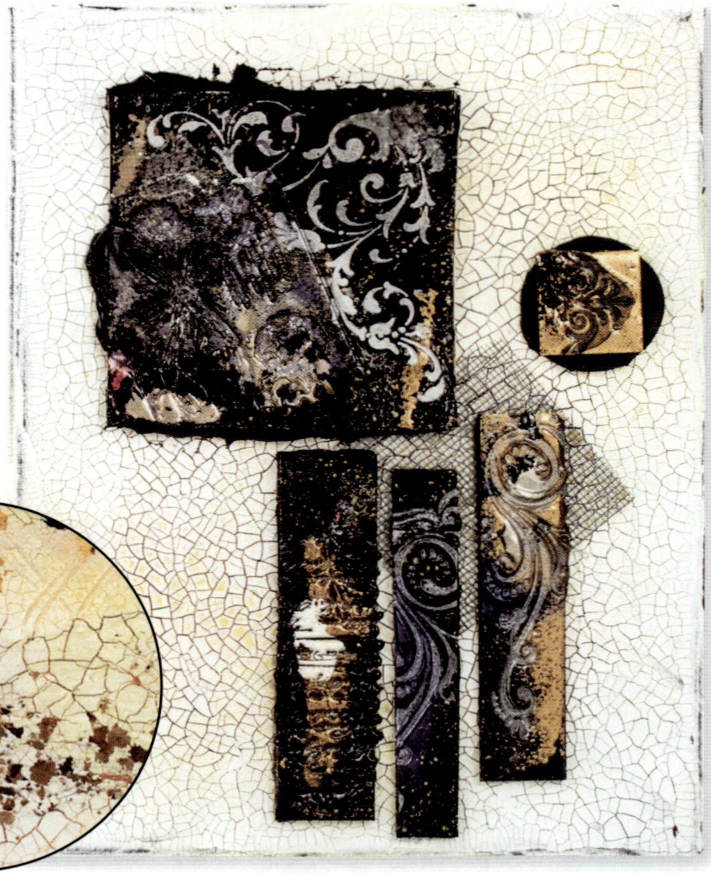

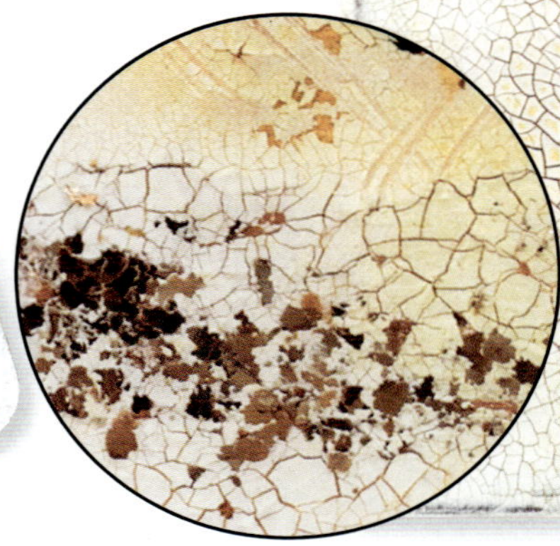

Crackle and texture: Crackle paste can be used under and over paint layers. Elements such as Mica, Fragments, or Crushed Glass Glitter can be embedded to air dry.

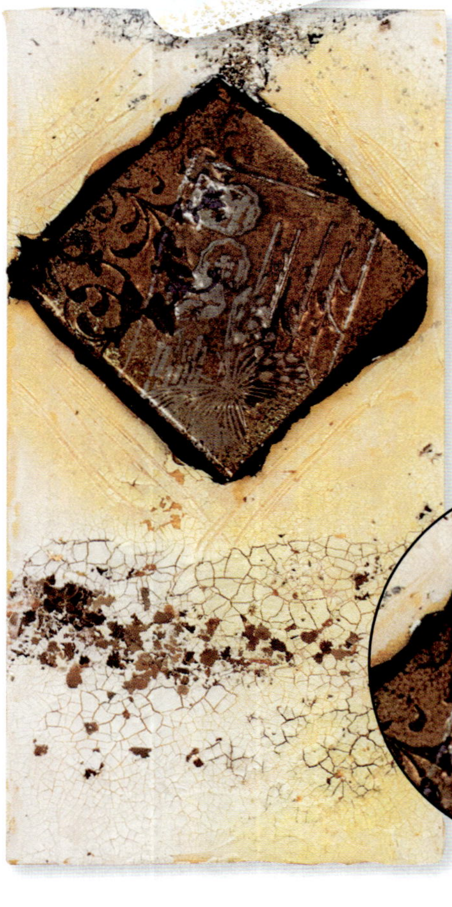

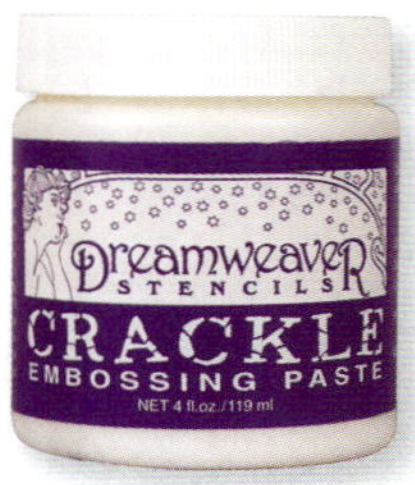

Paste to canvas is the ideal way to secure tiles to canvas. It may be hidden or pressed in for show.

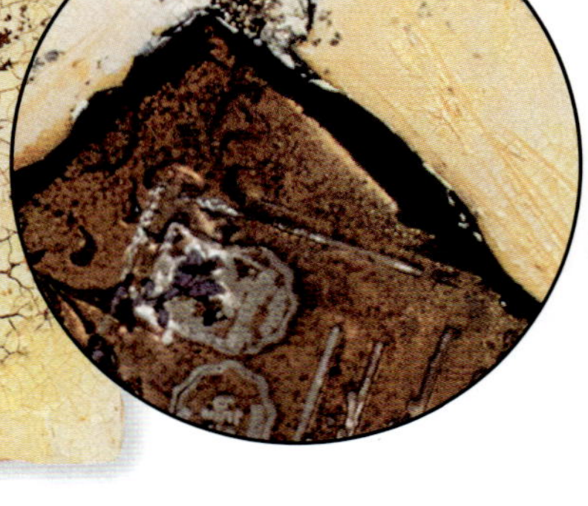

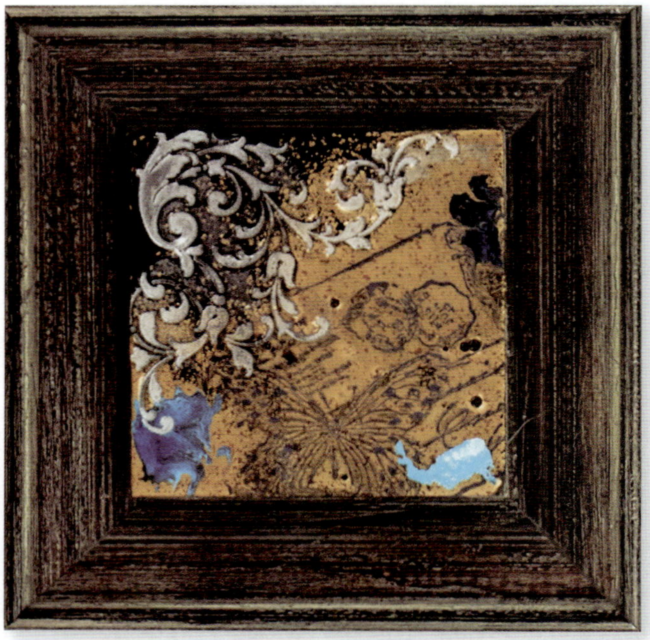

Frame tiles without glass. Enjoy the touch and feel texture.

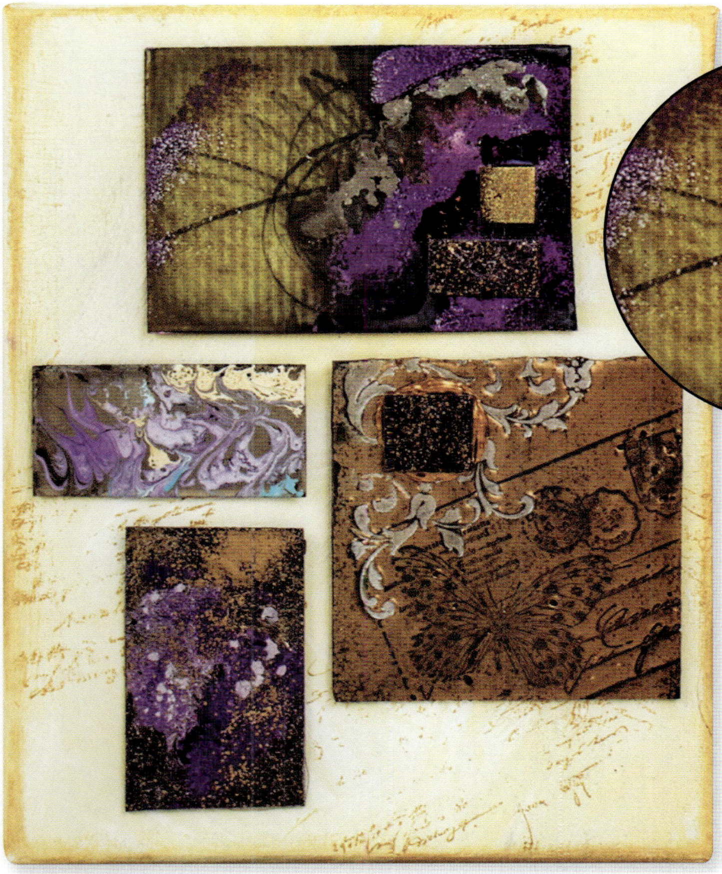

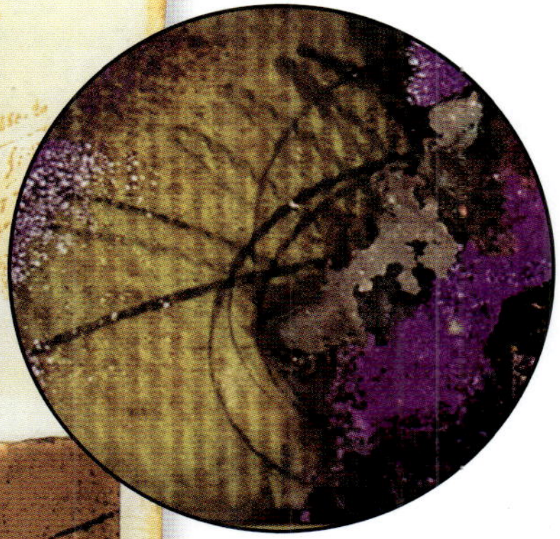

Melt wax in with Embossing Powders for a wonderful mixed media look. When molten it will be clear; when cool it will be milky and translucent with a soft texture all its own.

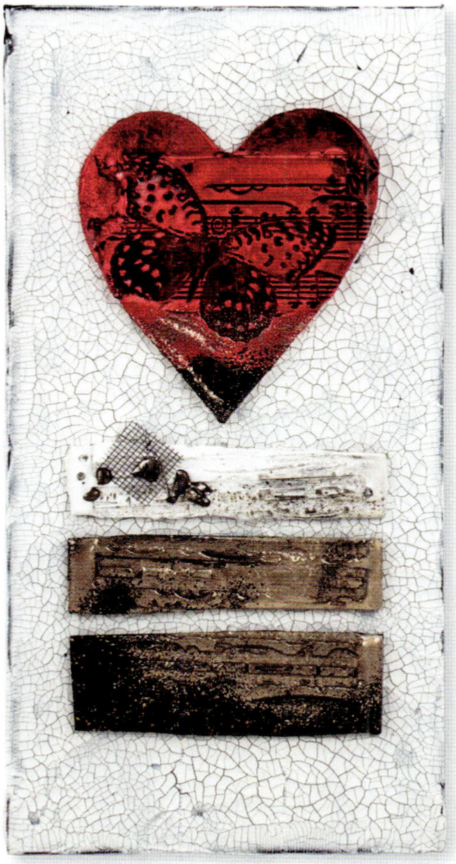

Clear embossing over other embossed colors often crackles. **Stencil** fern colors then cover with translucent paste for shine.

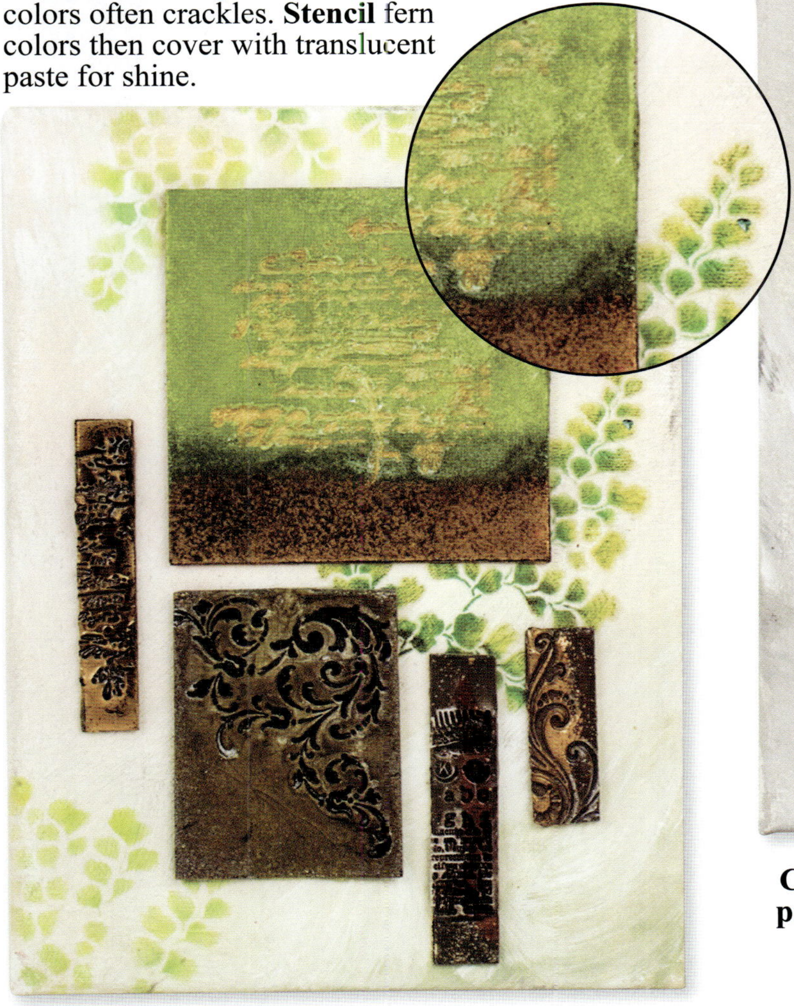

Clear embossing over paint or other embossed layers gives an aged, translucent quality.

DEEP IMPRESSION STAMPED TILES
ADVANCED EMBOSSING POWDER TECHNIQUE

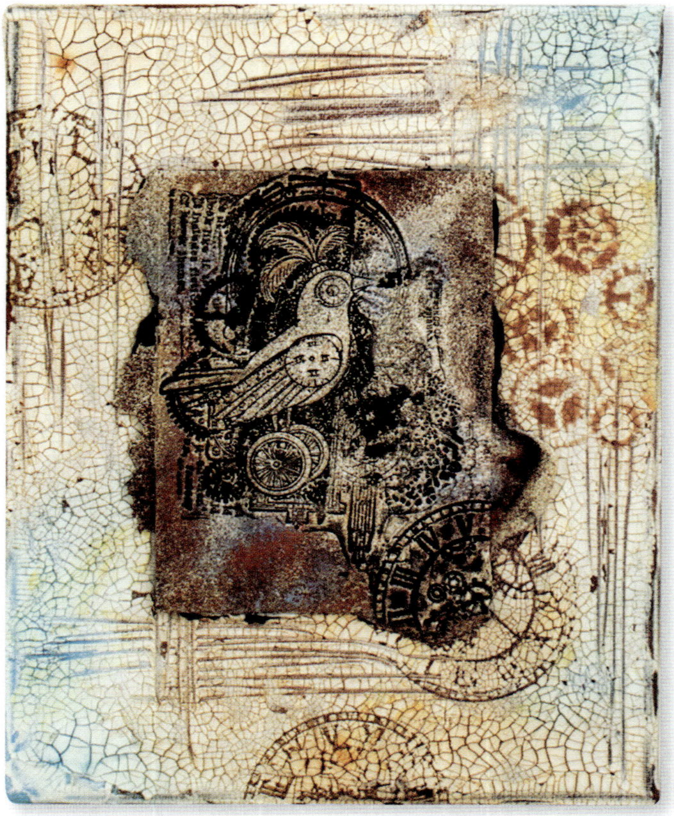

Color over crackle paste can be done with chalk or any number of paints or pigments as a dry rub once paste is dry.

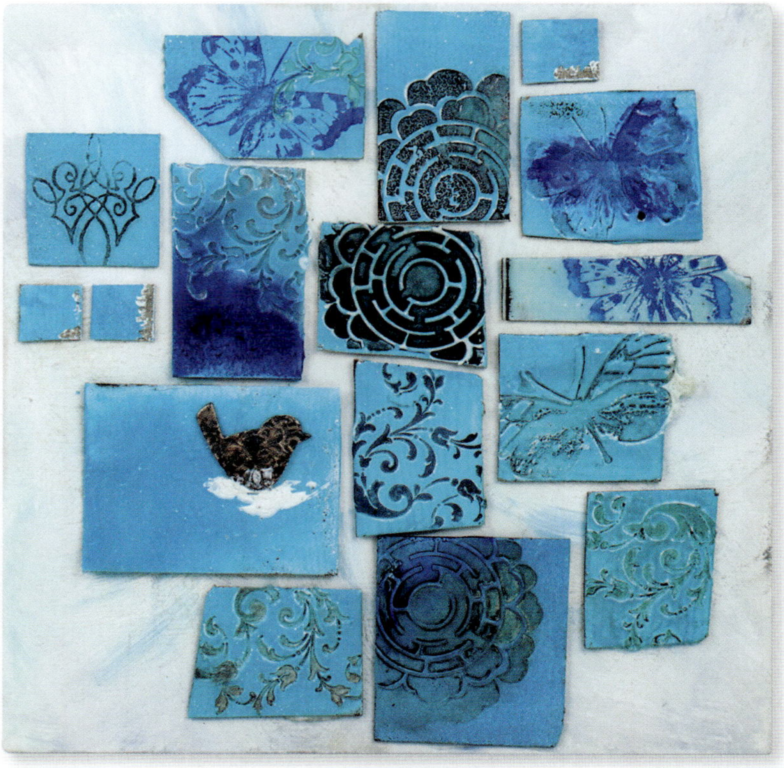

Mosaic of small tiles on a canvas becomes a home decor masterpiece. Create washes of acrylic paint on canvas. Stamping or stenciling can be added. Use Dreamweaver® Paste to secure tiles to canvas.

Stamp into paste to create texture. Let paste dry a bit. Scrub stamp clean before paste dries on stamp. Enhance with charcoal pencil to define as needed.

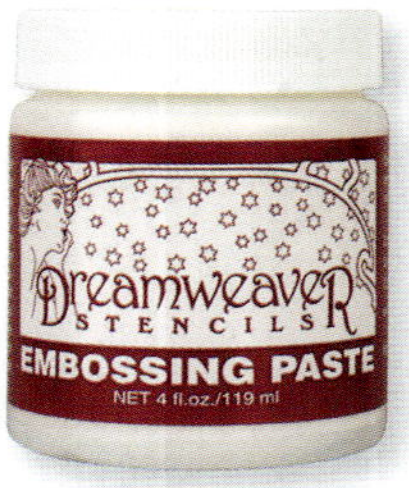

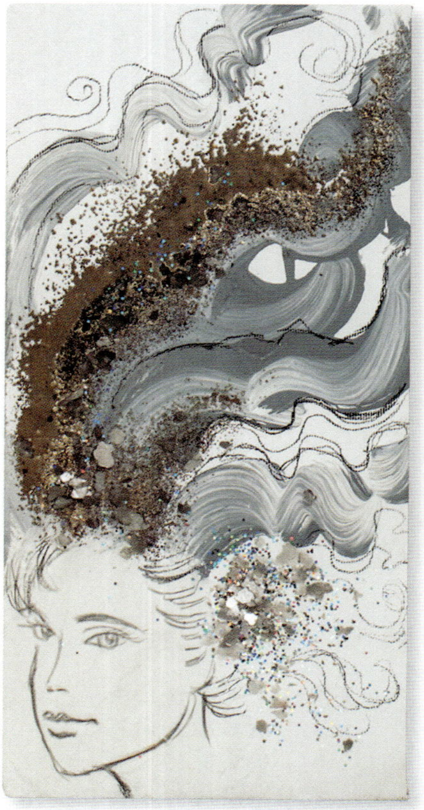

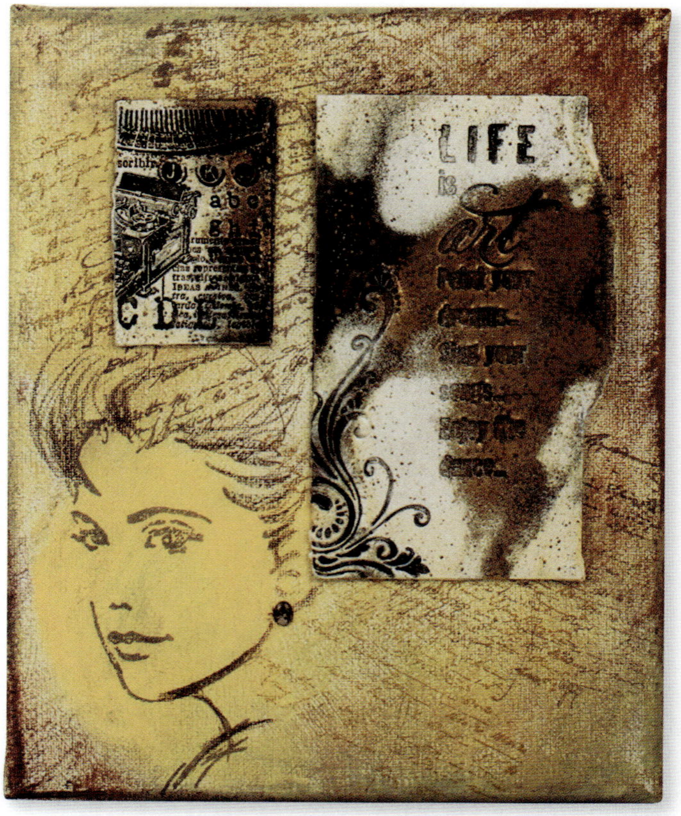

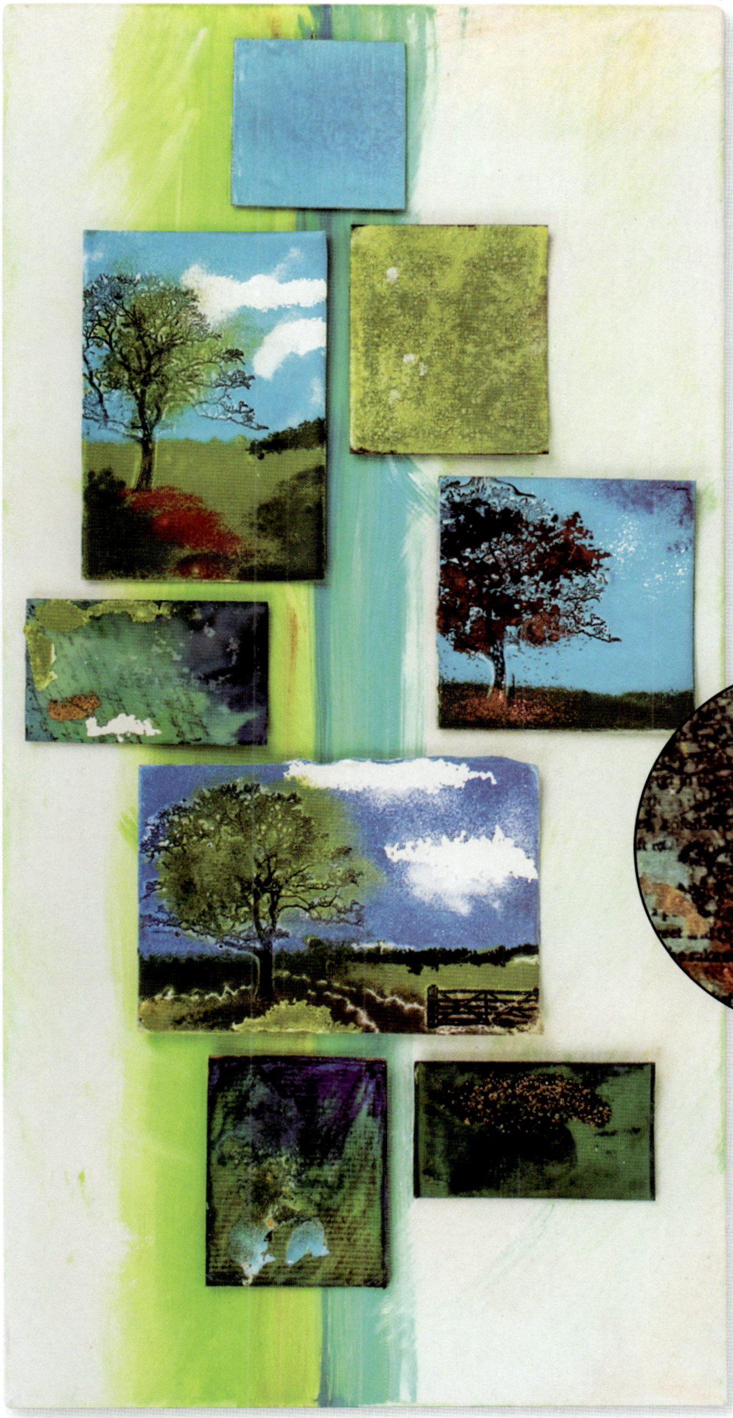

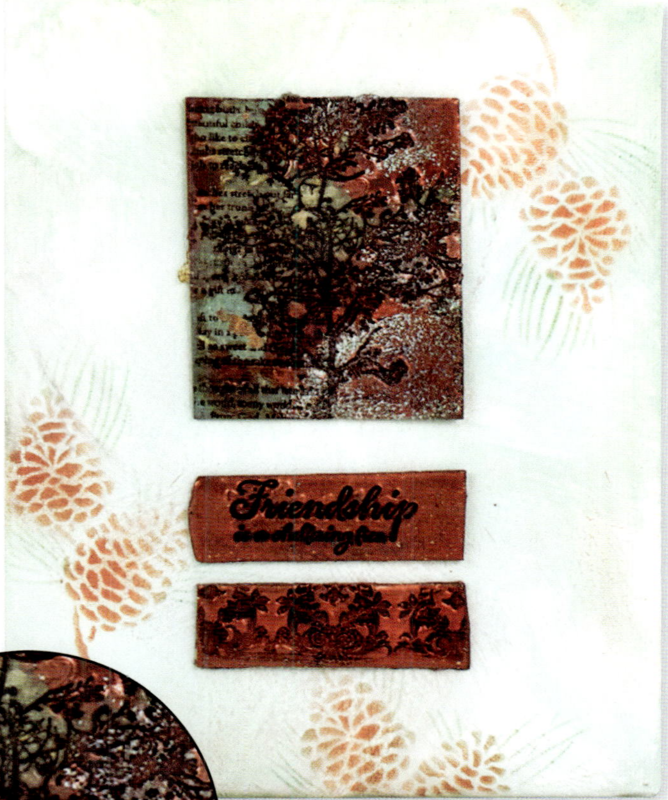

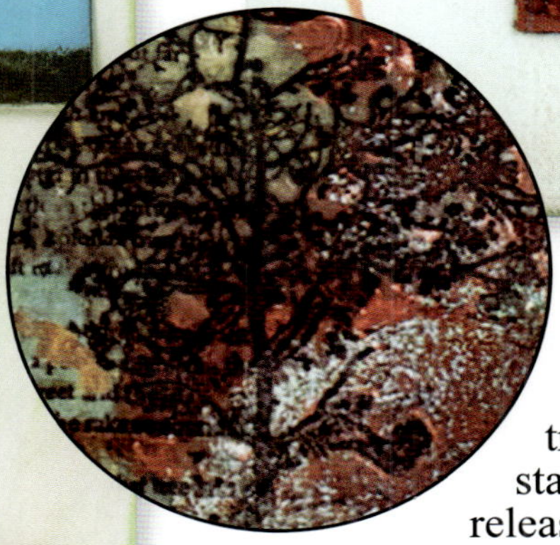

Raku Ceramic Look was created with black ink on tree stamp in Aged Copper Embossing Powder. Air was trapped in small compartments of stamp and took a while to cool and release. Use a brush to scrub bits of powder out of stamp.

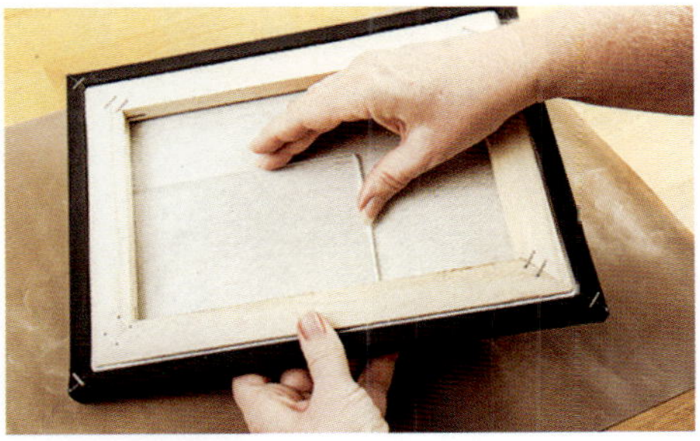

Level canvas for stamping or stenciling by inserting a jumbo handle from the back between canvas and frame to create a level surface. Press from both sides.

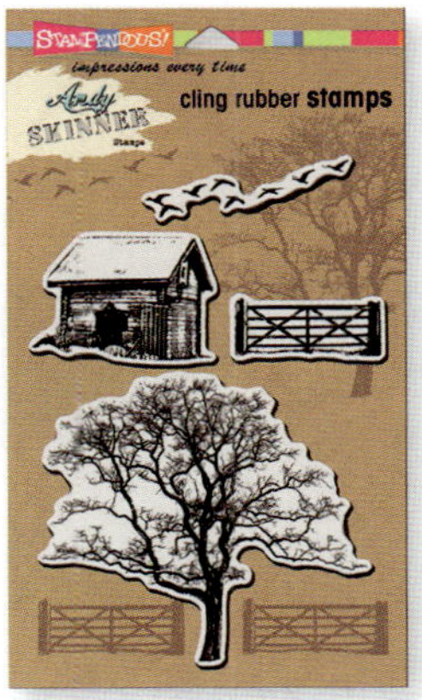

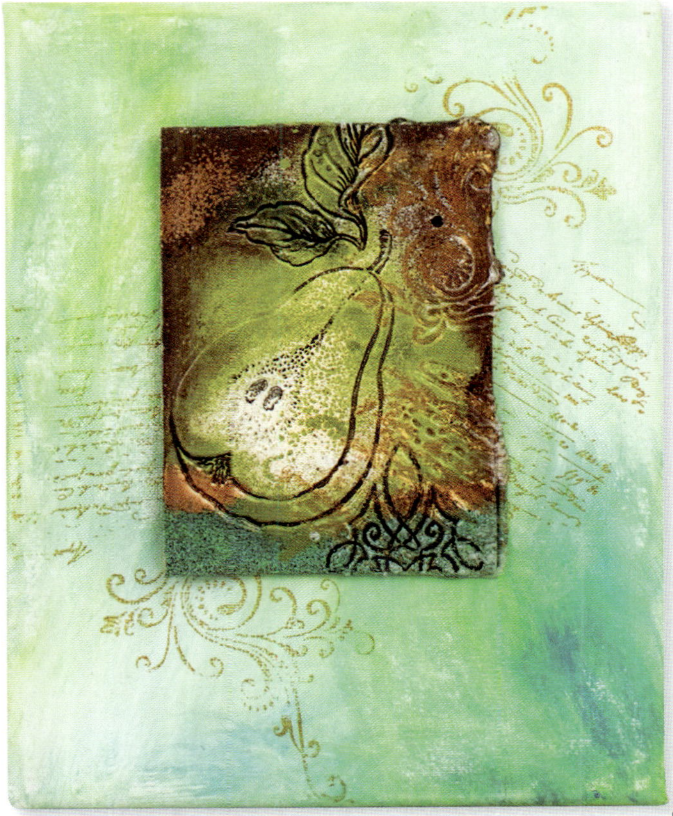

PAINTING WITH POWDER SCENIC TILES
EMBOSSING POWDER TECHNIQUE

These scenes can be as simple as 3 color stripes. Start at the top with the sky colors and work your way down to foreground. Pre-melt puddle shapes and drop them in over the background. Puddles are easier to work with than sprinkling. Some results are happy accidents. The more you practice, the more you can achieve the look you want. Use scenic photos for inspiration.

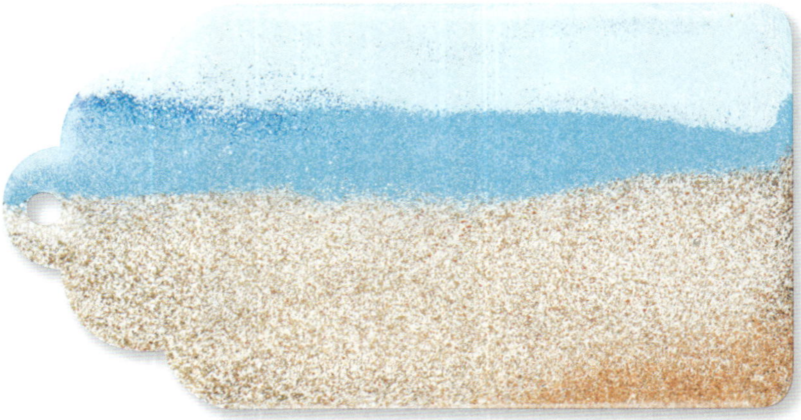

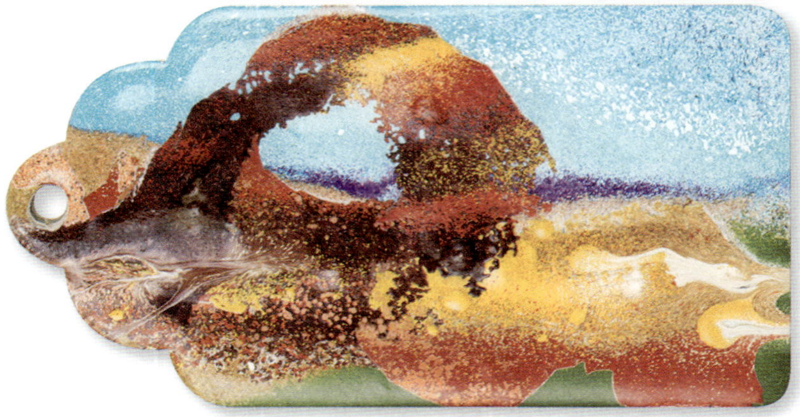

Puddle Painting Technique was used to make stone arch shapes. Create the puddles with earth toned powders, then drop them into place and melt over background.

PUDDLE PAINTING

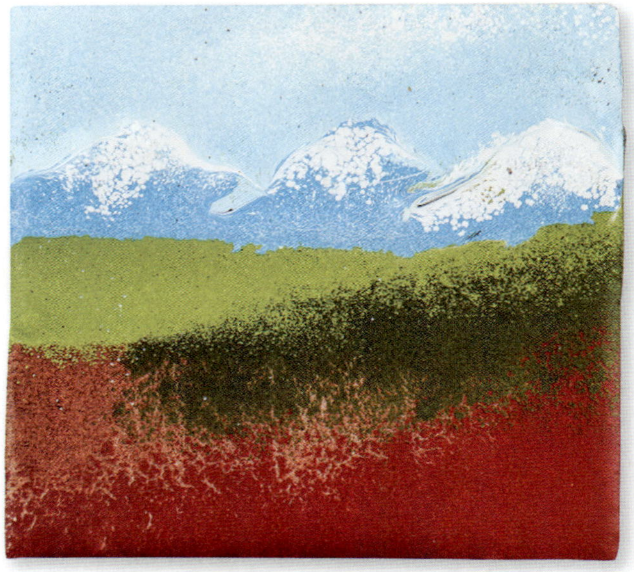

Puddle Painting Technique allows you to make snow caps with Chunky White Embossing Powder and drop into place over mountains.

14 Jar Embossing Powder Kit offers a great value and a variety of opaque colors ideal for this technique. A little jar goes a long way for making a wide variety of scenes.

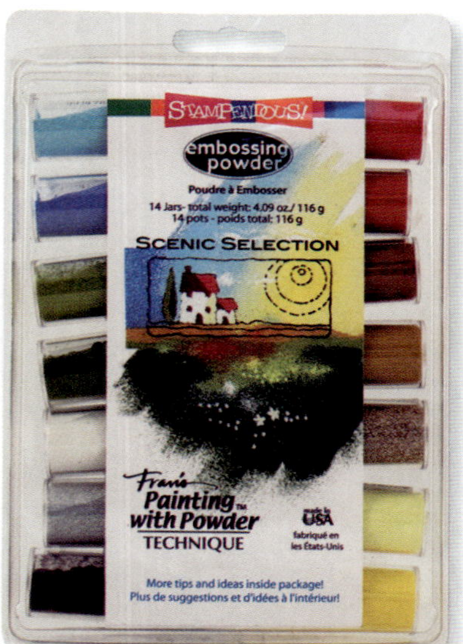

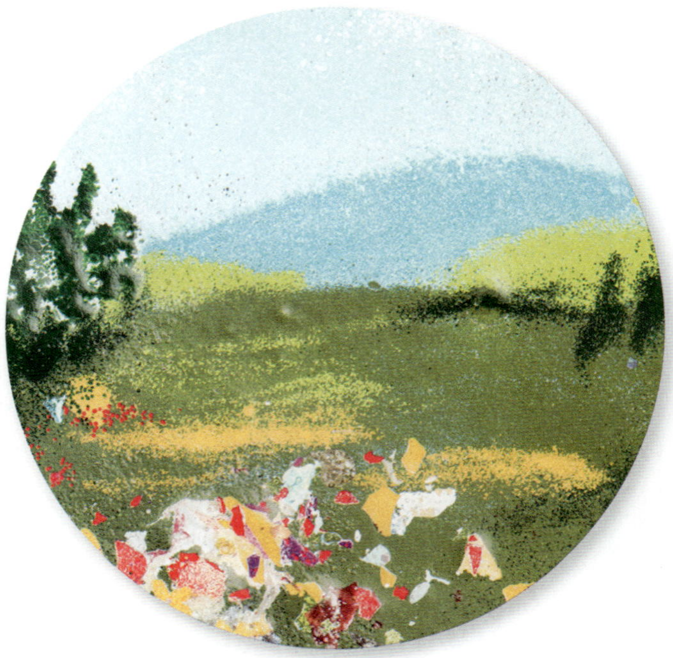

Puddle leftovers: Flowers in foreground are just crumpled up bits in interesting colors.

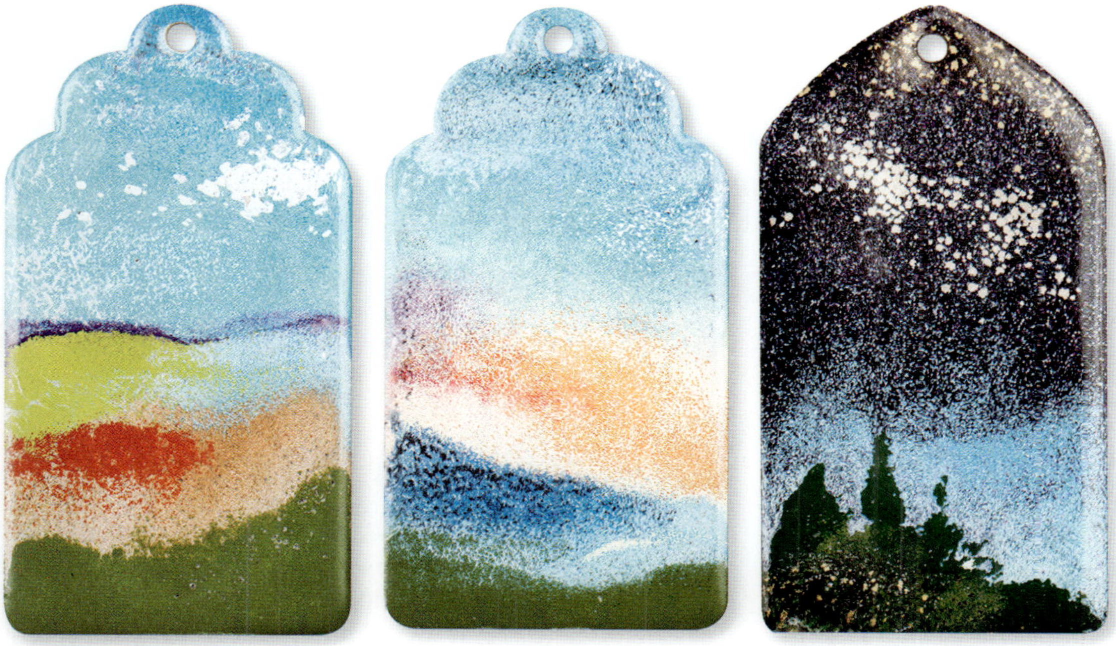

Clear powders over opaque colors allow for soft color blending. Try sunrise or sunset colors. Use Chunky White for clouds. Try Twilight for night sky. Dribble greens in a vertical drop for trees.

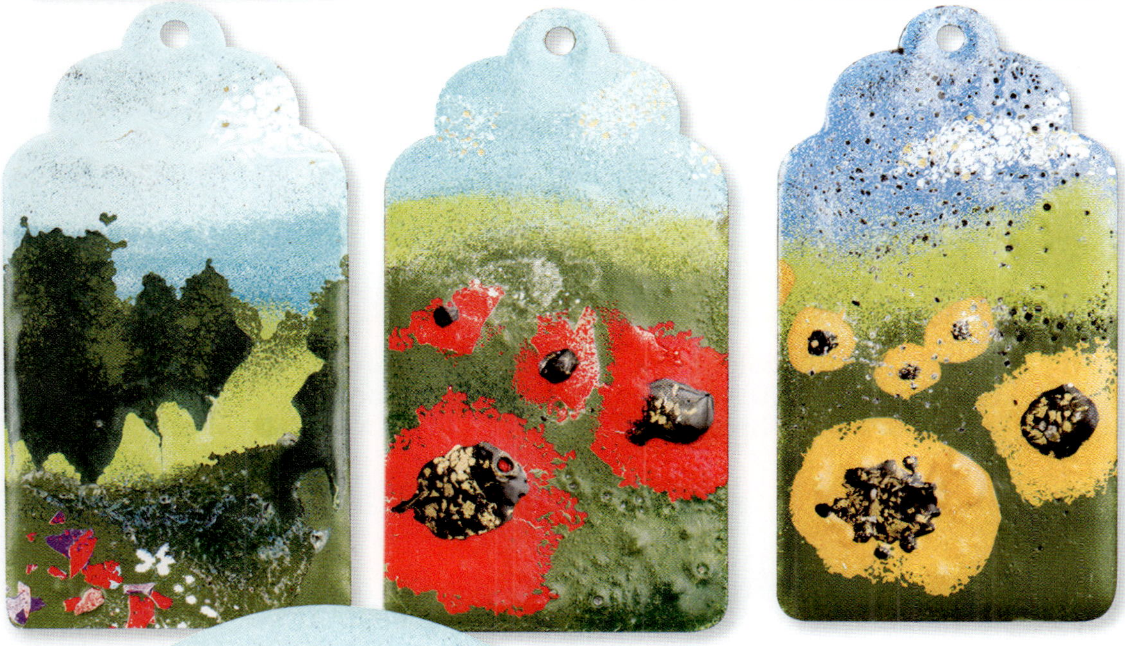

Puddle Painting Technique was used to make round flower shapes and centers that get dropped into place over the green backgrounds.

MARKER PAINTING

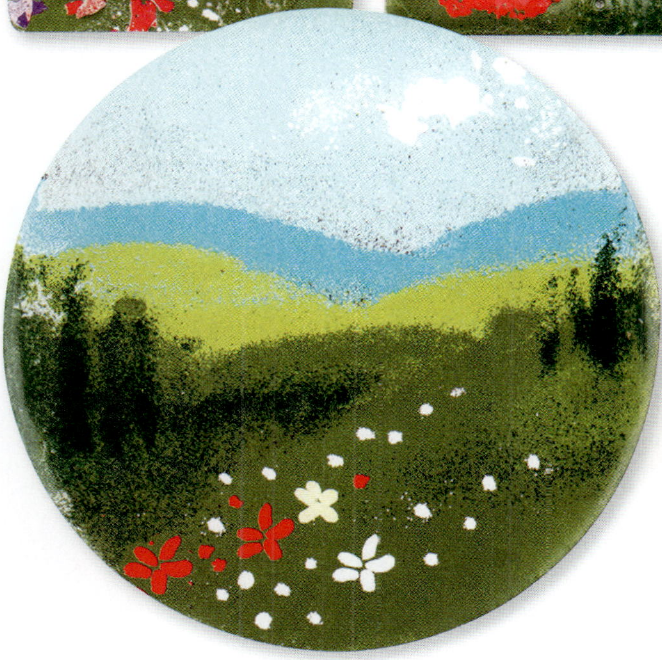

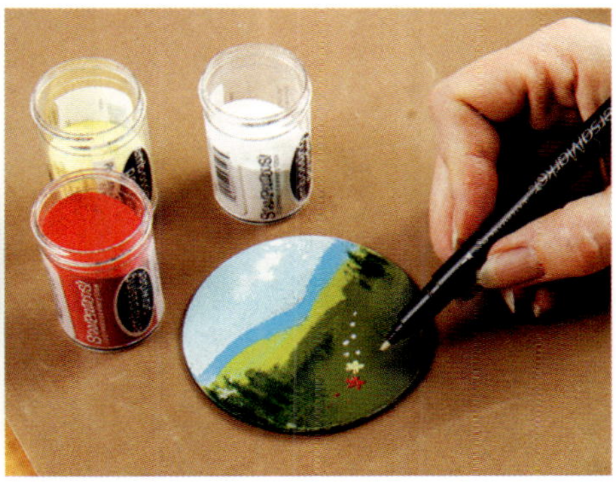

Marker detail can be added to the surface of any embossed tile by applying a VersaMarker™. Try a 5-dot flower and dust with contrasting color powder. Use heat tool just enough in that spot to not disturb the smooth surface.

PAINTING WITH POWDER SEASIDE GALLERY
EMBOSSING POWDER TECHNIQUE

Seaside tiles are a favorite and different each time. These tips and a bit a of practice will get you started. Favorite beach powders are listed in order used. Use scenic photos for inspiration.

Fran's Favorite Beach Powders:

Chunky Clear
Chunky White
Opaque Baby Blue
Opaque Sky Blue
Opaque Aqua
Clear Pacific Blue
Golden Sand

PUDDLE PAINTING

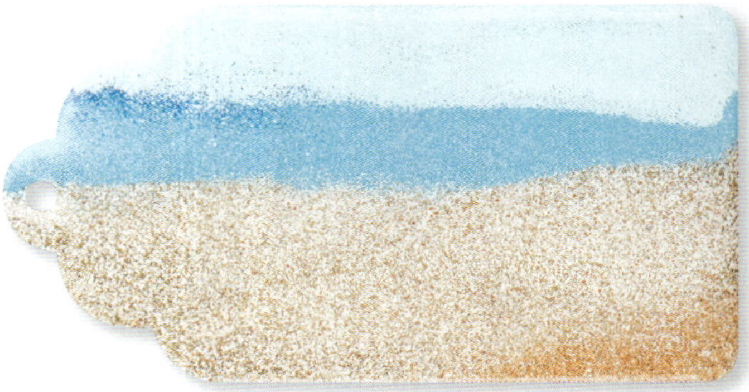

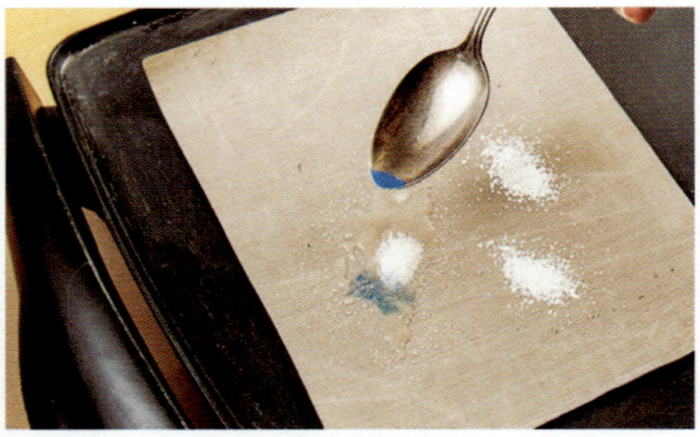

Pre-melt clear puddles of Chunky Clear with a bit of Clear Pacific Blue. Make White Chunky puddles. Remove and let cool.

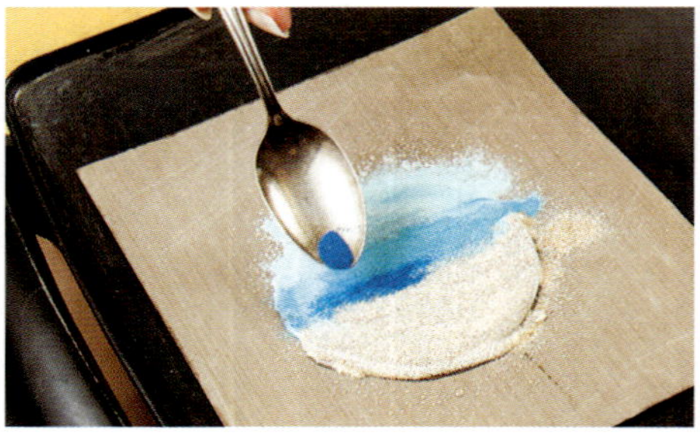

Melt beach colors from sky to water and sand. Add Clear Pacific Blue over opaque blues.

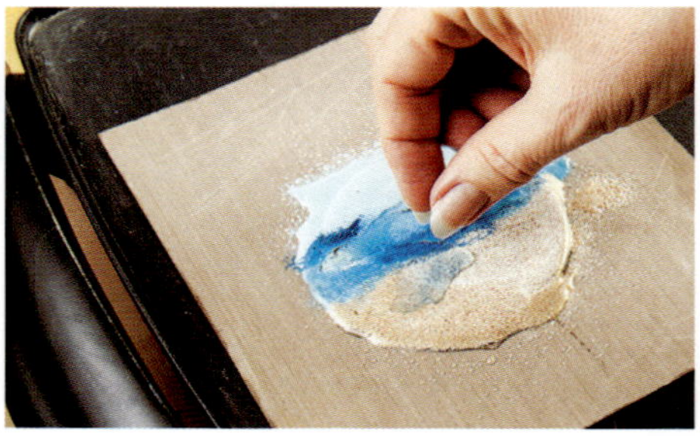

Add clear puddles for ocean waves and white puddles for clouds or surf. Sprinkle white too.

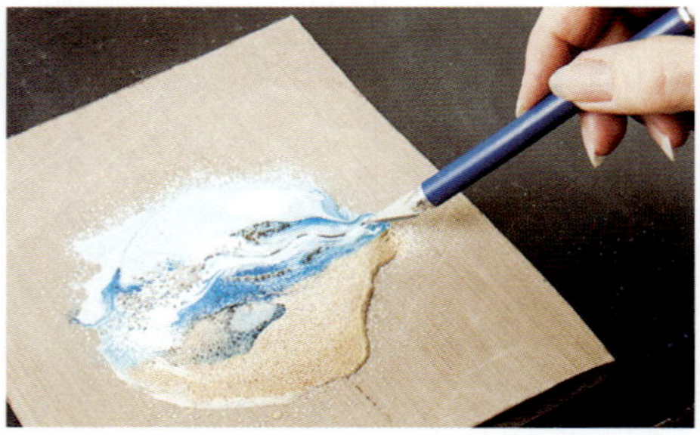

Swirl waves with a craft knife to pull and reshape them for that last little swirl or pull at the end.

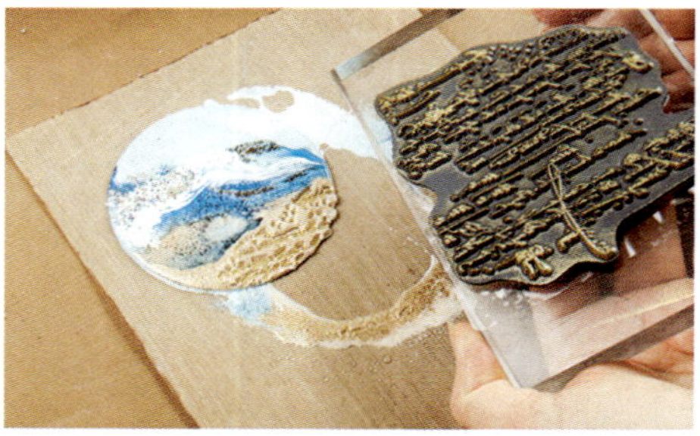

Pre-ink stamp with gold pigment ink be ready to stamp quickly as you remove it from heat.

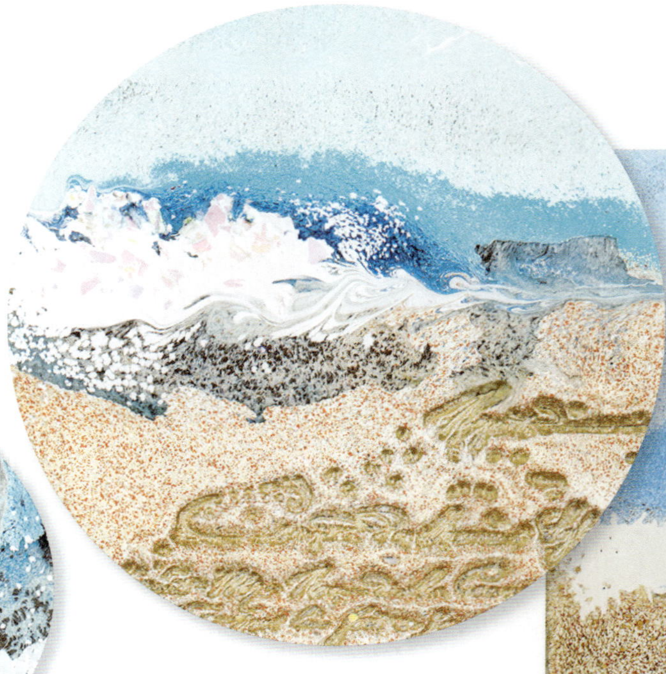

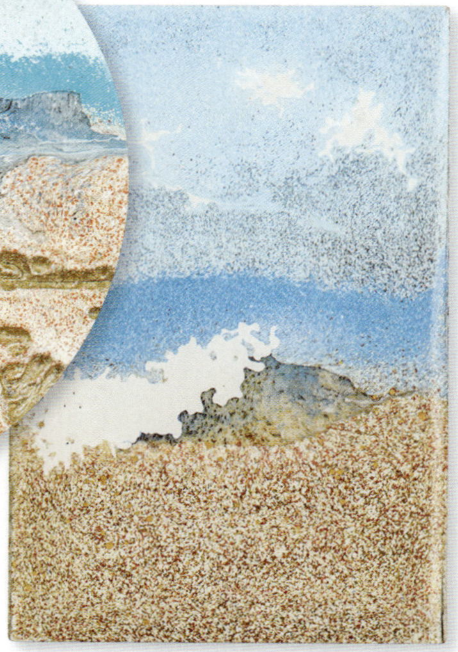

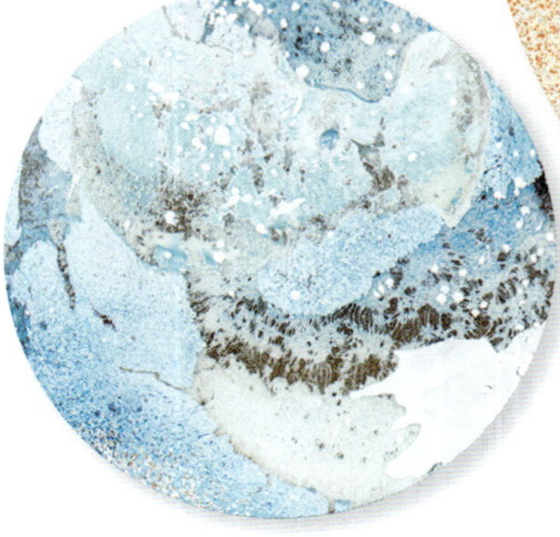

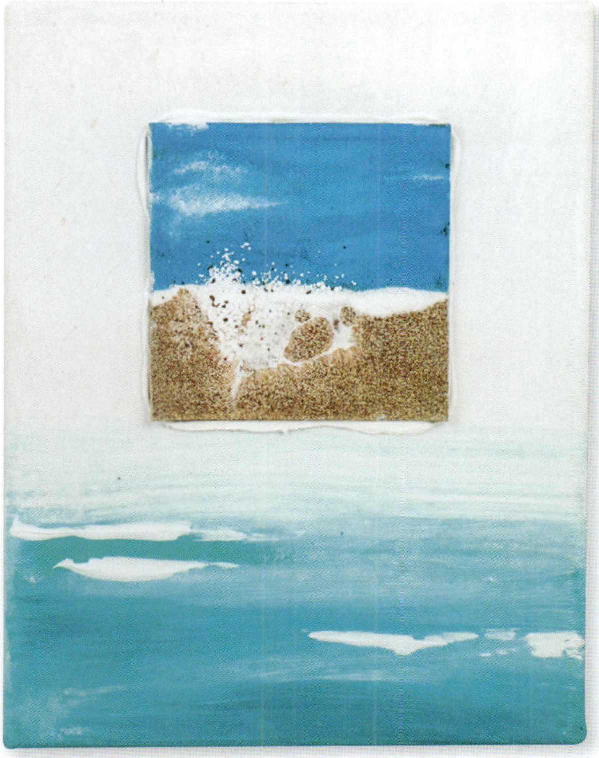

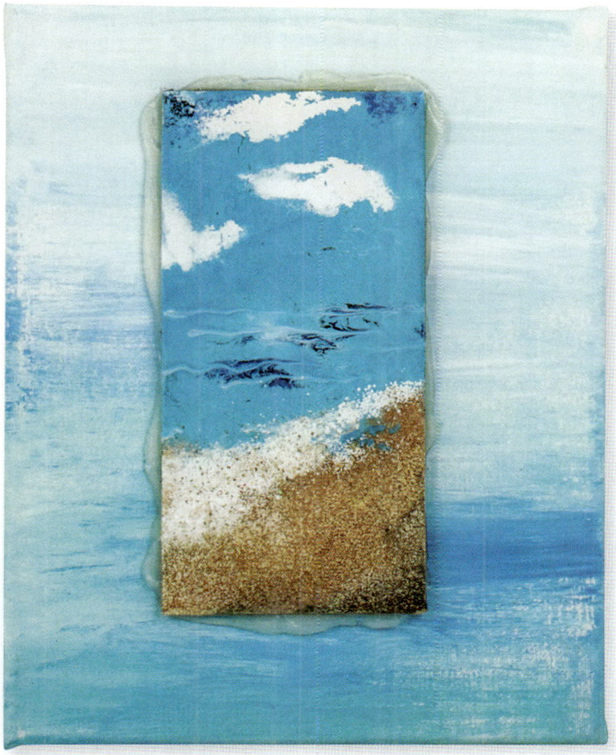

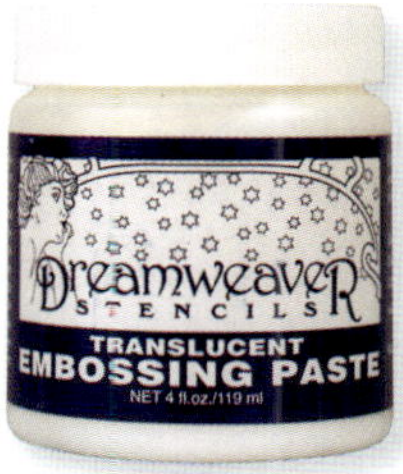

Translucent Paste or Glossy White Paste can be used on canvas. Apply with palette knife. Paste is also best way to attach tile to canvas. Paste remains flexible and durable.

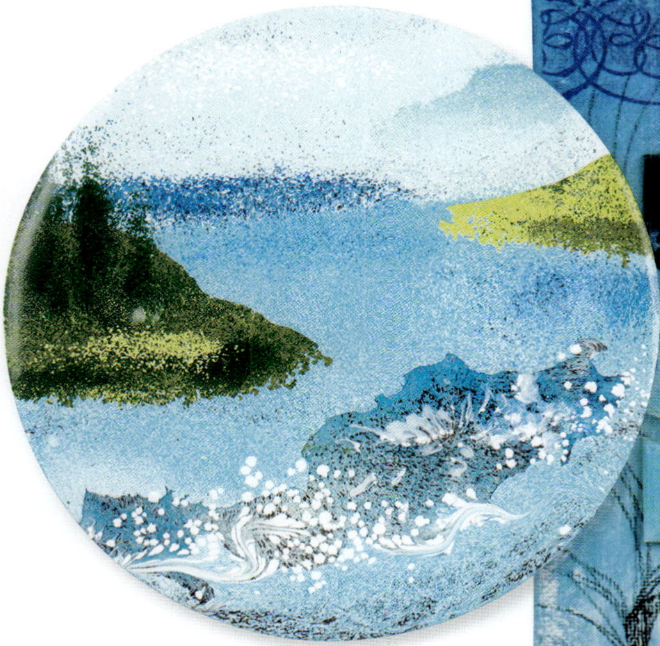

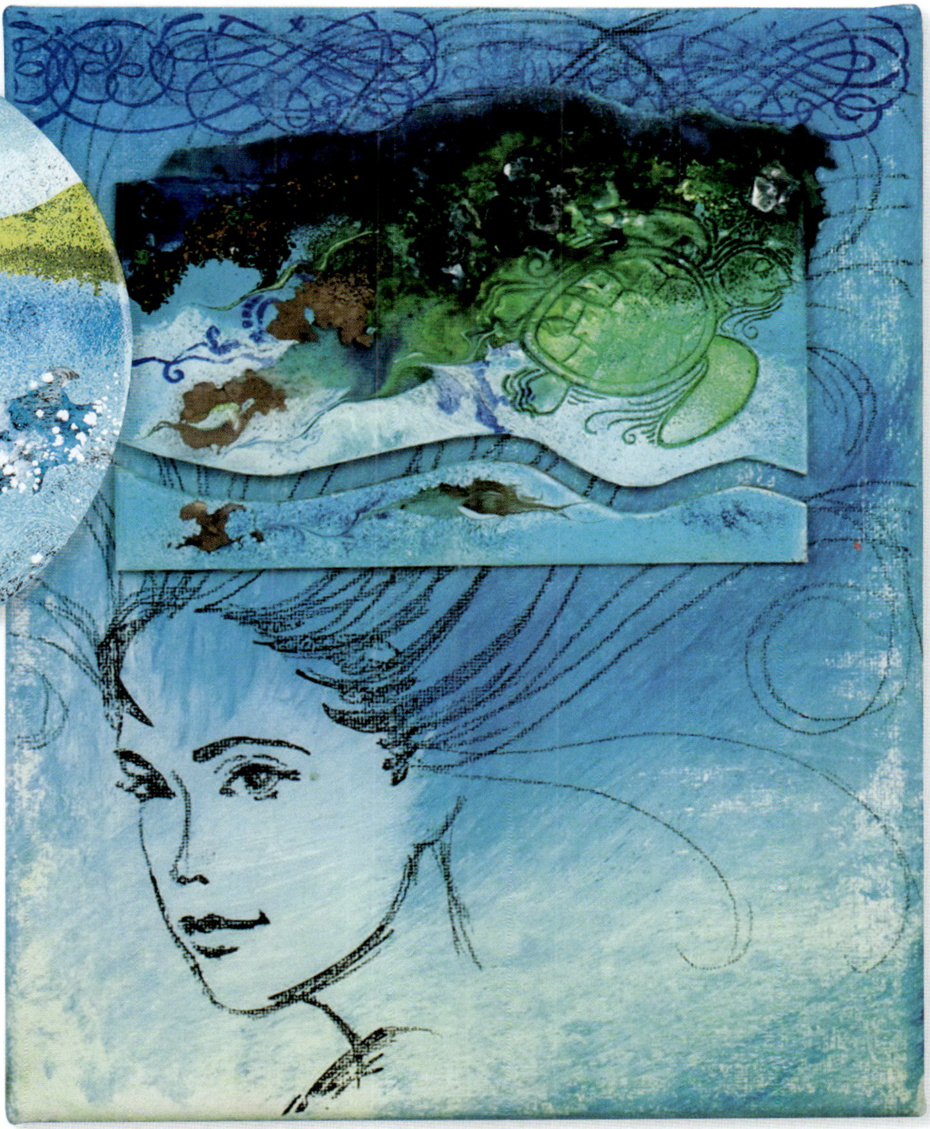

Pre-melted puddles are the easiest way to create island shapes. Clear puddles create wonderful currents.

Clear and Opaque Embossing Powders create the illusion of water. Use blues, greens, silver, and Mica or fragments. Stamped turtle was enhanced by painting it in with alcohol inks after it cooled.

PAINTING WITH POWDER PUDDLE PAINTING
ADVANCED EMBOSSING POWDER TECHNIQUE

Puddle Painting makes use of different colors and shapes of puddles that can be made on the griddle and cooled. Handle them with care. Dropping them in over background colors is easier to control than sprinkling.

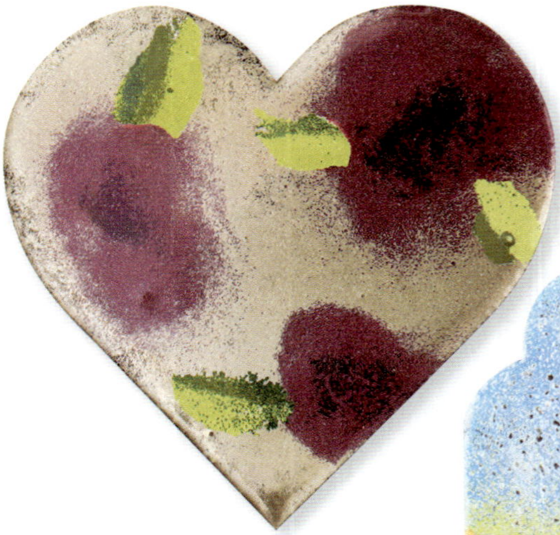

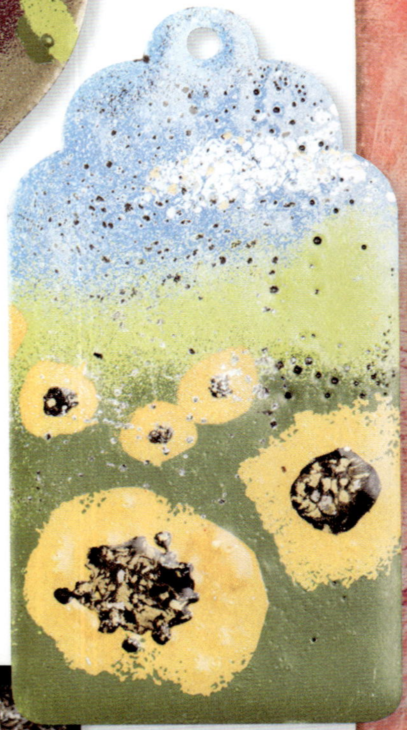

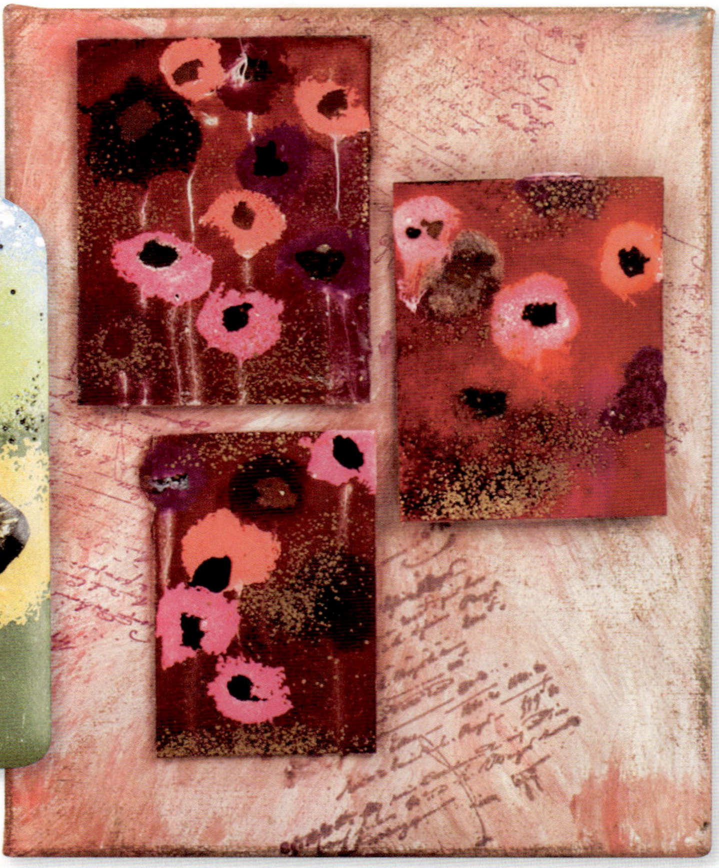

Sprinkle or pre-melt puddles: Heart above has soft sprinkled blossoms. Sunflowers and centers were pre-melted on a craft sheet and allowed to cool. Add them over background colors and allow to melt in.

PUDDLE PAINTING

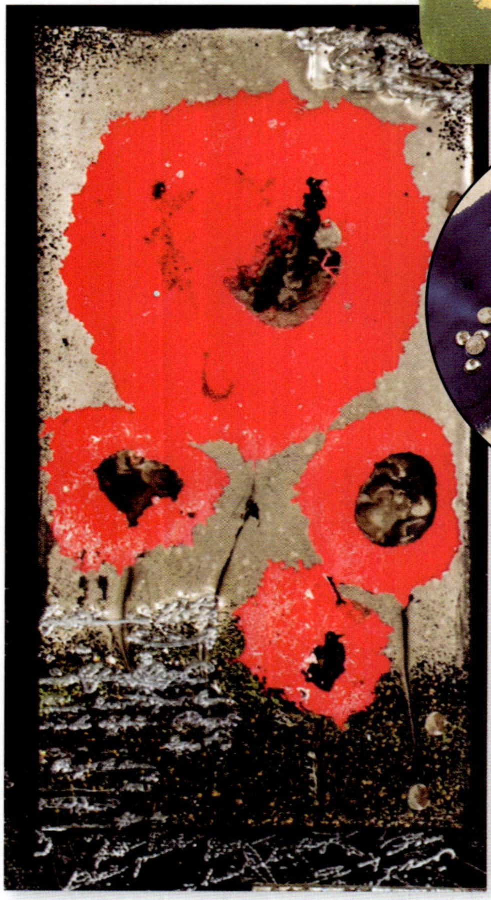

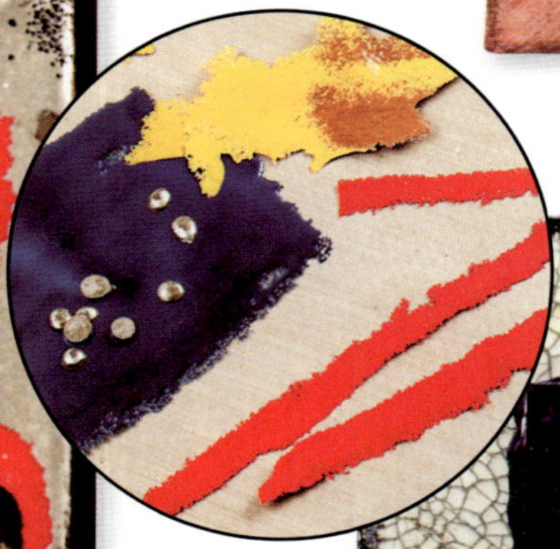

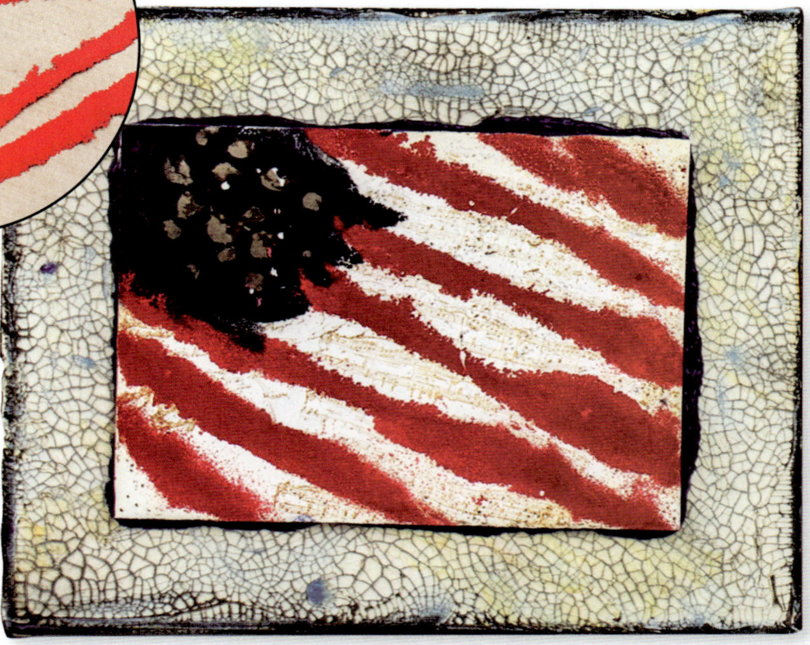

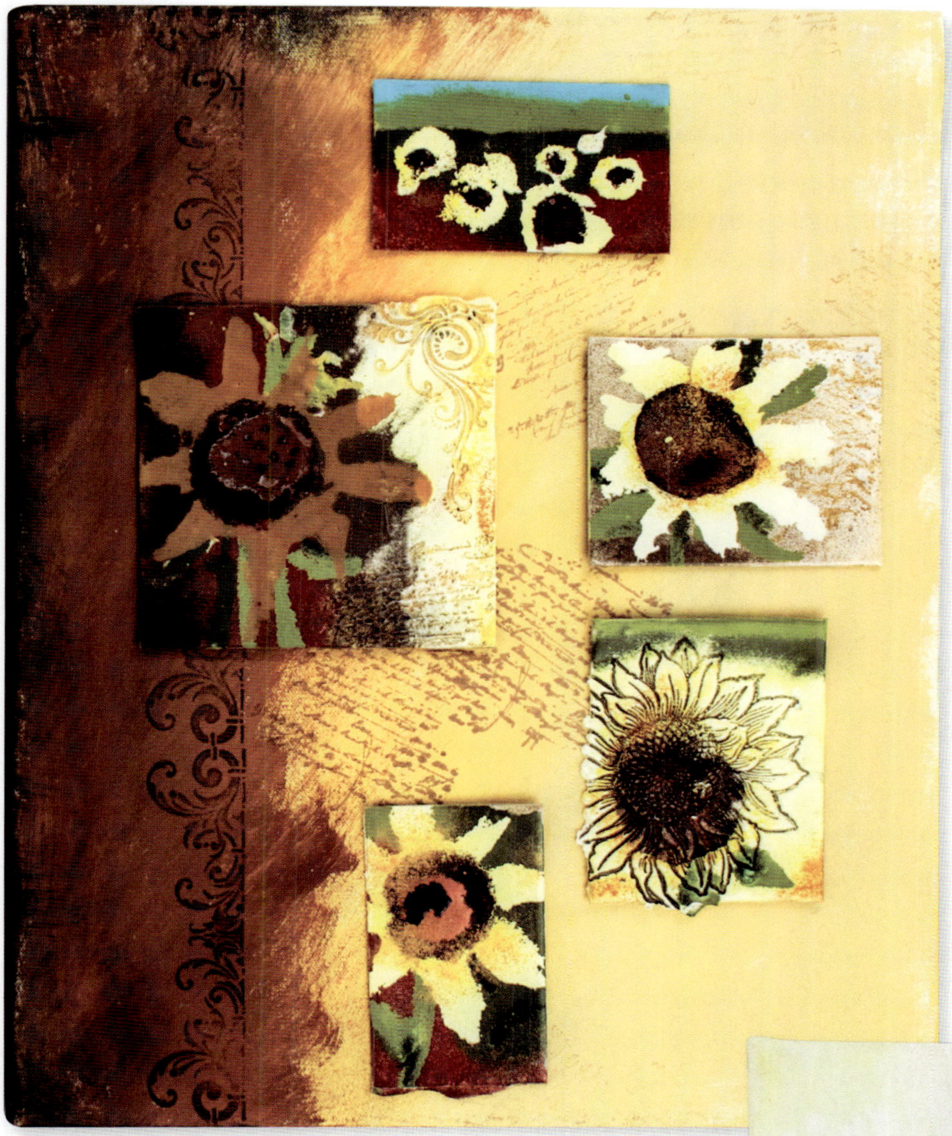

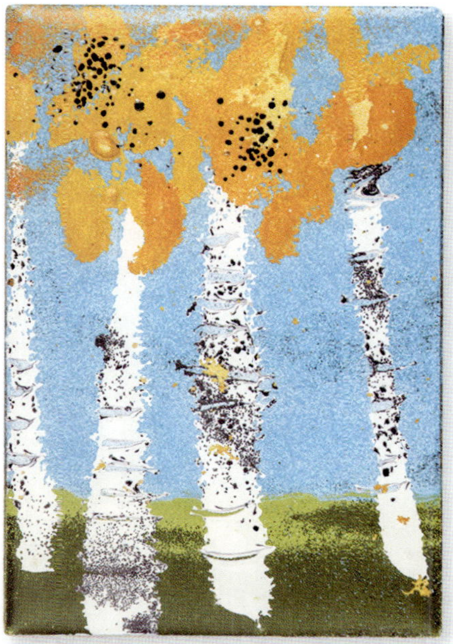

Break up puddles for Aspen leaves. Pre-melt tree trunks and score and sprinkle with a bit of chunky black.

Sunflower petals were also pre-melted shapes that were broken into triangular shapes.

Lavender Field is simply pre-melted stripes. Stamps and Stencils with paste were used on the canvas.

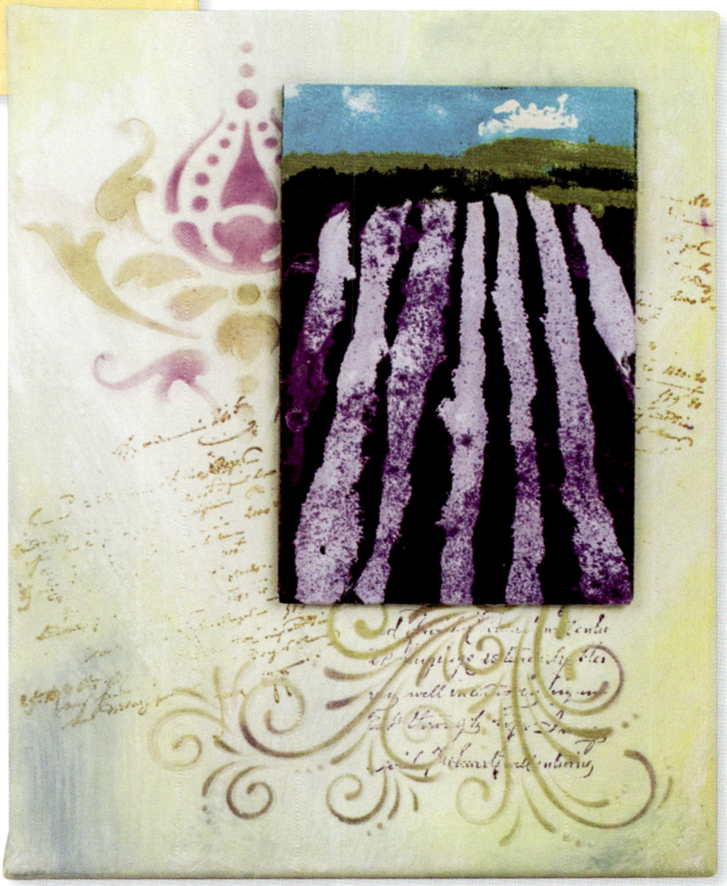

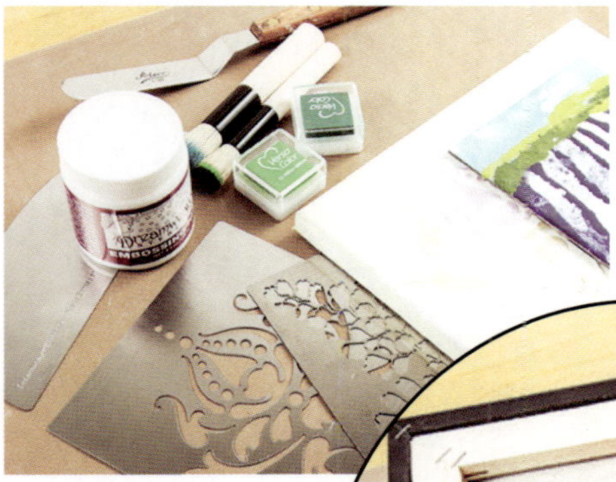

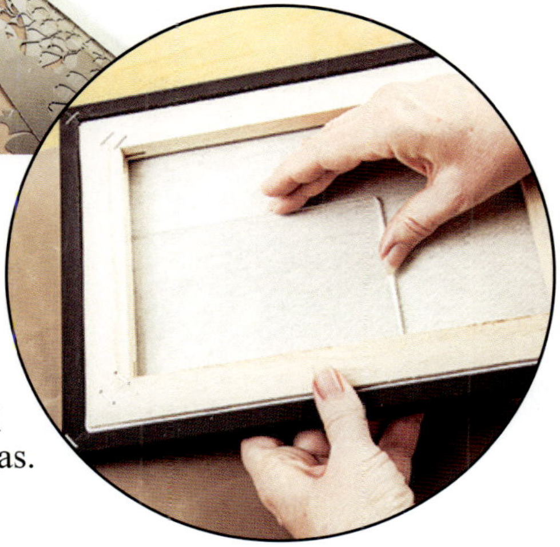

Stamping on Canvas Tip: Slide a jumbo acrylic handle in under canvas frame to support both stamping and stenciling on canvas.

MOLDING
WITH EMBOSSING POWDERS

Molten Embossing Powders can be poured into all sorts of molds you make or purchase for molding candy, soap, clay or other materials. Embossing Powders remain rather brittle even if wax pellets are added. Secure them to a flat surface with strong glue or Dreamweaver® Paste.

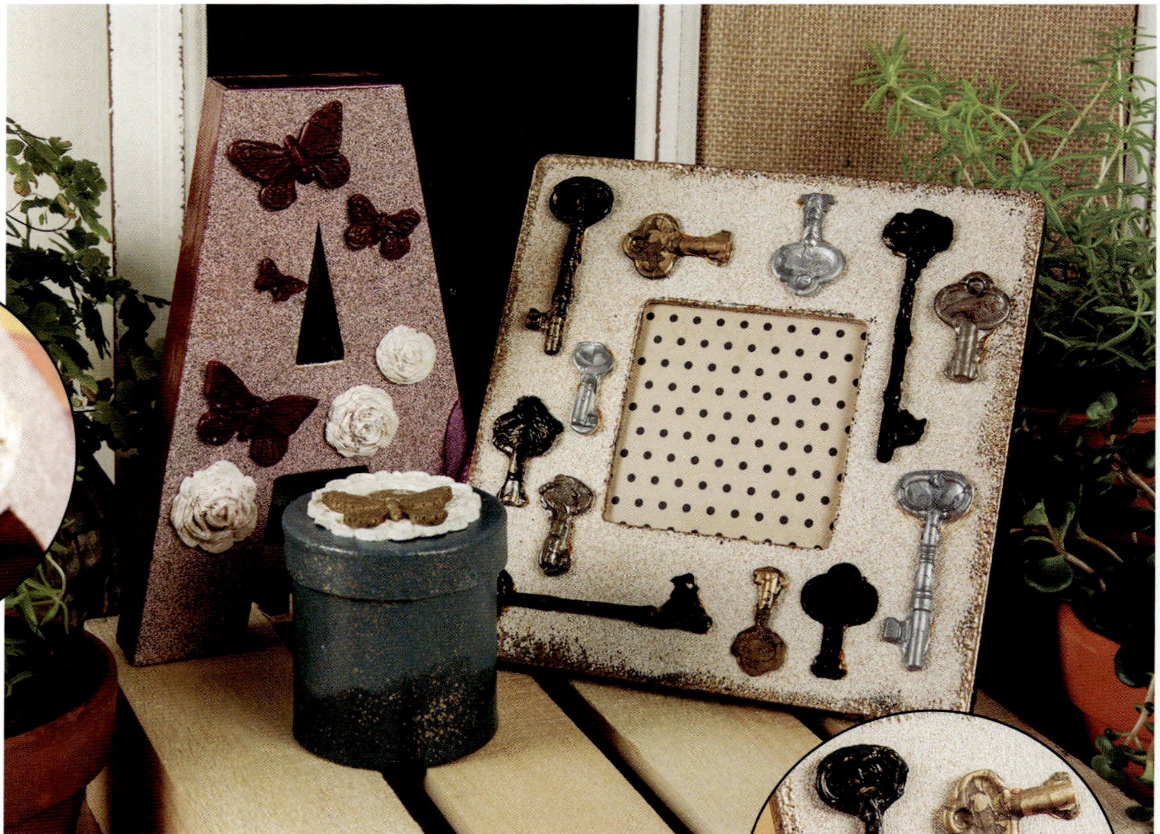

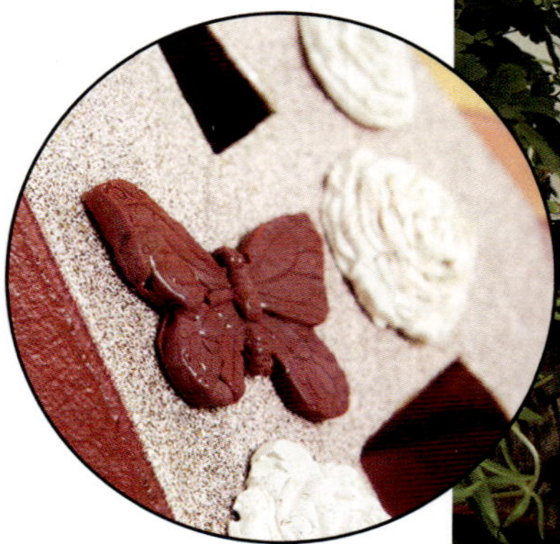

Butterflies made with Garnet PEARLustre™ Embossing Powders. **Roses** made with Frantage™ Shabby Pink Embossing Powder.

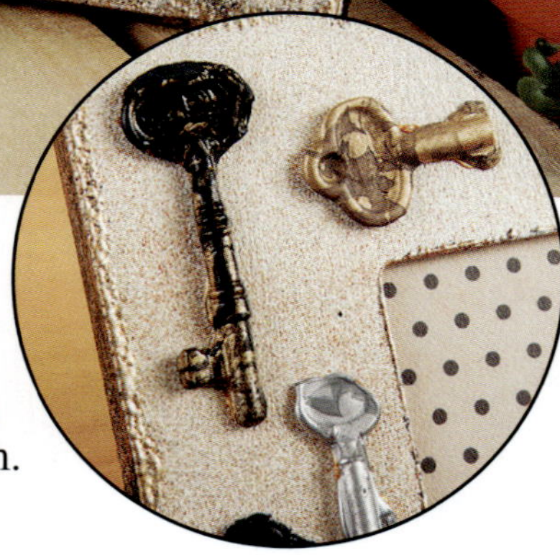

Keys made with metallic Frantage™ Embossing Powders: Aged Gold, Silver, and Black. They come out of the mold with a matte, old finish.

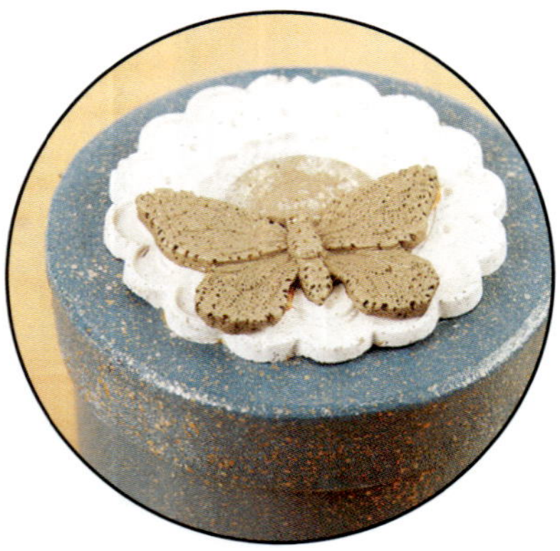

Butterfly made with Pirate Gold. **Medallion** made with Frantage™ Shabby Blue Embossing Powder.

MAKE YOUR OWN MOLDS

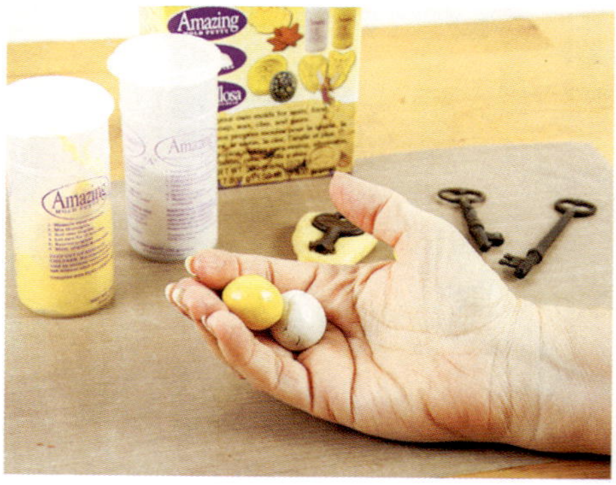

1. Mix equal parts: Follow directions of mold making materials. Roll out a ball of each color and knead until color is even.

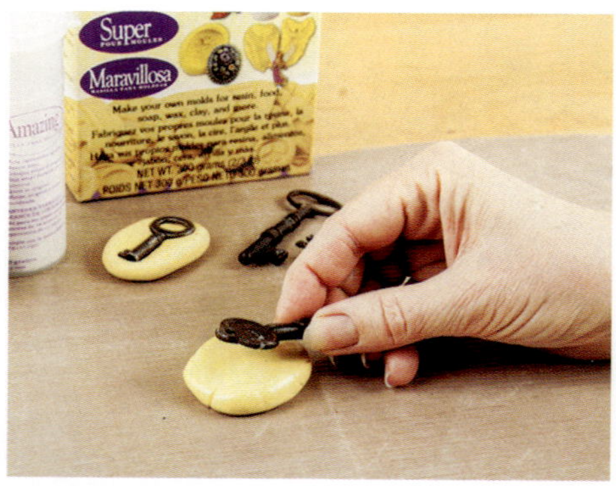

2. Press: Select item to be molded and press into material. Allow 20 minutes to cure on craft sheet.